Historical and Philosophical Foundations of Psychology

This textbook connects the big ideas and key thinkers of psychology and philosophy in a clear and cohesive theoretical narrative. Students are led to understand the relations between different schools of thought, and to connect the various thinkers, theories, and facts in psychology's history. Focusing on the major ideas that have reoccurred throughout history, such as the mind–body problem and the role of the mind in our experience, Martin Farrell shows how specific thinkers have explored the same ideas, but in different ways, leading to distinct schools of thought. The coherent narrative enables students to see the bigger picture, through which the historical and conceptual roots of psychology can be easily understood.

Martin Farrell is an Honorary Lecturer in the School of Psychological Sciences at the University of Manchester. With over 15 years' experience of teaching psychology, he has lectured on many aspects of the discipline but his main focus has always been on the interface between psychology and philosophy. He has lectured on the history of psychology for more than 10 years and on consciousness for 13 years, and has taught philosophy of science to postgraduate students for six years. This book is the fruit of this accumulated experience.

Historical and Philosophical Foundations of Psychology

Martin Farrell

CAMBRIDGE
UNIVERSITY PRESS

CAMBRIDGE
UNIVERSITY PRESS

University Printing House, Cambridge CB2 8BS, United Kingdom

One Liberty Plaza, 20th Floor, New York, NY 10006, USA

477 Williamstown Road, Port Melbourne, VIC 3207, Australia

314-321, 3rd Floor, Plot 3, Splendor Forum, Jasola District Centre, New Delhi - 110025, India

79 Anson Road, #06-04/06, Singapore 079906

Cambridge University Press is part of the University of Cambridge.

It furthers the University's mission by disseminating knowledge in the pursuit of education, learning and research at the highest international levels of excellence.

www.cambridge.org
Information on this title: www.cambridge.org/9780521184809

First published 2014

A catalogue record for this publication is available from the British Library

Library of Congress Cataloging in Publication data
Farrell, Martin, 1968–
Historical and philosophical foundations of psychology / Martin Farrell.
   pages   cm
ISBN 978-1-107-00599-0 (hardback)
1. Psychology – Philosophy.   2. Psychology.   I. Title.
BF38.F37   2014
150.1–dc23

                                                      2014001809

ISBN 978-1-107-00599-0 Hardback
ISBN 978-0-521-18480-9 Paperback

Additional resources for this publication at www.cambridge.org/farrell

For Donna

And my mother and father

Contents

Figures

Boxes

Preface

The sheer amount of information available to today's psychology student, and the ease with which that information can be obtained, is greater than it has ever been in the past. Though this is no doubt a blessing, it is not without its dangers. In particular, it is easy for the student to become bogged down in a mass of facts and details with little appreciation of how everything fits together. Knowing disjointed facts, no matter how vast that knowledge may be, does not constitute understanding. It is only when that knowledge is embedded within an overarching framework that understanding occurs. Knowledge of the historical and philosophical foundations of psychology provides such a framework.

But in order to achieve this, the historical and philosophical foundations of psychology cannot themselves be presented in a bitty and disjointed fashion. There must be some sort of narrative, not just a bunch of ideas and theories. There must be an indication of how ideas fit together, and of the pervasive influence of certain core ideas that resurface at various points throughout the history of psychology. That is what I have tried to do in this book.

This book grew out of a course on the history and philosophy of psychology that I taught at the University of Manchester. In preparing the course I had difficulty in finding a book that tied together the ideas and theories in quite the way I wanted. I felt that many of the available textbooks were repositories of factual information – useful factual information, no doubt – but that they did not present a coherent narrative. I also thought that there was a tendency to try to cover too much ground, too many thinkers, and that, as a result, the treatment of them was often a little cursory. My goal, then, was to provide more of a coherent narrative, and to discuss the ideas presented in greater depth.

The book is perhaps more selective than some others on the history and philosophy of psychology. I make no claims to its being comprehensive – nearly everyone will be able to point out some favourite psychologist or philosopher who has not been included or has not been given enough attention. But I thought it better to look in more detail at the work of a smaller selection of thinkers than to deal superficially with a large number of thinkers. It is also the case that concentrating on a smaller number of thinkers makes it easier to grasp the interconnections between their ideas than if one were to try to cover everyone of importance. I believe that, after having read this book, students will be equipped to locate the ideas of other thinkers not discussed in the book within the general framework that it provides.

The narrative presented in this book is, then, not the only story that could be told about the historical and philosophical foundations of psychology. It does, however, deal with what I believe to be some of the most important and recurring problems and issues concerning the foundations of psychology – issues such as the mind–body problem, the extent to which the mind itself constructs our experience, and the extent to which mental processes can be understood as being purely internal to the organism or essentially connected to the environment. These fundamental issues, and others like them, reappear throughout the book. These issues are discussed in relation to the thought of major philosophers, such as Descartes, Locke, Hume, and Kant, as well as the ideas of influential psychologists, such as William James and Wilhelm Wundt, and psychological movements, such as Gestalt psychology and behaviourism.

The book is organised in a roughly chronological order. It is sometimes the case that books on the history of ideas are organised around themes, but a chronological presentation seemed to me to be the most natural one for providing the narrative that I desired.

Features of the book

The book, as mentioned above, grew out of my undergraduate teaching, and so is aimed at undergraduate psychology students, though I hope that postgraduate students would also find something of value in it. I have tried to write the book as clearly as possible, but it is inevitable that some technical terms will feature in the text. Where these occur, they are printed in bold and are defined in a glossary at the end of the book.

To give the student some feel for the personal context in which ideas originated, I have included, in separate boxes, biographical information on the main thinkers discussed in the text. In addition to this, timelines at the beginning of each chapter relate the work of the thinkers discussed in that chapter to other historical events that were occurring at the same time. The student will also find revision questions at the end of each chapter.

Acknowledgements

I would like to thank the anonymous reviewers of draft chapters of this book, and Hetty Marx, Valerie Appleby, and Raihanah Begum of Cambridge University Press for all their help in helping me knock the book into shape. The book would have been a poorer one if it were not for their suggestions. Thanks are also due to my friend and colleague Professor Ivan Leudar, with whom I taught the course on which this book is based, for his constant encouragement. The biggest thanks of all go to my partner, Donna Lloyd, for all the love and support I could have wished for.

Part I
Philosophy of science

1 Logical positivism and Popper's falsificationism

Timeline

1914–18	First World War
1917	Russian Revolution
1929	Wall Street Crash
1939–45	Second World War
1953	Discovery of structure of DNA
1955–75	Vietnam War
1969	First Moon Landing
1989	Fall of the Berlin Wall

Karl Popper

1902	Born in Vienna
1934	First publication of *The Logic of Scientific Discovery*
1937	Moves to New Zealand
1945	First publication of *The Open Society and Its Enemies*
1946	Moves to England
1994	Dies in London

Introduction: why the philosophy of science?

I have chosen to start this survey of the historical and philosophical foundations of psychology with an examination of some of the major theories put forward in the philosophy of science. This might, at first sight, seem to be a rather unnatural place to start, but there are good reasons for it. Firstly, given that most psychologists think of their discipline as a science and of themselves as scientists, it is important to investigate ideas about what science actually is and what, if anything, are the characteristics that differentiate it from other, non-scientific, intellectual disciplines.

But there is another reason for looking at the philosophy of science to start off with, and that is that there is a good deal of overlap between ideas in the philosophy of science and psychology. Both the philosophy of science and psychology are concerned, at least in part, with the question of how we know about the world. As we shall see, many of the themes that will arise in the course of this presentation of the philosophy of science will re-emerge later in the history of psychology. Indeed, all of the philosophers of science that will be discussed in these three chapters make use of psychological ideas about the nature of knowledge.

One particularly influential view of human knowledge goes, roughly, like this: we gain knowledge of the world through the senses; events and objects in the world impinge on our sense organs, and the basic sensory information that they thereby transmit is the basis on which our knowledge of the world stands. This view has its counterpart in the philosophy of science in the theory that scientific knowledge is built up from observations of things and events in the natural world. According to this view, observational facts form the basis on which scientific knowledge stands.

These two views go hand in hand, and they are rejected by Karl Popper, the first philosopher of science that we are going to cover. He referred, dismissively, to the view of knowledge that has just been sketched as 'the bucket theory of knowledge' because it envisages the human mind as a sort of receptacle for factual information acquired via the senses. This view is also rejected by the three other major philosophers of science to be covered in these chapters: Thomas Kuhn, Imre Lakatos, and Paul Feyerabend. Though they disagree strongly with Popper on other matters, all agree that the bucket theory of mind gives an erroneous picture not only of scientific knowledge, but of human knowledge in general.

The bucket theory is traced by Popper, with some justification, to a school of philosophy called **empiricism**. This school of thought emphasises the importance of experience, and particularly sensory or perceptual experience, in gaining knowledge about the world. It is particularly associated with philosophers such as John Locke and David Hume, whose ideas we will consider in more detail in Chapters 5 and 6. According to the empiricists, the basic perceptual information that is provided by the senses is transformed into more elaborate knowledge through association: the different isolated bits of factual information become associated with one another, they become bound together, so as to create from a disconnected array of facts a coherent network of interconnected pieces of information. This idea of learning through association was to have great influence on the behaviourists (see Chapter 16). Again, this general view of human knowledge has its counterpart in the philosophy of science. According to the empiricist view of science, scientific theories are created by joining together the isolated facts and observations that scientists collect in the course of their research.

Empiricism assumes that the basic observations and facts that are the foundation of science are *given* to the scientist. The scientist has only to observe nature to be provided with the building blocks of scientific knowledge and these observations will be all the more accurate the less the scientist's mind is filled with expectations about what will be observed. Approaching the task of observing nature with pre-existing ideas about what one is going to find is, according to the empiricist approach to science, likely to bias or distort one's observations. The scientific ideal, then, is the completely open-minded and passive recipient of incoming information. It is only subsequent to having received this information that the mind can start to take an active role in the creation of scientific knowledge, by combining, associating, abstracting, and generalising ideas on the basis of the sure information provided by the unbiased operation of the senses. The bricks are *given* by nature; the building is constructed by mind.

The idea that science starts with the neutral observation of facts given to observation goes back to one of the earliest empiricists and thinkers on scientific method, Francis Bacon (1561–1626) (see Figure 1.1). For Bacon, the most important early step in scientific investigation was to remove from one's mind all pre-existing beliefs and expectations so that one can, as a scientist, make careful and unprejudiced observations of what one really sees, observations that are pure and uncontaminated. Bacon called the traditional or accepted beliefs that the scientist had to discard 'the idols of the tribe', and he was in no doubt that these idols had to be destroyed because they blocked the advance of

Fig. 1.1 Francis Bacon

scientific knowledge. The mind of the observer becomes cleansed and approaches as closely as possible to the blank slate on which empiricists believed nature could write its message unhindered. This purging of pre-existing beliefs and expectations has been likened by Lakatos (in his 'Falsification and the methodology of scientific research programmes'; see Chapter 3) to a sort of psychotherapy that the empiricist believes is necessary to prepare one's mind to receive the message of nature.

The four philosophers of science to be discussed in these chapters all reject the empiricist view of science. In its place they put forward an alternative view of science according to which the scientist is an *active seeker* of observations, not just a passive receiver. The scientist is not devoid of expectations or pre-conceptions, but, on the contrary, makes observations precisely in order to see whether these expectations are fulfilled. But the views of Popper, Kuhn, Lakatos, and Feyerabend go further than this. They assert that not only do a scientist's preconceptions guide her search for observations, but that they play an active role in actually structuring the observations themselves.

This alternative to the empiricist view of science has its roots in an alternative view of human knowledge and perception, which can be traced to the ideas of Immanuel Kant (1724–1804). According to Kant, whose ideas will be discussed in more detail in Chapter 6, the human mind does not passively record sensory impressions, but has a hand in constituting and constructing those impressions from the outset of perception itself. In particular, argued Kant, the mind has an innate structure, a built-in framework, through which we make sense of the world around us. The most obvious example of this is the physiology of the sensory apparatus itself – we can only hear a limited range of sounds or see a limited range of light frequencies. Thus, even our most basic perceptions are determined not only by what is out there in the external world, but by the form of our own minds. This fundamental Kantian insight formed the basic presupposition of psychologists such as Wundt (see Chapter 11).

The physiology of the perceptual systems is, however, not the only influence on the way that the mind structures perceptual experience. Another influence is the cultural experience of the perceiver, and it is on this factor that philosophers of science have focused. This, unlike the physiology of the perceptual systems, is not fixed, but can change as a result of learning. Popper, Kuhn, Lakatos, and Feyerabend all in their own ways argue that, just as the education and training of a literate person allows her to see lines and squiggles on a page as mean-ingful words, so the education and training of a scientist structures her obser-vations in particular ways. The expert naturalist has *learned* to see specific species of birds where the non-expert sees just undifferentiated 'birds'; the trained astronomer has *learned* to see the constellations whereas the non-expert just sees 'stars'. Contrary to empiricism, it is not just the edifice of knowledge that is constructed by the mind, but also the very building blocks of which it is made.

Logical positivism and the question of meaning

The empiricist view of science against which much of twentieth-century philosophy of science defined itself was given its most influential modern formulation in a school of thought called **logical positivism**. Logical positivism is particularly associated with a loose grouping of scientists and philosophers who worked in Vienna in the 1920s and 1930s, but was also promoted by English philosophers such as A. J. Ayer (1910–89). In order fully to understand the work of Popper and later philosophers of science it is useful, first of all, to understand what they were reacting against.

The logical positivists were particularly concerned with the question of what it is that makes a statement meaningful. They were concerned with this because they believed that a great deal of philosophy was nothing more than empty verbiage, high-sounding rhetoric that did not mean anything. This sort of grandiose philosophical jargon they dismissed as mere 'metaphysics'. To be truly rigorous in our thoughts, argued the logical positivists, we have to have some criterion that differentiates a truly meaningful statement from a superficially plausible one that does not have any meaning. We have to have some demarcation between sense and nonsense.

In trying to specify a criterion of meaning, the logical positivists took their lead from the eighteenth-century empiricist philosopher David Hume (whose ideas are discussed in more detail in Chapter 6), who recommended the following course of action:

> If we take in our hand any volume; of divinity or school metaphysics, for instance; let us ask, "Does it contain any abstract reasoning concerning quantity or number?" No. "Does it contain any experimental reasoning concerning matter of fact and existence?" No. Commit it then to the flames: for it can contain nothing but sophistry and illusion. (*Enquiries concerning Human Understanding and concerning the Principles of Morals*, p. 165)

For Hume, then, and for his latter-day followers among the logical positivists, any meaningful statement must fall into one of two categories: it must either contain 'abstract reasoning' or 'experimental reasoning'. The statements of mathematics would be examples of the first category of meaningful statement. 'Squares have four sides' or 'The sum of the internal angles of a triangle is 180 degrees' or '2 + 3 = 5' are all meaningful statements, but note that they are not arrived at from observing actual states of affairs in the world. The general statement 'Squares have four sides' is not obtained by going around counting the sides of every square that one encounters and *discovering* that squares have four sides. Rather, we would say that squares have four sides *by definition*. If someone were to announce that he had found a 'three-sided square', we would not hail this as a mathematical breakthrough but as evidence that the person in question did not know the meaning of the term 'square'. These mathematical statements are examples of *logical truths*. Logical truths are true in virtue of their structure and the definitions of the terms that they contain, not because they give us accurate information about the world. For example, the statement 'It is either raining or not raining outside my window' is true – it really *is* either raining or not raining – but it gives no information as to what the weather is actually like.

The second class of meaningful statements, according to Hume, consists of those statements containing 'experimental reasoning concerning matter of fact'. In contrast to logical truths, statements of this second type *do* give us information about the way that the world actually is. They are *observational statements*. In contrast to 'It is either raining or not raining outside my window', the statement 'It is raining outside my window' is an empirical statement; it says that a certain state of affairs exists in the world. It asserts a fact.

Empirical or observational statements, unlike logical truths, can be true or false, and we can check on their truth or falsity by actually making the relevant observations to see if the world actually is the way that the statement says that it is. We can, for example, look outside the window to see if it really is raining. If we see that the facts actually correspond to what the statement says, then we have *verified* the statement. An observation statement, then, is a statement that can, even if only in principle, be verified.

Ayer made the point as follows:

> The criterion which we use to test the genuineness of apparent statements of fact is the criterion of verifiability. We say that a sentence is factually significant to any given person, if, and only if, he knows how to verify the proposition which it purports to express – that is, if he knows what observations would lead him, under certain conditions, to accept the proposition as being true, or reject it as being false. If, on the other hand, the putative proposition is of such a character that the assumption of its truth, or falsehood, is consistent with any assumption whatsoever concerning the nature of his future experience, then, as far as he is concerned, it is, if not a tautology, a mere pseudo-proposition. (*Language, Truth and Logic*, p. 16)

Ayer goes on to give a quotation from the English philosopher F. H. Bradley as an example of the sort of meaningless metaphysics that the logical positivists sought to excise from philosophical discourse:

such a metaphysical pseudo-proposition as 'the Absolute enters into, but is itself incapable of, evolution and progress', is not even in principle verifiable. For one cannot conceive of an observation which would enable one to determine whether the Absolute did, or did not, enter into evolution and progress. (*Language, Truth and Logic*, p. 17)

We can conclude this section, then, by saying that, according to the logical positivists, for a statement to have any meaning at all it must fall into one of these two classes: it must either be true as a matter of logic or it must be an observational statement that gives us verifiable information about the way that the world is. It is because of this emphasis on the verification of empirical statements that the logical positivists' theory of meaning is sometimes referred to as **verificationism**.

The problem of induction

We have seen in the earlier sections of this chapter that, from the empiricist viewpoint, all science starts with observations. The statements or propositions that convey these observations clearly fall into the second of the logical positivists' two categories of meaningful statement: they assert the existence of some fact or facts about the world which can be verified by making appropriate observations.

But, though facts are important to science, science is not just a collection of facts. The scientist is not content with a large number of individual observations such as 'Steam was produced when a kettle of water was brought to boiling at 7.30 a.m. on 26th April 2013.' She does not just want to make statements about *individual* events, but wants to make *general* statements about whole classes of events: not just what happened when water was boiled this morning in a kitchen in Manchester, but what happens when water boils in general. Something has to be done with the individual facts collected by the scientist to convert them from reports of particular events or things into general statements. Bacon believed that general patterns would somehow emerge from a large number of observations, but the logical positivists wanted to be more rigorous in identifying how this might happen. Specifying exactly how general scientific statements or laws are derived from individual observations was particularly important to the logical positivists because they believed that the meaningfulness of any scientific law depended on its being built from verifiable facts.

The process by which general conclusions are drawn from a number of individual observations is called **induction**, and it is here that, according to

Popper, the whole programme of logical positivism foundered. To illustrate what is meant by induction or inductive reasoning it is useful to contrast it with **deduction** or *deductive reasoning.*

Here is an example of deductive reasoning. We have the following two premises:

1. All dairy products are made from milk
2. Cheese a dairy product.

If we accept that these two premises are true, then they necessarily entail the conclusion 'Cheese is made from milk.'

Here is another example of deductive reasoning. We have the following two premises:

1. All green things are made from grass
2. The carpet is green.

If we accept that these two premises are true, then they necessarily entail the conclusion 'The carpet is made from grass.'

Both of these are examples of valid reasoning. They are valid because the conclusions follow from the premises as a matter of logical necessity. It so happens that in the second example the premises are not actually true, but the *logical validity* of the argument is concerned not with whether the premises and conclusions really are true are false, but whether the conclusion follows logically from the premises if, *for the sake of argument*, we accept them to be true.

In both of the above examples of deductive reasoning we move from general statements in the premises (e.g. 'All dairy products are made from milk') to conclusions about particular things (e.g. cheese as a particular type of dairy product). But this type of reasoning, which goes from the general to the particular, cannot be used to derive scientific theories or laws from observations, because in this case the argument has to go in the opposite direction. We *start* with individual, particular cases and from them *arrive* at general conclusions.

It is here that we arrive at what is called the *problem of induction*, which was raised by Hume and then later used by Popper to undermine logical positivism. The problem of induction is simply that one cannot *logically* derive a general conclusion from a finite number of individual observations. If, for example, one has tested 20, 30 or even 1000 participants in an experiment, it does not follow that *all* people will perform in this way. There is no way of knowing whether the 21st, 31st or 1001st participant might perform in a completely different way. We might *expect* the 21st, 31st or 1001st participant to perform in broadly the same way as the preceding participants, but this is merely a subjective inclination rather than a logical necessity. For Popper, the invalidity of induction constituted a fatal flaw in the logical positivists' programme of rigorously demonstrating how scientific knowledge could be built on a foundation of observational statements. The

---

Box 1.1 **Karl Popper**

Karl Raimund Popper was born in Vienna in 1902 to a middle-class family. Though the family was Jewish in origin, both of his parents had converted to Protestantism before Popper was born. The atmosphere of the household was intellectual, and his parents were deeply interested in social and political issues as well as the arts and philosophy. Popper attended lectures in a variety of subjects – physics, mathematics, psychology, and philosophy – at the University of Vienna and later gained his doctorate in psychology. He was keenly interested in education and worked for a while as a social worker with deprived children and later as a teacher of mathematics and physics.

As a young man, Popper was active in left-wing politics and flirted with Marxism but later turned against it. His rejection of Marxism was, in part, prompted by the shooting dead of unarmed socialist demonstrators in Vienna by the police in 1919. Confronted by real bloodshed, Popper could no longer hope for the class war that the Marxists predicted and longed for. He was also disturbed by the dogmatic nature of what he was supposed to believe and was concerned that he himself had accepted these doctrines in an uncritical manner. Popper was also interested in the psychoanalytic ideas of Freud and Adler, but these too he came to suspect of being dogmatic.

Following the annexation of Austria by the Nazis in 1936, Popper left for New Zealand. Though he had been raised in an ostensibly non-Jewish household, his grandparents were all Jewish, which meant that Popper himself would have been classified as Jewish under the Nazis' racial laws. It was in New Zealand, spurred on by the rise of totalitarianism in Europe, that Popper wrote his most influential political work, *The Open Society and Its Enemies*. In this work he argued in favour of liberal democracy and against totalitarianism of both left and right.

At the end of World War II, Popper moved to England, where he worked at the London School of Economics and the University of London until his retirement in 1969 (see Figure 1.2), although he continued to write right up until his death in 1994. He was knighted in 1965.

Box 1.1 (cont.)

Fig. 1.2 Karl Popper

foundations themselves might be unassailable, but the construction of a theory upon them seemed to have no warrant in logic. Either the logical positivists' picture of science was seriously wrong or the logic of science was called into question.

The role of theory in observation

Induction was not the only problem that Popper saw with logical positivism. For him the observations made by scientists *were not firm and unassailable* in the way that the logical positivists thought they were. Whereas the logical positivists had argued that we start with observation and end up with a theory, Popper argued that we cannot even make observations unless we *already have* a theory which guides those observations and makes sense of them. The whole empiricist picture of the open-minded scientist making completely neutral observations, her mind purged as completely as possible of any preconceptions or expectations, was attacked by Popper as nothing more than a pernicious myth.

Popper (*Conjectures and Refutations*) recounted how he once asked a classroom of students to 'observe', and to write down their observations. The students were, not surprisingly, rather nonplussed by the vague instruction to 'observe'. 'Observe *what?*' was their understandable reaction. Even if the students had simply started to write down whatever observations struck them – the pen in their hand, the sun outside the window, a table made of wood, a floor with tiles on it – these would hardly have constituted anything approaching the coherence of a scientific theory. They would, on the contrary, have been nothing more than a random collection of unconnected facts. According to Popper, this little demonstration illustrates the completely unrealistic nature of the positivist idea that the scientist starts off by simply making lots of observations. For Popper, the scientist starts with a theory and *then* makes observations. Indeed, it is precisely in order to test the theory that the observations are made at all. This being the case, only certain, relevant observations will do, and it is one of the functions of a theory to guide the scientist in making those observations that are relevant to its testing.

But the problem with the positivist theory of completely neutral observation goes even deeper than this. It is, argues Popper, not only impossible to make coherent and relevant observations without the concepts and expectations contained in a guiding theory, it is impossible to make any observations *at all* without such preexisting knowledge. Even the student who, as in the above example, makes random observations of the pen, the table, the sun etc. can only do so on the basis of concepts that she already possesses. To perceive something as a table or the sun and to classify it as such requires pre-existing knowledge – one must already have the concept of 'table' in order to be able to class one of one's current observations as being an exemplar of this particular category. For Popper, then, even our everyday, non-scientific observations require a theory (albeit perhaps an implicit one). Some of this knowledge is learned but, in addition, according to Popper, "we are born with expectations; with 'knowledge' which ... is ... prior to all observational experience" (*Conjectures and Refutations*, p. 47). It is here that the Kantian idea of the mind's structuring of perception is most evident in Popper's thought.

The irrelevance of verification

The logical positivists argued that what differentiated real science from mere pseudo-science or metaphysics was that science could be verified through empirical observations whereas metaphysics and pseudo-science could not. This problem of differentiating between science and non-science was called the 'problem of demarcation' by Popper, and he pointed out that the logical positivists' answer to the problem, verification, did not successfully differentiate science from non-science. Astrologists, said Popper, can point to lots of supposedly verifying facts that support their claims – every stubborn Taurean counts as a verification – yet astrology is not a science. Verification, therefore, cannot be the mark of a science.

Popper's misgivings about the importance of verification were further exacerbated when he considered the difference between Einstein's theory of relativity and other supposedly scientific theories, such as Marxism, Freudian psychoanalysis, and the individual psychology of Adler. The followers of these theories, said Popper, could produce large amounts of data that appeared to verify the theories. Indeed, such was the explanatory power of these theories that they seemed able to provide an explanation of just about any occurrence that one could think of. A naïve, verificationist view of science would be impressed by a theory that can explain almost anything and has an enormous amount of empirical observations to verify it, but Popper was not so sure:

> It was precisely this fact – that they always fitted, that they were always confirmed – which in the eyes of their admirers constituted the strongest argument in favour of these theories. It began to dawn on me that this apparent strength was in fact their weakness. (*Conjectures and Refutations*, p. 35)

Einstein's theory, however, was a different matter. One aspect of it was a gravitational theory that predicted that light would be attracted to heavy bodies in the same way that material objects were. This would mean that light from a star that passed near to the Sun should be distorted by the Sun's gravitational field. As the light from such stars is not normally visible, because it is outshone by the Sun's own light, the only way the theory could be tested is during a solar eclipse, when the Sun's own light is masked by the passing of the moon. This is exactly what was done by the astrophysicist Sir Arthur Eddington in 1919, who led an expedition to the island of Principe, off the west coast of Africa, in order to observe the starlight during a total eclipse of the Sun. Eddington's observations confirmed Einstein's predictions and became front-page news around the world. These were the first empirical tests of Einstein's theory.

But it was not simply the confirmation of Einstein's theory that impressed Popper, it was what he saw as the risk involved in testing such predictions: there was a real possibility that the prediction might be wrong, and this would spell disaster for the theory that provided the prediction. "If observation shows that the predicted effect is definitely absent," said Popper, "then the theory is simply refuted. The theory is *incompatible with certain possible results of observation* ..." (*Conjectures and Refutations*, p. 36).

In contrast, then, to the theories of Marx and Freud, for example, Einstein's theory was distinguished by the fact that not all possible observations would fit with it. There were certain facts that could refute it. This, for Popper, was the strength of Einstein's theory, and this is what he argued should be regarded as the criterion of demarcation between science and non-science: "not the *verifiability* but the *falsifiability* of a system is to be taken as a criterion of demarcation ... *it must be possible for an empirical scientific system to be refuted by experience*" (*The Logic of Scientific Discovery*, p. 16, italics in original).

If we accept falsifiability as the criterion of a theory's scientific status, then we cannot accept the claims to scientific status of Marxism or psychoanalysis. Let us take psychoanalysis as an example. According to Freud, young boys are sexually attracted towards their mothers and, if these feelings are not resolved in the course of development, the unconscious desires, which Freud called the Oedipus complex, may linger and cause psychological problems in adulthood. If we were then to consider a man who was unusually affectionate and protective towards his mother, we could explain his behaviour as a manifestation of the Oedipus complex. But if we were to consider a man who was cold and unloving towards his mother this too could be 'explained' as a manifestation of the Oedipus complex. In this second case, it could be argued, the man is so disturbed by the attraction that he feels towards his mother that he acts contrary to the true nature of his feelings in an effort to deny the attraction. We have two opposite patterns of behaviour that can both be explained by the same theory; neither one behaviour nor the other can falsify the theory. This, for Popper, meant that psychoanalysis was not truly scientific.

The same was true of Marxism. Although interpreted by some as a genuine science of historical and economic development, there was always scope for making apparently inconsistent facts – such as the first Communist revolution occurring in relatively undeveloped Russia rather than, as Marx predicted, in the most advanced economies of the West – fit with the theory. It should be noted, however, that this did not mean that Popper thought that the ideas of Marx of Freud were devoid of any value whatsoever. It simply meant that they were not scientific.

The logic of falsification

We talk of trying to 'prove whether a theory is true or false' as if the proof of truth and the proof of falsity were on the same logical level. But, according to Popper, they are not. The problem of induction means that we can *never* prove an empirical theory to be true. There is always the possibility that a future observation may conflict with the theory. But by finding such conflicting observations we *can* prove an empirical theory to be false. Before Western Europeans went to Australia, for example, they believed that all swans were white. But though the general statement 'all swans are white' would have apparently been verified by thousands of observations of white swans, this did not prove it to be true. When, however, Europeans arrived in Australia they found that there were black swans there. This *was* enough to prove 'all swans are white' to be false. No number of confirmations, no matter how large, can ever prove a general statement to be true, but just one disconfirmation can prove it to be false.

Contrary to the logical positivists, then, Popper asserts that the rationality of science does not lie in the *creation* of theories, but in the *testing* of theories. In trying, unsuccessfully, to find the rationality of science in the logical construction of general theories from individual observations, the logical positivists were looking for the rational character of science in the wrong place. For Popper, how we arrive at a theory is unimportant; it is what we do with theories *after* we have created them that matters. A scientist may come up with a theory when daydreaming (there are cases of famous scientific discoveries that have arisen in this way) or even when asleep and dreaming. The source of a theory may be as intuitive and irrational as you like, but this is of no consequence as it is in the subsequent testing of the theory in an attempt to falsify it that rationality of science is to be found. Popper's philosophy of science is, therefore, sometimes referred to as **falsificationism.**

Popper's falsificationist logic has different – and what might seem counter-intuitive – consequences for what counts as a good scientific theory from verificationist or positivist accounts of science. The worth of a scientific theory, for Popper, is not to be gauged by how many facts that it explains, but by how many facts, or types of fact, that it *cannot* explain. It is, in other words, to be gauged by the number of potentially falsifying observations that could disprove the theory: the more highly falsifiable a theory is – i.e. the greater the class of observations that would disprove the theory – the better the theory is.

At first sight this criterion for determining the worth of a theory seems completely absurd, but Popper has powerful arguments to back up his position. The laws of nature, which science tries to discover, are, says Popper, not called 'laws' for nothing: like any other law, what they do is to rule things out, to prohibit certain states of affairs. "They do not," says Popper, "assert that something exists or is the case; they deny it. They insist on the non-existence of certain things or states of affairs" (*The Logic of Scientific Discovery*, p. 48). It is because they rule out certain facts that scientific theories are falsifiable; they are falsified by observing one of the facts that they have ruled out. And the more that a scientific theory rules out the more it actually tells us about the world.

This, again, this seems to make no sense at all, but let us follow Popper's argument. Imagine that we represent the set of all possible observations by a circle, like a pie-chart. Then let us shade in one of the sectors of the pie-chart to represent that class of observations that are incompatible with a scientific theory. If that theory rules out only a small class of observations, the sector will be small, as in Figure 1.3a; if the theory rules out a large class of observations, the sector will be correspondingly large, as in Figure 1.3b. The theory represented by Figure 1.3b is clearly more falsifiable than that represented in Figure 1.3a: it rules out a larger class of potential observations and, hence, there are more hypothetical observations that, if found, would falsify it. Now the theory depicted in Figure 1.3b actually tells us more about the world in which we live because it narrows down the possibilities to a greater extent than the theory in Figure 1.3a, which is so vague that lots of possibilities are consistent with it. We can think of the logic of science as analogous to a detective narrowing down the number of suspects who might be guilty of a crime – the greater the number of suspects that he can rule out, the closer he gets to finding the culprit. For Popper, the job of the

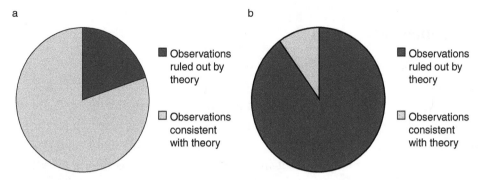

Fig. 1.3 The increase in empirical content of a theory as a function of how many possible observations are ruled out by the theory

scientist is similar: it is narrowing down the number of possible descriptions of the world so as to get closer to the description of the world as it actually is. A scientific theory, therefore, for Popper, is valuable for what it says *is not the case*, rather than what it permits.

Another consequence of Popper's falsificationist logic is that the disproof of a scientific theory is regarded as a good thing. The falsification of a theory means that another possible description of the world can be rejected. Falsification also forces the scientist to improve upon the rejected theory and thus pushes knowledge forward. We learn from our mistakes. For Popper, then, falsification is not merely the mark of a scientific theory but, when it occurs, it is the engine of scientific growth. It is therefore the job of the scientist to actively *try* to falsify theories, to submit them to the most rigorous tests that she can devise in an attempt to prove them wrong. It is only through the rejection of falsified theories and their subsequent replacement by more adequate theories, which have not yet been falsified, that science advances.

It is therefore a mistake in Popper's eyes for scientists to seek to protect their theories against falsification. It is always possible to do this by making ad hoc modifications to one's theory specifically to prevent it being falsified. For example, say we had a psychological theory that was supposed to predict the performances of all adults on a certain task, but that, though the male participants performed as expected, the female participants did not. One could either admit that the theory has been falsified by the female participants' performances or one could protect the theory by restricting its scope only to adult males. This latter course of action, the avoidance of falsification by ad hoc theory modification, is, for Popper, to be rejected. Of course it allows one to maintain that one's theory has not been disproved, but only by reducing its content; it is an entirely negative

Box 1.2 Popper and politics

Many of Popper's views in the philosophy of science, in particular the view that progress comes from the rational criticism of ideas and their subsequent revision, had their counterparts in his approach to politics. Just as no scientific theory could claim to have absolute truth, so no political ideas could justifiably claim to have the sure solution to all of society's ills. Popper argued against the idea that a dictatorship would somehow be more efficient in solving social problems than a liberal democracy. This is because totalitarian regimes stifle the very process of rational criticism that Popper believed was necessary for progress in solving any problem. Totalitarian regimes are therefore not only ethically despicable, they also do not work as well as democratic regimes. Though democracy may appear 'messy' compared to a totalitarian regime, it is actually this messiness that is a necessary factor in its success.

Popper was particularly critical of all forms of 'historicism', according to which the path of history inevitably tends in a certain direction, whether towards the classless society of Communism or the vague promise of 'progress'. The claim to have certain knowledge of what will happen in the future was as unacceptable in the political and social domain as it was in the scientific. In both cases, argued Popper, we have to accept the possibility that our ideas may be falsified by future events.

Though Popper the philosopher was tireless in his championing of tolerance and openness to criticism, Popper the man was not. His friend the philosopher and broadcaster Bryan Magee gives the following vivid description of Popper's domineering personality:

> My chief impression of him at our early meetings was of an intellectual aggressiveness such as I had never encountered before. Everything we argued about he pursued relentlessly, beyond the limits of acceptable aggression in conversation. As Ernst Gombrich – his closest friend, who loved him – once put it to me, he seemed unable to accept the continued existence of different points of view; but went on and on and *on* about them with a kind of unforgivingness until the dissenter, so to speak, put his signature to a confession that he was wrong and Popper was right. In practice this meant he was trying to subjugate people. And there was something angry about the energy and intensity with which he made the attempt. The unremittingly fierce, tight focus, like a flame, put me in mind of a blowtorch, and this image remained the dominant one I had of him for many years, until he mellowed with age.
>
> All this was the grossest possible violation of the spirit of liberalism exemplified and advocated in his writings. (*Confessions of a Philosopher*, pp. 231–2)

move. Accepting that the theory has been falsified, on the other hand, is actually a positive move. It forces us to confront a new question – why do males and females perform differently? – and to develop new theories accordingly. It pushes knowledge forward.

If Popper is right in saying that theories cannot be verified but only falsified, it means that we can never be sure that any scientific theory is true. The most that we can say of any theory is that it is the best that we have at any given time if it has been tested but not yet been falsified by any observation. We cannot, however, be sure that it won't be falsified by a future observation. It follows from this that all scientific knowledge is provisional rather than absolutely certain.

This conclusion constitutes another fundamental disagreement with the logical positivists, who thought that, by building scientific knowledge on verifiable observations, they could guarantee its certainty. Indeed, one could go further and say that Popper breaks with the predominant tradition of Western philosophy, which had, since the time of Descartes (see Chapter 4), sought absolutely certain knowledge as its goal. For Popper, such a goal is unattainable. There is no certain knowledge, only knowledge that has not yet been falsified.

Conclusion

We have seen, then, that Popper provides some serious arguments against the logical positivist, and more generally empiricist, view of science. Contrary to the empiricist view, science cannot start with observations. There must be, not only as a matter of fact but as a matter of logic, theory-based expectations and predictions *prior* to the making of any observations. Where these expectations come from does not matter, because rationality lies in the testing of them with an eye to their possible falsification and subsequent replacement with revised and improved expectations. It is here, in the replacement of old and falsified theories by new and as yet unfalsified ones, that scientific progress is to be found rather than in the accumulation of more and more observations.

Popper's anti-empiricist view of science means that science has to be understood not in terms of its theoretical solutions, but, first and foremost, in terms of its theoretical problems. It is not enough to be told about this or that theory without being aware of the problems, usually resulting from the falsification of previous theories, that they were supposed to solve. According to Popper, "every *rational* theory, no matter whether scientific or philosophical, is rational in so far as it tries to *solve certain problems*. A theory is comprehensible and reasonable only in its relation to a given *problem-situation*, and it can be rationally discussed only by discussing this relation" (*Conjectures and Refutations*, p. 199). Popper's view, then, draws our attention to the intellectual context in which science takes place. It is this context, and the questions to which it gives rise, that prompts the scientist to propose theories and to test them.

This means, according to Popper, that, as a scientist "you pick up, and try to continue, a line of enquiry which has the whole background of the earlier development of science behind it ... [W]e cannot start afresh ... we must make use of what people before us have done in science" (*Conjectures and Refutations*, p. 129). It because they thought that the scientist *does* start afresh, by making observations with no theoretical expectations, that the logical positivists, and other empiricists, were unable to formulate a credible philosophy of science.

Despite Popper's cogent criticisms of empiricism, however, there are nevertheless some problems with his own philosophy of science. In particular, the logic of theory falsification is not quite as clear as some of Popper's pronouncements might suggest. The example of falsification that is usually given in the literature (as I have also done above) is the observation of a black swan falsifying the statement that all swans are white. This is a perfectly good example to illustrate the concept of falsification, but the testing of real scientific theories is a good deal more complex than this. For example, if we obtain a result that seems to conflict with a previously held theory, how do we know that the theory is at fault rather than the design of our experiment or the equipment that it uses? Rather than the fault being in the theory, the fault could be in the observations that seem to falsify the theory. And even if we are sure that our experiment has been correctly designed, that the equipment works properly and that all the measurements have been done correctly, at what point do we deem a theory to be falsified and reject it? It would seem rash to reject a theory after only one conflicting observation. One would want the conflicting findings to be replicated by further research. But it is not clear how many replications would be needed to justify theory rejection.

For his part, Popper argues that these questions can only be decided by the agreement of interested scientists themselves: we cannot give a simple, one-size-fits-all, rule about how many falsifying observations are necessary to reject a theory. Science is a human activity and not just a set of algorithms to be implemented in the same way everywhere regardless of context. Popper himself points out that we can never conclusively disprove a theory:

> no conclusive disproof of a theory can ever be produced; for it is always possible to say that the experimental results are not reliable, or that the discrepancies which are asserted to exist between the experimental results and the theory are only apparent and that they will disappear with the advance of our understanding . . . If you insist on strict proof (or strict disproof) in the empirical sciences, you will never benefit from experience, and never learn from it how wrong you are. (*The Logic of Scientific Discovery*, p. 28)

But if there is no such thing as the conclusive disproof of a theory, and the decision to reject a theory and replace it with a new one hinges crucially on the collective decision of the scientific community, then what has become of the logic of falsificationism? Rational necessity seems to have been replaced by non-rational choice. That scientific theory change is not determined by rational factors is precisely what is argued by Thomas Kuhn, and it is to his work that we turn in the next chapter.

Revision questions

1. Why did Popper disagree with the empiricist approach to knowledge?
2. What, according to logical positivism, are the two classes of meaningful statement that can be made?
3. What is the problem of induction and why did Popper believe that it was fatal to the ambitions of logical positivism?
4. Why did Popper believe that verification was irrelevant to the scientific status of a theory?
5. What role, according to Popper, do theories play in scientific research?
6. According to Popper, is theory construction constrained by rational rules?
7. Why does a theory that rules out a large number of possible observations actually tell us more about the world than a theory that only rules out a small number of possible observations?
8. What, in practice, did Popper think determined whether or not a theory was falsified?

References

Ayer, A. J. ([1936]/1971). *Language, Truth and Logic*. London: Penguin.

Hume, D. ([1777]/1975). *Enquiries concerning Human Understanding and concerning the Principles of Morals*, 3rd edn (L. A. Selby-Bigge and P. H. Nidditch, eds.). Oxford: Clarendon Press.

Magee, B. (1998). *Confessions of a Philosopher*. London: Phoenix.

Popper, K. R. ([1959]/1992). *The Logic of Scientific Discovery*. London: Routledge.

Popper, K. R. (1963). *Conjectures and Refutations*. London: Routledge.

2 Kuhn and scientific revolutions

Timeline

1914–18	First World War
1917	Russian Revolution
1929	Wall Street Crash
1939–45	Second World War
1953	Discovery of structure of DNA
1955–75	Vietnam War
1969	First Moon Landing
1989	Fall of the Berlin Wall

Thomas Kuhn

1922	Born in Cincinnati
1962	First publication of *The Structure of Scientific Revolutions*
1996	Dies in Cambridge, Massachusetts

Introduction

We saw in the previous chapter how the positivist view of science – that it starts from the collection of facts and from these builds theories – was called into question by Popper. The logic of science could never lie in the creation of universal theories from finite facts simply because there was no logical way in which such laws or theories could be derived from facts. Instead, the theory had to come first and the logic of science – its particular claim to rationality – was to be found in the subsequent testing of theories once they had been invented.

Thomas Kuhn (1922–96), whose work is the topic of this chapter, agreed with Popper on a number of important points. Indicating these points of agreement, Kuhn himself stated: "neither Sir Karl nor I is an inductivist. We do not believe that there are rules for inducing correct theories from facts, or even that theories, correct or incorrect, are induced at all. Instead we view them as imaginative posits, invented in one piece for application to nature" ('Logic of discovery or psychology of research?', p. 12).

Kuhn also agrees with Popper that the image of the scientist making observations without any theoretical preconceptions or expectations is nothing more than a myth. "Sir Karl and I are united in opposition to a number of classical positivism's most characteristic theses," he states; "we both emphasize, for example, the intimate and inevitable entanglement of scientific observation with scientific theory; we are correspondingly sceptical of efforts to produce any neutral observation language" ('Logic of discovery or psychology of research?', p. 3).

For both Kuhn and Popper, then, science does not start with the observation of facts but with theory. Despite these points of agreement, however, there are major differences between the two thinkers. For Popper, as we have seen, falsification is the very engine of scientific progress. It is as though science is in a state of near-permanent revolution, with theories always on the brink of being rejected and replaced by new ones. Kuhn, on the other hand, argues that such theoretical revolutions are the *exception* rather than the rule. This is because, for Kuhn, the grip that any theory has on the minds of the scientists guided by it is far greater than is imagined by Popper. According to Kuhn, scientists *do not* normally try to test their theories to destruction, as Popper's falsificationism would advocate, but are usually content to work within the confines of the currently prevailing theory.

The Structure of Scientific Revolutions

Kuhn's philosophy of science is most famously put forward in his book, *The Structure of Scientific Revolutions* (1970). Despite its title, the main thrust of the argument in *The Structure of Scientific Revolutions* (hereafter referred to as *Structure*) is that scientific revolutions are relatively rare and that science is, for the most part, characterised by theoretical and methodological *conservatism*. What scientists do most of the time, what Kuhn calls 'normal science', is to work within a research tradition that they share with the rest of the scientific community. This shared tradition provides the scientific community with concepts and theoretically motivated questions to investigate, examples of accepted research methodology, and practical and technological tools with which to undertake research. These research traditions – these mixtures of theory, practice, and technology – are what Kuhn calls **paradigms**. For the most part, these paradigms are not questioned or tested in any way by the scientists working within them.

For Kuhn, it is the existence of such an accepted paradigm that marks out a particular field of scientific activity as a mature science. According to Kuhn, it is precisely because scientists agree on the fundamentals – because they no longer have to spend time and energy arguing with one another about the basic assumptions of their discipline – that science is so successful. Scientists can concentrate on a range of problems defined by the paradigm and explore these problems in greater and greater depth in a way that would not be possible were there no agreement on the foundations of their science.

Box 2.1 **Thomas Kuhn**

Thomas Samuel Kuhn was born in Cincinnati, Ohio, in 1922. He studied physics at Harvard and gained his doctorate there in 1949. He subsequently worked in several other US universities, moving to Berkeley in 1956 (where he discussed the ideas that were to develop into *The Structure of Scientific Revolutions* with Paul Feyerabend), to Princeton in 1964 and, in 1979, to MIT. He died in 1996.

As a young graduate student, Kuhn was asked by the President of Harvard, James Conant, to teach on a course on General Education in Science. This was a course

Box 2.1 (cont.)

designed to give humanities students a background in the history of scientific ideas. For Kuhn, already pursuing his PhD in theoretical physics, it was also his first exposure to many classics in the history of science, such Aristotle's *Physics*. Kuhn was perplexed by a seeming contradiction between the fact that Aristotle is generally regarded as one of the great thinkers of all time and the fact that much of his scientific work, interpreted from the viewpoint of the present day, seems hopelessly wrong. It was Kuhn's realisation that Aristotle approached his research with a different mindset from that of the present day scientist that sowed the seeds of the ideas that were to later result in *The Structure of Scientific Revolutions*. When one tried to understand the work of Aristotle, or any other historical scientist, in its own terms rather than those of today, it suddenly seemed to make much more sense. *The Structure of Scientific Revolutions*, first published in 1962, went on to become one of the most widely read works of twentieth-century philosophy. It was translated into over 20 languages and sold over 1 million copies in English alone. Its terminology of 'paradigms' and 'paradigm shifts' has found its way into the jargon of politicians, financiers, healthcare and education professionals, and pretty much anyone who advocates change of some sort or other. Needless to say, these terms are not always used in ways of which Kuhn would have approved, but the widespread use of the terminology testifies to the impact of his ideas.

Though the paradigm presents the working scientist with examples to emulate, the scientist does not simply aim at replicating the basic results of the paradigm over and over again. Rather she attempts to extend and deepen the paradigm by trying to apply it to new areas or to specify its fundamental ideas in greater detail, e.g. by using new technology to measure variables to a higher level of accuracy. The scientist does *not*, regardless of what Popper might say, attempt to disprove or test the paradigm. Indeed, Kuhn does not believe that the search for any sort of novelty – whether a groundbreaking theory or major new discovery – plays a part in the normal business of science. He states:

> No part of normal science is to call forth new sorts of phenomena . . . Nor do scientists normally aim to invent new theories, and they are often intolerant of those invented by others. Instead, normal-scientific research is directed to the articulation of those phenomena and theories that the paradigm already supplies. (*Structure*, p. 24)

This 'articulation' of the pre-existing paradigm – filling in its gaps and refining its details - Kuhn refers to as 'puzzle-solving', and it is this that most scientists do most of the time. The satisfaction gained by the scientist working in the normal research environment is in the use of his ingenuity to solve these puzzles thrown up by the paradigm.

Scientific revolutions

No paradigm explains everything; there will always be questions left unanswered and phenomena left unexplained. Indeed, any paradigm has to be sufficiently incomplete to give the scientific community ample scope for new research. But, in the course of this research, findings that are inconsistent with the paradigm, or which are difficult to accommodate within its framework, are bound to be obtained. Scientists do not thereby consider the paradigm to be falsified and reject it. On the contrary, says Kuhn, they will reject the troublesome observations as being somehow faulty or unreliable. We have already seen that even Popper recognised that this was a possible, and logically justifiable, reaction to the discovery of facts that seem to contradict a theory.

These observations that do not seem to fit with a paradigm are called **anomalies**, and, if they continue to be found consistently, the scientific community may start to take them more seriously. Changes will be made to the paradigm – concepts somewhat redefined, methods altered – to try to accommodate the anomalies. In tandem with the rejigging of the paradigm, there will be more and more research on the anomalies themselves in an effort to understand them. It is only with the effort, over many decades, to make sense of the anomalies in terms of the dominant paradigm that their true nature becomes clear. So, whereas Popper would have us believe that scientific advance results from the rejection of theories in the face of falsifying observations, for Kuhn it is precisely the conservatism of the scientific community, its unwillingness to abandon the paradigm that underpins all of its scientific work, that results in new knowledge.

Kuhn provides real examples from the history of science to back up his claims about the practice of science. One such example is **Ptolemaic cosmology**, according to which the Earth is the stationary centre of the universe. This theory was replaced by the Sun-centred model of the solar system associated with

Copernicus and, later, Galileo. As it is an example cited not only by Kuhn, but by Lakatos and Feyerabend, the two philosophers who are the topic of the next chapter, it is worth briefly describing its main characteristics. According to the Ptolemaic theory, which was dominant in the ancient world and in the Middle Ages, the Earth is stationary and is in the centre of the universe. The Sun, Moon, and other planets move around the stationary Earth in circular orbits. These 'heavenly bodies', unlike the craggy and mountainous Earth, are assumed to be perfect spheres. It was also believed that different physical laws operated on Earth from those that operated in the heavens. Thus, one could not extrapolate from explanations of Earth-bound phenomena in trying to explain celestial phenomena.

Kuhn points out that the Ptolemaic theory was consistent with many astronomical observations. Many of the predictions that it made, for example about the changing positions of stars and planets, were reasonably accurate. Other predictions, however, such as the timing of the equinoxes, were not quite right.

In this situation, what the scientists of the time did was not to completely reject the theory as being falsified, but to work within the paradigm to reduce the discrepancies between what the theory predicted and what was actually observed. In other words, the scientists engaged in puzzle-solving: they sought to refine and extend the paradigm so that its equinox predictions were improved. In order to do this, however, the theory itself had to be tweaked and altered here and there in order to try to get rid of the discrepancies. But this only led to the theory becoming more and more complicated as various tweaks and alterations accumulated. It got to the point where the elimination of a discrepancy in one aspect of the theory only succeeded in producing a discrepancy elsewhere. It is this inability of a paradigm to provide the solutions to the problems that it itself gives rise to, and not the mere existence of anomalies, that ultimately results in crisis and scientific revolution.

How, then, do scientists respond to a crisis in the prevailing paradigm. Again, says Kuhn, they do not simply reject the paradigm as the falisficationists would have us believe:

> No process yet disclosed by the historical study of scientific development at all resembles the methodological stereotype of falsification by direct comparison with nature . . . The decision to reject one paradigm is always simultaneously the decision to accept another, and the judgment that leads scientists to that decision involves the comparison of both paradigms with nature *and* with each other. (*Structure*, p. 77)

Scientists, then, do not reject a paradigm, no matter how problematic and unwieldy it has become, in favour of nothing. They do not reject a paradigm *and then* try to come up with something to replace it. They reject one paradigm in favour of a new paradigm that already exists, even if it is not yet fully developed. Indeed, for Kuhn, science *always* takes place within a paradigm. To reject the existing paradigm with nothing to replace it would, for Kuhn, be a rejection of science altogether, not merely of one paradigm.

It is the inability of a prevailing paradigm to accommodate anomalies that paves the way for the creation and acceptance of a new paradigm. As scientists tweak and alter the paradigm in order to try to square it with anomalous observations, they are driven to more and more drastic revisions of the prevailing theory. This effectively slackens the rules for scientific practice which had previously been relatively clearly defined by the paradigm. The criteria according to which one carries out and judges scientific work become increasingly unclear, and it is this lack of clarity that provides an entry point for new ideas to be considered by the scientific community. In the past, such ideas would not even have got a hearing as they would have been at variance with the paradigm, but in times of crises it is no longer clear what exactly *is* the paradigm, so pulled and pushed has it been in an attempt to make sense of anomalies.

It is, says Kuhn, only in times of crisis, when the rule-bound practice of normal science has collapsed, that the scientist resembles the picture that many people have:

> he will look almost like our most prevalent image of the scientist. He will . . . often seem a man searching at random, trying experiments just to see what will happen, looking for an effect whose nature he cannot guess. (*Structure*, p. 87)

The rejection of an old paradigm and the acceptance of a new one by the scientific community constitutes a **scientific revolution**. A scientific revolution is not usually an overnight thing. In the case of the replacement of the Ptolemaic Earth-centred theory of the planets by the Sun-centred **Copernican theory**, the process took centuries. Nevertheless, says Kuhn, the actual appearance of a new paradigm – its emergence into the crisis-stricken world of science – may be relatively sudden:

> the new paradigm, or a sufficient hint to permit later articulation, emerges all at once, sometimes in the middle of the night, in the mind of a man deeply immersed in crisis. What the nature of that final stage is – how an individual invents (or finds he has invented) a new way of giving order to data now all assembled – must here remain inscrutable and may be permanently so. (*Structure*, pp. 89–90)

Like Popper, then, Kuhn sees the actual process of coming up with a new theory as something that escapes analysis. A new theory may simply suddenly occur to a scientist in a moment of insight or inspiration; it is not necessarily something built up painstakingly bit by bit on the basis on past scientific findings. It is, rather, a new way of looking at things and the extent to which this new approach will bear scientific fruit is something that can only be discovered in the course of future research.

For both Kuhn and Popper, then, the appearance of a new theory or paradigm is not the end of scientific work or the culmination of research, but the start of research. The theory comes first, and then the scientist carries out research either to try to falsify the theory, as Popper would maintain, or to refine and extend it, as Kuhn argues. Both thinkers are fundamentally opposed to the positivist idea that we start with data and build theories on them.

Kuhn likens a scientific revolution to a political one. It is not the case that a political regime is overthrown in favour of nothing; it is overthrown in favour of a new political vision, a new model of society. But this vision is not yet fully worked out, it remains relatively vague, and it is the job of the revolutionaries to implement it. The new model of society, then, is accepted not because of what it has done – it has not yet been implemented and so has little in the way of concrete achievements to speak of – but because of what it promises: a new and better society. For Kuhn, scientific revolutions operate along similar lines. The new paradigm has not yet been fully worked out, and so it is incorrect to think that it wins out over the old because there is more evidence in favour of it or because it explains more phenomena than the old. Even though it may do a better job of dealing with the anomalies that have caused a crisis than the old paradigm, the wider range and application of the new paradigm is, by definition, unknown at the time of its adoption by the scientific community. This is because it is only in the acceptance of the new paradigm and the implementation of research under its rules and principles that its strengths and weaknesses can ultimately be known. The new paradigm is accepted not because of its achievements, but because of its perceived potential.

In psychology, the emergence of cognitive psychology over behaviourism as the dominant approach within psychology has been thought of as a scientific revolution, and, indeed, the whole period is sometimes referred to as the 'cognitive revolution'. We shall see in Chapter 17 how closely the change from behaviourism to cognitivism really exemplifies the characteristics of a scientific revolution as Kuhn saw it.

The non-rational nature of paradigm shifts

The fact that the success or otherwise of a new paradigm cannot be known in advance is just one of the reasons that, for Kuhn, a scientific revolution, with the replacement of one paradigm by another, is a *non-rational* affair. We saw in the previous chapter that the logical positivists attempted to locate the rationality of science in the building of theories based ultimately on observational facts. We saw also that Popper argued that there were no logical grounds on which the induction required by the positivists could proceed. Either science did not have the rational character that it was thought to have, or this rationality was located at some other point in the scientific process than the construction of theories. We saw that, for Popper, logic and rationality characterise the testing of theories once they have been created.

But for Kuhn the rejection of one paradigm in favour of another cannot proceed on rational grounds. This is one of the more controversial aspects of Kuhn's analysis of science: that the choice between two paradigms is not rational, it is not something that can be decided by simply examining the evidence and thereby determining which of the two competing paradigms gives us the most accurate picture of nature. This is not only because the fruit of the new paradigm cannot be known in advance, but for two other reasons. These are: the theory-laden nature of observation and the incommensurablity of paradigms.

Theory-laden observation

According to positivism we can have data or observations that are, in a sense, completely neutral when it comes to scientific theories: they are simply the observations that are given to any competent observer regardless of his or her theoretical beliefs or commitments. It is precisely because of this that the positivists believed that these basic observations could then form the basis for the construction of scientific theories. This, too, was the basis of the early empiricism of people like Francis Bacon, who enjoined scientists to rid themselves of preconceptions and prejudices – the 'idols of the tribe' he called them – so as to be able to observe the world of nature in a direct and unprejudiced way. This is a way of thinking that informed much of empiricism as well as philosophy of science. But Kuhn argues that such a view is wrong: there are no 'neutral' observations, there are no data independent of the observer's theoretical beliefs and commitments. Everything is seen through the prism of the particular paradigm to which the scientist subscribes. Evidence, data, observations are not the basic starting points from which we construct or judge theories, but are themselves the *products of theories*. It is only under the legitimating rules of a paradigm that anything can possibly count as data or observation.

And it is not only the methodological rules of a paradigm that allow a certain piece of data to count as a legitimate observation. Kuhn actually believes that scientists working under one paradigm see the world differently from those working under another paradigm. This is because their observations are **theory-laden**. This means that what they see is to some extent determined not only by what they are looking at, but also by the theories to which they subscribe. In effect, says Kuhn, scientists working within one paradigm live in a different world from those working within a different paradigm. This is one of the most radical of Kuhn's proposals and, at first sight, such an assertion may seem frankly outrageous. Surely the scientists live in the same world even if they have different beliefs about the nature of that world? Kuhn, however, has powerful arguments to back up his claim, and some of the evidence for his view comes from the psychology of perception, particularly from 'Gestalt shifts' in which the same figure can be seen in different ways.

Take the well-known example of the Necker cube (see Figure 2.1a). We can see this cube either as if we are looking down on it from above or up at it from below, and our vision can flip between these two different perceptions, sometimes at will. Yet nothing in the physical stimulus has changed at all. Nevertheless different perceptions are produced.

Another example give by Kuhn is the ambiguous figure of the duck–rabbit (see Figure 2.1b). Again, this figure can be seen in two ways – either as a duck, with its beak sticking out to the left, or as a rabbit, with its ears to the left and its mouth to the right – despite the fact that the physical stimulus has not changed.

Given, then, that our perceptions are driven not only by the physical world on which we gaze, but by other factors that are internal to us (rather than external in the environment), Kuhn argues that one of the things that a paradigm does is to induce in the scientist a certain way of looking at the world. Those who are educated in a particular paradigm will see the world differently from those who are not:

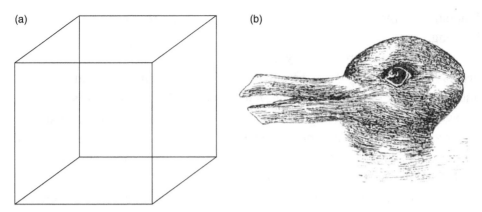

Fig. 2.1 (a) The Necker cube; (b) The duck–rabbit

What were ducks in the scientist's world before the revolution are rabbits afterwards. The man who first saw the exterior of the box from above later sees its interior from below. Transformations like these, though usually more gradual and almost always irreversible, are common concomitants of scientific training. Looking at a contour map, the student sees lines on paper, the cartographer a picture of a terrain. Looking at a bubble-chamber photograph, the student sees confused and broken lines, the physicist a record of familiar subnuclear events. (*Structure*, p. 111)

The education of the scientific student, then, has the effect of actually changing the way that he or she sees the world. To those committed to a positivist view of science, according to which one observes nature as it actually is and then makes constructions upon these basic observations, such a view seems ridiculous. Science supposedly starts with observation of the 'facts', which are objective and, at least in theory, accessible to anyone. What Kuhn says is that this is not the case: scientific observations are determined not exclusively by the objective reality that the scientist observes, but also by the training and education that the scientist has received.

Though such a view may seem outlandish, a few moments' reflection will reveal that it is, in fact, plausible. To someone who has never learned to read, the black marks on white paper that you are now perceiving will be no more than that – meaningless black lines and loops on white paper – whereas to you who have learned how to read they will be the vehicles of thoughts and ideas. They will have meaning. You literally see this page differently from someone who has not learned to read. Indeed, it is the meaning conveyed by words and letters that will be the most salient aspect of your perception, far more than the physical aspects, such as font. We are, then, in our own experience perfectly familiar with the altering of visual perception as the result of education and learning.

This shaping of perception by education is not, of course, something that occurs instantaneously; it is the outcome of prolonged immersion in the ideas and concepts of the paradigm. And, more importantly than this, it is *practical* engagement with the paradigm rather than simply learning about ideas that is important. The paradigm contains not only ideas, concepts, and principles of investigation, but practical methods, in which the student in the course of his or her education will be extensively trained.

Though the examples given by Kuhn are intuitively attractive illustrations of what might be engendered by a scientific revolution, there are important differences between these Gestalt switches and the changes in world-view wrought by paradigm shifts. In particular, we have, in the case of ambiguous figures like the Necker cube and duck–rabbit, independent knowledge of the figures themselves so that we know that they are not changing while our perception of them does change. We know this, for example, because we ourselves have actually created the figures and the physical page on which they stand. But we have no such independent knowledge of reality when it comes to paradigm changes. We have no knowledge of what is out there that is independent of our perception of it. In this sense, then, we cannot differentiate between our subjective perception and the objective reality of which it is a reflection in the same way that we can with the ambiguous figures. For the scientist, then, reality *is* what he or she observes. When what the scientist observes changes as a result of a scientific revolution, Kuhn's assertion that the scientist is now operating in a 'different world' is not as outlandish as it might have seemed at first.

It should also be noted that the perception of ambiguous figures can flip back and forth between the different perceptions whereas the perceptual changes brought about by scientific revolutions are, generally, one-way and irreversible. This is no doubt because of the prolonged immersion in a paradigm that is necessary to alter perception in a particular way: it is not a momentary or instantaneous 'flipping' of perception, just as learning to read is a prolonged rather than an instantaneous process.

According to Kuhn, then, "the scientist who embraces a new paradigm is like a man wearing inverting lenses. Confronting the same constellation of objects as before and knowing that he does so, he nevertheless finds them transformed through and through in many of their details" (*Structure*, p. 122). Indeed, says Kuhn, the idea that the scientist sees the world anew is corroborated by the reports of scientists themselves, who talk of the "scales falling from the eyes" or of a problem suddenly being illuminated by a metaphorical "lightning flash" (*Structure*, p. 122). All of these examples and metaphors attest to the wholesale nature of the switch of perception that occurs as a result of scientific revolution. It is not as though this or that specific phenomenon is now seen in a different way; on the contrary, the whole field is transformed, and nothing is quite as it was. And it is because of the wholesale (and irreversible) nature of the perceptual changes wrought by a scientific revolution, says Kuhn, that the process is non-rational. Because observations are structured by different paradigms pre- and post-revolution, there is no neutral, paradigm-independent, ground on which they can be compared.

This change in the perceptual world of the scientist is not confined to seeing old phenomena in a new way, it also allows the scientist to see phenomena that he or she could not have seen before. We saw above that, according to Ptolemaic cosmology, the heavenly bodies were supposed to be perfect spheres. Any observed imperfections, such as sunspots for example, would be inconsistent with the theory. But, says Kuhn, even though sunspots were visible to astronomers before the Copernican revolution overthrew the Ptolemaic paradigm, it was only *after* the new paradigm had been accepted that they began to be noticed. Because they did not fit in with the prevailing Ptolemaic paradigm, they were not seen prior to the paradigm change. It is important to realise that Kuhn is not simply saying that astronomers saw these phenomena but, because they did not fit in with their theory, decided to ignore them. Kuhn is arguing that astronomers literally did not see them.

Again, in order to accept this view, one has to divest oneself of the simplistic positivist–empiricist viewpoint that there is such a thing as pure, unadulterated perception which is direct perceptual contact with what is really there independent of attention and expectation. For scientists, just like the rest of us, are only apt to see what they are looking for and to filter out those things that they are not looking for. Again, the findings of perceptual psychology are relevant when it comes to understanding the role of paradigms in shaping the perception of the scientist. We all know from experience that we can fail to notice something that is right in front of us, and studies of **inattentional blindness** have demonstrated as much. In one well-known study (Simons and Chabris 1999), participants were shown a short video in which six people passed a basketball back and forth between them. The participants were asked to count the number of passes made by either those players with black vests or those with white vests. Part of the way through the video a man dressed in a gorilla suit walked across the screen, turned to face the camera, beat his chest, and then walked off on the other side of the screen. Despite the fact that the gorilla-suited man was visible on the screen for several seconds, a large proportion of the participants did not notice his presence. Because they were not expecting a man in a gorilla suit to walk across the screen, and because their attention was firmly fixed on counting the passes made by the basketball players, they literally did not see the man in the gorilla suit. This was even more marked when the participants had to count the number of passes made by the white team, which meant that they had to ignore the passes made by the black team. Filtering out people dressed in black may have contributed to their inability to see the man dressed in the black gorilla suit.

We have here a striking demonstration that we do not simply see what is right in front of our faces and that our expectations play an important part in our perception. It is therefore not outrageous to claim, as Kuhn does, that when Ptolemaic astronomers did not expect to see spots on the surface of the Sun, they did not see them, and that later astronomers did see them when the Copernican revolution made such observations legitimate.

Incommensurability

But there are other reasons as to why we cannot simply compare each paradigm against the data in order to determine rationally which one we should accept. One very important such reason is the fact that, according to Kuhn, different paradigms have different standards of evidence, different methodological rules, and different concepts and questions from one another. What counts as good, methodologically sound evidence for one paradigm will not count as legitimate evidence under the rules of its competing paradigm. Each paradigm will be superior to the other in terms of its *own* rules and methods, but will be inferior in terms of its opponent's rules and methods. The point here is that there is no such thing as 'evidence' that simply exists on its own outside the confines of a particular paradigm. Evidence or data are what scientists collect under the guidance of a particular paradigm. There is no evidence that is independent of a paradigm, and so there is no external yardstick relative to which the worth of different paradigms can be measured: each paradigm fulfils its own criteria while falling short of the criteria of its opponent. This lack of comparability between paradigms – because of the different observations that they engender and the different rules that they embody – is called **incommensurability**. Kuhn sums up his argument thus:

> Just because it is a transition between incommensurables, the transition between competing paradigms cannot be made a step at a time, forced by logic and neutral experience. Like the gestalt switch, it must occur all at once (though not necessarily in an instant) or not at all. (*Structure*, p. 150)

Rather than the outcome of rational argumentation, Kuhn claims that "[t]he transfer of allegiance from paradigm to paradigm is a conversion experience that cannot be forced" (*Structure*, p. 151).

The myth of the framework

The all-encompassing nature of the change wrought by a paradigm shift means that it is not open to the sort of discussion and rational deliberation that the likes of Popper believe lie behind the choice of scientific theory. Such a rational choice requires the existence of some findings that can adjudicate between rival theories, but, according to Kuhn, this is impossible. Popper, of course, is not naïve enough to believe that there is such a thing as **theory–neutral** observation. Indeed, he explicitly states:

> My point of view is . . . that our ordinary language is full of theories: that observation is always *observation in the light of theories*; that it is only the inductivist prejudice which leads people to think that there could be a phenomenal language, free of theories . . . (*The Logic of Scientific Discovery*, p. 37, footnote)

But though Popper believes that all our observations are theory-laden, he nevertheless believes that there is far more scope for discussion and deliberation between holders of different theories than does Kuhn. For Kuhn, the differences between pre- and post-revolutionary paradigms are so far-reaching – remember that scientists are said to live in different worlds – that there is no real common point of contact or shared ground from which discussion could start. The paradigms are incommensurable. Popper, however, believes that such discussion is possible. It may not be easy, but it can be done. Think, for example, of how different the world of the ancient Greeks must have been from our own. Not only did they have different scientific paradigms, for them the world was full of gods and supernatural events. The path of an individual through life was not determined by his or her own free choice, but was decreed by the fates. There can be no doubt that the ancient Greeks, living more than 2500 years ago (more, in the case of Homer) saw the world very differently from the way in which we do. We and they are, therefore, surely examples of peoples living in 'different worlds' as Kuhn would have it. Nevertheless, we *can* understand the world of the ancient Greeks, and we can translate their poetic, philosophical, and scientific writings into our own modern languages. This is not to say that such translation or understanding is easy – it is clearly not and requires a great deal of skill and knowledge – or that we can understand and capture every nuance of the ancient Greek mind – we probably cannot. Nevertheless, we can understand at least some aspects of the ancient Greek world-view, we are not in the position of living in different mental worlds that are so incommensurable that there can be no common understanding whatsoever. Common understanding between people guided by different paradigms – whether scientific or cultural – does occur. Kuhn, though he provides persuasive examples of the importance of paradigms in guiding the vision of scientists, perhaps draws too strong a conclusion when he states that this makes communication or comparison between different paradigms impossible.

Popper calls the overemphasis on theories, and belief systems in general, as insurmountable barriers to communication 'The Myth of the Framework'. According to Popper:

> The Myth of the Framework is, in our time, the central bulwark of irrationalism. My counter-thesis is that it simply exaggerates a difficulty into an impossibility. The difficulty of discussion between people brought up in different frameworks is to be admitted. But nothing is more fruitful than such a discussion; than the culture clash which has stimulated some of the greatest intellectual revolutions... a critical comparison of the competing theories, of the competing frameworks, is always possible. ('Normal science and its dangers', p. 57)

The importance of convention

We have seen above that there are many similarities between Popper and Kuhn: both attack the empiricist view that there is such a thing as neutral observation, which provides the scientist with facts with which she can then build her theory. Both also point to the overarching and pre-eminent role of theory, not only in guiding observation, but in actually constituting the very nature of our observations from the outset. They differ, however, on the essential goal of scientific activity – whether it is trying to falsify a theory or merely extending the reach of the current paradigm – and on the rationality of any decision on the part of the scientific community to change from one theory to another. For Popper this process of theory-testing and replacement is founded on a core of rationality; for Kuhn the incommensurability of paradigms means that such decisions cannot proceed on rational grounds.

But let us look more closely at the actual decision to test and, potentially, falsify a theory. One of the criticisms that Kuhn puts forward of Popper's falsificationism is that there are *always* falsifying data. No theory can ever explain everything, and will, therefore, *always* be falsified. According to Kuhn:

> If any and every failure to fit were ground for theory rejection, all theories ought to be rejected at all times ... if only severe failure to fit justifies theory rejection, then the Popperians will require some criterion of 'improbability' or 'degree of falsification'. (*Structure*, pp. 146–7)

Thus, the mere existence of facts or observations that do not fit with a theory does not suffice for it to be falsified. But then the question arises as to when observations can falsify a theory. Under what circumstances is theory rejection justified?

As we saw in the previous chapter, Popper himself recognises that a theory can never be conclusively disproved, because any finding that does not fit with a theory can be rejected as simply being an erroneous finding (rather than the theory itself being erroneous). For Popper, then, there is a *choice* about whether we accept apparently conflicting data as falsifying a theory. "Basic statements [e.g. observation statements]," he says, "are accepted as the result of a decision or agreement; and to that extent they are conventions" (*The Logic of Scientific Discovery*, p. 88). It is, of course, Popper's contention that, in general, it is a good thing to accept the falsification of theories, because this leads to the development of new and better theories. It is in this way that science advances.

But the idea that falsification depends crucially on the *decision* of the scientific community, which introduces an element of **conventionalism** into Popper's vision of science, raises difficult questions about the logic of theory rejection. The rejection of a theory is not forced upon the scientific community by logic, because there are always other possible reasons for the obtaining of observations that do not fit with the theory other than the falsity of the theory itself. It is just as logical to reject observations as erroneous or biased as it is to reject the theory. The scientific community, in the face of the opposing findings, *decides* that 'enough is enough' and that there is sufficient evidence of sufficient quality to reject the theory.

But if we accept the existence of such conventionalism – and it seems that we must – then Popper's philosophy of science runs the risk of succumbing completely to the vagaries of scientific and intellectual fashion. If all that is needed for a theory to be rejected are some observations that are inconsistent with it (and, as Kuhn argues, there are *always* some such observations) and a collective decision to reject the theory, then there seems to be little left of the logic and rationality that Popper sought to relocate from the building of theories to the testing of theories.

It was in order to prevent Popper's falsificationist scheme from collapsing into the perceived irrationalism of Kuhn's scientific revolutions that the next thinker that we will consider, Imre Lakatos, elaborated a new version of falsificationism. He wanted to avoid the irrationalism that he felt was inherent in Kuhn's philosophy of science and felt that a rejuvenated and more sophisticated version of falsificationism would allow him to do this. But, as we shall see, his main interlocutor, Paul Feyerabend, believed that the irrationalism suggested by Kuhn was not something to be avoided, but embraced.

Revision questions

1. What is a paradigm?
2. What, according to Kuhn, constitutes normal science?
3. What are anomalies and what role do they play in precipitating scientific revolutions?
4. Why do scientists decide to adopt a new paradigm over an old one?
5. What did Kuhn mean when he said that scientists before and after a scientific revolution can be thought of as living in different worlds?
6. What is theory-laden observation? Give examples from perceptual psychology to illustrate your answer.
7. Why did Kuhn believe that paradigm shifts are non-rational?

References

Kuhn, T. S. (1970a). Logic of discovery or psychology of research? In I. Lakatos and A. Musgrave (eds.) *Criticism and the Growth of Knowledge*. Cambridge: Cambridge University Press, pp. 1–23.

(1970b). *The Structure of Scientific Revolutions*, 2nd edn. Chicago, IL: University of Chicago Press.

Popper, K. R. ([1959]/1992). *The Logic of Scientific Discovery*. London: Routledge.

Popper, K. R. (1970). Normal science and its dangers. In I. Lakatos and A. Musgrave (eds.) *Criticism and the Growth of Knowledge*. Cambridge: Cambridge University Press, pp. 51–8.

Simons, D. J. and Chabris, C. F. (1999). Gorillas in our midst: sustained inattentional blindness for dynamic events. *Perception*, 28, 1059–74.

3 Lakatos and Feyerabend: research programmes and anarchism

Timeline

1914–18	First World War
1917	Russian Revolution
1929	Wall Street Crash
1939–45	Second World War
1953	Discovery of structure of DNA
1955–75	Vietnam War
1969	First Moon Landing
1989	Fall of the Berlin Wall

Imre Lakatos

1922	Born in Debrecen, Hungary
1950–53	Imprisoned for political beliefs
1956	Leaves Hungary for England
1974	Dies in London

Paul Feyerabend

1924	Born in Vienna
1942	Conscripted into German army
1960	Moves to Berkeley, California
1975	First publication of *Against Method*
1994	Dies in Genolier, Switzerland

Introduction

The two philosophers of science to be discussed in this chapter, Imre Lakatos and Paul Feyerabend, were both strongly influenced by Popper's falsificationism. In the case of Lakatos, this influence was positive and he sought to build upon Popper's ideas. In particular, he wanted to develop a more sophisticated falsificationist philosophy that maintained the rational core of Popper's approach while reflecting the actual practice of science and also minimising the risk of falsifying a theory prematurely. Feyerabend, on the other hand, although a one-time student of Popper's, reacted against the idea that falsificationism captures the essential feature of scientific method. Indeed, as will be seen, he questioned whether there was any single 'scientific method' and argued that science sometimes only progresses by breaking methodological rules.

Imre Lakatos

Imre Lakatos (1922–74) saw his task as improving on Popper's essential insights in order to avoid falling into what he thought of as Kuhn's irrationalism. Kuhn rejected falsificationism and, in so doing, had, according to Lakatos, replaced rationality with irrationality: "*in Kuhn's view scientific revolution is irrational, a matter for mob psychology*" ('Falsification and the methodology of scientific

---

Box 3.1 Imre Lakatos

Imre Lakatos was born Imre Lipschitz in Hungary in 1922. He studied mathematics, physics, and philosophy at the University of Debrecen. During World War II he joined the anti-Nazi resistance and changed his surname from the Jewish 'Lipschitz' to the non-Jewish 'Molnár' in order to avoid detection by the Nazis. His mother and grandmother, however, both died in Auschwitz. After the war he changed his surname for a third and final time to Lakatos, which means 'locksmith' in Hungarian. His choice of a working-class occupation as a name reflected his increasing Communist sympathies (Figure 3.1).

Box 3.1 (cont.)

Fig. 3.1 Imre Lakatos

Box 3.1 (cont.)

In 1947 he took up a position in the Hungarian Ministry of Education, but questioned some of the policies of the Stalinist regime. As a result he was imprisoned from 1950 to 1953 for his political views. Lakatos supported the Hungarian uprising of 1956 against Soviet control of Hungary. The rebellion was crushed by Soviet invasion, and, learning that he was due to be arrested, Lakatos fled first to Vienna and then to England.

In England Lakatos obtained a PhD in philosophy from Cambridge and taught at the London School of Economics from 1960 until his sudden and untimely death from a heart attack in 1974. He was, by all accounts, a lively and engaging personality, and his obituary in *The Times* gives a flavour of his personal charm:

> When he lectured, the room would be crowded, the atmosphere electric, and from time to time there would be a gale of laughter ... With his sharp tongue and strong opinions he sometimes seemed authoritarian; but he was 'Imre' to everyone; and he invited searching criticisms of his ideas ...

research programmes', p. 178; hereafter referred to as 'Methodology'). Given that there are no rational criteria for deciding between paradigms, or even comparing them, the switch from one to the other can only come about because of social factors, irrational preference, and faith. But, says Lakatos, Kuhn has rejected, and shown to be wrong, only a naïve and simplistic version of falsificationism. A more sophisticated falsificationism may avoid succumbing to irrationalism and mob psychology by finding rational grounds for theory change.

Like Popper and Kuhn (and Feyerabend; see the second part of this chapter), Lakatos believes that the idea of knowledge that can be proved conclusively to be true is an illusion. For centuries, scientists and philosophers equated knowledge with *proven knowledge*, and "*scientific honesty demanded that one assert nothing that is unproven*" ('Methodology', p. 94). We have already seen in the previous two chapters that, according to Popper and Kuhn, no scientific theory can be proven to be true. This is because of, among other things, the non-existence of inductive logic and the essential theory-ladenness of all observation. What falsificationism did, when faced with these problems, was to assert that, though one could never prove a scientific theory to be true, one could prove it to be false.

For Lakatos, however, a simplistic falsificationist position is also untenable, for it assumes that there exist absolutely firm observations, data, that can conclusively falsify a theory. But, as we have already seen in connection with Kuhn, this simple distinction between theoretical proposals on the one hand and 'hard facts' on the other cannot be maintained. The very facts themselves, the acceptance of a statement as a matter of observation, is only possible in the light of a theory for which *a certain statement plays the role of reporting an observation*. Moreover, says Lakatos, our theoretical expectations structure the very act of observation itself. Kant and Popper, says Lakatos, have shown that "there can be no sensations unimpregnated by expectations" ('Methodology', p. 99).

In addition to this, Lakatos points out (as had both Popper and Kuhn) that discrepant observations do not mean that a theory is definitely wrong; it could be the case something is amiss with the observations. Lakatos therefore rejects both the empiricism of the logical positivists and a naïve falsificationism that believes that observations can disprove a theory. He concludes that we can never prove a theory to be true *or false*.

Sophisticated falsificationism

Popper is what Lakatos calls a 'methodological falsificationist' (as opposed to a 'dogmatic falsificationist') in that he realises that it is a matter of *decision* on the part of the scientific community to accept that 'observations' have 'falsified' a theory – whether, for example, the potentially falsifying observations have been replicated a sufficient number of times. There is no absolute rule on this that says findings have to replicated ten or thirty times for them to falsify a theory. It is a matter of convention among scientists researching in a particular field as to whether a result has been replicated 'enough' to justify theory rejection.

The possibility is, of course, that in so doing we may reject a theory that is, in fact, true. "*The methodological falsificationist*," says Lakatos, "*separates rejection and disproof*" ('Methodology', p. 109). We have seen above that no theory can ever be conclusively disproved, but the methodological falsificationist is prepared to accept the possibility that a true theory may be rejected as a price that is worth paying for having some rational means of deciding between the worth of theories.

But, says Lakatos, there are problems with this sort of Popperian methodological falsificationism. Firstly, Lakatos argues, it does not fit in with the actual history of science. According to Popper, when a theory is falsified, and this is decided by the relevant part of the scientific community, it is rejected never to return. It becomes irrational to continue to work on that theory. But, says Lakatos, it is sometimes the case that a theory that is rejected may be reinstated as a result of appeals by upholders of the theory. The verdict, if you like, of the scientific community may be overturned and the once-rejected theory reinstated as something that is still worth working on.

A second problem with Popperian methodological falsificationism, according to Lakatos, is that it envisages theory-testing as comparing *one* theory with relevant observations. For Lakatos, in reality, a theory is not merely compared against observations, but against a rival theory as well. We have already seen that Kuhn makes a similar point when he argues that scientists do not simply reject one paradigm in favour of *nothing*, but reject one paradigm in favour of another. Lakatos therefore attempts to improve on Popper's falsificationism by arguing that we have to understand how theories relate to *one another* as well as to empirical observation. He argues that we should only treat a theory as having been falsified if there is a better theory available:

> For the naïve falsificationist any theory which can be interpreted as experimentally falsifiable, is 'acceptable' or 'scientific'. For the sophisticated falsificationist a theory is 'acceptable' or 'scientific' only if it has corroborated excess empirical content over its predecessor (or rival), that is, only if it leads to the discovery of novel facts. ('Methodology', p. 116)

In other words, Lakatos sees the scientific status of a theory not merely in terms of how it relates to observations (it can be falsified by them), but in terms of how it relates to other theories, i.e. it successfully predicts new findings.

It is this idea of theories being related to one another (and of improving on what has gone before) rather than just being related to observations, that is at the core of Lakatos's idea of the **research programme**:

> Let us say that such a series of theories is *theoretically progressive (or 'constitutes a theoretically progressive problemshift')* if each new theory has some excess empirical content over its predecessor, that is, if it predicts some novel, hitherto unexpected fact. Let us say that a theoretically progressive series of theories is also *empirically progressive (or 'constitutes an empirically progressive problemshift')* if some of this excess empirical content is also corroborated, that is, if each new theory leads us to the actual discovery of some *new fact*. Finally, let us call a problemshift *progressive* if it is both theoretically and empirically progressive, and *degenerating* if it is not. ('Methodology', p. 118)

The idea of research programmes also means, for Lakatos, that one is in the business of appraising series of theories rather than just a single theory taken in isolation. This shift to series of theories means that "Falsification can thus be said to have a *'historical character'*" ('Methodology', p. 120) – falsification can only occur when there is an improved theory that predicts new findings to take the place of the rejected theory. The mere presence of anomalies or troublesome findings does not falsify a theory. Indeed, it was one of Kuhn's points that there are always findings inconsistent with any theory and, if we take the rules of falsification literally, then all theories are falsified all the time. By arguing that we should only reject a theory when there is a better alternative, Lakatos tries to give some principled reason for maintaining a theory in the face of ever-present anomalies while, at the same time, providing some rationale for the theory's rejection if that is indeed the decision of the scientific community.

For Lakatos there is one major advantage that his theory has over the earlier form of falsificationism and that is, by shifting the emphasis to research programmes – series of theories – the procedure of rejecting theories becomes less risky. In the case of Popperian falsificationism, rejection is final. But given the risks inherent in theory rejection, Lakatos argues that there should always be room for a theory to be improved and for the interpretation of apparently falsifying data to be questioned. By applying rejection not to a single theory but to a research programme, Lakatos allows a series of theories more time to prove itself and to bear fruit before it is rejected. He thus believes that his sophisticated falsificationism runs a lesser risk of rejecting true theories.

The 'hard core' of a theory and auxiliary hypotheses

How is it, then, that a research programme can withstand the barrage of conflicting findings in order to be given a chance to prove itself and develop its full potential? According to Lakatos, such robustness is possible because not all parts of a research programme are equal. Some concepts and principles are clearly far more important than others and they form the essential commitments of the research programme. Lakatos calls these the **hard core** of the research programme. There are, however, other parts of a research programme that are more open to question. Lakatos gives the following example to illustrate the distinction. As was mentioned in the previous chapter, the cosmology put forward by Copernicus, and later defended by Galileo, put the Sun in the centre of the solar system with the other planets, including Earth, orbiting around it. This is a fundamental commitment of the Copernican research programme; it is part of its hard core. The precise nature of the planetary orbits is a question of more specific detail that is not as fundamental to the programme. Indeed, says Lakatos, early proponents of Copernicanism assumed that the planetary orbits were perfectly circular. As a result it was impossible to fit astronomical observations with the theory. But the hard core assumption of the Sun-centred cosmology was not thereby rejected; what was rejected instead was the less important assumption that planetary orbits are circular. Once this assumption was rejected and it was realised that the orbits were elliptical, the discrepancies between theory and observation were no longer as glaring.

It is these less fundamental aspects of a theory – what Lakatos calls **auxiliary hypotheses** – that can be questioned, changed, and improved in the course of a research programme. In the face of anomalous or apparently falsifying observations, these auxiliary hypotheses can be rejected without having to call into question the basic committments of the research programme. They thus form what Lakatos calls a **protective belt** around the hard core.

There are, says Lakatos, similarities between the idea of a research programme and Kuhn's idea of paradigms. Indeed, for Lakatos, a paradigm is nothing more than a research programme that has achieved monopoly status. But such theoretical monopolies, he says, seldom occur in the history of science, and more often than not we have several competing research programmes existing alongside one another. This, says Lakatos, is a healthy state of affairs for science because, as we have already seen, it is only when a theory has been falsified *and* a better alternative is available that, for Lakatos, rejection of the theory is justified.

Lakatos, then, tries to minimise the risk of rejecting a true theory by requiring that more time be available for ideas and theory variants to be developed, thus constituting a research programme. There is, says Lakatos, no such thing as 'instant rationality' in the evaluation of scientific theories. This was one of the faults of earlier versions of falsificationism: it treated rationality as a property of a single discrete event in time – the rejection of a theory as having been falsified in the face of conflicting data. But, says Lakatos, seeing rationality as being applicable only to historical traditions (i.e. research programmes) that, of their very nature, unfold and develop over time, is not only a more realistic picture of the way that science actually operates, it allows the rationality of falsificationism to still exist while minimising the risks of rejecting a true theory.

Despite its attractions, however, there is still a large amount of conventionalism in Lakatos's picture of science. Although Lakatos tries to provide a rational and objective way of deciding the relative merits of different research programmes, it is still not clear when one should change from one research programme to another.

How long should a research programme be accepted before it bears fruit? How does one know when a research programme is truly degenerating rather than just encountering temporary problems? It seems that there can be no strict answers to these questions, and that they can only be decided by the scientists who are themselves working in the relevant field rather than by abstract logic.

Paul Feyerabend

The idea that there might be no hard-and-fast rules in science is something that would have troubled Lakatos, but which was celebrated by his friend and philosophical sparring partner, Paul Feyerabend (1924–94). Feyerabend, in his most famous work *Against Method*, provocatively claimed to be putting forward an **epistemological anarchism**, according to which *there is no such thing as the scientific method*. He says:

> The following essay is written in the conviction that *anarchism*, while perhaps not the most attractive *political* philosophy, is certainly excellent medicine for **epistemology**, and for the *philosophy of science*. (*Against Method*, p. 9)

Feyerabend's point is that the world that we seek to know about is complex and multifaceted and so we should not restrict ourselves by preconceived ideas of what something called a 'correct' method should be. We need flexibility, sensitivity to different conditions and circumstances rather than rigidity, particularly a rigidity that follows not from experience or testing, but from a commitment to a **priori** abstract rules. Nothing, thinks Feyerabend, is more likely to stultify and inhibit the growth of scientific knowledge than the requirement that there is one true method which should always be followed regardless of the differing circumstances encountered in different investigations.

But as well as being, pragmatically, the most productive way of approaching science, an anarchistic or libertarian approach also has an ethical side. When we educate children, says Feyerabend, we want to encourage their individuality, their independence; a liberal education should not be about forcing thought into a preconceived conceptual straightjacket:

> The attempt to increase liberty, to lead a full and rewarding life, and the corresponding attempt to discover the secrets of nature and of man, entails, therefore, the rejection of all universal standards and of all rigid traditions. (*Against Method*, p. 12)

Box 3.2 **Paul Feyerabend**

Paul Feyerabend was born in Vienna in 1924. As a young man his twin passions were science and singing, both of which he studied in depth. In his autobiography, Feyerabend describes his youthful dreams of the future:

> The course of my life was ... clear: theoretical astronomy during the day ...; then rehearsals, coaching, vocal exercises, opera in the evening ...; and astronomical observation at night. (*Killing Time*, p. 35)

World War II brought these dreams to an end. Feyerabend was conscripted into the German army in 1942, finally reaching the rank of lieutenant, and saw action in Yugoslavia, Russia, and Poland. During a retreat from the advancing Soviet army, Feyerabend was hit by three bullets, one of which damaged his spinal nerves. He was paralysed from the waist down and required a wheelchair. He gradually learned to walk again, but only with the aid of a stick. His wounds continued to cause him pain and discomfort throughout his life.

After the war, Feyerabend studied the theatre before returning to physics. He studied under Popper at the London School of Economics in the early 1950s and was initially a supporter of his critical rationalist approach. After to moving to Berkeley in 1960 (where he met Kuhn), however, Feyerabend began to question the superiority of a scientific and rationalistic world-view.

Berkeley, like many another university in the mid and late 1960s, was the scene of student protests. These targeted not only the Vietnam War, but what was perceived to be the authoritarian nature of traditional social structures in general. Feyerabend sympathised with these protests, though he had little time for the student leaders, who he found every bit as authoritarian as the people and institutions that they criticised.

Feyerabend's unconventional approach to teaching at Berkeley (sometimes he told his students to go home if they wanted because the class notes would contain everything that they needed to know) did not always endear him to his colleagues, some of whom, he believed, tried to have him sacked. According to Feyerabend, they only gave up when they realised how much paperwork would be involved.

Feyerabend also taught at a number of other universities, including Bristol, Sussex, and Zurich (Figure 3.2). He also returned to teach at the London School of Economics, where he became close friends with Lakatos. Feyerabend was diagnosed with a brain tumour in 1993 and died the following year.

Box 3.2 (cont.)

Fig. 3.2 Paul Feyerabend

The history of science

Feyerabend claims that it is not merely his libertarian principles that argue in favour of methodological anarchism. He says that, if we look at the history of science, it is *in fact* characterised by methodological anarachism. On examining the history of science, Feyerabend says,

> [w]e find ... that there is not a single rule, however plausible, and however firmly grounded in epistemology, that is not violated at some time or other. It becomes evident that such violations are not accidental events, they are not results of insufficient knowledge or of inattention which might have been avoided. On the contrary, we see that they are necessary for progress. (*Against Method*, p. 14)

The breaking of rules, the refusal to follow a single methodological path, is not just what scientists, *in fact*, do, but it is good that they do it: it allows science to progress:

> This liberal practice ... is not just a *fact* of the history of science. It is both reasonable and *absolutely necessary* for the growth of knowledge ... given any rule, however 'fundamental' or 'rational', there are always circumstances when it is advisable not only to ignore the rule, but to adopt its opposite. (*Against Method*, p. 14)

Against falsificationism

The main target of Feyerabend's attack is Popperian falsificationism. We have already seen, in Chapter 1, that, for Popper, once a theory has been falsified it must be rejected for ever; there is no hope of its being rehabilitated. But, argues Feyerabend, such rejection of theories, even once they have been falsified, is to cut down the breadth of ideas that may, at some point, help us to understand the world and our place in it. In place of falsificationism, Feyerabend advocates theoretical **pluralism**; he believes there should be a wide range of theories in circulation, because it is only in comparing theories to one another, taking the best bits of each one, that we can hope for our knowledge to progress. We should seek guides to our understanding of the universe not only from officially sanctioned 'unfalsified' theories, but from wherever we can: "they may be taken from wherever one is able to find them – from ancient myths and modern prejudices; from the lucubrations of experts and from the fantasies of cranks" (*Against Method*, p. 33). Feyerabend points out that the idea that the Earth orbits the Sun (rather than being the stationary centre of the universe) was put forward in ancient Greece by Pythagoras only to be rejected by Aristotle and Ptolemy. Though displaced by the Ptolemaic theory, it was subsequently, and successfully, revived by Copernicus centuries later. No theory should ever be conclusively consigned to the dustbin of history – we can never be sure whether or not it might hold something of value.

To back up his anarchistic claims, Feyerabend gives examples from the history of science and goes into the case of Galileo in particular detail. Galileo (1564– 1642) argued in favour of Copernican cosmology, according to which the Earth was not the stationary centre of the universe, but was, along with the other planets, orbiting round the Sun. Some in the Roman Catholic Church, arguing that such a view was inconsistent with church teachings, tried Galileo for heresy. He was found guilty, placed under house arrest, and forced to recant his views. Though Galileo is often held up as a scientific hero, Feyerabend argues that he did not follow the path of rationality, particularly the logic of falsificationism, and that, had he done so, he would have been unable to make the progress that he did. It was only because he *departed* from strict rational criteria that Galileo succeeded in the end, says Feyerabend (Figure 3.3).

Feyerabend argues that, at the time of Galileo's trial, the weight of evidence and argument was actually on the side of the Ptolemaic theory of the stationary Earth. The most obvious piece of evidence in favour of the Earth being stationary is our own everyday observation: it seems blatantly obvious that the Earth is not moving around through space. If we truly were falsificationists, then, shouldn't this be enough to reject Galileo's theory?

Another, more complex, piece of evidence mentioned by Feyerabend is called the 'tower argument'. It goes like this: what would happen if you climbed to the top of a tall tower and dropped a weight from the top? Where would it land? Would it land at the bottom of the tower or would it land some distance away from the bottom of the tower? The answer is that it would land at the bottom of the tower. But the fact that it would land at the bottom of the tower seemed to disprove the idea that the Earth is in movement. The tower is on the Earth, which is rotating, so by the time that the weight lands, the Earth, and the tower which is on it, will have moved, and so the weight will not land at the bottom of the tower, but some distance away from it. To many astronomers at the time of Galileo, such observations clearly refuted the idea that the Earth is moving round in space rather than stationary. The logic of falsification would clearly demand that the Copernican theory be rejected.

Fig. 3.3 Galileo

It is clear, says Feyerabend, that Galileo himself recognised that the weight of evidence was against him. In a fictional dialogue, he writes to an imaginary supporter:

> You wonder that there are so few followers of the Pythagorean opinion [that the Earth moves] while I am astonished that there have been any up to this day who have

embraced and followed it. Nor can I ever sufficiently admire the outstanding acumen of those who have taken hold of this opinion and accepted it as true: *they have, through sheer force of intellect, done such violence to their own senses as to prefer what reason told them over that which sensible experience plainly showed them to be the contrary.* (Galileo, quoted in *Against Method*, p. 79, italics added)

Those who, like Galileo, hold to the Copernican view, do so *against the observational evidence*, not because of it. What Galileo has to do, therefore, is to try to persuade his opponents that the evidence of their everyday senses is wrong, and that better evidence can be obtained from "a superior and better sense" (*Against Method*, p. 81), which is the telescope. If we make our observations through the telescope rather than just with the naked eye, we will, he hopes, find that his theory is the correct one.

But telescopes were relatively crude pieces of equipment at the time of Galileo, and, because the technology had not been perfected, they were not always very reliable or accurate. Galileo therefore had trouble in persuading people that the observations that are made through a telescope are better than those obtained by the naked eye. Feyerabend quotes some of Galileo's contemporaries who looked through his telescope at the planets: "in the heavens it deceives one, and some fixed stars are seen double" (*Against Method*, p. 88). It thus seems that sometimes the telescope actually produced illusions, with two stars appearing where only one should be.

Another contemporary writes: "He has achieved nothing, for more than twenty learned men were present; yet nobody has seen the new planets distinctly" (*Against Method*, p. 88).

We have already seen in the course of these chapters on the philosophy of science that making an observation is not as simple an act as it might at first seem, and this is corroborated by these reports. Though Galileo invited people to look at the heavens through his telescope, not everyone agreed on what they saw and, in particular, not everyone saw what Galileo saw or wanted them to see.

There were more problems: the telescope appeared to distort things. The Moon, for example, appeared to have a smooth edge but a mountainous interior. Now, remember that one of the basic presuppositions of the Ptolemaic view was that the planets were perfect spheres because they were heavenly objects. Galileo, however, looked through his telescope and observed that the Moon, which *should* have been a perfect sphere, was not; it appeared to have many mountains in its interior, although its circumference or edge appeared perfectly smooth. But a problem arises when it is realised that, though the same face of the Moon is always towards Earth, the Moon nevertheless moves slightly so that different bits of the Moon will constitute the periphery at different times. Despite this, the periphery always appears smooth and the interior mountainous: it seems as though parts of the Moon that appear smooth when on its periphery as we view it are no longer smooth when they are no longer seen to be on the periphery. Conflicting observations such as these caused some to question the reliability of the telescope and the evidence that was gathered through its use.

All things considered then, says Feyerabend, the observational evidence at the time was, at best, of questionable reliability, and, at worst, ran completely counter to Galileo's view. Galileo can only win out in the end by refusing to accept, in the face of all the 'facts', that the Copernican theory has been falsified. Popperian logic would have required Galileo to abandon his position. Feyerabend concludes as follows:

> there are situations when our most liberal judgements and our most liberal rules would have eliminated a point of view which we regard today as essential for science, and would not have permitted it to prevail. These ideas survived and they *now* are said to be in agreement with reason ... *Copernicanism and other 'rational' views exist today only because reason was overruled at some time in their past.* (*Against Method*, p. 116)

For Feyerabend, science, far from proceeding according to strict methodological rules, is a much messier activity than most philosophers of science would have us believe. Feyerabend does not argue that there should be no rules, but only that the rules be flexible and sensitive to the particular historical context in which the investigation proceeds.

Against the idea of pure sensory data

In common with Popper, Kuhn, and Lakatos, Feyerabend argues that the empiricist ideal of pure, theory-neutral sensory knowledge of the world is a complete illusion. Even our most seemingly direct observations are influenced both by our historical and cultural background and by our sensory physiology:

> The sensory impression, however simple, contains a component that expresses the physiological reaction of the perceiving organism and has no objective correlate. This 'subjective' component often merges with the rest, and forms an unstructured whole ... (*Against Method*, p. 51)

In other words, even our most direct and seemingly simple observations are made up not only from what is out there – objective reality, as it were – but also from what is *in us* – the very nature of our perceptual systems. The final observation that we experience is a mixture of both subjective and objective contributions and they cannot be disentangled any more than we can isolate the individual ingredients of a cake once it has been baked.

As we have seen, thinkers of an empiricist persuasion (see also Chapters 5 and 6), such as Bacon, believed that we could, somehow, cleanse our observational apparatus of biases, prejudices, and expectations so as to be able to gaze on reality as it actually is, to make pure observations. These observations then, for the positivist, form the solid bedrock on which all of scientific knowledge can be erected. But, for Feyerabend, as for Kant, Popper, Kuhn and Lakatos, the inter-pretative concepts with which we approach observation are inseparable from the final observation itself, and, indeed, are necessary for observation even to be possible. Feyerabend puts the point as follows:

> It was Bacon's belief that natural interpretations [i.e. expectations and preconceptions] could be discovered by a method of analysis that peels them off, one after another, until the sensory core of every observation is laid bare. This method has serious drawbacks. First, natural interpretations of the kind considered by Bacon are not just *added* to a previously existing field of sensations. They are instrumental in *constituting* the field, as Bacon says himself. Eliminate all natural interpretations, and you also eliminate the ability to think and to perceive. Second, disregarding this fundamental function of natural interpretations, it should be clear that a person who faces a perceptual field without a single natural interpretation at his disposal would be *completely disoriented*, he could not even *start* the business of science ... It follows that the intention to start from scratch, after a complete removal of all natural interpretations, is self defeating. (*Against Method*, p. 60)

Box 3.3 **The genesis of *Against Method***

Feyerabend's most famous work, *Against Method*, was originally intended to be part of a larger work called *For and Against Method*, which would be co-authored with Lakatos. The book was intended to be a debate in which Lakatos argued for the existence of a rational method in science and Feyerabend argued against the existence of any such method. Though close friends, Lakatos and Feyerabend had very different philosophical positions and Feyerabend recounts that his lectures were sometimes interrupted by Lakatos in order to express disagreement:

Box 3.3 (cont.)

The lecture hall at the London School of Economics was directly opposite Imre's office window. In spring and summer, when the windows were open, Imre could hear every word I said. Feeling outraged, or simulating outrage at the drift of my story – with Imre you were never sure – he . . . came over, and tried to set things right. (*Killing Time*, p. 128)

It was Lakatos's idea that they should write a book together in which they argued their views with one another, but Lakatos died before he could write his part. In the Preface to *Against Method*, Feyerabend describes how the book came about:

In 1970 Imre Lakatos, one of the best friends I ever had, cornered me at a party. "Paul," he said, "you have such strange ideas. Why don't you write them down? I shall write a reply, we publish the whole thing and I promise you – we shall have lots of fun." I liked the suggestion and started working. The manuscript of my part of the book was finished in 1972 and I sent it to London. There it disappeared under rather mysterious circumstances. Imre Lakatos, who loved dramatic gestures, notified Interpol and, indeed, Interpol found my manuscript and returned it to me. I reread it and made some final changes. In February 1974, only a few weeks after I had finished my revision, I was informed of Imre's death. I published my part of our common enterprise without his response.

Many of the critics of *Against Method* objected not only to its philosophical content but also to its style, which they found not sufficiently scholarly or academic. Feyerabend responded by pointing out that his arguments were addressed to a friend and contained the irony, humour, and deliberate provocation that one would expect to characterise such an exchange. If critics found his style offputting, he said, it was only because they were unable to read the work in the spirit in which it was written.

The question of reality

But, if it is the case that all our observations, scientific and everyday, are at least in part subjective, and, therefore, not simply reflections of some objective external reality, then can we ever know what the nature of reality is in itself? Feyerabend would answer: "No." He argues that, although some scientists believe that science gives us the one, true picture of reality, such a view is mistaken. First of all, notes Feyerabend, there is not just one monolithic thing called science – there are not only different, and frequently mutually contradictory, schools of thought within single scientific disciplines, there are a large number of scientific disciplines as well. "Science," says Feyerabend, "is a mixed bag of opinions, procedures, 'facts', 'principles', not a coherent unit" (*Conquest of Abundance*, p. 212). Given this profusion of different approaches, different areas of investigation, and different conceptual frameworks, it simply cannot be true to say that 'the scientific world-view' gives us the 'true' picture of reality for the simple reason that there is no such thing as 'the scientific world-view'.

Feyerabend goes on to point out that, not merely do different scientific approaches exist, many of them are *successful* in their own domains, even though they may contradict approaches in other domains. "Nature," he concludes, "seems to respond positively to many approaches, not only to one" (*Conquest of Abundance*, p. 212). The choice of how to approach 'Nature', then, is not something that should be decided by inflexible, abstract rules that are set up in advance, but should be more pragmatic and fitted to the particular features of the field under investigation.

Plurality, then, rather than uniformity, is what characterises the different view-points that go to make up science. But, says Feyerabend, science is itself only one group of approaches amidst a plurality of non-scientific approaches, some of which may also, in particular circumstances, constitute successful approaches to nature. In particular, says Feyerabend, scientists sometimes argue that science tells us about what *really* exists whereas everyday experience provides us only with illusory, subjective appearances. This, he argues, is mistaken.

According to Feyerabend, our everyday world is full of variety. What science does is to cut down this variety, to categorise some things as real or objective, and other things as illusory or subjective. Thus some aspects of our everyday experience, such as colours, for example, are deemed by some scientists to be 'unreal'. Take the following example from neuroscientist Beau Lotto on the BBC website:

> The first thing to remember is that colour does not actually exist . . . at least not in any literal sense. Apples and fire engines are not red, the sky and sea are not blue, and no person is objectively 'black' or 'white' . . . What exists is light. Light is real. (www.bbc.co.uk/news/science-environment-14421303)

This is a view that goes back to the philosophers René Descartes and, particularly, John Locke (see Chapter 5). He famously distinguished between **primary** and **secondary qualities** of objects, the former being the 'real' properties of things, such as shape and mass, and the latter being the mere 'subjective' effect that things produce *in us*, such as sensations of colour, taste, and smell.

But, Feyerabend would argue, colours are just as real as anything else depending on the context within which one is working. The choice of which phenomena we are treat as real is a pragmatic rather than an absolute one. It is perfectly admissible for the physicist to treat colour as 'unreal' as it has no place in the world defined by physics, but the artist, gardener, or designer, pursuing different aims, is perfectly justified in treating colours as aspects of her fundamental reality. The world according to physics, Feyerabend would argue, is simply one perspective on a complex and multifaceted reality that cannot be encompassed by any single viewpoint. There are many things that do not feature in a physical picture of the world but which undoubtedly exist. Interest rates, for example, have no shape, or mass, or well-defined location in space, yet they undoubtedly are real: people's lives can be ruined by their fluctuations.

The picture of reality given us by the sciences, says Feyerabend, necessarily leaves things out. But this does not mean that those things do not exist, it merely means that they are not relevant for the science in question. Reality is so complex that there is no way in which we can hope to fully cognize the world of Nature in all its abundance. We need to order and make sense, to filter out some things, and we do this partly through choice and partly, involuntarily, as a result of our physiological constitution. "Only a tiny fraction of this abundance affects our minds," says Feyerabend, "[t]his is a blessing, not a drawback. A superconscious organism would not be superwise, it would be paralyzed" (*Conquest of Abundance*, pp. 3–4). The sciences provide one way of filtering and making sense of complex reality, but, says Feyerabend, "there are many such simplifications, not just one ..." (*Conquest of Abundance*, p. 241).

If we accept the idea that there is no single picture of reality that captures it in all its abundance, and that what we decide to designate as real is a pragmatic choice that depends on our goals and purposes, then can we just believe whatever we like simply because it suits us? Feyerabend answers "No": the fact that no one approach has *the* truth does not mean that some views cannot be better or more successful than others. But the superiority of one view over another, whether within the sciences or in a wider context, is a matter of practical utility in a particular situation rather than of abstract, universal criteria.

Conclusion

We have seen in this chapter how Lakatos tried to avoid what he felt were the irrational dangers of Kuhn's philosophy of science by developing the falsificationism that was first put forward by Popper. In particular, Lakatos argued that not only could no theory ever be proved true, but that no theory could ever be proved false. This meant that theories that were 'falsified' could possibly be true. Lakatos therefore believed that steps had to be taken to minimise the dangers of rejecting a true theory while also preventing scientific decision-making from becoming a matter of mere intellectual fashion or 'mob psychology'.

There are, nevertheless, aspects of Lakatos's thought that are resistant to formulation in terms of precise rules. It is unclear, for example, just when a research programme becomes degenerating. The length of time that a research programme should be allowed in order to prove itself is also difficult to specify in anything but the most general terms. Perhaps science can never be codified as a strict methodology.

This is precisely what was claimed by Feyerabend. He argued that a fixed and inflexible methodology, such as falsificationism, would actually inhibit the growth of scientific knowledge. The example of Galileo showed, according to Feyerabend, that a scientific breakthrough sometimes occurs only because the scientist has broken methodological rules.

There are, then, major differences between Popper, Kuhn, Lakatos, and Feyerabend in the extent to which they think that science can be differentiated from other pursuits in terms of its specific method and rationality. There is, none-theless, something on which all are agreed: science is not just the accumulation of observational facts and, moreover, that observations are not only guided by a scientist's theoretical framework, but are partially constituted by such frameworks. The framework leads the scientist to ask certain questions rather than others and actually colours the way that she subsequently sees the results of her investigation. To understand any science, then, one must know not only the 'facts' that it has discovered, but the theoretical and historical context within which those facts were discovered and interpreted. The following chapters are an attempt to describe some of that theoretical and historical framework for psychology.

Revision questions

1. On what grounds did Lakatos criticise Popper's falsificationism?
2. In what way did Lakatos believe his idea of research programmes improved on Popper's falsificationism?
3. What are the hard core assumptions and auxiliary hypotheses of a research programme?

4. How does Feyerabend use the example of Galileo to argue against a rigid scientific method?

5. Why does Feyerabend believe that science does not give us the one true picture of the world?

6. Does rejection of a rigid scientific method mean that there are no intellectual standards whatsoever?

References

Feyerabend, P. (1993). *Against Method*, 3rd edn. London: Verso.
Feyerabend, P. (1995). *Killing Time*. Chicago, IL: University of Chicago Press.
Feyerabend, P. (1999). *Conquest of Abundance*. Chicago, IL: University of Chicago Press.
Lakatos, I. (1970). Falsification and the methodology of scientific research programmes. In I. Lakatos and A. Musgrave (eds.) *Criticism and the Growth of Knowledge*. Cambridge: Cambridge University Press, pp. 91–196.

Part II

Historical development of the philosophy of mind

4 Descartes and the mind–body problem

Timeline

1562–98	French 'Wars of Religion' between Catholics and Protestants. An estimated 3 million people died.
1580	Montaigne publishes the first edition of his *Essays*
1603	Earliest edition of Shakespeare's *Hamlet*
1610	Galileo discovers the four largest moons of Jupiter
1618–48	The Thirty Years War
1633	Galileo condemned for heresy by The Inquisition

René Descartes

1596	Born in La Haye, France
1618	Enlists in the army of Maurice of Nassau
1628	Moves to Holland
1637	Publishes the *Discourse on Method*
1641	Publishes the *Meditations*
1649	Leaves Holland for Sweden to be tutor to Queen Christina
1650	Dies in Stockholm

Introduction

Descartes (see Box 4.1) is often thought of as the inaugurator of modern (as opposed to ancient or mediaeval) philosophy. Any chopping up of intellectual history into distinct periods is, of course, going to be somewhat arbitrary but Descartes does nevertheless represent an appropriate starting point for our discussion of the philosophy of mind, not only because of his canonical status as the

Box 4.1 **René Descartes**

Descartes (1596–1650) was born in the small town of La Haye (now renamed Descartes–La Haye in his honour) in northern France. He was sent to the Jesuit-run school of La Flèche, then considered to be one of the most prestigious and progressive educational institutions in Europe. He was, however, disappointed with what he was taught there. In particular, Descartes was surprised that, even in such an excellent school, much of what was taught was speculative and uncertain.

As a young man he enlisted as a soldier in one of the many armies fighting in the wars of religion that raged throughout Europe at that time (one of his early works was a treatise on fencing) and travelled throughout Germany, Holland, and Bohemia. He returned to France at the age of 30 and, settled in Paris, he involved himself in the new scientific and philosophical ideas that were being discussed there (Figure 4.1).

Then, in 1628, Descartes left France for Holland, where he said he could "live a life as solitary and retired as if [he] were in the most remote deserts" (*Discourse on Method*, p. 30). War was still raging in various parts of Europe, but Holland was relatively peaceful. Descartes was to remain there for nearly the rest of his life and it was in Holland that he entered into the most productive phase of his career, publishing the *Meditations* and various other works. He was finally persuaded to leave Holland for Sweden in 1649 by Queen Christina, who was so impressed by his works she invited him to join her court to give her personal tuition in philosophy. Unfortunately for Descartes, she preferred to have her philosophy lessons at 5 o'clock in the morning, and these early rises, combined with the cold Swedish

Box 4.1 (cont.)

climate, led to Descartes becoming ill. He died in February 1650, only six months after leaving for Sweden.

Fig. 4.1 René Descartes

starting point of modern philosophy, but because of the immense influence of his ideas on later developments in psychology and philosophy.

The roots of many contemporary debates, from the question of innate linguistic representations to the relationship between the mind and the body, are to be found in Descartes, and many psychologists and philosophers still define themselves explicitly as aligned with or – more commonly – in explicit opposition to Descartes' ideas. For this reason, the intellectual framework within which much psychological thinking proceeds is still largely **Cartesian,** even if the thinking in question is only an attempt to get away from the Cartesian framework. Descartes is still the reference point relative to which many psychologists and philosophers define their stances. Nowhere is this truer than in the context of the relationship between mind and body. Descartes effectively changed the intellectual landscape so that nearly all discussions of the **mind-body problem** today will start with an account of Descartes' own thoughts on the topic. And this is with good reason – the mind–body problem in its modern guise really did start with Descartes. The body and the mind were, thought Descartes, completely different substances: whereas the body was made out of the same matter as the rest of the physical world, the mind, argued Descartes, was a non-physical substance. Explaining how two such different entities could possibly interact with one another is the nub of the mind–body problem, and the difficulty of providing such an explanation has, as we shall see, provoked many thinkers to argue that there must be something fundamentally wrong with the idea that body and mind are different substances.

We shall also see that Descartes' characterisation of the mind and body as different substances stemmed from his own attempts to provide a solid foundation for scientific knowledge. It was, in part, the seeming certainty with which we know our own thoughts in contrast to the fallible knowledge that we have of the world outside ourselves that led Descartes to think of the mental and the physical as two radically distinct realms. This concern with the foundation of scientific knowledge was not merely of theoretical interest to Descartes, but had great practical importance. Descartes himself was a scientist – he was part of the scientific revolution of the early seventeenth century that also produced Galileo – and he was determined to give his own scientific work a secure basis. Because Descartes' views on the mind and body emerged from this new scientific knowledge and its justification, we shall start this chapter with an account of the change in world-view that underpinned the scientific revolution of which Descartes was part.

The new mechanical science

The 'scientific revolution' of the early seventeenth century changed the way that we look at the universe and our position within it. It can best be understood in contrast with the preceding world-view, which it sought to overthrow. This world-view had been dominant throughout the Middle Ages and was derived largely from Aristotle (Figure 4.2). In the Aristotelian philosophy, the universe and everything in it was animated by its own particular essence, which it attempted to fulfil and which, therefore, governed its behaviour. According to Aristotelian science, for example, we can explain the fact that a stone, when dropped, will fall to the ground because the ground is its natural home and where its stony essence dictates it should be. When removed from its natural home the stone will 'try' to get back to where it should be, and, if any barriers to its doing so are lifted, by our letting go of the stone for example, then the stone will return to where it should be, on the ground. A similar account can be given of why fire rises upwards: the stars were believed to be made of fire so that, when one lights a fire, the flames attempt to go up to the heavens, their natural place in the order of things. Of course, neither Aristotle nor the mediaeval scholastic philosophers who followed him believed that stones and fire were possessed of volition in the same way as living things, let alone humans, but they nevertheless accepted that everything had its own fundamental nature that it strove to express.

The view of the universe put forward by Descartes (and Galileo) (see Box 4.2) was a form of **mechanism**, and was radically different from this Aristotelian view. Whereas the Aristotelian world was full of living entities with their own particular essences that they sought to fulfil in their own particular ways, for Descartes, the physical universe was entirely mechanical. Rather than the different behaviour of stones and fire and trees being explained with reference to their own qualitatively different essences, they were all explained according to the same laws of mechanics. There were no qualitative differences between these phenomena – they were all just different manifestations of matter moving mechanically in different ways. The victory of the new mechanical philosophy was called, and for good reason, the 'disenchantment of the world' by the sociologist Max Weber. Gone were the essences and vital principles that animated everything in the universe, replaced only by universal laws of mechanics that recognised no qualitative distinction between one phenomenon and another.

Fig. 4.2 Aristotle

Box 4.2 Descartes the scientist

Though Descartes is today largely regarded as a philosopher and it is the philosophical aspects of his work that are most commonly studied, Descartes was just as much a scientist and mathematician as he was a philosopher. Or, it may be more correct to say that, at the time that Descartes was working, there was no division between science and philosophy of the sort that exists today: for Descartes, all thinking was part of the same enterprise to understand the world and our place in it. Indeed, one of the reasons that Descartes turned to philosophy was to find a firm foundation upon which his scientific work could be built. Among the 'scientific' subjects that Descartes investigated were meteorology (in *Meteors*), geometry (in *Geometry*), and the physics of light (*Dioptrics*).

One of Descartes' major projects was a description of the physics of all natural phenomena which was to be published under the title *The World*. As *The World* was being readied for publication, Descartes heard that Galileo had been condemned by the Church for teaching that the Earth, far from being the stationary centre of the universe, moved round the Sun. Descartes' book also included a discussion of the movement of the Earth (albeit only as a hypothesis) and he therefore decided not to publish it. He nevertheless continued to work on it throughout his life, incorporating some of the less controversial parts of it into his other published work. The original treatise was eventually published after Descartes' death.

Mechanising the soul

This disenchantment of the world applied not only to inanimate things such as stones and fire, but applied also to plants, animals, and people. Descartes wanted to explain as much as he could of human and animal behaviour in terms of pure mechanism. For Descartes, the functions of growth, nutrition, sensation, and motion that we see in plants and animals could all be explained in purely mechanical terms without recourse to the idea of some inner animating principle. He may, in part, have been inspired by the hydraulically powered **automata** that were popular at that time among the aristocracy. It was fashionable in Descartes' day for kings and queens to have mechanical figures of human beings and animals placed in various locations around their gardens, and visitors would marvel at the apparently autonomous behaviour of these artificial models. The 'behaviour' exhibited by these figures demonstrated that even complex functions could be the result of purely mechanical forces. For Descartes, then, the bodily movements of people and animals did not need a soul to explain them. The **reflex** withdrawal of one's hand from a fire can be accounted for in terms of a physiological connection between the hand and the brain; there is no need to invoke a mind or soul to explain this action. The adaptation of motor behaviour to different circumstances could also be explained mechanistically through the changes in the mechanical linkages between the parts of the body. Figure 4.3 shows, for example, how visual information from the eye can guide movements of the arm through their mutual connection via the brain's pineal gland. In essence, what we have here is an early example of a **feedback loop** whereby motor behaviour is controlled with reference to visual information.

There were, however, some aspects of human existence that Descartes thought could not be explained in purely mechanical terms. One such feature was conscious perception, i.e. not merely responding to a stimulus, but actually having a conscious subjective perceptual experience. Another such feature was the intelligent use of language. Although the functions of plants, animals, and the human body had been mechanised, Descartes thought that a rational, human soul or mind was necessary to account for these abilities that could not be mechanised. The mind in which these abilities resided was, therefore, something radically different from the purely mechanical body. Given that the physical world was defined entirely in terms of mechanical matter, the mind had to be non-physical and **immaterial**. The question of the relationship between the non-physical mind and the physical, mechanical body is one that has bedevilled psychology and philosophy ever since Descartes made this distinction between them. But to understand why Descartes made this distinction in the way he did requires, first of all, some understanding of the motivation behind the intellectual revolution that Descartes wrought.

Descartes' world: the fruit of scepticism

The world into which Descartes was born was one marked by two major events in European thought: the **Renaissance** and the **Reformation**. Both of these, in different ways, had questioned previously existing thought and authority and

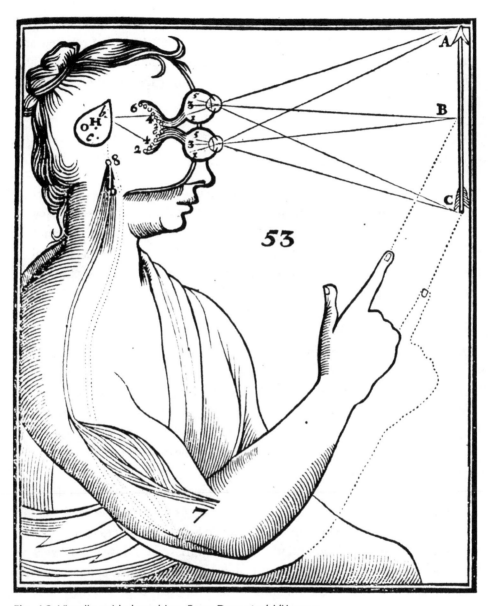

Fig. 4.3 Visually guided reaching. From Descartes' *L'Homme*

had brought about crises in knowledge. In many ways Descartes was himself a representative of the Renaissance tradition that questioned the authority of the Aristotelian **scholasticism** that had held sway in the middle ages. We have seen that Descartes, too, in his quest for a new science had opposed the scholastic world-view. But the questioning urge of the Renaissance, perhaps most evidently displayed in the writings of Montaigne, had not found anything positive to replace the now rejected world-view. The reigning philosophy, then, was one of **scepticism** about knowledge in general: the old beliefs had been rejected and human knowledge had thus been shown to be fallible. But, given this fallibility, what hope was there of ever attaining true knowledge? In the absence of

---

Box 4.3 Scepticism: the example of Montaigne

No thinker exemplifies the sceptical trend of thought in the sixteenth century better than Michel de Montaigne (1533–92). In his *Essays*, Montaigne asks himself "What do I know?" and, in the course of treating many diverse topics ranging from thumbs to freedom of conscience, he presents a variety of different opinions from classical literature and his own experience, and thus emphasises the sheer variety of different points of view that obtain on pretty much any subject one cares to mention. Given such variety, the suggestion seems to be, it is foolhardy to assert one single point of view as the absolute truth.

Montaigne also devotes a good deal of time to the examination of himself. Given the variability of opinion on so many other matters, perhaps, thinks Montaigne, meditation upon himself – that thing that he knows best of all – will provide surer knowledge. Even when examining himself, however, Montaigne can find nothing fixed or stable; he himself is a mass of constantly changing perceptions, feelings, thoughts, and opinions. For Montaigne, then, human knowledge is ephemeral and fallible – we can never know anything for certain.

The emphasis on doubt, the preparedness to question the validity of conventional wisdom and customary beliefs, and the realisation that one must, therefore, take oneself as the starting point for any theory of knowledge all find echoes in the work of Descartes. But there is one important difference: in Descartes' case, he believes that the methodical application of doubt ultimately leads not to disillusionment and acceptance of fallibility, but to certain knowledge.

When investigating himself, Montaigne finds nothing stable – just a constantly changing pattern of thoughts and feelings. For Descartes, however, it is not the content of these thoughts (which does indeed change) that is important, but the very fact of their existence. The content of the thoughts does not matter – it can be as unsteady, changeable, or wrong as you like – but the fact that there *are* thoughts is all that Descartes needs. He has found that one stable point from which he can construct the whole of his science and metaphysics.

certainty, the only attitude to adopt was that of resigned acceptance of human intellectual weakness (see Box 4.3).

The Reformation too had shaken the established order. Though Descartes was and remained a faithful Roman Catholic throughout his life, the Europe that he was born into was riven by religious wars in which not only Catholic and Protestant were in conflict, but even rival Protestant denominations fought with one another. All of these denominations claimed to have a monopoly on religious truth and that the others were heretics.

Descartes' world, then, was one that appeared to have lost its intellectual bearings and, despite being educated at one of the most prestigious schools of the day – the Jesuit-run college of La Flèche – Descartes was later to claim that little of what he learned there remedied this lack of sure knowledge. It was, indeed, this intensely felt need on the part of Descartes to find a new, secure footing for human knowledge that provided the impetus for all his subsequent philosophy.

Box 4.4 Education and method

As a child, Descartes says, he was led to believe that education would help him towards "a clear and assured knowledge of all that is useful in life" (*Discourse on Method*, p. 9). On completing his formal education, however, he says that "I found myself embarrassed by so many doubts and errors, that it seemed to me that the only profit I had had from my efforts to acquire knowledge was the progressive discovery of my own ignorance" (*Discourse on Method*, p. 9). He concludes that his inability to find the certain and sure knowledge that he desires is not due to any fault in himself or in his school, but because "there was no science in existence that was of such a nature as I had previously been given to believe" (*Discourse on Method*, p. 9). It became Descartes' work to try to found such a science himself.

The idea for the development of this new science came to Descartes on 10 November 1619. Descartes, at that time a soldier, was on his way to rejoin his regiment when he was forced to break his journey by the onset of winter. He took refuge in a stove-heated room in the German town of Ulm, where he shut himself up to meditate on his thoughts. It was in this heightened state of concentration and agitation that Descartes had dreams and visions which, he thought, were divine revelations that pointed the way to the future science of certain knowledge that he desired. The way to that new science was a method. The first cornerstone of this

---

Box 4.4 (cont.)

method was that Descartes take *himself and his own thoughts* – not the varied opinions of the academic authorities – as the starting point of this new science. The second was to submit his own thoughts to the test of reason. This latter principle is a version of the 'method of doubt' that Descartes also employed in the *Meditations.*

As he himself said in his *Discourse on Method,* "I always had an extreme desire to learn to distinguish truth from falsehood in order to have clear insight into my actions and proceed in this life with assurance" (p. 13) (see Box 4.4).

How, then, was one to distinguish truth from falsehood? How was one to come by true knowledge? Descartes' radical solution was to start from scratch: to reject, at least provisionally, all the knowledge that he personally had accumulated in his lifetime and that had been accumulated too throughout history. He hoped to find knowledge that was secure, that "presented itself to my mind so clearly and distinctly that I had no occasion to doubt it" (*Discourse on Method,* p. 20). Such knowledge would then form the unshakeable foundation on which Descartes would then attempt to reconstruct the whole of human knowledge.

The *Meditations*

Descartes attempted to find this certain knowledge by employing what he called the **method of doubt.** What he did was to consider all the different sources of knowledge that we believe ourselves to have and to ask whether this alleged knowledge could possibly be false. If it could be false, said Descartes in the *Meditations,* then one must reject it. By employing this strict criterion and by examining the sources of knowledge in a systematic way, Descartes hoped to arrive at knowledge that could not be doubted and, therefore, could not possibly be false.

The first possible source of knowledge that Descartes considers are the senses. But, says Descartes, "I have sometimes caught the senses deceiving me; and a wise man never entirely trusts those who have once cheated him" (*Meditations,* p. 62). It is indeed possible, says Descartes, that even the impression he has of sitting by the fire writing is merely a dream. Indeed it is possible that he has no body at all, but only the erroneous impression that he has a body. All these beliefs are derived from the senses, but the deliverances of the senses are open to doubt and, hence, the senses must be rejected as possible sources of true knowledge.

Perhaps, then, mathematical reasoning rather than sensory input is a surer basis for knowledge: as Descartes notes, "Whether I am awake or asleep, two and three add up to five, and a square has only four sides; and it seems impossible for such obvious truths to fall under a suspicion of being false" (*Meditations*, p. 63). But, says Descartes taking his method of doubt to the most radical extreme, suppose that instead of an all-powerful and benevolent God, there is an all powerful and malevolent demon, who takes great pleasure in misleading me so that, no matter how sure I am that I am right, I am in fact wrong – even when this concerns the most self-evidently true statements, such as $2 + 3 = 5$:

> I will suppose, then, ... that there is an evil spirit, who is supremely powerful and intelligent, and does his utmost to deceive me. I will suppose that sky, air, earth, colours, shapes, sounds, and all external objects are mere delusive dreams, by means of which he lays snares for my credulity. I will consider myself as having no hands, no eyes, no flesh, no blood, no senses, but just having a false belief that I have all these things. (*Meditations*, p. 65)

Descartes, of course, does not believe that such a demon really exists, but as his goal is to find certain knowledge, the mere possibility that it does exist is enough for him to reject anything that could be a delusion produced by the demon. Is there, then, anything that is immune from this extreme doubt? Descartes concludes that there is: his own existence. Even if there is an all-powerful deceiver, says Descartes, that being cannot deceive him about the fact that he exists when he is thinking: "If he deceives me, then . . . I undoubtedly exist; let him deceive me as much as he may, he will never bring it about that, at the time of thinking that I am something, I am in fact nothing . . . this proposition 'I am', 'I exist', whenever I utter or conceive it in my mind, is necessarily true" (*Meditations*, p. 67). If he is thinking, even if he is thinking wrongly and is mistaken, nevertheless in order to be mistaken he must exist. This, for Descartes, is a necessary truth that cannot possibly be false and it is the source of the famous Cartesian dictum: "I think, therefore I am."

Through employment of the method of doubt, Descartes has arrived at something that cannot possibly be doubted. But what is this 'I', this self, this thinking thing that necessarily exists when it engages in the act of thinking? It is a "conscious being . . . [a] being that doubts, understands, asserts, denies, is willing, is unwilling; further, that has sense and imagination" (*Meditations*, p. 70). The necessarily existing 'I' cannot be identified with the body because the very existence of the body (or the entire physical world) is doubtful, whereas the 'I' necessarily exists. This mind that does the thinking, the reasoning, and the willing must, therefore, be non-physical. This is **Cartesian dualism**: the idea that the body is a physical mechanism (however elaborate) and that the mind or soul, the seat of thought and consciousness, is a non-physical substance.

The logical leap that Descartes makes from doubting the existence of his body to the conclusion that he is something non-physical that is distinct from his body has been called "one of the most notorious **nonsequiturs** in the history of philosophy" (Cottingham 1992, p. 242). Descartes, however, has other reasons for believing the mind to be different from the physical, mechanical body. One of these, which is particularly important in the history of psychology, is his argument that no purely mechanistic entity could ever use language in the flexible and creative way that people do:

> they [machines] could never use words or other constructed signs, as we do to declare our thoughts to others. It is quite conceivable that a machine should be so made as to utter words, and even utter them in connexion with physical events that cause a change in one of its organs; so that e.g. if it is touched in one part, it asks what you want to say to it, and if touched in another, it cries out that it is hurt; but not that it should be so made as to arrange words variously in response to the meaning of what is said in its presence, as even the dullest men can do. (*Discourse on Method*, pp. 41–2)

Descartes' argument that linguistic ability has to be something more than the mechanistic response to external stimuli not only provides another reason for his distinction between body and mind, but as we shall see in a later chapter on the 'cognitive revolution' in psychology, prefigured Chomsky's attack on Skinner's *Verbal Behaviour*. Chomsky argued that Skinner's behaviouristic theory of language was too mechanistic and could not do justice to the creativity and flexibility of human language use and, therefore, that innate capacities had to be invoked to explain language. As we shall see later in this chapter, the importance of **innate ideas** was also something that was stressed by Descartes. Given his anti-mechanistic view of language and postulation of innate ideas, it is not surprising that Chomsky was to title one his books *Cartesian Linguistics*.

Mind–body interaction

We have, then, seen some of the reasons that Descartes put forward in support of the dualism of physical body and non-physical mind. But the question of how these two radically different entities can interact with one another – the mind–body problem – is one that Descartes never solved. How one physical thing interacts with another physical thing – how one billiard ball hits another and causes it to move, for example – would seem to be unproblematic. But the difficulty of conceiving how a non-physical substance could interact with a physical substance has appeared to many thinkers to be insurmountable.

The mind–body problem is usually conceived of by contemporary thinkers in terms of how the non-physical mind could influence the physical body. After all, if our actions are to follow from our conscious decisions and volitions, there must be some way for the mind that makes these decisions and forms these volitions to influence the body that ultimately enacts these decisions in the physical world. But if the mind is a non-physical thing, it is hard to understand how it could have any purchase on the physical body.

There is good reason to believe that the mind–body problem as envisaged in this way by later thinkers was not a serious problem for Descartes. There seemed to him to be no particular problem with different substances interacting with one another. For Descartes, the apparent difficulty of mind–body interaction "proceeds from a supposition that is false and that cannot be proved, namely that if body and soul are two substances with different natures, that prevents them from being able to act on one another" (letter to Clerselier, 1646, cited in Rozemond 1999, p. 445). There was, then, no prima facie reason why the interaction of two different substances was any more problematic than the interaction of two substances identical in nature. After all, we know from experience that the mind and the body *do* interact with one another, even if we can give no clear account of this interaction.

The converse relationship – how matter could influence the more elevated substance of mind – was, however, considered by Descartes to be more problematic. For Descartes the motions induced in the physical matter of the brain by external stimuli acted as signs for the mind to evoke and perceive innate ideas within itself. Although today the mind–body problem is usually phrased in terms of the 'downward' causal effect of the mind on the body – how does the mind control the actions of the body? – the 'upward' causal relationship of the body on the mind is nevertheless still with us today in the problem of consciousness and the question of how physical events in the brain give rise to qualitative subjective experience.

Despite the problems with Cartesian dualism, there are nevertheless some modern-day thinkers who put forward something like a substance dualist view of mind–body interaction. Karl Popper and the neurobiologist John Eccles argue in *The Self and Its Brain* (1977) that causality between physical things is no easier to understand than that which might obtain between physical and non-physical things. They therefore do not see any particular reason why an entity on one level, such as the human mind, should not be able to cause changes in entities at another level, such as the human body. But this is very much a minority view. Most psychologists and philosophers have rejected Cartesian substance dualism and argue that we must conceive the relationship between mind and body in a different way.

One such different way of conceiving of the relationship between body and mind is called **property dualism**. According to this view, the mind and the body are not two different substances: they are one and the same substance. There are, however, different properties that attach to this substance, some of which are mental or psychological properties, and others of which are physical properties. Most property dualists nowadays would accept that matter is the single substance in which the mental and physical properties inhere. If, however, the matter in question is sufficiently complex and organised in the right way – as a human brain might be, for example – then it will also give rise to mental properties in addition to the physical properties of mass and extension in space that are exhibited by all matter. In this case, mental properties are said to be **emergent**. An example given by the philosopher John Searle (*Minds, Brains and Science* 1989) nicely illustrates this idea of emergent properties. Water is wet, it is liquid, it has a certain colour. A molecule of water on its own, however, has none of these properties: it is not wet, it is not liquid, it doesn't have a colour. But a sufficient number of molecules that themselves are not wet, when put together in a certain way, will give rise to the higher-order property of wetness. Global features can emerge from the organisation of local elements without being reducible to the properties of the local elements themselves. The relationship between the body, specifically the brain, and the mind is supposed to be understood in an analogous way. The higher-level properties of thought and consciousness are supposed to emerge from the way in which neurons are organised and connected in the brain, but such properties cannot be reduced to the basic physical properties of neurons; they only appear at a higher, non-basic level.

Property dualists, although they oppose substance dualism, nevertheless agree with substance dualists that the question of the mind–body relationship constitutes a genuine problem that demands a solution. There is, however, another point of view, according to which the mind–body problem is completely misconceived. This approach, associated with the English philosopher Gilbert Ryle (1900–76), considers the mind–body problem to be a **pseudo-problem** that has stemmed from a misunderstanding of what mentalistic terms, such as 'understand', 'wills', and 'doubts', actually mean. If we examine how these concepts actually work, says Ryle, we will find that the mind–body problem is not a real problem at all; rather than solving the problem, we *dissolve* the problem and come to realise that it was never actually a problem in the first place. Ryle, in *The Concept of Mind* (1949), argues that our mentalistic concepts are not attributes of a mysterious non-physical substance, but are ways of talking about our actions. Take, for example, 'understanding'. What does it mean to understand something? It means that a person can solve a problem without difficulty, can explain how the solution is arrived at, can go on to solve other problems of the same type. Or it may mean that a person can communicate successfully using a particular language. Looked at in this way 'understanding' does not refer to the attributes of an immaterial mind, but to whether certain tasks, such as problem-solving or communicating with other people, are performed effectively or not. Take 'willing' as another example. To do something willingly is to do it enthusiastically and without complaint; it does not mean that the action is preceded by some act of will or volition on the part of a non-physical mind. When we attribute 'will-power' to someone, we mean simply that he or she will perform unpleasant but necessary actions even in the face of temptations not to do them; we do not mean that his or her immaterial mind is especially efficacious. Rather than referring to the properties of a Cartesian mind or soul, our mental state vocabulary is really a way of talking about actions and the way in which these are performed. According to Ryle, the mind–body problem has arisen because philosophers have failed to understand this point. They have made what Ryle calls a **category mistake** by erroneously taking words of one logical category to be members of another, quite different, logical category. When, however, we realise that what we are talking about is publicly observable behaviour rather than another, non-physical, substance, we realise that there is no mind–body problem.

Probably the most influential approach to the mind–body problem in cognitive psychology is called **functionalism**. Functionalists would disagree with Ryle and would claim that mentalistic terms are not just ways of talking about action. There are, they would argue, genuine mental states. Of course, these mental states must be connected to overt behaviour in some way, but they are not *just* aspects of overt behaviour. Indeed, according to functionalism, mental states are defined by their connections to overt behavioural outputs and perceptual inputs. Take, for example, the thought "It is raining." We can define this thought, in function-alist terms, as that mental state that is, on the one hand, caused by seeing the rain falling down and, on the other hand, causes the person who has that thought to put on a coat and take an umbrella when going out. The thought, then, is defined, not by its own intrinsic characteristics or by its inherence in a particular sub-stance, but by the *function* that it performs in linking perception and behaviour. Any state of any system that performs the appropriate function can be said to be a mental state. The nature of the substance in which this state is instantiated is irrelevant for functionalism, as long as it permits the performance of the required functions.

An example (again from Searle) that makes clearer the difference between function and substance is money. Money can be made out of paper and metal, but at different times and in different places different things would have served as money: sacks of grain or sheep, for example. Often today money is, physi-cally, nothing more than a pattern of electrical changes in a computer. What makes something money is not what it's made out of but the functions that it performs, such as allowing people to buy things with it. The intrinsic, physical characteristics of the thing that does the job do not matter, it is the job that is done that matters. Functionalists tend to think of mental states in an analogous way, and that is why functionalism has been so important in the development of cognitive psychology and artificial intelligence. If it is the case that the material out of which a system is made is irrelevant then there is no reason why we cannot investigate human mental states using, for example, computer models. The fact that computers and brains are made out of completely different materials does not matter. As long as computers can be built to perform the same functions as a human brain, they can be used as legitimate tools of investigation. For functionalists, the functions performed are analogous to computer software and the system that performs those functions, whether a brain or computer, is analogous to hardware on which the software runs. It is, according to function-alists, the software that is important in thinking about mental states. However, other psychologists and philosophers of a more **reductionist** outlook seek to identify mental states with particular patterns of brain activity. To have or to be in a particular mental state is simply to be in a particular brain state. So, in contrast to functionalism, the hardware, the actual material make-up of the system, does matter, and the ultimate goal of psychology is to reduce mental states to the brain states.

Innate ideas

We have now seen some of the major characteristics of the Cartesian philosophy: firstly, a characterisation of the physical world as entirely mechanical and an attempt to explain as much as possible about the universe on the basis of this mechanistic science and, secondly, a characterisation of the mind as a non-physical, thinking thing whose existence cannot be doubted. There is, however, another aspect of his philosophy that has great importance in the development of psychology: the doctrine of innate ideas.

First of all, Descartes gives a new sense to the notion of 'ideas'. He says: "by the term 'idea' I mean in general everything which is in our mind when we conceive something, no matter how we conceive it" (letter to Mersenne, 1641; cited in Ariew and Grene 1995, p. 90). This conception of 'idea' as an internal, mental representation was relatively novel at the time that Descartes was writing – prior to the Renaissance, ideas were only thought of as existing in the mind of God – but Descartes gave this new, psychological notion of ideas yet another twist. The prevailing view of ideas at the time was that they were caused by external objects and somehow resembled them. Ideas were, essentially, images of the external objects that had produced them. Descartes, however, argued that ideas need not be sensory; they could be purely conceptual.

This conceptual understanding of ideas is another manifestation of Descartes' distrust of the senses, which we have already seen in the arguments of the *Meditations*. True knowledge is intellectual and rational rather than sensory. Indeed, for Descartes, even knowledge based on the senses had, ultimately, to be intellectualised if it was to constitute real knowledge. Descartes' most famous argument for this point of view is that of the perception of a piece of wax:

It has just been extracted from the honeycomb; it has not completely lost the taste of the honey; it retains some of the smell of the flowers from which it was gathered; its

> colour, shape, size are manifest; it is hard, cold, and easily handled, and gives out a sound if you rap it with your knuckle ... (*Meditations*, p. 72)

But then, says Descartes, he brings the wax close to the fire and its sensory characteristics change as it begins to melt.

> It loses the remains of its flavour, the fragrance evaporates, the colour changes, the shape is lost, the size increases; it becomes fluid and hot, it can hardly be handled, and it will no longer give out a sound if you rap it. (*Meditations*, p. 72)

But nevertheless, even though all these sensory qualities have changed, Descartes continues to perceive it as a piece of wax. It therefore follows that perception must be something over and above the reception of changing sensory qualities. It must be largely intellectual and rational:

> perception of the wax is not sight, not touch, not imagination ... it is a purely mental contemplation. (*Meditations*, p. 73)

Ideas, then, even perceptual ideas, are intelligible rather than sensed.

This **intellectualist** approach to knowledge is further evident in Descartes' contention that our ideas are innate. Not only did Descartes believe that certain ideas, such as that of God, were innate, he believed that *all* knowledge was, strictly speaking, innate. Sensory stimulation of the body might cause us to have ideas, but the ideas themselves were already within the mind; the physical stimulation of the body was merely the signal that caused them to be evoked.

Descartes' innatist vision, then, is about as far as one can get from the empiricism of the Aristotelian scholastics. For them, nothing was in the mind that was not first in the senses. For Descartes, by contrast, there is nothing in the senses that is ever in the mind. All the senses can do is to provoke the mind to call up ideas that are already in it. Descartes states this explicitly:

> anyone who pays proper attention must believe that however far our senses extend and whatever it is exactly that can reach our faculty of thought from them, it is never the case that the ideas of things as we form them in our thought, are exhibited to us by them [the senses]. Therefore there is nothing in our ideas which is not innate in the mind or faculty of thinking, except only for the circumstances that concern experience. For this reason we judge that certain ideas that we now have present in our thought are referred to certain things placed outside us. We do not do so because those things sent the ideas themselves to our mind through the organs of the senses, but because they sent something, which gave occasion to our mind to form these ideas

---

Box 4.5 **Cartesian linguistics**

According to Chomsky, one of the hallmarks of language is its creativity: there is a huge discrepancy between the linguistic input that a language user is exposed to and the number of sentences that can be (and are) produced by the language user. This is to say nothing of the novelty of the sentences that can be produced. Chomsky, therefore, argues that we must be possessed of an innate grammar that specifies the rules according to which language operates. This grammar is universal and applies to all languages – a child in an English-speaking environment will learn English just as easily as a child in a French-speaking environment will learn French or a child in a Chinese-speaking environment will learn Chinese. The innate grammar does not, therefore, encode the rules of any specific human language, but is sufficiently abstract and general to apply to all human languages. The child will apply these rules to whatever language is encountered in the particular culture in which he or she is raised.

Chomsky defines the rationalist approach to knowledge (of which Descartes is a notable example) as the view that the structure of knowledge is innate and that the role of experience is to evoke these innate structures. Chomsky sees his own thinking regarding the learning and use of language as fully in line with this tradition. We do not, according to Chomsky, derive our linguistic knowledge from stimulation; the stimulation serves to awaken the knowledge within the mind: "stimulation provides the occasion for the mind to apply certain innate interpretative principles, certain concepts that proceed from 'the power of the understanding' itself, from the faculty of thinking rather than from external objects" (Chomsky 1967, p. 10). There are obvious similarities between this view and Descartes' view that sensory stimulation simply serves to evoke innate ideas that are already there in the mind.

by means of a faculty innate to it at this time rather than another time. (*Comments on a Certain Broadsheet*, 1648; cited in Rozemond 1999, p. 449)

This Cartesian belief that environmental stimulation serves as a spur to awaken knowledge that is already present in the mind finds a modern counterpart in Chomsky's linguistic theory, in which exposure to language activates innate linguistic knowledge (see Box 4.5).

Conclusion

We have seen, then, how Descartes defined the mind as a non-physical thinking thing that was distinguished from the physical, mechanical body to which it was attached and, indeed, from the entire mechanical universe. The realm of the mind was the realm of thought, meaning, and rationality, whereas the realm of the physical was that of meaningless mechanism. Such a sharp distinction between the mental and the physical, however, made it very difficult to see how these two realms could possibly interact with one another, and the mind–body problem continued to trouble philosophers and psychologists after Descartes. In particular, many thinkers believed that the problem could only be solved by rejecting wholesale the mind–body distinction as conceived by Descartes. Other ways of conceptualising the mind, the body, and the relationship between the two, such as property dualism and functionalism, were therefore proposed. Others believed that the mind–body problem was not really a problem at all and only appeared to be so because philosophers had failed to understand the nature of the concepts in which it was framed.

Descartes' distinction between the body and the mind emerged, as we have seen in this chapter, from his desire to find true knowledge that could not possibly be doubted. The locus of this certain knowledge was to be found within the mind itself and its sure consciousness of its own existence. Information provided by the senses, in contrast, was suspect and fallible. A corollary of this view is Descartes' doctrine of innate ideas, according to which all real knowledge is already present within the mind at birth. Sensory experience only has the role of calling forth this already existing knowledge rather than providing any new knowledge itself. But this downplaying of the importance of sensory experience, along with belief in innate ideas, was attacked by another group of philosophers, the empiricists. They, in contrast to Descartes, argued that knowledge really did come, ultimately, from the senses. It is two of the most important empiricist philosophers, John Locke and George Berkeley, who are the topic of the next chapter.

Revision questions

1. How did the new science, exemplified by Descartes and Galileo, differ from the Aristotelian world-view?

2. What were the historical circumstances that prompted Descartes' search for certain knowledge?

3. How did Descartes arrive at the conclusion that the mind and the body were separate?

4. What aspects of the mind or soul did Descartes think were not amenable to mechanistic explanation?

5. How have thinkers tried to solve the mind–body problem?

6. What is a category mistake?

7. What are emergent properties?

8. What are innate ideas?

References

Ariew, R. and Grene, M. (1995). Ideas, in and before Descartes. *Journal of the History of Ideas*, 56, 87–106.

Chomsky, N. (1967). Recent contributions to the theory of innate ideas. *Synthese*, 17, 2–11.

Cottingham, J. (1992). Cartesian dualism: theology, metaphysics, and science. In J. Cottingham (ed.) *The Cambridge Companion to Descartes*. Cambridge: Cambridge University Press, pp. 236–55.

Descartes, R. ([1637]/1970). *Discourse on Method*, trans. E. Anscombe and P. T. Geach. In E. Anscombe and P. T. Geach (eds.) *Descartes: Philosophical Writings*. London: Thomas Nelson, pp. 5–57.

Descartes, R. ([1642]/1970). *Meditations*, trans. E. Anscombe and P. T. Geach. In E. Anscombe and P. T. Geach (eds.) *Descartes: Philosophical Writings*. London: Thomas Nelson, pp. 59–124.

Popper, K. R. and Eccles, J. C. (1977). *The Self and Its Brain*. London: Springer.

Rozemond, M. (1999). Descartes on mind–body interaction: what's the problem? *Journal of the History of Philosophy*, 37, 435–67.

Ryle, G. (1949). *The Concept of Mind*. London: Penguin.

Searle, J. R. (1989). *Minds, Brains and Science*. London: Pelican.

5 Locke, Berkeley, and empiricism

Timeline

1642–51	English Civil War
1649	Charles I executed
1651	Thomas Hobbes publishes *Leviathan*
1653	Oliver Cromwell becomes Lord Protector of England, Scotland, and Ireland
1660	Restoration of the monarchy. Charles II becomes king. Official foundation of the Royal Society
1666	Great Fire of London
1687	Publication of Newton's *Principia Mathematica*
1689	The 'Glorious Revolution'. William of Orange replaces James II as King
1707	Act of Union between England and Scotland
1726	Publication of Swift's *Gulliver's Travels*
1745–6	Jacobite Rebellion
1755	Publication of Samuel Johnson's *Dictionary of the English Language*

John Locke

1632	Born in Somerset
1652	Goes to Oxford University
1683	Goes into exile in Holland for political reasons
1689	Returns to England. Publication of *An Essay concerning Human Understanding*
1704	Dies in Essex

George Berkeley

1685	Born in County Kilkenny
1700	Enrols at Trinity College, Dublin
1709	Publishes *An Essay towards a New Theory of Vision*
1710	Ordained an Anglican priest. Publishes *Principles of Human Knowledge*
1728	Goes to live in America for 3 years
1733	Publishes *The Theory of Vision Vindicated and Explained*
1734	Is made bishop of Cloyne, County Cork
1750	Resigns bishopric
1753	Dies in Oxford

Introduction

We saw in the previous chapter that Descartes, in his search for absolutely certain knowledge, argued that real knowledge was innate and was not derived from the senses. The senses, he believed, were often misleading and could not, therefore, be the source of the true and infallible knowledge that he sought.

But not all thinkers agreed with this position. In contrast to Descartes, they argued that sensory experience was the ultimate source of knowledge. This school of thought is called **empiricism**. In this chapter, we will discuss the work of two major empiricist philosophers, John Locke and George Berkeley. These two thinkers built on an established tradition of philosophy that emphasised the importance of experience. We have already seen in Chapter 1 that Francis Bacon (1561–1626) argued for the importance of empirical observation in the building up of scientific knowledge. Another important forerunner of the later empiricism of Locke and Berkeley was Thomas Hobbes (1588–1679). Hobbes was a contemporary of Descartes and, indeed, published a set of objections to Descartes' *Meditations* to which Descartes subsequently replied in an attempt to rebut Hobbes's criticisms.

Hobbes believed that we derived our ideas as a result of physical objects impinging on our bodies and thus producing 'motions' within us. For Hobbes, then, ideas were nothing more than particular sorts of physical events occurring within the body. Those ideas that are produced immediately through the causal impact of external bodies are sensations, but some motions will continue to reverberate within the body even after the object that has caused them is no longer present. These are memory images. For Hobbes, then, "there is no conception in a man's mind, which hath not at first, totally, or by part, been begotten upon the organs of sense" (*Leviathan*, p. 1). Here we have the first of the hallmark ideas of empiricism: experience as the source of knowledge.

A second crucial idea of empiricism is the **association of ideas**. The ideas that we derive from our senses, says Hobbes, are not just a chaotic jumble but are connected to one another in trains of thought. These connections or associations between ideas reflect the associations between the original sensations of which the ideas are the continuing echo:

> When a man thinketh on any thing whatsoever, His next Thought after, is not altogether so casuall as it seems to be. Not every Thought to every Thought succeeds indifferently. But as wee have no Imagination, whereof we have not formerly had Sense, in whole, or in parts; so we have no Transition from one Imagination to another,

whereof we never had the like before in our Senses. The reason whereof is this. All Fancies are Motions within us, reliques of those made in the Sense: And those motions that immediately succeeded one another in the sense, continue also together after Sense: In so much as the former comming again to take place, and be predominant, the later followeth, by coherence of the matter moved ... (*Leviathan*, pp. 8–9)

That knowledge, firstly, consists of ideas derived from the senses and that these are, secondly, associated with one another according to the way in which they were originally experienced are two of the fundamental ideas of empiricism and are shared to some extent by all thinkers that fall under the empiricist heading, including Locke and Berkeley, the two thinkers to be discussed in the present chapter. They are also shared by Hume (Chapter 6) and form the cornerstone of much behaviourist psychology (Chapter 16).

Locke's empiricism was, as we shall see, much more down to earth in its aims than the rationalism of Descartes. In particular, Locke was happy to accept that knowledge, which is ultimately derived from the senses, is never absolutely certain in the way that Descartes demands. But lack of certainty does not mean worthlessness. All it means is that we have to be aware that our knowledge is partial and fallible and that we must be prepared to change our views in the light of evidence or argument.

Locke's goal was to identify those questions on which we might expect the human mind to be able to make some progress or to possess some knowledge, however fallible. This was in distinction to those questions that are simply beyond the reach of the human mind. As far as these questions are concerned, we simply have to content ourselves with knowing that we have reached the limits of our understanding. We should refrain from arguing about such matters and turn our attention to those questions that are more tractable to our finite mental powers.

To this end, Locke examines the sorts of ideas that are to be found when examining the mind – just what are the sorts of contents that are found there? These are the natural constituents of the human mind. Locke provides a sort of natural **taxonomy** or categorisation of the sorts of ideas that the mind contains and investigates their sources. As has already been indicated, Locke believes that all our ideas derive, ultimately, from experience. Nowhere, says Locke, is there any evidence for the innate ideas postulated by the likes of Descartes.

In keeping with his practical approach to knowledge, Locke does not come to any final conclusion on the mind–body problem. We simply do not know whether thinking takes place in an immaterial substance or whether it is the result of purely physical processes in the material body, he says; it is one of those questions that is beyond human understanding. But, on a pragmatic level, we can understand personality as a *psychological* phenomenon regardless of whether it inheres in the physical body or in a non-physical mind. The psychological is something that is within the bounds of our experience and, hence, serves as our marker of the mind and the person for all practical purposes.

Just as we understand the mind practically in a psychological sense without having knowledge of the substance that underlies it, so all we know practically of objects is the ideas or sensations that they produce in our minds. The nature of the substances that produce such ideas is, again, something that is beyond the realm of our possible experience and hence beyond the scope of human knowledge.

This idea of not going beyond the bounds of our experience was to find a more radical expression in the works of Berkeley. If, said Berkeley, all we know of reality is our experience of it then why postulate the existence of some unknowable something that lies behind or beyond that experience? If all we know of physical objects, for example, are the sensations that they produce in us then why should we not say that physical things really are nothing more than our sensory experiences of them. This outlook, radical though it seems, was to find more modern adherents in the positivism of Mach (Chapter 11) and the radical empiricism of William James (Chapter 14).

Berkeley viewed learning though the association of ideas as of paramount importance. It was precisely through associating visual ideas with the sensations of touch that accompanied them that we came to be able to interpret and understand the information that we receive from the eyes. The idea of learning to perceive, which has been immensely important in perceptual theory, has one of its most influential expressions in the work of Berkeley.

John Locke

The spur for Locke's writing of the *Essay concerning Human Understanding* (1689; hereafter referred to as the *Essay*), his most important work in the philosophy of mind, was the disagreements that he and his friends and colleagues frequently fell into when discussing intellectual matters. Locke (see Box 5.1) believed that such disagreements might be particularly likely to arise when discussion turned to matters about which we can have little in the way of real knowledge. On such topics, he thought, we can never come to any firm decision and, instead of arguing interminably over such problems, we would do better to

Box 5.1 **John Locke**

John Locke was born in Somerset in 1632. He studied at Christ Church college in Oxford and was probably initially intended to become a clergyman (which is what most undergraduates did at the time), but his interests later switched to medicine and natural science, and it was as a doctor that he was initially employed (Figure 5.1).

Fig. 5.1 John Locke

Box 5.1 (cont.)

In 1666 Locke met the future Earl of Shaftesbury, a member of the court of King Charles II and a leading political figure of the time (he served for several years as Chancellor of the Exchequer). Locke became employed as a member of Shaftesbury's household, on one occasion supervising an operation on Shaftesbury's liver. The success of the operation led Shaftesbury to credit Locke with saving his life.

Under Shaftesbury's patronage, Locke served in a number of political and administrative roles, but Shaftesbury, at one time a close ally of the king, was later to become one of his fiercest opponents. Charles II had dissolved parliament several times to prevent it passing legislation that would exclude his brother James from ever becoming king (James was a Roman Catholic). Shaftesbury and other radical members of the Whig party believed that the king was overstepping the bounds of his legitimate authority in doing this and infringing on the rights of the elected members of parliament. Locke, as Shaftesbury's secretary, was implicated in this controversy and may have helped Shaftesbury to write political pamphlets urging opposition to the king. Shaftesbury, aware that he was likely to be found guilty of treason, escaped to Holland, where he died shortly afterwards. Locke, too, escaped to Holland in 1683, after opponents of the king started to be arrested for plotting to assassinate him and his brother. There is no evidence that Locke himself was involved in any such plot, but given his close association with opponents of the king, he prudently escaped to Holland while he still could. The English Crown tried to have Locke (as well as other political exiles) arrested by the Dutch authorities and extradited back to England, but no arrest was ever made.

Locke finally returned to England in 1689 after the victory of the Protestant William of Orange over the Catholic James II and shortly after published his most famous works: *An Essay concerning Human Understanding* and *Two Treatises of Government*. Locke served as a political advisor to the new regime and as an administrator on the Board of Trade. Despite his increasingly poor health, Locke continued to publish works on diverse subjects, such as economics and religion. He died in 1704.

accept that their solution is beyond the boundaries of our intellectual abilities and turn to problems that do hold out some hope of resolution. Locke therefore argues that we should investigate the nature of our minds themselves in order to find out what sort of ideas they are capable of dealing with. We will then, says Locke, be able to distinguish between those topics about which we may reasonably expect our inquiries to produce something like reliable knowledge and those for which this is not a possibility. It is the former to which we should devote our attention.

In some respects, then, Locke's problem was similar to that of Descartes: both wanted to investigate the nature of human knowledge and to establish, as far as possible, how reliable and how wide that knowledge was. But they approached this problem in different ways. Whereas Descartes was concerned to find absolutely certain knowledge even at the expense of doubting everything, Locke was altogether more modest and more commonsensical in his approach: he did not intend nor did he expect to find absolutely certain knowledge. He merely wanted to know the scope within which normal human knowledge, fallible though it may be, could be expected to work with some degree of reliability and accuracy.

Locke set about this task by providing a kind of survey of all the different contents of the human mind that he found when he reflected upon it. A naturalist observes the natural world and organises the things that he or she finds there into a coherent taxonomy, and Locke sought to do the same for the contents of our minds by providing an inventory of the different sorts of ideas that we have. Those ideas that are naturally found in the mind are likely to correspond to those things that the mind is naturally suited to dealing with. It is therefore about these sorts of things that we may reasonably expect knowledge to be attainable (see Box 5.2 for the relationship between Locke's philosophy and science).

Box 5.2 **Locke and science**

Locke was associated with eminent scientists of his time, such as Isaac Newton. Indeed, Locke claimed that it was the intention of his philosophy to clear the way for the progress of science. He viewed himself as an 'Under-labourer' employed in "removing some of the Rubbish, that lies in the way to Knowledge ..." (*Essay*, Epistle to the Reader, pp. 9–10). Among the 'rubbish' to be removed was "the learned but frivolous use of uncouth, affected, or unintelligible Terms" and the "Vague and insignificant Forms of Speech, and Abuse of Language" which have passed for "Mysteries of Science" (*Essay*, Epistle to the Reader, p. 10). By clarifying the sorts of topics that the mind can know something about (and identifying those that are beyond the scope of human knowledge), Locke thought he could be of service to science: the energies of the scientist could be devoted to tractable questions rather than being wasted in speculating on unresolvable ones.

Empiricism and nativism

As part of his survey of the contents of our minds, Locke asks where these contents come from. We saw in the previous chapter that, for Descartes, our ideas are present in the mind from birth, but for Locke, in contrast, all our ideas are ultimately derived from experience. This dichotomy, between **nativists** (those who believe most of our knowledge is innate) and empiricists (those who believe that it is largely acquired) is one that has a long history and it continues to be felt in psychology today. As far back as ancient Greece, for example, we find Plato arguing that knowledge is already present in the soul before birth whereas his pupil, Aristotle, places much more emphasis on experience and observation of the world in the development of knowledge. In the present day, the so-called **nature–nurture debate** concerning the genetic or environmental sources of many psychological characteristics is a modern manifestation of this same disagreement.

For Locke, the mind at birth is what he called a **tabula rasa**, a blank slate, which only comes to be filled with ideas through experience. He spends the first book of the *Essay* arguing against innate ideas. If there are indeed such inborn ideas, says Locke, then everyone should believe in them. But, he argues, this has never been shown to be the case; it may be shown that *many* people agree about certain ideas, but this is not enough to show that the ideas in question are innate. For that to be the case, *everyone* must hold these same ideas. And there are no such ideas, according to Locke. Moreover, even if it could be proved that there are certain ideas about which everyone agrees, this would not guarantee that the ideas in question are innate. It could equally be the case that everyone learns these ideas very early in life (and so no one remembers learning them) or simply that the ideas in question are so self-evidently true that everyone agrees with them. Everyone would no doubt agree that two is greater than one, but this hardly proves that our ideas of number are innate. That two is greater than one is simply an obvious truth that everyone learns very early in life.

Like Descartes, Locke believes the mind to be transparent to itself. There is nothing in the mind that is hidden from our awareness or introspection in principle. Locke therefore challenges the readers of the *Essay* to reflect on the contents of their own minds and to find ideas that are not somehow derived from experience. To the suggestion that there may be innate ideas of which we are unaware, Locke replies:

> To imprint any thing on the Mind without the Mind's perceiving it, seems to me to be hardly intelligible. (*Essay*, Bk I, Ch. II, 5)

In his survey of ideas, then, Locke finds no examples of innate ideas. There are no convincing logical arguments for the existence of such ideas either and so we therefore have to conclude that they do not exist.

The way of ideas

We have seen that Locke's task was to provide a wide ranging survey of the ideas that the mind can form and, by so doing, to provide a sort of guide as to the sorts of things about which human beings could reasonably be expected to be able to gain knowledge. But what was an 'idea'? Locke defined an idea as "whatsoever is the Object of the Understanding when a Man thinks" (*Essay*, Bk I, Ch. I, 8) or "the immediate object of Perception, Thought, or Understanding" (*Essay*, Bk II, Ch. VIII, 8). For Locke, when we think, our thoughts must be directed towards something, they must be *about* something; there is no such thing as just thinking without any topic of thought. That which our thoughts are about, the object towards which they are directed, is an idea. We can thus think of ideas as the contents of our thoughts. Locke's survey of ideas is, therefore, a survey of the sorts of things that we think about.

The different kinds of idea

For Locke, as we have seen, the source of all our ideas is experience. But, Locke notes, there are different kinds of experience: there is, on the one hand, experience of the external world of things brought to us through our senses and, on the other hand, experience of the workings of our own minds brought to us by our own inward reflection or introspection. This, then, is the first great division in Locke's taxonomy of ideas: **ideas of sensation** and **ideas of reflection**.

Now, whether our ideas come from sensation or from reflection, sometimes those ideas can be broken down into simpler, more basic ideas. The idea of a cat, for example, can be analysed into more basic ideas of furriness, colour, and shape. Other ideas, however, cannot be analysed in this way: the idea of white, for example, cannot be broken down any further into constituent elements. White is just white, and we cannot get any simpler than that. This distinction, then, between ideas that can be broken down into more basic ideas and those that cannot constitutes a second major classification of ideas in Locke's scheme. This is the division between what Locke calls **simple ideas** and **complex ideas**. A simple idea is "uncompounded" and "contains in it nothing but *one uniform Appearance*, or Conception in the Mind, and is not distinguishable into different

Ideas" (*Essay*, Bk II, Ch. II, 1). Simple ideas of sensation include those of "*Yellow, White, Heat, Cold, Soft, Hard, Bitter, Sweet*" (*Essay*, Bk II, Ch. I, 3); simple ideas of reflection include the basic activities and processes of the mind: "*Perception, Thinking, Doubting, Believing, Reasoning, Knowing, Willing*, and all the different actings of our own Minds" (*Essay*, Bk II, Ch. I, 4). Complex ideas, of course, are those ideas that are compounds or amalgamations of these simple ideas.

Such complex ideas can be given to us directly in experience, such as when we perceive a composite object such as a tree (which can, of course, be analysed in simpler ideas of trunk, leaves, colours, basic shapes etc.), or they can be constructed by the mind itself from the ideas furnished by experience. Thus, says Locke, our minds can put together the ideas of "a rational Creature, consisting of a Horse's Head, joined to a body of humane shape, or such as the *Centaurs* are described" (*Essay*, Bk II, Ch. XXX, 5). Such complex ideas created by the mind may or may not correspond to anything that really exists outside the mind.

Ideas of primary and secondary qualities

The possibility that our ideas, the contents of our thoughts, may or may not correspond to what really exists or depict things as they really are has important consequences for Locke. We have here a distinction between things as they appear to us in our thoughts and things as they really are in themselves. One of the most important ways in which this distinction manifests itself in Locke's philosophy is in another classification of different kinds of idea: ideas of **primary qualities** and ideas of **secondary qualities**. This distinction was not new with Locke (versions of it can be found in the works of both Galileo and Descartes), but it is with his name that it is most closely associated today.

Ideas of primary and secondary qualities are perceived qualities or characteristics of things. But they differ from one another in terms of whether they actually correspond to qualities that really exist in the thing in question. Primary qualities are those qualities that can really be said to belong to a thing. Among such qualities, Locke mentions "Solidity, Extension, Figure, Motion, or Rest, and Number" (*Essay*, Bk II, Ch. VIII, 9). These qualities are primary in the sense that they *must* really be possessed by any thing. Any material thing must have size and shape, for example; without such qualities it would not even be a thing.

Secondary qualities, however, are not inherent in the thing itself, but are, properly speaking, sensations or experiences produced in the mind of a person when he or she perceives a thing. The thing produces inner states in the perceiver, but these are qualities of the perceiver, not the thing. Examples of secondary qualities are colours, sounds, and tastes. For Locke, a thing is not inherently coloured. It does, however, by virtue of its physical constitution, have what Locke calls the 'power' to produce a sensation of colour in us when we observe it. This colour sensation – like sensations of sound and taste – is, however, a purely subjective phenomenon and, unlike size or shape, not a real characteristic of the thing in itself.

Another example that Locke gives of a secondary quality is the heat of fire. We might be tempted to say that heat is a property of the fire, but as we move closer to the fire, the heat that we experience changes to a sensation of pain. No one would be tempted to say that pain is 'in' the fire as one of its intrinsic qualities; it is clear that pain is a sensation produced *in us* by the fire. Even though we admit this, says Locke, people are nevertheless prone to think that heat or warmth *are* really in the fire. But, says Locke, the case is exactly analogous to that of pain: heat is a sensation produced in us by the fire just as much as is the pain. Nothing about the fire itself changes as we move towards it. The change, rather, is in us and, consequently, the change from heat to pain is not a change from a primary quality to a secondary quality, but from one secondary quality to another.

Primary qualities, then, really do belong to the thing in question, whereas secondary qualities are merely effects that the thing produces in us. Our *ideas* of primary qualities, how they appear to us, therefore actually do resemble or represent genuine aspects of the external world. Our ideas of secondary qualities, however, do not as they cannot be said to truly belong to the thing in question at all. This distinction is an important one for Locke's somewhat sceptical view of knowledge. Locke recognises that human knowledge is partial and does not necessarily reflect things as they really are. All we have to go on at bottom is our own experience; we can only know things as they are experienced by us. But things as they are experienced by us are not things as they really are independent of our experience of them. It is only the ideas of primary qualities that correspond to qualities that exist in things independent of our perceiving them (see Box 5.3 for the relationship between Locke's view of knowledge and his political philosophy).

Knowledge

Locke's conception of knowledge is intimately bound up with his conception of ideas. Knowledge is, for him, entirely based on ideas. But though it is based on ideas, knowledge is not, for Locke, simply the passive reception of sensory stimulation. That is merely the starting point. Sensory information has to be manipulated and put into connection with other ideas in order for it to constitute

Box 5.3 Locke's politics

Locke is as well known as a political thinker as he is as a philosopher concerned with the nature of mind and knowledge. His political thought was an influence on both the American and French revolutions as well as on the development of modern liberalism. In the *Two Treatises of Government*, for example, he argued that it was right, under some circumstances, to resist illegitimate political power. Locke's moderate scepticism forms a link between his thoughts on mind and knowledge and his political philosophy. Given that we can never have absolute knowledge that is true with certainty, we should, says Locke, be more cautious about trying to impose our views on others and be aware that they might be right and that we might be wrong. Moreover, as we derive all our knowledge ultimately through the senses, it is to experience rather than to tradition and authority that we should turn in trying to understand the world and how we should conduct ourselves in it. Locke's vision of society is one that is pluralistic and tolerant:

> For where is the man that has incontestable evidence of the truth of all that he holds, or the falsehood of all that he condemns, or can say that he has examined to the bottom all his own, or other men's, opinions? The necessity of believing without knowledge, nay often upon very slight grounds, in this fleeting state of action and blindness we are in, should make us more busy and careful to inform ourselves than constrain others. (*Essay*, Bk IV, Ch. 16, 4)

Locke's sober and practical approach to philosophical questions militates against both absolute knowledge and absolute political power.

knowledge. Indeed, Locke defines knowledge as the seeing of connections between ideas:

> Knowledge is the perception of the agreement or disagreement of two ideas. Knowledge then seems to me to be nothing but the perception of the connexion of and agreement, or disagreement and repugnancy of any of our ideas. In this alone it consists. Where this perception is, there is knowledge, and where it is not, there, though we may fancy, guess, or believe, yet we always come short of knowledge. For when we know that white is not black, what do we else but perceive, that these two ideas do not agree? When we possess ourselves with the utmost security of the demonstration, that the three angles of a triangle are equal to two right ones, what do we more but perceive, that equality to two right ones does necessarily agree to, and is inseparable from, the three angles of a triangle? (*Essay*, Bk IV, Ch. I, 2)

This conception of knowledge may seem unremarkable, but it follows from it that knowledge is entirely within the mind of the individual person and that know-ledge has only an indirect link with the exercise of any ability in the everyday public world. We may think that for someone to have knowledge of the French language, for example, is for them to be able to get by when on holiday in a French-speaking country; we might think that mathematical knowledge is the ability to solve mathematical problems when confronted with them. But Locke would disagree – these practical abilities do not, in themselves, constitute knowl-edge. At most they can only be the manifestations of *real* knowledge: that which resides within the privacy of the mind of the individual subject and which consists in that subject's ability to perceive the connections between different ideas. These connections may be perceived more or less directly – we immediately perceive, for example, that three is greater than two – or the connection might have to be recognised more indirectly through several intermediate steps. We do not perceive directly, for example, the connection between the idea of the angles of a triangle and the idea of 180 degrees, but the connection can be made through the intermediate steps of a mathematical proof, which demonstrates that the sum of the internal angles of a triangle is 180 degrees. In either case, however, it is the recognition of the relations and connections between ideas that constitutes knowledge.

This notion that knowledge consists in the connectedness of ideas has had great influence in the development of modern psychology. For example, one popular approach to knowledge in cognitive psychology considers our knowledge of the world to take the form of a semantic network. Here is an influential early example of such a network from Collins and Quillian (1969) (see Figure 5.2).

As you can see, this representation of our knowledge takes the form of a network consisting of interconnected concepts or ideas, some of which corre-spond to things and some of which correspond to qualities possessed by things. These concepts are arranged in a hierarchical fashion so that each thing possesses not only the qualities directly attached to it, but also the qualities associated with the more general category to which it belongs. For example, CANARY possesses not only the quality of yellowness, which is directly attached to it, but also the quality of having feathers, which attaches not directly to CANARY but the more general category of BIRD. CANARY also has the qualities of breathing and moving about that attach to the even more general category of ANIMAL.

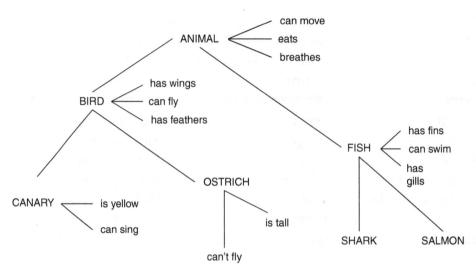

Fig. 5.2 An example of a semantic network (Collins and Quillian 1969)

Knowledge of the world as represented in such a semantic network conforms to Locke's view of knowledge: it consists of having concepts or ideas that are joined to one another in more or less direct ways. When Collins and Quillian (1969) gave participants sentences that they had to evaluate as true or false (e.g. "A canary can sing"), the participants were quicker to recognise a sentence as true the more direct the link between the concept and the qualities attached to it. For example, participants were quicker to respond to "A canary is yellow", in which the quality attaches directly to the concept in the semantic network, than "A canary has feathers", in which the quality of having feathers attaches only indirectly to the concept CANARY via the intermediate, more general concept of BIRD. So, not only is knowledge represented as connected ideas, the time that it takes to access this knowledge is a reflection of how far apart things in the network are from one another. If we were to interpret such findings in Lockean terms, we could say that the time that it takes to access the knowledge is a reflection of how long it takes the participant to perceive the connection between the relevant ideas.

Locke's view of thinking as the manipulation and transformation of ideas that are ultimately derived from sensation also anticipates important aspects of cognitive psychology. We have already seen above that, for Locke, more complex ideas can be created by joining together simple ideas. We have just seen that knowledge consists in putting ideas in connection with one another. But there are other ways in which ideas can be manipulated. We can, for example, take a number of discrete sensory ideas and select their common qualities to create general abstract ideas. We have the idea of whiteness, but we never experience the abstract quality of whiteness itself. We do, however, experience lots of different white things and, for Locke, one of the operations of mind is to be able to generate the general abstract idea of whiteness by extracting what is shared by all the concrete instances of white objects that we encounter.

This idea of performing operations on and transforming the information that we receive through the senses is basic to much of modern cognitive psychology. In one of the foundational texts of cognitive psychology, Ulric Neisser states that

> the term 'cognition' refers to all processes by which the sensory input is transformed, reduced, elaborated, stored, recovered, and used. (Neisser 1967, p. 4)

The mind–body problem and personal identity

As already mentioned, Locke's main concern was to delineate the boundaries of human knowledge. We had to accept, thought Locke, that our knowledge was limited. But he also thought that this limited knowledge, although it fell short of the absolute certainty sought by Cartesian rationalism, was often perfectly adequate to guide our everyday activities. Locke's view of knowledge, then, was a modest and pragmatic one, and nowhere is this more clearly demonstrated than in his approach to the mind–body problem.

We are aware, says Locke, of the workings of our own minds, their properties and the powers they possess, through ideas of reflection, but we have no direct experience of the underlying substance that possesses these qualities. For Locke the substantial nature of the mind – whether it is a non-material substance as Descartes thought, or whether it is physical – was something that was beyond our knowledge. Indeed, Locke believed that both substance dualism and materialism were, strictly speaking, incomprehensible. It is simply beyond our intellectual capabilities to understand how thinking could inhere in purely physical substance. But it is equally beyond our powers to understand how a non-physical mind could interact with the physical world. One of these views, thinks Locke, must be true, but we cannot know which one: "he who will ... look into the dark and intricate part of each Hypothesis, will scarce find his Reason able to determine him fixedly for, or against the Soul's Materiality" (*Essay*, Bk IV, Ch. III, 6).

Locke, however, is not content to rest at this sceptical conclusion. If we look at the question from a more practical perspective, do we really need certain knowledge of whether or not the soul is material? For Locke the answer is: "No." For practical purposes, we want to know about the soul or mind because that is where the self, the real, inner person, is supposed to exist. And we want to know about persons so that they can be rewarded or punished for their actions. When it comes to this *practical* question, whether the soul is a material or non-material substance is irrelevant; what matters is *psychological* continuity regardless of the substance that underlies that continuity.

When, for example, someone is punished for his evil deeds, it is essential, for Locke, that he remembers having done the deeds for which he is being punished and remember these deeds *as his own*. It is essential that the guilty person realises that he is being punished for particular deeds that he has committed. If the punished person had no memory or awareness of the deeds, it would just seem as though bad things were happening to him for no reason. Whether or not the same substance continues over time does not enter into the question. If there was continuity of the same substance over time, whether that substance was a non-physical soul or a physical body, but no continuity of mental states, then we would not be able to punish or reward appropriately. The psychological continuity that is necessary would be lacking and, hence, we would not be dealing morally and legally with the same person.

What counts, then, when we decide whether John is the same person now as he was last year is that John has memories of what he experienced last year, and these memories create a psychological bridge between the present and the past. This principle can be extended to cover longer time periods. It need not be the case, for instance, that we remember in the present things that happened when we were small children in order for us to be the same person now as we were then. We may not directly remember when we were five years old, but we do remember when we were ten years old. And when we were ten years old we *did* remember when we were five. We therefore still have psychological continuity with our five-year-old selves, even though it is by way of our ten-year-old selves. The psychological connection is there even though that connection is not always through the same memories, just as a single rope may not have one continuous strand running through it but may be made of shorter strands each of which has a connection with the immediately preceding and succeeding strands.

Locke gives us several thought experiments designed to demonstrate the priority of psychological continuity over continuity of substance in determining personal identity. Imagine, he says, that a cobbler wakes up one day with the memories of a prince, while the prince wakes up with the memories belonging to the cobbler. We have the body of the cobbler with the prince's memories and the body of the prince with the cobbler's memories, but which is now the prince and which the cobbler? Locke believes that our inclination would be to say that it is the memories that are important and that the person of the prince is now in the body of the cobbler and vice versa. We therefore spontaneously use psychological continuity as our criterion rather than bodily continuity.

Locke's approach to personal identity is an important forerunner of later psychological ideas. In the functionalist approach to psychology, which was touched upon in the previous chapter, mental states are thought of in terms of their functions rather than in terms of the substance in which they are instantiated. That is one of the reasons why, according to this approach, mental states can be investigated through computer modelling, even though computers are made out of different substances than are brains. The substance is irrelevant; it is the function that a mental state performs in relation to other mental states that is important just as for Locke it is the function that memory performs in providing a psychological link between the past and the present that is important. The nature of the substance that underlies the performance of this memory function is of no consequence.

Locke: conclusion

As we have seen, then, Locke presents us with a philosophy that attempts to delineate the boundaries of human knowledge. The conclusions that he arrived at were of great importance in the future development of psychology. Firstly, we have the emphasis on experience as the source of knowledge rather than innate ideas, and hence the importance of *learning* as a topic of scientific and philosophical investigation. Secondly, we have the notion of *ideas* as the immediate objects of our experience and as the vehicles of knowledge (knowledge being the perception of relations between ideas). Thirdly, we have Locke's psychological approach to personal identity: it is the functional and pragmatic criterion of psychological continuity, rather than substance, that is the crucial factor. As we shall see in the next chapter, however, Locke's dismantling of the substantial self in favour of the psychological self was to be taken a step further by another empiricist philosopher, David Hume. For Hume, there seemed to be very little evidence for a continuing self – even a purely psychological self – at all.

George Berkeley

For an empiricist like Locke, experience is the ultimate source of knowledge. Experience also marks the boundary of reliable knowledge: if all our ideas come from experience, then to go beyond the bounds of that experience is to enter the realm of speculation about which we can never have clear understanding. Nevertheless for some other empiricist philosophers, Locke was not radical enough in his insistence on the fundamental importance of experience. One of these thinkers was the Irishman George Berkeley (see Box 5.4).

Box 5.4 George Berkeley

George Berkeley was born in 1685 in County Kilkenny in Ireland. He studied at Trinity College in Dublin and was ordained as an Anglican priest (see Figure 5.3). It was while he was a fellow at Trinity that he published his most famous philosophical works: *An Essay towards a New Theory of Vision* (1709) and *A Treatise concerning the Principles of Human Knowledge* (1710). Berkeley left for London in 1713 in order to have some of his work published there and he became involved with many of the intellectual and literary figures of the time, including his fellow Irishman Jonathan Swift, author of *Gulliver's Travels*.

In 1722 Berkeley had come up with a plan to open a college in Bermuda, which was intended to train missionaries to help the conversion of native Americans to Christianity. The college was to have a mainland base in Rhode Island in America, and Berkeley lived there for several years with his wife before the project fell through because a promised government grant never materialised.

While at Rhode Island, Berkeley published work defending Christianity against what he saw as a rising tide of atheism and unorthodox religious views. In 1734 Berkeley returned to Ireland as Bishop of Cloyne. During his time as bishop, as well as carrying out his ecclesiastical duties, he published work on improving the economic and social problems in Ireland. Berkeley died in Oxford, where he had gone to oversee his son's education, in 1753.

Much of Berkeley's philosophy, even when it is not explicit, was designed to combat the materialistic and mechanistic philosophy of the likes of Newton. Berkeley considered that one of the results of such a philosophy would be to undermine traditional Christian belief. His arguments for immaterialism in the

Box 5.4 (cont.)

Principles of Human Knowledge and his semiotic theory of perception in *Essay towards a New Theory of Vision* both have this theological underpinning.

Fig. 5.3 George Berkeley

Berkeley is known in the history of thought for two particular contributions. Firstly, there is his **immaterialism**, according to which there are no things in themselves apart from our experience of them (a doctrine presented in his *Principles of Human Knowledge*). Secondly, there is his influential theory of vision, according to which seeing is based on learning rather than on innate visual capacities. Both of these aspects of Berkeley's thought foreshadowed later ideas in psychology. This is most obvious in the case of perceptual learning, but even the more metaphysical doctrine of immaterialism was to influence the development of psychology through the radical empiricism of William James and the positivism of Ernst Mach.

Immaterialism: to be is to be perceived

Locke, as we have seen, argued that the immediate objects of our perception are *ideas*. Berkeley, too, took this as his starting point. But from this common beginning, Locke and Berkeley went on to draw very different conclusions. Locke believed that lying behind the ideas that we perceive there were things that existed independently of our perception of them. Our ideas of sensation were effects caused in us by objective things impinging on our sense organs. But for Berkeley, if we are being true to empiricism, we have no warrant for asserting the existence of things that exist independently of our experience. In claiming that there are independently existing things Locke is, for Berkeley, flouting his own principles in going beyond what is given in our perceptual experience. Berkeley, on the other hand, is much more radical in his empiricism: according to him, there are no things separate from the ideas that we perceive. To put it another way, 'things' simply *are* perceived ideas and qualities; they are *not* substances that cause ideas in us, but are the ideas themselves. For Locke there are ideas, minds that perceive those ideas, and substances that cause those ideas to be perceived by minds, but for Berkeley there only minds and the ideas perceived by those minds.

At first glance, this theory seems to be completely implausible – it would appear that Berkeley is denying the existence of the external world and claiming that everything we see is simply a figment of our imagination. And this is, indeed, how many people have interpreted him. But the interpretation is wrong. Berkeley is *not* saying that the world that we perceive, of cats and tables and chairs, does not exist, but that this world is a collection of perceptual experiences rather than independently existing substances that lie beyond our experience. In this way he is even truer to empiricism than is Locke. For Berkeley, the world that we experience *is* the real world, whereas for Locke it is a subjective reflection of an objective real world that we can never experience directly. This is the root of the famous Berkelean maxim, *esse est percipi* (Latin for "to be is to be perceived"). An object, according to Berkeley, is the sum of a particular set of perceptual experiences; without those perceptual experiences the object would not exist because it simply *is* those perceptual experiences.

Berkeley's immaterialism, despite its seemingly fantastic nature, is, he would argue, actually closer to common sense than the theory that the world consists of independently existing substances that produce subjective effects in us. Berkeley might ask: what do we actually *mean* when we say, for example, that there is a cat on the mat? We cannot be talking about something mysterious that lies outside our experience. On the contrary, we are talking about the sensory experiences that we are having. When we say that we see the cat, we are, in effect, saying that we are having certain perceptual experiences. 'The cat', then, is nothing more than a name for a certain group of perceptual experiences, 'the mat' a name for another set of sensory experiences. If we accept that this is what we normally do in everyday life, then we have to conclude that Berkeley's theory is closer to common sense that it first appears.

In effect, what Berkeley is offering to us is a pragmatic theory of things that has something in common with Locke's approach to personal identity. For Locke, as we have seen, the question of whether the self resides in a continually existing non-material soul or a material body is unanswerable. What matters, from a practical point of view, is that there is psychological continuity, and the presence or absence of such continuity is a normal feature of our everyday experience. Berkeley's view of things is analogous to this. We have no experience of, and can know nothing about, any hypothesised things that exist independently of our perception. They simply cannot play any part in our everyday business, just as the substance of the soul (whether material or non-material) cannot play a part in deciding personal identity. What *counts* as a thing in everyday life is a certain group of perceptual experiences just as what *counts* as a person is the continuity of experiences in memory.

The idea that the world is fundamentally nothing more than the sum of experiences was to resurface later in the work of William James, who even wrote an essay called 'A world of pure experience'. It would also form a fundamental part of the positivism of Ernst Mach, which was to have a great influence not only on psychology, but on the philosophy of science in general. Indeed, the disagreement between thinkers who take the world of experience as the funda-mental reality and those who believe it to be merely a secondary manifestation of something more real that lies behind it is a theme that will recur at many points throughout this book.

Berkeley's theory of vision

Whereas Berkeley's immaterialism encountered opposition and some ridicule in his lifetime, his theory of vision (put forward in *An Essay towards a New Theory of Vision* and *The Theory of Vision Vindicated and Explained*) met with greater public success. Berkeley saw himself as combating a particular approach to perception that was associated with thinkers such as Descartes and Isaac Newton. According to this approach, visual perception, particularly perception of distance and depth, was to be understood in mathematical terms. The ques-tion of depth perception was problematic because the retina gives us only a flat, two-dimensional image yet we undoubtedly perceive the world in three dimen-sions. The source of the third dimension of depth was, therefore, of particular interest to perceptual theorists. Descartes argued that we can determine the position of a point in depth "by a sort of innate geometrical knowledge shared by all men" (*Dioptrics*, VI, cited by Berkeley, 1709/1975, p. 57). The analogy that Descartes gives is that of a blind person holding a stick in each hand with which he or she touches the same object. Descartes argues that the blind person can judge the distance of the object on the basis of the angles formed by the two sticks: the angle between the two sticks at the object will be larger the closer the object is to the blind person. Similarly, we have to turn the eyes through greater or lesser angles to focus on objects depending on how far they are from us. The axes of the eyes, then, were thought to be analogous to the two sticks held by the blind person and people such as Descartes thought we could judge distance by perceiv-ing the angle between the eyes' axes.

Berkeley, as an empiricist, found such a view unacceptable because sensory experience had to be supplemented with innate mathematical abilities to account for our perceptions of a three-dimensional world. Berkeley pointed out that, when perceiving things around him at various distances and directions, he had no awareness of doing any mathematical or geometrical reasoning. He also pointed out that those who were poor at mathematics or who had never learned it nevertheless perceived just as well as those were skilled in geometry. Whatever this mysterious geometrical ability was, it was something of which we were completely unaware and which was completely independent of education and training. For Berkeley there was, therefore, no evidence for such 'innate geometrical knowledge'. In addition, Berkeley argued that we do not perceive the optic axes (the lines of sight radiating from the eyes), whereas the blind person does perceive the sticks that he holds. Given that neither the supposed geometrical computations nor the data on which they are supposed to operate are to be found anywhere in experience, Berkeley, taking experience as his yardstick, rejects both.

Rather than thinking of distance perception as a matter of mathematical calculation, Berkeley thinks of it as learning and understanding a language. Just as the words of a language are arbitrary, so the signs of the visual language are arbitrary. In English, for example, the fact that we use the word 'cat' to refer to a certain group of animals is purely arbitrary; there is nothing in the written or spoken word that resembles or otherwise connects it to cats. Similarly, in the sensations that are produced by the eye, there is nothing that intrinsically would allow us to perceive distance. There is no necessary reason, for example, why things that are further away from us should give us a fainter impression than those that are nearby, says Berkeley. We nevertheless learn to interpret the faintness of a visual sensation as meaning that the perceived object is further away than an object that gives a more vivid sensation. The same goes for size: a book that is in front of us on the table will produce a larger retinal image than a book on the other side of the room, but this information in itself tells us nothing about the respective distances of the two books from us. Again, we have to learn to interpret these differing visual sensations as meaning that one book is further away than the other.

We learn to make such interpretations by learning the association between, on the one hand, visual sensations and, on the other, touch and motor sensations. Unlike vision, the sense of touch, according to Berkeley, does give us direct perception of distance and depth. A greater movement is needed to reach a longer distance than a shorter one, and this difference is apparent in the sensations generated by limb movement. The association of visual sensations with those of movement and touch allow us to interpret the visual sensations in terms of distance. We come to associate, for example, less distinct visual sensations with a greater depth or distance (as provided through touch) than those that are more distinct and vivid. This is the aspect of Berkeley's theory, sometimes referred to as the **touch teaches vision** theory, that met with the longest-lasting success. It again exemplifies the importance of learning and experience for empiricism.

But this idea of vision as a language has a wider and more philosophically profound context. For Berkeley, the language of vision was created by God:

> how comes it to pass that a set of ideas [i.e. visual ideas], altogether different from tangible ideas, should nevertheless suggest them to us, there being no necessary connection between them? To which the proper answer is, that this is done in virtue of an arbitrary connexion, instituted by the Author of Nature. (*The Theory of Vision Vindicated*, sect. 43)

For Berkeley, then, the visual world was a series of signs through which God communicates with us.

Berkeley's theory of vision was, therefore, a manifestation of his deep antipathy to the mechanistic and materialistic philosophy that had developed with modern science since the seventeenth century. As we saw in the previous chapter (Chapter 4: 'Descartes and the mind–body problem'), the scientific revolution had 'disenchanted' the world by conceiving it in purely mechanical and mathematical terms. Scientists and philosophers in the Middle Ages and the Renaissance had thought of nature as a text, as a reflection and expression of the mind of God. It was the job of the scientist (or natural philosopher as they would have been called in those days) to try to understand the 'Book of Nature' that had been 'written' by God. Science, then, was not something opposed to religion (as is sometimes thought today), but a profoundly religious activity: understanding nature brought one closer to an understanding of its creator. With the rise of mechanistic science, however, the world could be understood in purely materialistic terms. The role allotted to God, if any, was now that of a divine engineer who constructed the mechanical universe and set the mechanism in motion, but who then played a minimal part in its running.

Such a mechanistic world-view was, for Berkeley, a step on the road to atheism pure and simple. In Berkeley's own time, the mechanistic science of Newton (with Locke as its philosophical underlabourer) seemed to reduce the role of God and to remove meaning and significance from the universe, and it was this view that Berkeley sought to attack. In his theory of vision, Berkeley harked back to the older view of nature as a meaningful text rather than a machine. This is why he argued that vision was a language made up of signs that had meaning rather than the result of mechanical causation or mathematical calculation.

It was, as mentioned above, the perceptual learning aspect of Berkeley's theory of vision that met with most acceptance by later thinkers. Nevertheless, there are also aspects of Berkeley's linguistic approach to vision that still have echoes today, albeit shorn of their original theological context. The contemporary idea that vision consists in the interpretation of visual cues or making sense of ambiguous data is in many ways a modern version of Berkeley's idea of visual language. Of course, many contemporary psychologists also hold that perception is a mechanistic, causal process, which is the view that Berkeley's theory attacked.

Conclusion

Both Locke and Berkeley, then, emphasise the importance of experience and learning as the sources of our knowledge as opposed to innate ideas. They also believe that *ideas* are the objects of our perception, although for Locke ideas are subjective effects caused by objective things, whereas for Berkeley ideas are things. Both also try to give accounts of concepts that can be 'cashed out' in terms of everyday experience rather than speculative metaphysics. Locke does this with his psychological approach to personal identity; Berkeley does it with his immaterialist approach to things. In the next chapter we shall see how Hume takes empiricism a step further in which the very ideas of self and causality are called into question from the standpoint of experience.

There are, nevertheless, important differences between Locke and Berkeley, even thought they start from the same empiricist principles. These differences are particularly manifest in their differing approaches to the idea of an objective reality that exists independently of our experience and in their opposed theories of perception. In the first case, Berkeley can be thought of as a more radical empiricist than Locke in that Berkeley rejects any notion of things that exist independently of experience. In the case of perception, both Berkeley's linguistic approach and Locke's mechanical/causal approach, though opposed to one another, have echoes in more modern psychological theories of perception.

Revision questions

1. What was Locke's goal in examining the contents of the mind and how did it differ from Descartes' approach to knowledge?

2. Why did Locke not believe in the existence of innate ideas?

3. What is the difference between simple and complex ideas?

4. What is the difference between ideas of primary qualities and ideas of secondary qualities? Give an example to illustrate the difference.

5. What, for Locke, constitutes the essence of knowledge?

6. In what does continued personal identity consist, according to Locke?

7. What does Berkeley mean when he says that to be is to be perceived?

8. How did Berkeley's theory of depth perception differ from that of Descartes?

References

Berkeley, G. ([1709]/1975). *An Essay towards a New Theory of Vision*. In *Berkeley: Philosophical Works*. London: J.M. Dent, pp. 1–59.

Berkeley, G. ([1710]/1975). *Principles of Human Knowledge*. In *Berkeley: Philosophical Works*. London: J.M. Dent, pp. 61–127.

Berkeley, G. ([1733]/1975). *The Theory of Vision Vindicated and Explained*. In *Berkeley: Philosophical Works*. London: J.M. Dent, pp. 229–50.

Collins, A. M. and Quillian, M. R. (1969). Retrieval time from semantic memory. *Journal of Verbal Learning and Verbal Behavior*, 8, 240–7.

Hobbes, T. ([1651]/1904). *Leviathan* (A. R. Waller, ed.). Cambridge University Press.

Locke, J. ([1689]/1979). *An Essay concerning Human Understandings* (P. H. Nidditch, ed.). Oxford: Oxford University Press.

Neisser, U. (1967). *Cognitive Psychology*. New York: Appleton–Century–Crofts.

6 Hume, Kant, and Enlightenment

Timeline

1719	Daniel Defoe publishes *Robinson Crusoe*
1727	Death of Isaac Newton
1750	Start of the Highland Clearances in Scotland
1771	First edition of the *Encyclopaedia Britannica*
1774	Discovery of oxygen independently by Joseph Priestly and Karl Scheele
1776	American declaration of independence from Britain
1783	First manned hot-air balloon flight
1789	Storming of the Bastille. Start of the French Revolution
1793	French revolutionaries execute Louis XVI and Marie Antoinette by guillotine
1801	Act of Union of Great Britain and Ireland
1804	Napoleon Bonaparte is crowned French Emperor

David Hume

1711	Born in Edinburgh
1739–40	Publishes *A Treatise of Human Nature*
1748	Publishes *An Enquiry concerning Human Understanding*
1754–62	Works as librarian in Edinburgh. Writes and publishes his 6-volume *History of England*
1776	Dies in Edinburgh

Immanuel Kant

1724	Born in Königsberg, East Prussia
1755	Obtains academic position at the University of Königsberg. Proposes nebular hypothesis of the formation of the solar system
1781	Publishes the *Critique of Pure Reason*
1788	Publishes the *Critique of Practical Reason*
1804	Dies in Königsberg

Introduction

The ideas of Hume and Kant, which we will be examining in this chapter, are of great importance for the future development of psychology. In particular, the contrasting ways in which they conceived of human experience formed the metaphysical bedrock of differing approaches to psychology. The Humean conception of experience as consisting of, fundamentally, discrete sensations only held together by fortuitous associations underpinned such schools of psychology as structuralism and behaviourism. The Kantian view of experience as something intrinsically structured, on the other hand, was a philosophical presupposition of thinkers such as Helmholtz and Wundt. Such profoundly differing conceptions meant that the psychologists who held them not only disagreed in the answers that they gave, but in the questions that they asked in the first place.

Hume and Kant were both creatures of the **Enlightenment**. The Enlightenment was the outcome of and fulfilment of a general trend in European thought that, since the time of Descartes and the scientific revolution, had distrusted and questioned traditional authorities. Its proponents argued against what they saw as superstition and urged instead that we put our trust in human reason. In the words of Kant, the motto of the Enlightenment was "dare to know". One should have the courage to use one's own reason instead of just accepting what tradition or authority tells one to believe, even if that means questioning and rejecting long-standing beliefs or indeed whole belief systems. This spirit of Enlightenment was above all manifested in the progress of science, particularly in the work of Isaac Newton. In his physics he seemed to many of his contemporaries to have discovered the fundamental laws of the universe, and was proof of the heights to which human reason could soar when unhampered by tradition and superstition.

Many philosophers were inspired by Newton and sought to do for human beings and society what he seemed to have done for the physical universe. Just as Newton had discovered the fundamental laws of the physical universe, they wanted to discover the fundamental laws and character of human nature. Such a quest was not merely of academic interest: it had a real practical outcome too. The philosophers of the Enlightenment thought that if one could discover what human nature, the real essence of human beings, is, then one could reorder society in order to fit in with human nature. Human nature, then, would not be oppressed and perverted by traditional forms of authority but would flourish in a society adapted to the needs and inclinations of its citizens. This 'enlightened' search for human nature had, however, an important consequence for subsequent ideas about the mind because reason itself, as part of human nature, came under scrutiny. As a result, in different ways in the works of Hume and Kant, the traditional optimistic view that human reason unaided can discover virtually everything began to be called into question. Reason itself came to be seen as partial and limited.

David Hume

Nowhere was this critical examination of human reason and knowledge more evident than in the work of the Scottish philosopher David Hume (1711–76). Hume is often grouped together with Locke and Berkeley as an exponent of empiricism. Though there were many differences between these philosophers they nevertheless shared an emphasis on the importance of experience, particularly sense experience, for the attainment and growth of knowledge. Hume, as we shall see, certainly proposed this view. But, by taking this empiricist notion of the importance of experience to its logical extreme, he arrived at conclusions that had potentially devastating effects on how we understand ourselves and our place in nature.

The importance accorded to experience by Hume is clear in his most famous work, *A Treatise of Human Nature* (1739–40), which is subtitled "An attempt to introduce the experimental method of reasoning into moral subjects." By the experimental method Hume did not necessarily mean carrying out actual experiments in a scientific laboratory, though that would certainly be one possible example of it, but something more general: using experience as the yardstick and the guarantee of knowledge. We must, in other words, take whatever knowledge that we have and test it against experience, whether that be in an experiment or our everyday lives. And the meaning of that knowledge, the very sense of the concepts in which it is expressed, lies in its being ultimately derived from sensory experience.

Hume and causality

Hume distinguishes two different sorts of mental content: there are **impressions** and there are **ideas**. "*Impressions*," according to Hume "are our lively and strong perceptions: *ideas* are the fainter and weaker" (*Treatise*, p. 647). We thus have actual perceptual experiences and we have ideas derived from them, ideas that can be likened to faint copies or images of the original experiences. It is this connection between our ideas and perceptual experience that gives them their

Box 6.1 **David Hume**

David Hume was born in Edinburgh in 1711. He was a bright child and enrolled at the University of Edinburgh shortly before his 12th birthday. He studied a wide range of subjects, including science and history as well as philosophy, but his single-minded devotion to his philosophical studies over a number of years left him mentally exhausted and he decided that a less isolated and intense lifestyle would be better for his health. He worked for a while as a clerk in a Bristol sugar importer before moving, in 1734, to France, where he resumed his philosophical investigations. It was at the famous college town of La Flèche, where Descartes had studied, that Hume wrote *A Treatise of Human Nature*.

Hume was disappointed by the lack of reception that the book received and stated that it fell "dead-born from the press". He later, in *An Enquiry concerning Human Understanding*, recast the book's ideas in what he believed would be a more readable style, although the resulting book was not much more successful. Hume did, however, have notable literary success in his lifetime as the author of a six-volume work, *The History of England* (1754–62), which sold well enough to provide Hume with an independent income for the rest of his life. Indeed, during his lifetime, Hume was far better known as a historian than as a philosopher.

Hume had a reputation as a religious sceptic, and it was rumoured that he might even be an atheist. He was consequently turned down for academic positions at both the University of Edinburgh and the University of Glasgow. Hume's actual position on the existence of God is, however, not entirely clear. Though there is no doubt that he was critical of many aspects of religion and, in particular, of belief in miracles, it seems that he never completely ruled out the possibility that there might exist a deity, or deities. He did not, however, believe in life after death.

Hume was, by all accounts, an open, generous, and cheerful personality (Figure 6.1). He had worked as a diplomat in the British Embassy in Paris between 1763 and 1766 and had been hugely popular in the salons of Paris, where he made the acquaintance of the leading figures of the French Enlightenment, such as Diderot and D'Alembert. His friend, the economist Adam Smith, described Hume "as approaching as nearly to the idea of a perfectly wise and virtuous man as perhaps the nature of human frailty will admit".

Hume spent his last years back in Edinburgh and died in 1776.

Box 6.1 (cont.)

Fig. 6.1 David Hume

sense. Any idea that is not traceable back to experience is nothing more than nonsense. Experience is not only the source of our knowledge but the yardstick against which it is to be measured. As Hume says: "When we entertain any suspicion that a philosophical term is employed without any meaning or idea (as is but too frequent) we need by enquire, *from what impression is that supposed to be derived*" (*Enquiry*, p. 22). This view of knowledge was to be hugely influential, particularly in the approach of positivists such as Mach and Ayer, in the early twentieth century.

If we grant that all our knowledge comes from experience there nevertheless arises a further question: how do these impressions and these ideas derived from them become organised in our minds? A mind that consisted of nothing but disjointed sense impressions and images could scarcely be said to have knowledge at all. What is also necessary for knowledge is that impressions and ideas be related in appropriate ways. They may, for example, be linked through resemblance so that the image of one particular person may call to mind that of another person who has some sort of physical resemblance to the first. They might be related in terms of what Hume calls contiguity in time and space, i.e. they tend to occur together. So, for example, the idea of thunder will tend to bring to mind the idea of lightning because the two corresponding impressions are linked together closely in time, and so the ideas that are derived from them become associated with one another. For Hume the most important way in which ideas and impressions are linked together is in terms of cause and effect:

> 'Tis sufficient to observe, that there is no relation, which produces a stronger connexion in the fancy, and makes one idea more readily recall another, than the relation of cause and effect betwixt their objects. (*Treatise*, p. 11)

Such linking together of ideas and impressions is, of course, fundamental to our idea and to our experience of an ordered and coherent world. Events do not just happen in a random way; they are connected causally to one another. Thus, to use Hume's own example, if we see a flame and then subsequently feel the sensation of heat, we experience the flame as having caused the heat. We do not experience the flame and the heat as two sensations that just happen to have occurred together arbitrarily. In a more formal context, the necessary linking of causes and effects is also crucial for the validity of Newtonian science.

It is here, however, with the importance accorded to causality, that Hume's enquiries take a more troubling, sceptical turn. We have already seen that, for Hume, for an idea to be meaningful, it has to be derived ultimately from some sensory impression. But what then is the impression from which the idea of causality is derived? According to Hume, there is no such impression: we never actually observe a causal connection. When, for example, you see a snooker ball rolling along the table and hitting another ball, causing it to move, you do not actually receive an impression of a causal connection. You have an impression of one ball rolling along the table and then an impression of another ball rolling along the table. You see two discrete events, but do not see a causal connection between these two events.

Yet, it is undeniable that we do experience the flame as the cause of the heat and the motion of the first snooker ball as the cause of the motion of the second. For Hume, though, this is just a matter of habit: we experience the constant conjunction of the flame and heat and of the motion of one ball followed by the motion of the other and come to conclude that the former is the cause of the latter in each case. There is nothing in the cause itself that would lead us to expect what its effect was going to be. A young child without the appropriate experience would not expect the flame to cause heat nor the motion of one snooker ball to cause motion of the other. But through experience, he or she would become accustomed to expect the occurrence of one event given the occurrence of the other. Such expectations, however, are not logically justified: it does not necessarily follow that, because event A is constantly precedes event B, A is the cause of B. Nor, as we have seen, is there any impression corresponding to a causal connection. Our idea of causality, therefore, has neither a basis in sensation nor justification in logic. It is simply a matter of habit, of what we have become accustomed to. It is Hume's apparent demonstration that causality – what we might think of as the glue of the universe – has no firmer a foundation than human habit that was to prove such an impetus to Kant in his own philosophising.

Hume and the self

Hume's sceptical gaze was not only turned outwards towards the world of physical events and objects, it was also turned inwards to the mental world. And just as Hume could find no firm basis for what was thought to tie physical events together, causality, he could find no firm basis for the existence of what was thought to tie mental events together, the self.

We have already seen in the work of Descartes, for example, the idea that, although sceptical doubts may be applied to the external universe, internal knowledge, knowledge that we have of ourselves, seems to be particularly privileged. For Descartes and his followers it was immune from the same sort of doubt that may apply to knowledge of the external world. Take for example the idea that there is such a thing as a stable, continuing self, an entity that is the real you and is the thing that *has* your thoughts and experiences. For Descartes nothing could be more certain than the existence of such a self, but for Hume the inner self cannot escape scepticism any more than can the external world.

Self-knowledge too must be assessed with respect to its grounding in experience. And, just as we never have an impression of causality, we never seem to actually have an impression of the self:

> For my part, when I enter most intimately into what I call *myself*, I always stumble on some particular perception or other, of heat or cold, light or shade, love or hatred, pain or pleasure. I never can catch *myself* at any time without a perception, and never can observe anything but perception . . . I may venture to affirm of the rest of mankind, that they are nothing but a bundle or collection of different perceptions, which succeed each other with an inconceivable rapidity, and are in a perpetual flux and movement. (*Treatise*, p. 252)

There is, in other words, no such thing as a substantial self that exists through time; there is no such thing as the continuous bearer of perceptions, merely the perceptions themselves. This is sometimes referred to as the **bundle theory of the self**.

Humean scepticism, therefore, potentially threatens not only how we understand the physical universe, but how we understand ourselves. It calls into question the existence of those very things, necessary causal connection and a stable self, that seem to be required to give coherence to both the outer and the inner worlds. And where there is no coherence, no understanding is possible. Sceptical reasoning, carried to its conclusion, seems to be self-destructive and to undermine the foundations of any claims to knowledge whatsoever. Nobody, however, as Hume himself realised, can live in the midst of such doubt. Belief in the necessity of causal connections, for example, is required if we are to function at all, even if we can find no rational justification for such a belief. And so reason has to give way to what Hume called our "natural beliefs" – those things, such as belief in causality, that we cannot but believe and which we are predisposed to believe by nature, but which cannot, ultimately, be justified. Unlike some Enlightenment thinkers, then, Hume does not think that reason can be the sole guide to human activity because it destroys those very beliefs that are necessary for us to live normal everyday lives. Rational enquiry shows that reason itself is limited.

Immanuel Kant

It was Hume's questioning of the supremacy of reason and of the rational justification of many of our fundamental beliefs that provided the spur for Kant's revolution in philosophy. Kant had been trained in a particular tradition of philosophy – the rationalism that we associate with Descartes and Leibniz – according to which one could obtain, through reason, absolute knowledge of the universe, of people, and of their place in that universe. Kant accepted this received view until he came across the work of Hume:

> I openly confess, the suggestion of David Hume was the very thing, which many years ago first interrupted my dogmatic slumber, and gave my investigations in the field of speculative philosophy quite a new direction. (*Prolegomena*, p. 7)

In particular, it was Hume's account of our idea of causality that sent Kant on his new intellectual path. Kant, as well as being a philosopher, was also a scientist interested in astronomy and physics, and he was therefore perturbed by Hume's idea that causality was just a matter of habit and that there was no necessary causal connection between one event and another. This seemed to destabilise the Newtonian world-view that was the cornerstone of the new, enlightened science.

Humean scepticism seemed to raise doubts about the extent and applicability of reason and Kant saw his task as finding out where the bounds of reason lay. One would then know those areas in which one could have confidence in rational human knowledge and those areas in which one could not have such knowledge and in which, consequently, unverifiable faith, perhaps, could be one's only guide. This was what he attempted to do in what is probably his most famous work, *The Critique of Pure Reason*. Here Kant employed what are known as **transcendental arguments**. Instead of trying to derive knowledge (such as our knowledge of causality) from experience, as the likes of Locke and Hume had tried to do, Kant asked a different sort of question. He said: given that we do have

Box 6.2 Immanuel Kant

Immanuel Kant was born in 1724 in Königsberg in East Prussia (today the city is named Kaliningrad, after one of Stalin's allies, and is the centre of a small pocket of Russian territory on the Baltic Sea). Kant's family was of modest means (his father made horse harnesses) and devoutly religious. They were adherents of Pietism, an austere form Lutheran Protestantism, which emphasised personal faith and inner religious feelings over formal institutions and theology. It was at a Pietist school that Kant was educated and where he found the strictness and narrowness of the tuition to be frustrating. Though Kant never argued against

Box 6.2 (cont.)

religion in total and, indeed, agreed with many of Christianity's ethical teachings, he found Pietism's emphasis on personal emotional experience at the expense of reason to be distasteful.

Kant studied at the University of Königsberg from the ages of 16 to 22, after which he worked as a private tutor for several years. He finally, at the age of 31, was given permission to teach at the university but was paid directly by the students rather than receiving a salary from the university. This was a common arrangement in German-speaking universities and many of the other thinkers discussed in this book, such as Wundt, all started their academic careers as unsalaried lecturers of this sort. Kant taught a wide variety of subjects, including anthropology and geography, but his main interests were in astronomy and mathematics. Indeed, Kant was one of the first people to propound the nebular hypothesis of the origins of the solar system. According to this view, the planets were created when vast clouds of gas and dust collapsed because of gravity and thereby formed denser bodies. A modern version of this basic idea is widely accepted today. He was finally given a professorship (and a salary) in philosophy at the age of 46. At this point he devoted himself to philosophy and used his lectures to expound and develop the thoughts that he would later publish in his most famous works, such as the *Critique of Pure Reason*. Kant was said to be an engrossing lecturer and students had to arrive an hour before he was due to teach in order to be sure of having a place in the packed lecture theatre. The overall impression that Kant gave, according to the recollections of some of his students, was of someone thinking fresh thoughts on the spot rather than mechanically working his way through the requirements of an approved syallabus.

Kant's personal habits were notoriously regular: it was said that the citizens of Königsberg could set their clocks by the passing of Kant by their houses as he went on his afternoon walk around the city. But this regularity does not indicate a dry and dusty character. On the contrary, Kant was well known as a witty conversationalist and host (Figure 6.2). He retired from teaching in 1796. His mental powers gradually declined and it is thought that he may have suffered from a form of dementia. Kant died in 1804. News of his death quickly spread through Königsberg and, though he had stipulated his preference for a quiet funeral, many thousands of his fellow Königsbergers followed the coffin.

Box 6.2 **(cont.)**

Fig. 6.2 Immanuel Kant

experience of a certain sort, what must be the case in order for us to have such experience in the first place? Kant, therefore, seeks to go further back than the empiricists. For them everything is grounded in sensory experience, but for Kant this experience itself depends on pre-existing factors. It is in going beyond and behind experience, in *transcending* it, and in finding out its enabling conditions that Kant believed the solution to sceptical doubts lay. This is so because scepticism itself is only possible given certain experiential foundations.

Kant argues that for us even to be able to raise sceptical questions about causality, the self, and the external world, it is necessary for us to have experience of a certain sort in the first place. Specifically, to ask ourselves whether things really are the way that they seem to be, we have not only to have experience, but self-conscious experience. This is because it is only when experience is self-conscious, when we are aware of ourselves as having experiences, that we can stand back and objectify our experience and ask whether it conforms to the way that the world actually is. My feeling that all my experiences are owned by me is therefore a precondition of scepticism.

What, then, has to be the case for us to have the self-conscious experience that is necessary for scepticism even to arise? Let us take for example my doubting that the desk in front of me is really there, as Descartes might have done. For this even to be possible I must have the experience of an object (in this case the desk) existing apart from me at a particular point in space. But where does the idea of space come from? From what impression, as Hume might say, is it derived? Kant's answer is that it is not derived from any impression. Rather, any having of impressions of external objects at all presupposes the existence of the idea of space, otherwise these objects would not even be experienced as external to ourselves. Hume was wrong in saying that all knowledge must be derived from experience. On the contrary, there are some ideas, such as space, that are necessary for the existence of our experience, and so cannot be derived from it. They must exist prior to experience. Similar reasoning applies to time. Kant argues that it is impossible for the idea of time to be derived from experience. For this to be possible, one would have to be aware of one event occurring before, after, or simultaneously with another. Through repeated experiences of this sort, one might derive the idea of time. But to experience any event as occurring before, after, or simultaneously with another presupposes that they are *already* experienced in time. Both time and space, then, because they are necessary characteristics of our experience, are not themselves drawn from experience but are preconditions of it.

That any possible experience must have certain characteristics meant, for Kant, that we can make meaningful statements about it that are not the result of observation nor are logically necessary truths. For Hume and for the logical positivists who followed him in the twentieth century, there were only two sorts of meaningful statement. There are statements that are true by definition ('All triangles have three sides', for example), and these are referred to as **analytic**. There are statements that are true in terms of their conforming to the facts of the empirical world. The statement 'It is raining outside' would be an example of the latter. Such statements are referred to as **synthetic**. According to logical positivism, any statement that does not take one of these forms is, strictly speaking, meaningless.

Analytic statements can be known to be true **a priori**, that is before experience. To know that the statement 'All triangles have three sides' is true, it is not necessary to check it against impressions of actually existing triangles. It is true by definition. Synthetic statements, on the other hand, could only be known to be true **a posteriori**, that is after experience. To know whether the statement 'It is raining' is true or not I have to look out of the window to check the statement against the facts of experience. Analytic statements, because they are true by definition, do not tell us anything about the world. 'All triangles have three sides' does not tell us whether or not there are any triangles and it would be true regardless of the existence of any actual triangles. Synthetic statements, on the other hand, do tell us about the world (whether or not it is raining, for example). That is why their truth can only be verified by checking them against our experience of the world.

We have, then, analytic statements that are true *a priori* and which do not tell us anything about the world; and synthetic statements whose truth can only be established *a posteriori* and which do tell us something about the world. These correspond to Hume's and the logical positivists' two classes of meaningful proposition. But Kant said that there is a third class of meaningful statement: statements that tell us something about the world but are true before experience, and thus do not require checking in relation to experience. These statements are synthetic but are true *a priori*. Such propositions describe the basic forms of experience, and they are necessarily true of it. Thus, that we experience the external world in terms of space tells us something about the external world – it has spatial characteristics. But we know this without consulting our experience of the external world because our experience of it *must* be spatial. If it were not spatial, then it would not be experience of an external world. Space is not an idea that can be derived from experience itself. Space is something that must be there prior to experience of an external world.

The ideas of space and time, then, cannot be derived from experience as they are the presuppositions of any experience whatsoever. The empiricist notion that all knowledge comes from experience or needs to be checked with respect to experience is wrong. The mind is not a blank slate, but has an inherent structuring activity from the outset, and it is necessary for it to do this structuring in order for us to have experience. *All* our experiences, whether of ourselves or of the external world, are mediated by particular structures that are not themselves experienced, but which structure that experience. This can be likened to going through life with coloured glasses on that you can't take off: we see everything through ever-present filters.

As well as space and time, another of these ever-present structuring principles built into our minds is causality. That there is no 'impression' from which the idea of causal connection can be derived does not, ultimately, have the damaging consequences for Kant as it does for Hume. This is because Hume did not realise that causal connection is not the name of an impression, but of a principle that organises impressions. For the world that we do experience, therefore, it is necessarily true that there are causal connections and so Hume is wrong: we cannot but experience things in terms of causal connections (and in terms of space and time), and these connections are necessary, not just a matter of habit.

But Kant's demonstration that the mind has an active role in constructing experience does have one particular consequence whose radical nature it would be impossible to overstate: we can never know or experience the world as it is in itself. Because we have our coloured glasses on, and can't take them off, we can never actually see reality except as it appears to us through the coloured lenses of the mind's structuring principles. Kant called reality as it is in itself the **noumena**; but we only come into contact with **phenomena**, the appearances of reality.

This idea has important consequences for the scope of human knowledge: if we can never experience things as they really are in themselves, there is another realm of existence or reality that we can never say anything about because we are inherently finite beings who can only experience things according to the ways that our minds themselves are structured. For Kant, we cannot go beyond the bounds of space, time, and causality, which are the bounds of any possible experience, and so attempting to say anything about the world as it is in itself will inevitably result in confusion and nonsensical metaphysical speculation. In showing that absolute knowledge of reality was impossible, Kant administered a fatal blow to centuries-old pretensions of philosophy and science.

It is important to realise that the mind's inherent organising principles, although they are not derived from experience, are not the same as the innate ideas invoked by some philosophers, such as Descartes. For Descartes, the innate idea of God is an idea with a specific content, but for Kant the innate ideas of space, time, and causality are forms that structure and organise content provided by sensation. Kant is therefore sometimes seen as proposing a sort of middle road between extreme nativism, on the one hand, and extreme empiricism, on the other. It is also important to realise that, for Kant, the existence of the mind's inherent organising principles is rationally demonstrable. Nativism of this sort is not a refuge of last resort to be exploited when one has not been imaginative or diligent enough to identify the sources of knowledge in experience, but a realisation that experience itself is not the simple entity that empiricism takes it to be, and that something else must lie behind it.

But, as we have seen, this structuring of experience applies not only to the external world, but also to inner sense. Our experience of our own mental states is also mediated by inherent structuring principles, and these principles are themselves not objects of experience. Thus, just as we cannot have direct contact with the world as it is in itself, we cannot have direct contact with our own minds; we can only have experience of our phenomenal selves. "[I]nner sense," says Kant, "by means of which the mind intuits itself, or its inner state, gives . . . no intuition of the soul itself, as an object" (*Critique of Pure Reason*, p. 67). The Cartesian idea of a direct and incorrigible knowledge of ourselves as stable, continuing substances is, then, an illusion. But so is the Humean claim that what we call the self is merely a bundle of sensations. Again, Hume makes the fundamental mistake of thinking that all ideas must come from experience, whereas the whole point of Kant's arguments is that this *cannot* be the case. The non-existence of an impression corresponding to self does not mean that there is no such thing as the self. It means, rather, that the experiencing self is not something that is part of our direct experience, but is something that lies behind it. The following analogy, made by the twentieth-century philosopher Ludwig Wittgenstein, may serve to illustrate this idea of the self. A visual field necessarily implies the existence of the eye whose visual field it is. But the eye is not itself part of the visual field and is not itself seen. In a similar way the existence of the self is necessary for experience – it does the experiencing – though it is not experienced. It is like the eye of an observer, which does the seeing but is not seen.

It may appear obvious that, contrary to Kant, we do have experience of ourselves: we are, after all, aware of our thoughts and feelings every day. But Kant would argue that even this seemingly direct self-knowledge is mediated by the same structuring principles that apply to the external world. We experience our thoughts and feelings in time – we may, for example, feel a sudden pang of sadness that lasts for a few moments, or we may feel sad for a whole day. But time itself, like space and causality, is one of the mind's inherent structuring principles and so even experience of ourselves is organised by the mind rather than being direct. Just as we never experience the world as it is in itself, we never experience ourselves as we really are. One's real self, sometimes referred to as the **transcendental self**, is the entity that does the organising of experience and it is only the empirical or **phenomenal self**, which is only an appearance, that is experienced.

Given his doubts about the possibility of self-knowledge, Kant had a somewhat dismissive attitude towards the idea that psychology could be a truly scientific enterprise. (But then again he thought that chemistry wasn't a truly scientific enterprise either – only physics seemed to Kant to be properly scientific.) Any attempt to introspect or observe our own inner states was bound to miss the mark. In addition, because thoughts do not have spatial extent like objects, they cannot be measured and so cannot be the subject matter of objective science, which is mathematical. Psychology might not be completely fruitless, but all that it could produce would be qualitative descriptions yielded by a suspect introspection rather than truly scientific knowledge.

We can, therefore, never know anything for certain about the experiencing mind or self. We do have self-conscious experience which we feel is associated with a particular unified point of view and we identify this with ourselves. But for Kant that is all we can say about the self. It is not a part of the empirical world, because we never experience this point of view itself: we experience the empirical world *from* this particular point of view. What we can do, and what Kant has done, is to try to find out what the structures of the mind must be in order for us to have the type of experience that we do. But this is not the result of observation of our own minds; it is inferred from the nature of our experience.

It has to be stressed that Kant is not making an empirical point; he is not talking about how the human nervous system just happens to carry out information processing. He saw himself as making absolute claims that applied to *any experience whatsoever*, claims that were prior to, and more fundamental than, any empirical questions. Later thinkers, particularly early experimental physiologists and psychologists, did, however, try to transpose the spirit of Kant's ideas into the empirical realm by investigating how experience was *in fact* structured by the human organism. Other psychologists, however, followed the Humean path. Assuming that any combination of impressions or ideas occurred simply through habit, these psychologists saw identifying the elements of experience as their main task.

Box 6.3 Kant's ethical thought

Though Kant's *Critique of Pure Reason* is the most important of his works from the point of view of the history of psychology, Kant's ethical philosophy, which he described in the *Critique of Practical Reason*, is also intimately connected with his view of the human mind. Just as Kant had developed his idea of the *a priori* concepts of space, time, and causality as a reaction against Hume's sceptical empiricism, so his ethical theory can also be constrasted with Hume's ideas.

For Hume, passions were the driving forces behind our actions. Though we may use reason instrumentally in figuring out the best way to satisfy those passions, the ultimate wellsprings of our actions are not rational, they are emotional. The ethical praise or blame that we attach to any particular action is also a matter of feeling or sentiment. For Kant it followed from such ideas that there could be no objective moral laws: if everything is, at bottom, merely a question of subjective feeling, then nothing is right or wrong in any absolute sense.

Kant argued against this view. He believed that there were objective moral laws and that these did not spring from feelings but from rationality. Unlike Hume, Kant argued that reason does not merely play a role in deciding the means to satisfy the ends dictated by the passions, but that reason itself decides the ends of action. For Kant, it is only when we act in accordance with reason that we can be said to be exhibiting free will. Simply fulfilling our passions is a form of slavery; freedom means liberation from one's own capricious desires.

The essence of Kant's rational ethics is expressed in an overarching moral principle that he called the **categorical imperative**. According to this principle one should "act only in accordance with that maxim through which you can at the same time will that it become a universal law". In other words, one should act in the way that you would want all other people at all other times to act. To act otherwise would not only be ethically wrong, but rationally self-defeating.

Conclusion

In this chapter we have seen how the questioning attitude of the Enlightenment came, in the work of Hume, to question the validity of human knowledge itself. Taking experience as his touchstone, Hume could find nothing in our experience that justified belief in the real existence of causality or of a stable self. Our beliefs in such things were merely habits of thought rather than true reflections of objective reality. Hume's arguments rely on the empiricist presupposition that all our knowledge has its basis in sensory impressions. Sense experience is fundamental, primary, and is the bedrock on which the rest of knowledge is built, and any empirical ideas that cannot be traced back to some sensory origin are, for Hume, fictions. This sensory experience in which all genuine empirical knowledge has its source consists essentially of discrete sensations or impressions. Many of these discrete sensations, particularly those that are experienced closely to one another in space and time, become associated with one another and so an element of connection and order is introduced into our experience. But this, for an empiricist such as Hume, should not detract from the fact that it is with discrete sensory impressions that we start.

Kant saw the potentially devastating consequences that Humean empiricism might have for human knowledge and sought to save it by questioning the very basis of Hume's philosophy. Sensory experience, said Kant, is not primary but itself relies upon something more fundamental: the structuring activity of the human mind. Because this structuring lies behind experience, its nature can only be inferred from experience rather than being directly observed itself.

With Hume and Kant, then, we have two opposing sides on a fundamental question that was to be a major theme in the work of early psychologists: is experience, at bottom, inherently structured or simply a jumble of discrete sensational elements? The opposing answers to this question given by different pioneering psychologists meant that, from the outset, they worked on the basis of different philosophical presuppositions. As we shall see, some psychologists, such as Wundt (see Chapter 11), took their cue from Kant and tried to investigate how the mind structured experience. The approach of his student, Titchener (see Chapter 12), however, was Humean: for Titchener, the goal of psychology was to identify the basic sensations of which our experience consists. Later psychologists, such as the behaviourists (see Chapter 16), were also strongly empiricist in orientation. In the next chapter, however, we examine a philosopher, Schopenhauer, who explicitly took the philosophy of Kant as his starting point. For Schopenhauer, one of the essential consequences of the Kantian philosophy is that we do not experience all that is going on in our own minds. The outward show of our conscious experience is, for Schopenhauer, merely the relatively slight product of a vast amount of activity that is going on behind the scenes. In arguing such a point Schopenhauer was, as we shall see, anticipating many ideas later put forward by Freud (see Chapter 10).

Revision questions

1. What, according to Hume, is the difference between impressions and ideas?
2. Why was Hume sceptical about the reality of causality?
3. Why was Hume sceptical about the reality of the self?
4. How did Hume waken Kant from his 'dogmatic slumber'?
5. What is a transcendental argument?
6. What is the difference between *a priori* truth and *a posteriori* truth? Give examples.
7. What is the difference between phenomenon and noumenon?
8. For Kant, what is the source of our ideas of space, time, and causality? What role do these ideas play?
9. What implication does Kant's distinction between phenomena and noumena have for self-knowledge?

References

Hume, D. ([1739–40]/1978). *A Treatise of Human Nature*, 2nd edn (L. A. Selby-Bigge, ed., revised by P. H. Nidditch). Oxford: Oxford University Press.

Hume, D. ([1748]/1975). *An Enquiry concerning Human Understanding*. In *Enquiries concerning Human Understanding and concerning the Principles of Morals*, 3rd edn (L. A. Selby-Bigge, ed., revised by P. H. Nidditch). Oxford: Oxford University Press.

Kant, I. ([1781]/1989). *Critique of Pure Reason*, trans. N. Kemp Smith. Basingstoke, UK: Macmillan.

Kant, I. ([1783]/1949). *Prolegomena to any Future Metaphysics*, trans. P. Carus. Chicago, IL: Open Court.

Kant, I. ([1788]/1997). *Critique of Practical Reason*, trans. M. Gregor. Cambridge University Press.

7 Schopenhauer and Nietzsche

Timeline

1813	Birth of Richard Wagner
1815	Defeat of Napoleon at the Battle of Waterloo
1848	Revolution throughout Europe. Marx and Engels publish *The Communist Manifesto*
1854–6	Crimean War
1859	Darwin publishes *On the Origin of Species*
1870–1	Franco-Prussian War
1874	Wundt publishes *Principles of Physiological Psychology*
1896	First modern Olympic Games are held in Athens

Arthur Schopenhauer

1788	Born in Danzig (now Gdańsk)
1819	Publishes the first volume of *The World as Will and Representation*
1820	Briefly becomes a lecturer at the University of Berlin, but fails to attract students
1833	Settles in Frankfurt
1844	Publishes the second volume of *The World as Will and Representation*
1860	Dies in Frankfurt

Friedrich Nietzsche

1844	Born in Röken, Saxony
1868	Befriends Richard Wagner
1872	Publishes his first book, *The Birth of Tragedy*
1883–5	Publishes *Thus Spake Zarathustra*
1889	Collapses in Turin
1900	Dies in Weimar

Introduction

In the previous chapter we examined the work of Hume and Kant. We saw how Kant's 'Copernican revolution' constituted a major shift in the understanding of the place of human beings in the universe. No longer was the mind thought of as a passive recipient of experience that impinged upon it from outside. Kant had shown that experience was *made* by the mind rather than just received by it. Such a view, we saw, has major consequences for the extent to which we can have knowledge of the world. If we can only experience reality through the organising filters of our own minds, this means that we can never experience reality as it is in itself. Or, to put it in Kantian terms, we can only experience the world of phenomena, not that of noumena.

This restriction on knowledge applies also to our own minds. Because the mind is active in constructing experience, we do not have direct knowledge of the mind as it is itself. Any perception that we have of the mind is mediated by the same organising framework as perception of the external world. The mind as it is in itself is therefore something that lies behind experience. This conclusion marks a fundamental shift from the Cartesian position according to which the mind is the thing that we know most directly and securely. Descartes, as we saw in Chapter 4, argued that it was contents of the mind that we could be most certain about. It was knowledge of the outer world that was problematic. A similar view obtained with Locke – the only things that we perceive directly are ideas in the mind. And, though Locke believed that these ideas were caused by external substances, we could never know these substances directly in the way that we knew our own ideas.

With Kant a new view emerges. The mind, for him, is not just a receptacle or a blank slate: it is an active force. And because this active force structures experience, the fundamental nature of the mind is something that cannot be experienced. Just as we see *through* the eye, and hence do not see the eye itself, we experience *through* the mind, and hence do not experience the mind itself. It may be the case that we can infer what some characteristics of the mind may be – this, after all, is what Kant did in his transcendental arguments – but we can never experience it directly as it is itself. It is just as out of reach as anything else in the world.

The idea that the operations of the mind are hidden is one that has enormous significance in the development of psychology. The concept of unconscious processes that forever lie below our awareness is one that is found throughout psychology, from the forbidden desires of **psychoanalysis** to cognitive psychology's unconscious perceptual processes that construct a representation of the external world. In this chapter I will discuss two thinkers for whom this idea of the unconscious mind was of great importance. The first, Schopenhauer, considered himself to be a follower of Kant, but he also disagreed with important aspects of Kant's philosophy and sought to correct what he perceived as errors. He nevertheless accepted the Kantian idea that we can never experience the world-in-itself, but only the world of phenomena. He also accepted that the mind was also subject to this stricture on direct experience. But he differed from Kant in seeing the mind not as a rational agent, but as fundamentally composed of unconscious, irrational, **instinctual** desires. In this way he prefigured some of the ideas that were subsequently to feature strongly in the work of Freud.

The second thinker to be discussed in this chapter is Nietzsche. Nietzsche was, as a young man, profoundly influenced by Schopenhauer and, though he came to reject important aspects of Schopenhauer's (and Kant's) thought, Nietzsche, too, argued that our thought and action have an instinctual basis. In particular, he argued that even the most refined and civilised of our behaviours have their roots in a basic desire to exert and feel power.

Arthur Schopenhauer

Schopenhauer thought of himself as both a follower of Kant and a corrector of some of the errors in Kant's philosophy. He believed, along with Kant, that what we perceive depends not only upon what is there to be perceived, but also on the way in which we are constituted as perceivers. Our experience, even when we simply open our eyes and gaze at an object in front of us, is never direct: it is always mediated by our own conceptual and sensory apparatus, which structures and organises the incoming sensory data. Without this structuring there would be nothing recognisable as experience at all. There would not even be a chaos of sensations as even a chaos is situated in space and time, and for both Kant and Schopenhauer space and time are supplied by us. There would simply be nothing conceivable as experience at all.

Kant had, through his transcendental arguments, attempted to show that the categories of space, time, and causality were the inherent structuring principles that any mind capable of experience would have to apply to sensory data. For Schopenhauer, in the particular case of human beings, these structuring principles and the act of structuring itself were instantiated in the operations of the brain and the sensory organs. Schopenhauer remarked that while the nerves of the sense-organs invest the appearing objects with colour, sound, taste, smell, temperature, and so on, the brain imparts to them extension, form, impenetrability, mobility, and so on, in short, all that can be represented in perception only by means of time, space and causality. (*The World as Will and Representation,* vol. 2, p. 20)

In other words, the senses supply the qualitative sensory aspects of experience and these are organised within spatio-temporal and causal frameworks by the brain. This idea that, in the case of humans, the physiological constitution of the body was a particular manifestation of the Kantian structuring of experience was to be of great importance in the development of physiological psychology. It meant that what Kant had shown for all possible beings by metaphysical argument could, in the particular instance of human beings, be investigated empirically by researching how the brain and the sense organs structure experience. The translation of Kantian metaphysics into sensory physiology, exemplified in the above quotation, was a great motivation to the work of early physiologists, such as Helmholtz, as we shall see in the next chapter.

Box 7.1 Arthur Schopenhauer

Arthur Schopenhauer was born in Danzig (now Gdańsk in Poland) in 1788 into a wealthy trading family. His early education was patchy as he frequently was taken by his parents on their travels throughout Europe and he spent significant periods of time in France and England (where he learned to speak the respective languages) as well as in Germany. This early experience of foreign places and peoples was intended to prepare Schopenhauer for a future in the family business and was thought to be more important to that end than a formal academic education.

At the age of 17, Schopenhauer was employed in the offices of the family firm, but he had already developed an interest in philosophical questions and, following his father's death, his mother gave him permission to follow his inclinations and to study at university. Because of the large inheritance that he received from his father, Schopenhauer was able to support himself for the rest of his life and had no need to seek paid employment. He was, therefore, completely free to devote himself to philosophy.

Box 7.1 (cont.)

Fig. 7.1 Arthur Schopenhauer

In 1818 he published his magnum opus, *The World as Will and Representation*, but few people seemed to notice: sales were tiny and there were very few reviews. Thinking that he might be able to make his philosophy more widely known through teaching, Schopenhauer arranged to give a lecture course at the University of Berlin. The most famous philosopher in Germany at the time, Hegel, also taught at Berlin, but Schopenhauer regarded him as a charlatan and deliberately

Box 7.1 (cont.)

timetabled his own lectures at the same time as those of Hegel. As a result no one came to Schopenhauer's lectures and the course was cancelled.

Schopenhauer eventually settled in Frankfurt in 1833, and was to stay there for the rest of his life (Figure 7.1). Like his philosophical inspiration, Kant, Schopenhauer adopted an unchanging schedule that he followed every day. After rising between 7 and 8 o'clock, he wrote until noon, practised the flute, and went to lunch (always in the same restaurant). Following an afternoon walk, he would read *The Times* in the library before going to the theatre and, finally, finished up with a meal in the same restaurant that he went to for lunch.

In 1853, Schopenhauer finally received recognition for his work. *The World as Will and Representation*, a second edition of which (more than twice the length of the first) had been published in 1844, was reviewed in the *Westminster Gazette* and the review was soon translated into German. Reviews of his work shortly appeared in Denmark, Italy, and France and, before long, lecture courses in his work were a feature of several universities. After being ignored for most of his life, Schopenhauer, now in his late sixties, was famous. He died of a heart attack in 1860 knowing that his life's work had received the respect and acknowledgement that he always thought it deserved.

This structuring of experience according to the categories of space, time, and causality is, of course, completely outside of conscious awareness. The workings of our own minds are, therefore, largely hidden from us. With Kant and particularly with Schopenhauer we are moving decisively away from the Cartesian idea of a transparent self-knowing subject. Indeed, for Schopenhauer, as we shall see, there is little that we know *less* well than our own minds. This applies not only to the unconscious processes that lie behind our experience, but our motivations, drives, and inner nature as well. In this connection, Schopenhauer's ideas foreshadow those of Freud.

To understand the importance of unconscious forces and drives in Schopenhauer, one must first of all consider how he saw himself as differing from and improving upon the philosophical doctrines of Kant. We saw in the previous chapter that, for Kant, we are never in touch with things as they are in themselves (noumena) but only with things as they appear to us (phenomena). This is a consequence of the fact that our experience is not direct but is structured and organised by our minds.

Schopenhauer accepted this doctrine as far as it went but did not think that it went far enough. Kant, in Schopenhauer's eyes, had still not fully broken away from the empiricist idea that our representations of reality, how things appear to us, must resemble reality in some way. We saw in the work of Locke, for example, the notion that our ideas are, in some sense, copies, albeit imperfect ones, of the substances that cause them. But such a view is inconsistent with Kantianism. If we follow through the implications of Kantianism, we have to recognise that our representations, including our perceptual representations, can be nothing like the noumenal world. The noumenon would lack features of experience such as space, time, and causality because those are ingredients that *we* supply and which cannot be said to apply to that which lies outside our experience. This is what Schopenhauer thought that Kant had missed. Kant had, in a way, not been Kantian enough and Schopenhauer felt that it was down to him to spell out the implications of the Kantian philosophy in their fullest form.

One consequence of this Schopenhaurian completion of Kant was the realisation on Schopenhauer's part that Kant was wrong to talk about *things* in themselves in the plural. Things can only be differentiated from one another in terms of space and time and, because these are categories of the *phenomenal* world rather than the noumenon, that noumenon cannot be differentiated in this way. Speaking correctly, then, there is only *one* thing-in-itself. Kant sometimes talked as if there was a thing-in-itself corresponding to each phenomenal thing; as if, for example, there is the table in front of me as it appears in my experience and there is the table as it really is in itself. But this is what Schopenhauer thought was inconsistent with Kant's own principles. For Schopenhauer, then, the true upshot of Kantianism was that reality was a single, undifferentiated thing that manifested itself in the multiplicity of our experience. This single, undifferentiated reality lay behind *everything* in our experience: people, objects, everything. Schopenhauer called it **Will**:

> only the *will* is *thing in itself* ... It is that of which all representation, all object, is the phenomenon ... It appears in every blindly acting force of nature, and also in the deliberate conduct of man, and the great difference between the two concerns only the degree of the manifestation, not the inner nature of what is manifested. (*The World as Will and Representation*, vol. 1, p. 110)

We must, however, be careful not to think of this metaphysical Will in human terms. When we speak of a person's act as wilful, we mean that the act was deliberate, intended, and perhaps preceded by a conscious resolution to carry through the act. Schopenhauer's noumenal Will has none of these characteristics: it is best thought of as an unconscious, blind, impersonal force. Everything, including ourselves, is a manifestation and vehicle of this force. It may seem strange, even outrageous, to believe that what we experience as the world of differentiated objects is actually fundamentally one thing that shows itself in an infinite variety of ways, but some (e.g. Magee 1997) have suggested that Schopenhauer's philosophy is in accord with much of modern physics, for which all of the physical world is the manifestation of the one basic entity, which is energy.

Even though it appears to us that we are in rational, conscious control of our lives, this is a false impression. Behind this facade lies the reality that we too are simply the vehicles and manifestations of Will. It is the metaphysical Will, in its senseless striving to realise itself, that lies behind all our actions and our very existence. Conscious rationality is just the surface appearance of what is, in truth, an unconscious force struggling for expression. We are, here, moving away from the clear self-understanding rationality of Descartes to something closer to the Freudian **id**, the unconscious driving force behind the **libido**.

That we are driven by a senseless impersonal force is the reason for Schopenhauer's deep pessimism. Schopenhauer is probably the most famous exponent of philosophical **pessimism**. For him, life is bound to be tragically unfulfilled and it would be better not to be born at all. But it is important to realise that this pessimism is not just a quirk of Schopenhauer's personality, but is logically entailed by his philosophy. There is no God who created an ordered, meaningful universe. The world and everything in it is nothing more than the manifestation of the same irrational metaphysical Will. And we ourselves are nothing more than the insignificant expressions of this, at bottom, meaningless force. All that we are and do is driven not by reasons or meanings but Will. Our lives are, then, ultimately futile and pointless. They are also ultimately frustrated and unfulfilled. The Will that drives us seeks blindly to fulfil itself. But, because it is not rational, it can never be satisfied; no matter how much it has realised itself, it always requires more fulfilment, more expression. And because we are the vehicles of this insatiable Will, we too are doomed never to be satisfied. For Schopenhauer it is not merely a matter of sad fact, but a matter of metaphysical necessity, that all life is, ultimately, unfulfilled and unfulfilling.

Here too Schopenhauer's thinking prefigures that of Freud: the id, like the Will, cannot be reasoned with. It operates, says Freud, according to the **pleasure principle** – it demands immediate, constant, and complete satisfaction regardless of whether this satisfaction is reasonable or even possible. It is only with the development of the conscious **ego**, which operates according to the reality principle, that the unconscious, irrational demands of the id can be held in check and adapted to reality. Satisfaction of desires can be delayed or repressed by the ego if they conflict with what is physically possible or socially desirable.

And, just as the Freudian ego is in a sense the servant of the id in that it tailors the id's demands to reality, so for Schopenhauer the conscious intellect is the tool of the unconscious Will. Whereas for many of the thinkers that we have considered so far – Descartes, Locke, Kant – the intellect or reason is the primary characteristic of human beings, that which underlies our thought and action, for Schopenhauer the intellect is secondary – it is merely there to serve the irrational instincts that are the real root of all our being and all our activity.

Of course, we may not want to acknowledge that we are driven by irrational instincts and desires. Indeed, we may be completely unaware of the fact. But this does not alter the reality of the situation. And it is here that Schopenhauer again foreshadows developments later to be seen in the work of Freud. For Schopenhauer, we may refuse to acknowledge our true nature as driven by the Will because it does not agree with the exalted picture that we have of ourselves as rational and reasonable beings:

> The will . . . makes its supremacy felt in the last resort. This it does by prohibiting the intellect from having certain representations . . . We often do not know what we desire or fear. For years we can have a desire without admitting it to ourselves or even letting it come to clear consciousness, because the intellect is not to know anything about it, since the good opinion we have of ourselves would inevitably suffer thereby. (*The World as Will and Representation*, vol. 2, p. 208)

This idea that we can have desires that we deliberately refuse to admit consciously to ourselves is later echoed in the Freudian theory of **repression**, in which our conscious self is protected from unconscious desires that are too powerful or too disturbing to acknowledge by defence mechanisms, such as denial, which prevent awareness of these desires. And for Schopenhauer, as for Freud, these desires are, in the case of human beings, ultimately sexual. Sex, says Schopenhauer, "is the ultimate goal of almost all human effort" (*The World as Will and Representation*, vol. 2, p. 533) and he claims that "The genitals are the focus of the will" (*The World as Will and Representation*, vol. 2, p. 514). This is because the Will, of which we are the vehicles and manifestation, is always seeking to maximise its realisation. Given that one of the ways in which it realises itself is in people, we are driven by the Will to reproduce and thus multiply its manifestations.

Schopenhauer, then, is important in the history of psychology for his doctrine of the Will, in which he drew out some of the consequences of the Kantian philosophy. In particular, in emphasising the point that we are not conscious

Box 7.2 Schopenhauer's influence on the arts

Schopenhauer's philosophy had as great an influence on artists and writers as it did on philosophers. In no one is this influence more prominent than the composer Richard Wagner (1813–83). Wagner became acquainted with Schopenhauer's philosophy in 1854, just as the philosopher was becoming famous throughout Europe, and it was to be, according to Wagner himself, the most important intellectual discovery of his life. Schopenhauer had argued that the arts, and music in particular, were expressions of the metaphysical, noumenal Will. It is likely that Wagner had somehow felt that he wanted to write music that was timeless and that expressed the underlying universal truths about reality, but he found this difficult to harmonise with his professed beliefs that art should be engaged with current (and, therefore, transient) social questions. By providing Wagner with a philosophical justification for the type of music that he really wanted to produce, Schopenhauer liberated Wagner from his concerns with the ephemerality of politics and allowed him to conceive his work in terms of enduring metaphysical questions. In addition to Wagner, Schopenhauer was a vital influence on many major writers, including Thomas Hardy, Joseph Conrad, Leo Tolstoy, and Thomas Mann.

of much of what goes on in the mind, he expounded important ideas about the irrational, unconscious motivations of our behaviour and prefigured important ideas concerning sex and repression that were to be developed in psychoanalysis.

Friedrich Nietzsche

Nietzsche was, as a young man, profoundly influenced by Schopenhauer. He was, nevertheless, later to reject major aspects of Schopenhauer's philosophy, as we shall see later. For the moment, though, let us concentrate on some of the similarities that his philosophy bears with that of Schopenhauer, particularly the idea that human conduct, far from being the outcome of pure, rational thought, has its roots in basic, instinctual drives. Nietzsche proposes that all our drives and motivations can be seen ultimately as manifestations of the one fundamental drive, which he called the **will to power**:

Suppose, finally, we succeeded in explaining our entire instinctive life as the development and ramification of *one* basic form of the will – namely the will to power ... suppose all organic functions could be traced back to this will to power and one could also find in it the solution of the problem of procreation and nourishment – it is *one* problem – then one would have gained the right to determine *all* efficient force univocally as – *will to power*. (*Beyond Good and Evil*, p. 36)

It is the desire to increase our feeling of power that lies behind all that we do. It is common nowadays to assume that human beings are driven to increase their happiness and pleasure, but Nietzsche would disagree. He would also disagree with the proposal that we are ultimately driven by the desire to preserve our own lives. On the contrary, Nietzsche pointed out that people frequently expose themselves to danger and discomfort in pursuit of some other goal, a goal that would serve to increase their feelings of power. One of the most eminent writers on Nietzsche, Walter Kaufmann (1974), gives the example of mountain climbing. If a life of placid contentment was really the supreme goal of human existence, then no one would risk their lives and voluntarily subject themselves to the extreme hardships that come with a climbing expedition. For the mountaineer, the feeling of power and mastery that comes with the conquering of a mountain far outweighs any desire for pleasure and comfort.

Box 7.3 Friedrich Nietzsche

Friedrich Nietzsche was born in the small town of Röken in Germany in 1844. His father was a Lutheran minister, who died when Nietzsche was only 4 years old. Nietzsche studied literature and classics in Bonn and Leipzig and, aged only 24, was appointed professor of philology at the University of Basel in Switzerland in 1869 (Figure 7.2). He worked at Basel for 10 years, although this was interrupted by a period of military service as a medical orderly during the Franco-Prussian war of 1870–1. During his military service, Nietzsche contracted dysentery and diphtheria and returned to his post at Basel. Nietzsche's health was poor, and he was to suffer throughout his life from severe migraines, vomiting, and eye problems which, at times, rendered him virtually blind. Indeed, so severe were his health problems, and so frequent and prolonged the absences from work that they entailed, that Nietzsche was given early retirement on the grounds of ill health from his university post in 1879. He was awarded a small pension from the university and he lived frugally on this meagre income for the rest of his life.

Box 7.3 **(cont.)**

Fig. 7.2 Friedrich Nietzsche

Box 7.3 (cont.)

It was while he was a young professor that Nietzsche became a close friend of Richard Wagner and was a frequent visitor to his house. The two men were united in their interest not only in music and Greek tragedy but, more particularly, in the philosophy of Schopenhauer. Nietzsche had picked up a copy of Schopenhauer's *The World as Will and Representation* in a secondhand bookshop, and it had the same sort of stimulating effect on him as it had on Wagner. Nietzsche, although he later repudiated much of Schopenhauer's thinking, always acknowledged the formative influence that the latter had had on him, and titled one of his works *Schopenhauer as Educator.*

Nietzsche was also to repudiate and to break with Wagner. Nietzsche came to feel that his friendship with Wagner was preventing him from developing his own individual ideas. Moreover, he came to see Wagner as having betrayed his own principles and increasingly as the proponent and embodiment of a rising tide of German nationalism, militarism, and anti-Semitism that followed the German victory in the Franco-Prussian war.

Nietzsche lived a peripatetic existence, living in boarding houses in various locations in France, Switzerland, and Italy. The locations were often chosen because their climate, Nietzsche thought, would be beneficial to his fragile health. During this time he wrote and published numerous works, but they failed to attract much notice and sold poorly.

In 1889, Nietzsche collapsed, insane, in the street in Turin. He never recovered his sanity and was taken back to Germany where he was cared for by his mother and sister. He died in 1900. The cause of Nietzsche's mental collapse is not known for certain, but many scholars believe that a likely cause was syphilis (possibly contracted when Nietzsche was a student), which, in its tertiary stages, attacks the nervous system.

Most people would not, of course, put themselves through the hardships faced by a mountaineer, but, for Nietzsche, the will to power can manifest itself in a myriad of more subtle and less obvious ways than in the exercise of purely physical strength. Indeed, it is a failure to understand this point and, consequently, to interpret power in purely physical, political or military terms that has led to Nietzsche being associated, erroneously, with Nazism. For Nietzsche (and later for Freud) it is crucial that we realise that, rather than being expressed directly, unconscious desires and drives can be expressed in a higher form through their **sublimation**. What this means is that the energy and force associated with an instinct can be channelled into other outlets. According to Nietzsche, even our most artistic and intellectual desires and motivations find their roots in the will to dominate. Think, for example, of a novel, or a painting, or a scientific theory. What do these things do? The novel may highlight certain features of the social attitudes and mores of a certain society; the painting may attempt to capture a particular characteristic mood of a person or a landscape; the scientific theory may attempt to describe and explain a particular set of natural phenomena. What they all have in common is that they attempt to capture, to get a hold on, to fix some features of the ever-changing flux of experience. In their attempts to restrain or control certain aspects of experience, even momentarily and even in verbal or symbolic terms, they are exercises in power and dominance over

Box 7.4 Nietzsche and the Nazis

Nietzsche is sometimes portrayed as a philosophical precursor of Nazism. Part of the reason for this is the role played by Nietzsche's sister, Elizabeth. Elizabeth was an ardent German nationalist and she married Bernhard Förster, a prominent anti-Semitic agitator. Together the couple went to Paraguay to found a pure, Aryan colony to be called Nueva Germania, but the project collapsed and they had to return to Germany. There is no doubt that Nietzsche was appalled by his sister's marriage to Förster in particular and by anti-Semitism in general. In one letter to Elizabeth, Nietzsche states: "It is a matter of honour to me to be absolutely clean and unequivocal regarding anti-Semitism, namely *opposed*, as I am in all my writings" (cited in Kaufmann 1974, p. 45).

Elsewhere Nietzsche was to describe himself as an anti-anti-Semite, but none of this stopped Elizabeth from trying to co-opt her brother's work to the cause of racist nationalism. Following Nietzsche's death, Elizabeth established a Nietzsche archive, to which she invited Hitler and which, on a trip to the Wagner festival in Bayreuth, Hitler did indeed visit. It was Elizabeth who tried, and to some extent succeeded, in persuading the Nazis that her brother was *their* philosopher. The Nazis did indeed try to twist Nietzsche's thought to their own ends in order to give their movement some sort of intellectual credibility, but, as is evidenced by Nietzsche's own writings and letters, this is something that he would have abhorred.

the empirical world. They are, of course, far more subtle exercises of power than brute physical force, but they are exercises of power nonetheless. Thus, even our most sophisticated cultural products, says Nietzsche, are sublimations – transformations and channelings – of the basic will to power: all "our drives are reducible to the will to power" (unpublished notes, cited by Kaufmann 1974, p. 216). We might think that the desire to feel and to exercise power is something cruel, but Nietzsche's point is that all that we consider most refined and civilised has its roots in this basic desire for dominance: "Those of his abilities which are awesome and considered inhuman are perhaps the fertile soil out of which alone all humanity . . . can grow" (unpublished notes, cited by Kaufmann 1974, p. 193). For Nietzsche, then, the will to power is not about giving free rein to our most cruel and aggressive impulses, but about controlling and making use of these forces in a creative way.

The idea of controlling and directing basic impulses can be further illustrated by what Nietzsche says about sex. For Nietzsche, the sexual instinct is one way in which the will to power can be manifested: "The will to rule," he says, is "a mark of the most sensual men; the waning propensity of the sex impulse shows itself in the relenting of the thirst for power." But he then goes on to say that "[t]he feeling of power has so far amounted highest in abstinent priests and hermits" (unpublished notes, cited by Kaufmann 1974, p. 222). The will to power is manifested to a higher degree in the **ascetic** than in the **hedonist** because the former have been able to exert control over their impulses rather than simply giving in to them. The abstinent saints have been able to exert their own will to power *over themselves*. They have thus succeeded in overcoming their own instinctual selves and effected a self-transformation from a creature completely at the mercy of its instincts to one that is in full control of all its energies.

It was because even the most spiritual and civilised values had their roots in basic instinctual desires for dominance that Nietzsche was critical of traditional Christian morality. Nietzsche was the son of a Protestant pastor and had been devoutly religious as a youth, but he came to question and then to criticise vehemently what he saw as the Christian repudiation of the striving for dominance and power. Christianity, with its glorification of the weak and the poor and its elevation of pity, seemed to Nietzsche to specifically set itself against the values of power and strength that he championed. But it was more than a simple conflict of values. According to Nietzsche, as we have seen, all the good things in life have their roots in the will to power. Christianity, in denying this will, undermined all that was good and beautiful. In trying to *eliminate*, rather than to *sublimate*, what it deemed to be sinful desires, Christianity was, for Nietzsche, inimical to civilisation and culture. In the gospel of Mark, for instance, Christ says: "If thine eye offend thee, pluck it out." The Christian doctrine is to renounce and to remove characteristics that are sinful. But such a doctrine therefore also renounces the drives and impulses that are behind all that is most admirable in human life: "Instead of employing the great sources of strength ... this most shortsighted and pernicious mode of thought [i.e. Christianity] ... wants to make them dry up" (Nietzsche, *Will to Power*, cited by Kaufmann 1974, p. 225).

But it is not only the case that Christian morality teaches us to renounce our basic impulses, it teaches us that these impulses are, in themselves, evil. We therefore develop feelings of guilt and what Nietzsche calls '**bad conscience**' because we have such impulses:

> Hostility, cruelty, joy in persecuting, in attacking, in change, in destruction – all this turned against the possessors of such instincts: *that* is the origin of 'bad conscience'.

Here again Nietzsche's thought prefigures themes later to appear in the work of Freud. As well as the unconscious, instinctual id and the rational, conscious ego, Freud conceived of a third component of the human mind, which he called the **superego**. The superego internalises the moral demands of our family and society and, like the id, it demands complete satisfaction. It makes no allowance for our natural desires and inclinations, but demands total adherence to the most strict and unrealistic moral standards. We cannot but fail to live up to the demands of the superego and we are thus punished by feelings of guilt and shame.

The demands of Christian (and Christian-derived) morality, too, cannot be satisfied, as they force us to deny certain fundamental aspects of our own selves. Bad conscience is the result. Nietzsche, of course, does not see the solution of this problem in indulging our every desire and inclination in a guilt-free, hedonistic way. Christian morality is right that we should be hard on ourselves, but it is wrong in thinking that this hardness towards oneself should be expressed through extinguishing rather than controlling our basic impulses.

Pleasure and power

Although Schopenhauer and Nietzsche, in their own ways, emphasise the importance of unconscious drives as the engines of human behaviour, there are, nevertheless, important differences between them. One way in which they differ is in their understanding of what constitutes a psychologically healthy way of life. For Schopenhauer, as we have seen, everything we are and do is a manifestation of the unconscious and irrational Will. And, because this Will is insatiable, our lives are bound to be unsatisfying and unfulfilled. The Will, in the phenomenal world of our experience, manifests itself in an infinity of competing desires and forces: aggression and competition between people, the endless striving for money, fame, sex, power, the perpetual struggle of animals to survive. All of these are manifestations of the Will in the phenomenal world. The only way in which we might give some meaning to our lives is to turn our backs on these phenomenal aspects of the Will, and instead of ceaselessly struggling, to try, as far as we can, to understand the noumenal world – the real world of the Will in itself – which lies behind all of these phenomenal manifestations. For Schopenhauer, this is best done through the appreciation of art, particularly music. It is art that, of all human endeavours, gets us closest to the hidden reality that underlies everything. Schopenhauer, therefore, advocated an attitude of renunciation in which, instead of being driven by the insatiable desires of the phenomenal Will, we try to concentrate on what is really worthwhile and eternal.

In his insistence that an attempt to free oneself from the endless striving of the Will is the best way to achieve something like health and happiness (even though we can never achieve these completely), Schopenhauer's thought has a great deal in common with some of the foundational ideas of Buddhism, which also counsels us to free ourselves from our desires and from the futile striving that accompanies them. Schopenhauer discovered these ideas independently of Buddhism but, when translations of Buddhist scriptures became available in German, he was fulsome in his praise of Buddhism, thinking it a far superior religion to Western Christianity.

The idea of being freed from our desires and drives is one that is also apparent in the work of Freud. For Freud, the tension that arises as a result of an unfulfilled drive is painful to the organism in question, and the goal of all behaviour is the reduction of this tension and the achievement of a state of equilibrium in which the organism is not disturbed by its instinctual drives. This removal of tension, and the arrival at a more stable state of equilibrium, is pleasure. The final state of equilibrium is, of course, death, in which all striving and struggle ceases. It is for this reason that Freud, later in the development of psychoanalysis, postulated the existence of a **death instinct** to supplement the sexual instinct. "The aim of all life," said Freud, "is death" (*Beyond the Pleasure Principle*, p. 70).

In this sense, Nietzsche differs markedly from both Freud and Schopenhauer. For him, pleasure is not the goal of life, but, as we have seen, it is the exercise of the will to power. Rather than seeking a state of passive equilibrium, we seek to exercise our power, and, though pleasure and happiness may be the by-products of this exercise of power, they are not the desired ends of our activities. Indeed, it is precisely in the perpetual striving to overcome obstacles, to master oneself, to deploy one's energies, that happiness lies. "What is happiness?" asks Nietzsche, and answers: "The feeling that power is *growing*, that resistance is overcome" (*The Anti-Christ*, p. 2). To withdraw from the struggles of life, as Schopenhauer advises, would, for Nietzsche, be to withdraw from that which is most valuable in life. It is *in* the struggle, not outside it, that life at its richest is to be found.

Self-overcoming and the *Übermensch*

Nietzsche, as has already been said, was, in his youth, an ardent admirer of Schopenhauer. He became, however, adamantly opposed to Schopenhauer's view. It was, for Nietzsche, a sign of weakness to withdraw from life, to try to free oneself from one's drives. It was the mark of people who could not control and master their own impulses and desires that they seek to deny and escape from them. Nietzsche had a different attitude to what would be the most fulfilling, valuable, and psychologically healthy kind of life.

He believed, along with Schopenhauer, that our lives were driven by unconscious desires and urges, but, as we have seen, these, for Nietzsche, were not to be denied, but were to be channelled into creative activities. This is the process of sublimation, which has been referred to earlier. One has not to suppress or deny or try to separate oneself from these drives. Neither has one to simply give them free rein. One has to master them, and make them harmonise with one another in the service of a greater, creative goal.

We are all, for Nietzsche, a mass of competing drives and desires:

> In the present age human beings have in their bodies the heritage of multiple origins, that is opposite and not merely opposite drives and value standards that fight each other and rarely permit each other any rest. (*Beyond Good and Evil*, p. 200)

Psychological health and strength consists, not in suppressing or denying these drives, but in controlling them. The healthiest person is the one who can channel these drives into a single goal, who can harmonise all his or her chaotic energies under an overarching purpose. For Nietzsche, therefore, the healthy person is the one in whom these drives are the most *integrated* with one another. Of course, this exercise of control and integration over one's own conflicting inner drives is another manifestation of the will to power. Indeed, this is one of the highest manifestations of the will to power – mastery of oneself – whereas the attempt to dominate others is a lesser manifestation of the will to power among those who are not strong enough to dominate themselves. The person who can dominate him- or herself, the highest form of human being, Nietzsche called the **Übermensch**. This term is, unfortunately, often translated into English as *superman*, but a more correct translation is *overman*. This captures Nietzsche's sense of individuals who have succeeded (and continue to succeed) in *overcoming* their own natures and bending their own energies to their wills in a continuous effort at self-mastery.

The failure to integrate all one's energies with one another has two possible consequences. One is that one is simply the slave of one's passions: one is driven this way and that by one's desires which, because they are conflicting, cannot ever be fully satisfied. This is the way of the hedonist, who thinks that psychological health lies simply in allowing free expression to all one's desires and inclinations. For Nietzsche, however, this is not a recipe for happiness or fulfilment, but chaos. It is a manifestation of a weak and sick personality.

The other possibility of the failure to integrate one's drives is the splitting off, the separation, of some drives from others. Those drives that we acknowledge or that we deem valuable, are our conscious motivations in what we do. But the other drives, because they cannot be mastered, are simply suppressed. Separated from our other drives, they can find no fulfilment in our activities. This failure to integrate one's drives and the concomitant suppression of some of them is, for Nietzsche, another type of psychological unhealthiness.

Conclusion

We have seen how both Schopenhauer and Nietzsche emphasise the unconscious nature of the drives that lie behind our actions. For Schopenhauer these drives stem, ultimately, from the metaphysical Will that lies behind all phenomena; for Nietzsche, our thoughts and actions are manifestations of the will to power. Both thinkers recognise that we may be blind to the real nature of the forces that propel us, and that we may suppress or refuse to recognise these forces. In so doing, they both prefigure ideas that were to be fundamental to the development of depth psychology, particularly in the work of Freud. Nevertheless, despite these commonalities, Schopenhauer and Nietzsche differed markedly in their view of how we should deal with our instinctual drives in order to live a psychologically healthy and fulfilling life. For Schopenhauer, we should seek to release ourselves from the incessant striving of the Will in a life of renunciation; for Nietzsche, we should try to master and integrate our drives towards a higher goal.

Revision questions

1. In what way did Schopenhauer modify the ideas of Kant?
2. Outline Schopenhauer's concept of the Will.
3. Why was Schopenhauer a pessimist?
4. Why did Schopenhauer think sex was important?
5. Outline Nietzsche's concept of the will to power.
6. What is sublimation?
7. Why did Nietzsche criticise Christianity?
8. How do Schopenhauer and Nietzsche differ from one another in their attitude to life?
9. What did Nietzsche mean by *Übermensch*?

References

Freud, S. (1920). *Beyond the Pleasure Principle*. Standard Edition, vol. 18.

Kaufmann, W. (1974). *Nietzsche: Philosopher, Psychologist, Antichrist*, 4th edn. Princeton, NJ: Princeton University Press.

Magee, B (1997). *The Philosophy of Schopenhauer*, revised edn. Oxford: Oxford University Press.

Nietzsche, F. ([1886]/1973). *Beyond Good and Evil*. London: Penguin.

Nietzsche, F. ([1887]/1989). *On the Genealogy of Morals*, trans. W. Kauffmann and R. J. Hollingdale. New York: Vintage Books.

Nietzsche, F. ([1888]/1968). *The Anti-Christ*. London: Penguin.

Schopenhauer, A. ([1819]/1969). *The World as Will and Representation*, vol. 1, trans. E. F. J. Payne. New York: Dover.

Schopenhauer, A. ([1844]/1966). *The World as Will and Representation*, vol. 2, trans. E. F. J. Payne. New York: Dover.

Part III
Psychology

8 Psychophysics and physiological psychology

Timeline

1805	Battle of Trafalgar
1813	Jane Austen publishes *Pride and Prejudice*
1833	Abolition of slavery in the British Empire
1838	Coronation of Queen Victoria
1845–52	Irish Famine
1860	Charles Dickens publishes *Great Expectations*
1861–5	American Civil War
1865	Assassination of Abraham Lincoln
1871	Bismark becomes Chancellor of Germany
1876	Alexander Graham Bell makes first telephone call
1888	Sir Arthur Conan Doyle publishes the first Sherlock Holmes story

Gustav Fechner

1801	Born in Gross Särchen, Saxony
1818	Goes to study medicine in Leipzig
1839	Begins experimentation on colour vision
1840	Suffers breakdown
1849	Publishes *Nanna, or On the Soul Life of Plants*
1860	Publishes *Elements of Psychophysics*
1887	Dies in Leipzig

Johannes Müller

1801	Born in Koblenz, Germany
1834	Appointed lecturer in physiology at Berlin
1834–7	Publishes *Elements of Physiology*
1858	Dies in Berlin

Hermann Helmholtz

1821	Born in Potsdam, Prussia
1839	Studies medicine in Berlin
1850	Invents ophthalmoscope
1858–67	Publishes *Handbook of Physiological Optics*
1870	Appointed professor of physiology at Berlin
1894	Dies in Berlin

Introduction

In the mid nineteenth century, scientists started to investigate human mental life experimentally. The mind had, up until this point, mainly been the topic of theoretical or logical discussion or, when empirical, based on the everyday observations of thinking and feeling. Now, however, the new methods and equipment of laboratory science were turned towards the investigation of the mind. But though the methods of science were mobilised in this direction, this did not mean that the investigators in this new field had completely jettisoned philosophical ideas about the mind as put forward by some of their predecessors. Indeed, as we shall see in this chapter, developments in the scientific approach to mind were explicitly informed by philosophical theories and the resulting empirical work was an attempt to make concrete the theoretical ideas of certain philosophers. Two philosophers in particular had an important influence on the development of physiological psychology. One of them was Kant, who has already been discussed in Chapter 6; the other is Spinoza.

Spinoza, as we shall see, believed that the mental and the physical were not metaphysically separate realms but two aspects of one and the same reality. It follows from this that every event that occurs in the physical body can also be seen as a mental event, and vice versa. It was this conceptualisation of the mental and physical that lay behind the work of psychophysicists, such as Gustav Fechner, who tried to find out the relationship between these two aspects of reality. Inspired by Spinoza, Fechner sought not to *explain* the mental in terms of the physical (or the physical in terms of the mental) because neither the mental nor the physical was more important or fundamental than the other. Instead he sought to provide a mathematically precise characterisation of the way in which the mental and the physical were correlated with one another.

The influence of Spinoza is also seen in the work of another physiologist, Johannes Müller. Müller argued that, if the mental and physical are indeed two aspects of one and the same thing, then our psychological experiences can be thought of as the mental aspect of physical events in the nervous system. What we really experience are not things in the external world but states of ourselves. Different stimuli, then, if they stimulate the same nerves, will give rise to the same mental experience.

This idea, deriving from Spinoza, that we essentially experience changes in our own bodies, was also taken up by Müller's student, Hermann von Helmholtz, who was to be one of the most important scientists of the nineteenth century. But Helmholtz's thought also showed the unmistakeable stamp of Kantian philosophy. Helmholtz believed that in studying how the nervous system organises perceptual experience he was investigating, in concrete terms, an example of the structuring principles that Kant had argued lay behind experience.

Given, then, the importance of Spinoza for Fechner, Müller, and Helmholtz, I will now describe his ideas in a little more detail.

Spinoza

The ideas of Spinoza (see Box 8.1) on the relationship between mind and body were of great importance in the development of physiological approaches to psychology. We have already seen that Descartes defined the mind and the body as mutually exclusive substances: things either had the property of being extended in space (physical things, such as the body) or the property of thought (non-physical things, such as minds). The mind–body problem concerned how these two different substances could possibly interact with one another. Spinoza, however, rather than trying to find a way in which the physical body and the immaterial mind might affect one another, completely rejected Cartesian substance dualism from the outset. For Spinoza there was only one substance, and that comprised the whole of reality. This substance (which Spinoza identified with God and Nature) did, however, have different attributes or features; one of these attributes was that of physicality or extension in space and time, the other attribute was that of mentality. Spinoza, then, conceived the mental and the physical as different attributes of one and the same thing rather than the defining characteristics of two distinct things. He states that "the mind and the body, are one and the same individual which at one time is considered under the attribute of thought, and at another under that of extension" (*Ethics*, Ch. 2, Prop. 21). It is because the mental and the physical are two aspects of the same thing that Spinoza's approach is sometimes referred to as the **double-aspect theory** of the mind–body relation.

The idea that the whole of reality has both the attributes of thought and the attributes of physicality means that thought or mentality is found throughout nature. This is a view called **panpsychism**. Again, this is very different from the Cartesian view that we have discussed previously. For Descartes, as we have seen, most of what exists does not have thought or mentality. The natural world, the world of physics, is, for Descartes, defined precisely by the absence of thought: it is

Box 8.1 **Baruch Spinoza**

Baruch (later Benedict) Spinoza (1632–77) was born in Amsterdam to a Jewish family of Spanish and Portuguese origin. The family had moved to the relatively tolerant atmosphere of The Netherlands in order to escape the Spanish Inquisition, which was forcing Jews to convert to Christianity or to emigrate. At this time, The Netherlands was a centre of scientific innovation, and Spinoza, in addition to his traditional education in the Jewish religious school, became interested in the new ideas that were being discussed by Dutch scholars. Exposure to these views, including the philosophy of Descartes (himself a long-time resident in The Netherlands), led to Spinoza's dissatisfaction with the established rabbinical teaching. The rabbis, aware of what they thought of as the increasingly unorthodox nature of Spinoza's thought (it was said that he believed that God had a body), charged him with heresy. He was found guilty and excommunicated from the synagogue and expelled from the Jewish community. Spinoza changed his name from the Hebrew "Baruch" to the Latin "Benedictus" (both mean "blessed"). This expulsion was a serious matter – it meant that no one in the Jewish community was even allowed to speak to Spinoza – but Spinoza accepted it with forbearance, maintaining nonetheless that there was nothing in his philosophy that contradicted the teachings of the Bible.

Spinoza finally settled at The Hague, where he lived a relatively secluded existence developing his philosophy (Figure 8.1). It was an austere life, marked by dedication to his work, but it suited Spinoza; he even turned down the offer of a university professorship as such a position would have taken him away from the routine to which he had become accustomed. Spinoza's life was not, however, completely devoid of creature comforts: he was said to enjoy smoking a pipe and drinking beer.

The burgeoning of scientific enquiry in The Netherlands of the seventeenth century had produced an increasing demand for lenses, which were used in scientific instruments, and for years Spinoza had augmented his income by working as a lens grinder. It is likely that this work hastened his death. He was already suffering from consumption and the condition was probably worsened by breathing in the glass dust produced by the grinding of lenses. By the time of his death, and despite his simple and secluded life, Spinoza's renown as a wise and learned man had spread, and many important members of Dutch society came to pay their respects to him at his funeral.

Box 8.1 (cont.)

Fig. 8.1 Baruch Spinoza

pure mechanism. Mentality, he believed, is only found in that portion of reality that lies outside the bounds of the natural, physical world in the immaterial mind of human beings. Spinoza rejected this postulate from the outset – mentality was not found in a separate realm outside the physical world, but was a characteristic of that very same world, albeit that same world seen from a different point of view.

The idea that the whole of the natural world is somehow imbued with mental life as well as physical characteristics might seem almost mystical to us today, but it has had a long presence in Western philosophy as well as in Eastern thought (Skrbina 2003). Spinoza's panpsychism does not entail that everything, from animals and plants to stones and trees, has mentality in the same way as human beings do, let alone that everything is conscious or has subjective experience; different things will have mental qualities to different extents and in different ways. Nevertheless, the attributes of mind "are altogether general, nor do they refer more to man than to other individuals, all of which are animate, although in different degrees" (*Ethics*, Ch. 2, Prop. 13). As we shall see below, panpsychism was one of the motivating forces behind the thought of Gustav Fechner, one of the founders of psychophysics in the nineteenth century.

The idea that the mental and the physical are attributes of one and the same substance has important consequences for the mind–body relation. According to Spinoza, it is a misunderstanding to look for some causal connection between the mind and the body, as if stimulation of the body or events in the brain *cause* certain mental states. Such a causal relationship can only hold between *different* things and it is entirely compatible with Cartesian dualism, in which physical states are indeed said to cause or bring about, however obscurely, mental states. But neither does the view that 'the mind and the body are one and the same thing' mean that the mental states can be reduced to physical states. Such a reductionist view, which is not unusual among psychologists and neuroscientists today, would mean that the physical picture of the world is somehow more fundamental, somehow truer, than a description in terms of the mental. But for Spinoza, and for the early physiological psychologists inspired by his thought, neither the mental nor the physical has priority over the other. Both are true, albeit different, descriptions of the same thing. When we experience mental states, such as thoughts and sensations, these are indeed, seen from one point of view, physical events. They are, says Spinoza, "modifications of our body" (quoted by Bernard 1972, p. 209). But they are also, when seen from another, equally valid point of view, mental events. One example that illustrates this idea of the double aspect of one and the same thing is a curved line (Lewes 1891). The curve, from one point of view, can be seen as convex (i.e. curving outwards), and from another point of view it can be seen as concave (i.e. curving inwards). Nevertheless, these are two aspects of one and the same line. Similarly, according to Lewes, the mental and the physical are attributes of one and the same substance, understood in different ways. Persons, therefore, are neither primarily mental nor physical, because mental events and physical events are the same things viewed from different perspectives.

Fechner and psychophysics

Spinoza's panpsychism and, in particular, his view that the mental and physical were are two attributes of the same substance, was of immense importance for Fechner's development of **psychophysics**. For Fechner (see Box 8.2), panpsychism provided a solution to the mind–body problem, which he saw as arising from Descartes' exclusion of mind from the natural world. According to Fechner, "[t]he foremost difficulty of our task lies . . . not in the fact that we are accustomed to regard the mind as a rule, but as an exception in nature" (*Zend-Avesta*, cited by Woodward 1972, p. 384).

Box 8.2 Gustav Theodor Fechner

Gustav Theodor Fechner (1801–87) was born in Gross Särchen, Saxony, the son of a Lutheran pastor. At the age of 17 he went to study medicine at Leipzig, a city in which he lived for the rest of his life and which he rarely left. Though he qualified in medicine, he never went into medical practice. Instead, Fechner lectured on physics at Leipzig and, starting in 1838, undertook a large number of experiments on subjective colour experience (frequently using himself as the experimental participant).

It is not known how far this prolonged experimentation on himself contributed to Fechner's subsequent illness, but in 1840 Fechner suffered a serious breakdown. His eyesight had seriously deteriorated and for long periods he was virtually blind. He often found it difficult to tolerate light and for much of the time had to stay in darkened rooms. Accompanying these difficulties were periods of intense pain in the eyes and teeth and a recurring inability to stomach food so that Fechner did not eat anything for days on end. The period of illness lasted for three years, during which time Fechner came close to death on several occasions (see Figure 8.2).

Box 8.2 (cont.)

Fig. 8.2 Gustav Theodor Fechner

Box 8.2 (cont.)

It is clear that, whatever the causes of this breakdown, Fechner himself felt it to be something more than a prolonged period of physical illness. He also felt it to be a spiritual crisis. In particular, he felt that he had, up until the period of his illness, not been true to his own philosophical beliefs. While working within the materialistic physics and physiology of his day, Fechner had also been interested in an approach to science called *Naturphilosophie*, which was associated with Romantic thinkers, such as Schelling (1775–1854). According to this view, which diametrically opposed itself to the mechanistic physics of Newton, the universe was not to be conceived of as a large piece of clockwork, but as a dynamic organism. It was a view that had clear affinities with Spinoza's panpsychism. Fechner believed that, although temperamentally attracted to such views, he had tried to pretend to himself that he was really a materialist and in so doing denied his own conscience. Following his crisis, he began to take his own metaphysical inclinations more seriously.

The problem with Cartesian dualism is fundamental: it denies mentality of any sort to the whole of the physical world and conceives of mind as mysteriously attached to only a small proportion of physical objects, i.e. human bodies. But, asks Fechner, why should we accept such a view? Why, rather than viewing mind as the exception in nature, should we not view it as the rule? Why should we shrink from attributing some degree of mental life to plants, for example? Fechner asks:

> is not the plant quite as well organized as the animal, though on a different plan, a plan entirely of its own, perfectly consonant with its idea? If one will not venture to deny that the plant has a life, why deny it a soul? For it is much simpler to think that a different plan of bodily organization built upon the common basis of life indicates only a different plan of psychic organization. (*Nanna*, cited by Skrbina 2003, p. 25)

If we think that the mental is the physical seen in a different way, then there is no principled reason why it should not be present in all organised physical things, although, as Fechner notes in the above quotation, the nature of the mental life in question will differ as the physical organisations of the things in question differ from one another.

Fechner explicitly connects his view with that of Spinoza:

> Spinoza's view permits, as does ours, the double, materialistic and mentalistic, conception of the realm of existence by conceiving the One identical, essential being (the substance) now as bodily (under the attribute of extension) and then again as mental (under the attribute of thought). In all this we fully agree with Spinoza. (*Zend-Avesta*, cited by Bernard 1972, p. 213)

The apparent problem of how the mind and the body might causally interact with one another is, therefore, based on a fundamental misconception of what mind and body are. If, instead of conceiving of them as two different substances, we conceive of them as two attributes of the same substance, then a different question arises: the question of how these two attributes are correlated with one another. According to Fechner, "man leads both an outward and an inward life in this world; the one visible and perceptible for everyone in his looks, words, and deeds; the other perceptible only for himself in his thoughts and emotions" (*On Life after Death*, cited by Woodward 1972, p. 371). It is the relationship between the 'inward' world of sensations and thoughts as experienced by an individual subject and the 'outward' public world of objective events that Fechner wished to discover.

For Fechner, the nature of this relationship can be established through scientific investigation. This is what psychophysics tries to do: by presenting participants with stimuli of different intensities and correlating them with the reports or judgements of the participants (e.g. by determining the magnitude by which a stimulus must be increased for the participant to notice a difference), a psychophysical law could be established linking the mental and the physical. Most famously, Fechner found, building on the work of Weber, that the relationship between stimulus intensity and intensity of sensation was **logarithmic**.

Fechner's insights, with their basis in Spinozist panpsychism, were of great importance for the development of psychology as a laboratory science. In particular, the idea that the mental could be measured constituted a revolutionary change in scientists' approach to the mind. Since Descartes, the physical world had been defined as that aspect of reality that could be measured and described mathematically. What could not be treated in this way was, by definition, not physical. As we have seen, for Descartes, the human mind was not physical in this sense. With Locke, too, we saw that there was a difference between primary qualities, which were mathematically describable and which really belonged to objects, and secondary qualities, which were purely subjective mental states and were not mathematically describable. In the same vein, Kant had later denied that psychology could be a true science because mental states were not mathematically describable. For many thinkers, then, the mental world was defined as the realm of *quality* rather than *quantity*. Mental states were understood to differ in terms of their intrinsic qualities, but to try to quantify them was not thought to make sense. One cannot say, for example, that the sensation of red is bigger or smaller than the taste of coffee: they are simply qualitatively different.

For Fechner, by contrast, the mental and the physical were not two separate realms, one characterised by quality and the other by quantity; "Body and Mind act together; a change in one corresponds to a change in the other" (*Elemente der Psychophysik*, cited by Bernard 1972, p. 214). And so, a change in the intensity of one should correspond to a change in the intensity of the other. The mental and the physical are, therefore, both mathematically describable. Fechner would, of course, not deny that there are qualitative differences between sensory modalities – the sensation of red *is* qualitatively different from the taste of coffee – but by measuring sensations in terms of the **just-noticeable difference** (the amount that a stimulus has to be increased to produce a just-noticeable difference in the magnitude of the sensation), Fechner found a way of treating all sensations – those of brightness, weight, loudness – in a mathematical way regardless of their differences in quality. Fechner, therefore, represents an important departure for the development of psychology – its suitability for quantification – that seems to bring it within the purview of natural science defined as the mathematical description of nature. It must not be forgotten, however, that the philosophical orientation that enabled him to do this was characterised by a very different conception of nature – nature as animate rather than nature as mechanical – than that which characterised much of science and philosophy since the seventeenth century. For Fechner, mind could only be investigated by natural science by changing the conception of nature from that of a dead mechanism to that of a living organism. As has been pointed out by one commentator, it was Fechner's "philosophical, even mystical, views which led to the first precise measurements in psychology" (Bernard 1972, p. 214).

Müller and the doctrine of specific nerve energies

The influence of Spinoza on the development of early physiological psychology was also manifested in the work of Johannes Müller (see Box 8.3). Müller was a figure of immense importance in the development of laboratory psychology. This

Box 8.3 Johannes Müller

Johannes Müller (1801–58) was born in Koblenz, Germany. He was the son of shoemaker. As a child he had been passionately interested in nature and collected plants. Müller had strong religious inclinations and considered studying theology at university, but it was his scientific interests that won out in the end and he studied medicine and physiology in Bonn and, in 1833, became a lecturer in physiology at Berlin.

Physiology was a new science at the time, gradually establishing itself as independent from the science of anatomy, and Müller was at the forefront of these developments. Müller's physiological interests were wide-ranging: he studied stimulation of the brain and spinal cord, the eye and the ear, the reproductive organs, among many other things. Indeed, both through his personal scientific work and through the very many eminent scientists (such as Helmholtz) who trained with him, Müller was one of the most influential scientists of the nineteenth century (Figure 8.3).

Bonn, where Müller trained, was a stronghold of *Naturphilosophie* (see Box 8.2), and its Romantic outlook coloured Müller's own views throughout his life. In particular, he was opposed to a purely materialistic physiology and promoted a variation of **vitalism** instead. According to vitalism, living things cannot be explained by purely physical/chemical mechanistic laws – there is something extra (e.g. a life force or soul) this is needed to account for life itself. Müller himself believed that there was an organic life force that organised and coordinated the various organs but which was not located in any single location in the body. He argued that, from a purely physical point of view, there was nothing in terms of material composition to differentiate between a fresh corpse and a living body. The difference between them, then, must lie in the presence of some force in the latter that is no longer present in the former.

Müller's students, including Helmholtz, strongly disagreed with their teacher's vitalism and some of them were outspoken advocates of materialism and reductionism. Nevertheless, despite this fundamental disagreement, good relations were maintained between teacher and students. Müller often suffered from severe depression and he was found dead in his bed in 1858. There were no obvious signs of illness and it has been suggested that the most likely cause of death was suicide by drug overdose.

Box 8.3 (cont.)

Fig. 8.3 Johannes Müller

was not only because of his own theories and scientific work, but also because of the many eminent scientists who started off as his students. These included Helmholtz, who will be discussed later in this chapter, and Wundt, who will be discussed in Chapter 11.

The influence of Spinozist ideas on Müller was particularly evident in what has come to be known as his doctrine or law of **specific nerve energies**. This doctrine, which Helmholtz later rated as highly as Newton's theory of gravitation in scientific importance (Finger and Wade 2002a), states that a nerve gives rise to the same sensation regardless of how it is stimulated. Whether the optic nerve, for example, is stimulated by a flash of light, by physical pressure on the eyeball from the finger, or by an electrical current, it always gives rise to a sensation of light. Each different sensory system seems to have specific qualities associated with its stimulation, and this is why hearing something is qualitatively different from seeing something or tasting something. The important point here is that the subjective sensory quality that is produced by stimulation is associated with the nerves themselves, not with the stimuli.

We have already seen above that, for Spinoza, the mental and the physical are two attributes of the same substance and that when we experience mental states we are experiencing 'modifications of our body'. This is echoed in Müller's thought: we do not experience external things, but the states of our body produced by those things. What we are aware of is the inner aspect of the physical changes wrought in us by external objects. The objects serve to set off the physiological response, but it is in this response, or 'modification', in which the experienced qualities inhere rather than in the object that caused the response. According to Müller:

> If the modifications of the retina are what we sense in vision, then we also may say that by the act of vision the retina feels itself in some state, or that the sensorium perceives the retina in some state. (*Handbuch der Physiologie des Menschen*, cited by Pastore 1974, p. 379)

And this is why stimulation of a particular sensory nerve always produces the same type of sensation regardless of how the stimulation was produced: we are, in vision, experiencing activity in the optic nerve and anything that stimulates the optic nerve will produce sensations with a visual quality. The same also holds for the other sensory modalities: any stimulation of the auditory nerve, regardless of the cause, will produce auditory sensations and any stimulation of the tactile receptors will produce the sensations of touch. This is because it is the activity of the sensory apparatus itself that we perceive. Müller says that our sensations are "of the nerves of sense themselves" and that "these qualities of nerves themselves are in all different, the nerve of each having its own peculiar quality or energy" (*Handbuch der Physiologie*, cited by Bernard 1972, p. 210). There is a clear link between this view and Spinoza's ideas about the relationship between the physiological and the mental, and Müller himself remarked that many of his ideas were similar to those of Spinoza.

The doctrine of specific nerve energies, with its Spinozist foundation, provided the underpinning of much of Helmholtz's work on sensory physiology. Helmholtz (see Box 8.4) agreed with his teacher, Müller, that what we are directly aware of are the states of our own bodies: "What ... we directly apprehend is not the

---

Box 8.4 Hermann Helmholtz

Hermann Helmholtz (later von Helmholtz) was born in Potsdam, Prussia, in 1821. Helmholtz was one of the great polymaths of the nineteenth century: he made important contributions to anatomy, physiology, physics, mathematics, medicine, and aesthetics as well as what was to become psychology.

At the age of 17, Helmholtz went to study medicine at the University of Berlin. He had originally intended to study physics, but his father persuaded him that medicine would be more likely to provide him with the means to make a living. Helmholtz later went on to teach physiology, physics, and anatomy in Königsberg (the home town of Kant), Bonn, and Berlin (Figure 8.4).

Helmholtz made many contributions to physiology, particularly sensory physiology. For example, he measured the time of sensory nerve impulses, a task that many before him had thought impossible, because of the supposed speed of such impulses. One of the methods that Helmholtz used was to stimulate the toe and the thigh of a human subject, who had to make a motor response when the stimulus was felt. By stimulating different parts of the body, Helmholtz found that the reaction time was longer the greater the distance of the stimulated area from the brain. It was this method that was later, in the hands of people such as Wundt, to become modified to the reaction time paradigm that is still used today to measure psychological (as opposed to physiological) processes.

Another of Helmholtz's contributions was the invention of the ophthalmoscope in 1850. This device used a mirror to direct a beam of light into the eye of the patient and, by using a lens to focus and magnify the light as it was reflected back by the retina, it allowed the observer to examine the state of the retina and therefore diagnose eye problems and diseases. The ophthalmoscopes used today operate on similar principles to the instrument constructed by Helmholtz.

In 1883 Helmholtz was awarded the addition of the aristocratic 'von' to his name by Kaiser Wilhem I (an honour similar to receiving a knighthood in the UK) in recognition of his outstanding scientific achievements. He died in 1894, at the age of 73, following a stroke.

Box 8.4 **(cont.)**

Fig. 8.4 Hermann von Helmholtz

immediate action of the external exciting cause upon the ends of our nerves, but only the changed condition of the nervous fibres which we call the state of *excitation* or functional activity" (*Popular Lectures*, p. 204). Helmholtz, however, took the idea behind the doctrine of specific nerve energies a stage further. For Müller, it was the specific qualities associated with different nerves (optical, auditory etc.) that accounted for the different subjective 'feels' associated with the different sensory modalities, but Helmholtz applied this idea *within* as well as between sensory modalities.

An example of this is Helmholtz's **trichromatic theory of colour vision**. This is the idea that colour vision is underpinned by three different types of nerve, each of which responds preferentially to light of a different wavelength. As well as qualitative differences between sensations of vision and sound, for example, there are qualitative differences *between* different visual sensations, such as different colours, or the sounds of a guitar and those of a flute. In these cases, it is not the case that one sensation is quantitatively different from the other – blue is not bigger or smaller than red – but that it is different in terms of its subjective *quality*. For Helmholtz, these qualitative differences in colour sensations could be accounted for by different nerves within the visual system:

> The eye is provided with three distinct sets of nervous fibres. Stimulation of the first excites the sensation of red, stimulation of the second the sensation of green, and stimulation of the third the sensation of violet. (Finger and Wade 2002b, p. 241)

Through laboratory studies of colour vision and studies of colour blind people, Helmholtz was able to collect empirical evidence to back up this theory.

Helmholtz and Kant

As well as the Spinozist doctrine of the substantial identity of mind and body, the ideas of Kant also were important in providing a philosophical grounding for the physiological work of Müller and Helmholtz. According to Helmholtz, Müller himself stated that

> The concept of space cannot be acquired; rather it would seem that the apperception of space and time is a necessary assumption, is itself a form of apperception for all sensations. As soon as there is any sensation, the sensation is in these forms of apperception ... (Helmholtz, *Treatise on Physiological Optics*, cited by Pastore 1974, p. 379)

Here, Müller echoes the Kantian idea that space and time are innate structures of the human mind and that, rather than being experienced, they are necessary for there to be any experience at all.

Helmholtz had a rather different, less Kantian, view of space perception than did his teacher (see Box 8.5), but the influence of Kant on his thought was nevertheless strong in other areas. We have seen in Chapter 6 that one of the major points of Kant's philosophy was that experience is structured by our own

---

Box 8.5 Helmholtz and empiricism

In tracing the lines of influence from Müller to Helmholtz, it is the Kantian strain of thought that is most evident. But Helmholtz was not a 'pure' Kantian; he was also influenced by empiricism. This influence is most clearly seen in his account of space perception. The perception of visual space, and particularly the perception of depth, was a topic of intense debate among psychologists, philosophers, and physiologists at the end of the nineteenth century. Some, such as Helmholtz's main opponent, Ewald Hering (1834–1918), argued that the perception of space was innate. The visual system, according to this view, was constructed in such a way as to immediately produce sensations of depth and space whenever it was stimulated. According to Helmholtz, however, we have to learn to see depth through experience. Visual sensations could only be given a spatial quality through learning. It was their association with motor movement and touch that provided spatiality to the retinal 'local signs'. It is in this respect that Helmholtz most clearly departs from the Kantian notion that space is an *a priori* category of the mind and, rather, has more in common with the empiricism of Berkeley, who also argued that we have to learn to interpret perceptual signs as indications of depth.

---

minds. Kant attempted to prove that this was necessarily so of any being whatsoever that was capable of having anything that we would recognise as experience. In the particular case of human beings, Helmholtz thought that this structuring of experience was done by our sensory apparatus. By investigating the physiology of the sense organs and their relationship to sense experience, in particular how they structured sense experience, Helmholtz saw himself as investigating one particular concrete instance of the general principle that underpinned Kant's philosophy. Helmholtz stated it thus:

> The character of our perceptions is conditioned just as much by the nature of our senses as by the external things ... What the physiology of the senses has demonstrated experimentally in more recent times, Kant tried to do exactly that for the ideas of the human mind in general. (*Über das Sehen des Menschen*, cited by Pastore 1974, p. 387)

Of particular importance in Helmholtz's theory of perception was the Kantian idea of causality. As we saw in Chapter 6, this was, for Kant, along with space and time, one of the inbuilt structures of the perceiving mind. Indeed, it was causality, and Hume's scepticism about it, that provided Kant with the impetus to undertake his *Critique of Pure Reason*. According to Kant, we spontaneously structure our perceptions in terms of causal connections. This idea was important for Helmholtz because it provided a bridge between subjective sensations and the external world of objects. One of the problems faced by any theory of perception, such as those of Müller and Helmholtz, that states that what we immediately sense are the states of our own bodies is the question of how we perceive anything outside ourselves at all. After all, when we reflect on our own experience, most of our perception has as its object things outside ourselves. As I write these words, I *do not* perceive changes in my retina or activity in my visual cortex; I perceive the computer screen in front of me on the desk. When we hear something, we don't hear it *in* the ear even though the physical changes are taking place in the ear; we hear the events as taking place in space out there, at some distance from us. In general, then, there is frequently a distinction between the place where sensory excitation takes place, which is indeed in our bodies, and the place where we perceive a thing to be or an event to take place, which is outside our bodies. Indeed, it could be argued that the whole point of perception is that it tells us about what is going on out there in the world, not what is going on inside our organs.

How can such observations be squared with the idea that we are most directly in touch with the processes that are going on in our nervous systems? For Helmholtz the leap from experience of internal sensation to experience of external objects can be made if one recognises that sensations are *signs* of the external objects that cause them. The idea that sensations function as signs of the external world is one that we have already come across in connection with the empiricism of Berkeley and Locke. And indeed Helmholtz was influenced by empiricism as well as by Kant (Turner 1977). Nevertheless, this empiricist theory of signs is one that has crucial Kantian foundations in the *a priori* idea of causality. It could, after all, be asked why sensations should functions as signs of external objects: there could be, as Berkeley argued, no independently existing objects that lie behind our subjective sensations. For Helmholtz, however, the *a priori* principle of causality – the innate knowledge that every event has a cause – meant that sensations were immediately interpreted as being events caused by something outside ourselves.

In order, however, to get from sensations to the actual perception of the external world, something more than the bare framework of causality is needed. This additional process is **unconscious inference**, a notion for which Helmholtz is particularly well known. It is on the basis of the sensations that we receive that we infer that there are objects outside of us and what the nature of these objects is. This inference, however, relies on the basic Kantian notion of causality to get it going: it is only on the basis of the principle that every event has a cause that we can then make the inference from the subjective, internal sensations that we receive to the external, objective things and events that are their causes. Importantly, however, this inferential process proceeds without our awareness. The inference is not the result of a deliberate conscious decision on our part, but takes place involuntarily beneath the level of conscious experience. What we experience consciously is the outcome of that process.

Another thinker associated with the idea of unconscious inference (and who was read avidly by Helmholtz) is John Stuart Mill (1806–74). Mill summarises the idea of unconscious inference in perception thus:

> we may fancy that we see or feel what we in reality infer. A truth, or supposed truth, which is really the result of a very rapid inference, may seem to be apprehended intuitively. It has long been agreed by thinkers of the most opposite schools, that this mistake is actually made in so familiar an instance as that of the eyesight. There is nothing of which we appear to ourselves to be more directly conscious than the distance of an object from us. Yet it has long been ascertained, that what is perceived by the eye, is at most nothing more than a variously colored surface; that when we fancy we see distance, all we really see is certain variations of apparent size, and degrees of faintness of color; that our estimate of the object's distance from us is the result partly of a rapid inference from the muscular sensations accompanying the adjustment of the focal distance of the eye to objects unequally remote from us, and partly of a comparison (made with so much rapidity that we are unconscious of making it) between the size and color of the object as they appear at the time, and the size and color of the same or of similar objects as they appeared when close at hand, or when their degree of remoteness was known by other evidence. The perception of distance by the eye, which seems so like intuition, is thus, in reality, an inference grounded on experience ... (*A System of Logic*, p. 20)

This idea that we do not perceive things directly but have to infer their existence through some rational process of logical inference or problem solving is one that has had immense influence on the psychology of perception, right through the twentieth century to the present day. For example, the influential perceptual psychologist Richard Gregory states:

> We are so familiar with seeing, that it takes a leap of the imagination to realise that there are problems to be solved ... We are given tiny distorted upside-down images in the eyes, and we see separate solid objects in surrounding space. From the patterns of stimulation on the retinas we perceive the world of objects, and this is nothing short of a miracle. (*Eye and Brain*, p. 7)

There is, according to this view, a gap between the sensory stimulation that we receive ("tiny distorted upside-down images") and the eventual content of our conscious perceptions ("the world of objects"). According to Gregory, "perception involves going beyond the immediately given evidence of the senses ... the senses do not give us a picture of the world directly" (*Eye and Brain*, p. 11). For Gregory, and for many other perceptual theorists today, this "going beyond the immediately given evidence of the senses" requires unconscious processes of logical inference and problem-solving.

This logical process of unconscious inference gives us a very different conception of the unconscious to that put forward by Schopenhauer and Nietzsche. For Schopenhauer and Nietzsche the unconscious is irrational and full of seething sexual desires and urges. The conscious, rational mind is qualitatively different from the unconscious, though it is its servant and curbs and channels unconscious desires into socially acceptable outlets through sublimation. With the unconscious of Mill and Helmholtz we have, in contrast, the idea of a *rational unconscious*, one that engages in logical thought and problem solving (Reed 1998). To a large extent, this unconscious is not qualitatively different from the conscious mind – it carries out many of the same rational tasks and thought processes. It differs only from the conscious mind in that it does these tasks unconsciously.

The existence of sensations

As we do not consciously experience the sensations themselves (we experience external, physical objects), any inference that we make on their basis cannot be conscious. But an important question arises here in connection with both Mill and Helmholtz: given that we consciously experience things rather than bare sensations, what evidence do we have that there are such things as sensations at all? As we shall see in later chapters, the existence of such sensations was by no means taken for granted by all psychologists. Some, such as William James (see Chapter 14) and the Gestalt psychologists (see Chapter 13), argued that the basic atomistic sensation was a purely fictional entity for which there was no evidence. They did not, of course, dispute that we have complex perceptual experience of external objects or that the sense organs played an essential role in providing us with such experience. But they did dispute the idea that there was an unconscious level of basic sensations and logical processing that gave rise to this complex conscious experience.

What, then, was the warrant for postulating the existence of such entities given that they are not to be found in our experience or through introspection upon that experience? For Helmholtz, the evidence was physiological rather than psychological: we assume that each nerve produces a particular qualitative sensation. Based on the presupposition that each nerve has a subjective 'inner' sensation corresponding to its objective stimulation, we can infer from the physiological structure of our organs that basic sensations that go into making up our conscious experience must exist. Because we have discrete nerve cells, we can infer that we have discrete sensations and that this is, ultimately, what our experience is made out of. According to Helmholtz, "here we have to do with mental activities, of which self observation cannot give us any information at all, whose existence can only be inferred from the physiological investigation of the sensory organs" (*Über das Sehen des Menschen*, cited by Pastore 1974, p. 388). A clear example of this is the different receptors in the visual system, which respond differentially to different wavelengths of light. The physiology of the visual system provides evidence that our colour vision is made up of different basic colour sensations corresponding to the stimulation of these different receptors. In this sense, then, the argument for the existence of sensations rests ultimately on the Spinozist theory that we sense the states of our own bodies.

But as well as this Spinozist influence, there is also an echo of Kant in Helmholtz's approach. We have seen above that Helmholtz's study of physiology was a variation on Kantianism in the sense that it sought to investigate how experience is constructed. In the case of human beings, this construction is carried out by the nervous system. One essential point of the Kantian philosophy is that the structuring processes that go into making our experience are not themselves part of experience. Kant, as we saw in Chapter 6, inferred their existence not through direct introspective experience of them but through inferring their existence on the basis of the experience that we do have. This essential point is echoed in Helmholtz's sensory physiology: the structuring processes, among which we can include the unconscious inferences and judgements working on basic sensations, are not experienced. Their existence and the existence of the sensations on which they work is *inferred* rather than observed. As we shall see in Chapter 11, Wundt (who was a student of Helmholtz) also held the idea that the psychologist has to infer processes that are hidden from direct experience because they create that experience. Attitudes towards this idea constituted a clear divide between those psychologists who can be thought of as intellectual descendants of Kant (like Helmholtz and Wundt) and other positivist-inclined psychologists (such as Wundt's student, Titchener) who can be thought of as intellectual descendants of Hume. For this latter group, there were no hidden processes lying behind experience.

Conclusion

In this chapter we have seen how Spinoza offered a different view of the relationship between mind and body than the substance dualism of Descartes. The mental and the physical were seen by Spinoza as two aspects of one and the same substance. Everything physical also had a mental aspect and vice versa. This had the consequence that not just human beings, but everything in nature has mentality to some degree. This is a view known as panpsychism. It was panpsychism, partly inspired by Spinoza, that lay behind the psychophysics of Fechner. Fechner believed that scientific investigation could uncover the relationship between the mental and the physical aspects of human beings.

A second major influence on the development of physiological psychology was Kant. Kant's idea that mind structured experience rather than just passively receiving it was translated into the physiological realm by scientists such as Müller and Helmholtz. They argued that the organisation of the sensory systems shaped the structure of experience because what we experience most directly is not the external world but the activity of the sensory systems themselves. Perception of the external world, rather than being direct, is, according to this view, the outcome of a process of unconscious inference based on the basic sensations furnished by stimulation of the sensory organs.

Revision questions

1. How did Spinoza view the relationship between the mental and the physical?

2. How did Fechner's psychophysics draw on the ideas of Spinoza?

3. What was Müller's doctrine of specific nerve energies and how did it have its basis in the ideas of Spinoza?

4. In what way did Helmholtz believe his research to be updating the ideas of Kant?

5. What is unconscious inference and what is its relevance to perception of the external world?

6. How does the idea of the unconscious found in Helmholtz and J. S. Mill differ from the idea of the unconscious found in Schopenhauer and Nietzsche?

7. What reasoning did Helmholtz give for postulating the existence of individual sensations?

References

Bernard, W. (1972). Spinoza's influence on the rise of scientific psychology: a neglected chapter in the history of psychology. *Journal of the History of the Behavioral Sciences*, **8**, 208–15.

Finger, S. and Wade, N. J. (2002a). The neuroscience of Helmholtz and the theories of Johannes Müller. Part 1: Nerve cell structure, vitalism, and the nerve impulse. *Journal of the History of the Neurosciences*, **11**, 136–55.

Finger, S. and Wade, N. J. (2002b). The neuroscience of Helmholtz and the theories of Johannes Müller. Part 2: Sensation and perception. *Journal of the History of the Neurosciences*, **11**, 234–54.

Gregory, R. L. (1966). *Eye and Brain*. London: Weidenfeld & Nicolson.

Helmholtz, H. von (1904). *Popular Lectures on Scientific Subjects*. London: Longman.

Lewes, G. H. (1891). *The Physical Basis of Mind*. Boston, MA: Houghton, Mifflin.

Mill, J. S. (1882). *A System of Logic*. New York: Harper & Sons.

Pastore, N. (1974). Re-evaluation of Boring on Kantian influence, nineteenth century nativism, Gestalt psychology and Helmholtz. *Journal of the History of the Behavioral Sciences*, **4**, 375–90.

Reed, E. S. (1998). *From Soul to Mind: The Emergence of Psychology, from Erasmus Darwin to William James*. New Haven, CT: Yale University Press.

Skrbina, D. (2003). Panpsychism as an underlying theme in Western philosophy. *Journal of Consciousness Studies*, **10**, 4–46.

Spinoza, B. ([1677]/1949). *Ethics* (J. Gutman, ed.). New York: Hafner Press.

Turner, R. S. (1977). Hermann von Helmholtz and the empiricist vision. *Journal of the History of the Behavioral Sciences*, **13**, 48–58.

Woodward, W. R. (1972). Fechner's panpsychism: a scientific solution to the mind–body problem. *Journal of the History of the Behavioral Sciences*, **8**, 367–86.

9 Evolution and psychology

Timeline

1801	Act of Union of Great Britain with Ireland creates United Kingdom
1832	Great Reform Act extends voting rights
1838	Coronation of Queen Victoria
1847	Emily Brontë publishes *Wuthering Heights*
1854–6	Crimean War
1871	Legalisation of Trade Unions in Britain
1871–2	George Eliot publishes *Middlemarch*
1901	Death of Queen Victoria

Herbert Spencer

1820	Born in Derby
1837–41	Works as a railway engineer
1847	Works as a journalist for *The Economist*
1852–3	Romantic relationship with writer George Eliot, but the couple decide against marriage
1855	Publishes *The Principles of Psychology*
1864–7	Publishes *The Principles of Biology*
1879–82	Publishes *The Principles of Sociology*
1902	Nominated for the Nobel Prize for Literature
1903	Dies in Brighton

Charles Darwin

1809	Born in Shrewsbury
1825	Studies medicine at the University of Edinburgh
1828	Starts BA at Cambridge in preparation for becoming an Anglican clergyman
1831–9	Voyage of the *Beagle*
1839	Starts publication of his *Journal of researches into the geology and natural history of the various countries visited by H.M.S. Beagle*
1858	Meeting of the Linnean Society at which Darwin and Wallace both present the theory of evolution by natural selection
1859	Publishes *On the Origin of Species*
1882	Dies in Kent

Introduction

The idea that species changed through evolution was one that preceded Darwin by a good many years, perhaps even centuries. Traces of such ideas can be found as far back as the works of Aristotle and evolutionary ideas were particularly prevalent among eighteenth-century naturalists, such as Buffon (1707–88). Pre-Darwinian approaches to evolution were not necessarily inimical to religion and many saw evolution as the unfolding of God's design; it was creation in action. This meant that nature had a purpose: the instantiation of the divine plan through evolution. Humanity, as the pinnacle of God's creative plan, was, therefore, the last to emerge from the evolutionary process.

The fundamental idea behind these approaches to evolution was that of progress. The evolutionary process was understood as naturally tending towards the appearance of more and more sophisticated species. Even those who rejected the idea of a divine plan and who had a secular understanding of evolution nevertheless held it to be something progressive. One of these theorists was Herbert Spencer (1820–1903), one of the most influential and widely read scientists and philosophers of the nineteenth century. It was Spencer who was the first thinker to bring the idea of evolution to bear on psychology in a major way.

Herbert Spencer and evolution

Spencer believed that evolution tended to produce more and more sophisticated species as time went on. The original idea came to Spencer from studies of embryology. The biologist von Baer (1792–1876) had appeared to show that all vertebrate embryos are alike at early stages in their development, and that it is only gradually, through their development, that they come to be differentiated into separate and identifiable species. That evolution also follows this plan – that it moves from the undifferentiated to the differentiated – was the essential core of Spencer's approach to everything; his overarching principle was "the truth that all organic development is a change from a state of homogeneity to a state of heterogeneity" (*Reasons for Dissenting from the Philosophy of M. Comte*, quoted by Smith 1982, p. 58). The animal kingdom, for example, has simple homogeneous organisms at the lowest end of the scale and, at the other end of the scale, humans, with highly differentiated body parts. The evolution of humans from other, simpler, species seemed to Spencer to follow the same pattern as the development of the vertebrate embryo.

But this pattern of evolution was not, for Spencer, restricted only to the world of biology: he believed that it characterised everything, from the evolution of the universe itself (from a homogeneous state to differentiated planets and stars) to that of society (from homogeneous primitive societies to highly sophisticated and heterogeneous developed societies).

This pattern of progress, however, was not for Spencer the unfolding of a divine plan, but was to be understood in purely scientific, even materialistic, terms. It is the case, said Spencer, that a single event has multiple consequences. This means that effects will naturally, automatically, tend to be more differentiated and complex than their cause. It is simply through the operation of physical cause and effect that

---

Box 9.1 **Herbert Spencer**

Herbert Spencer was born in Derby in 1820. Through his father he became acquainted with the theories of evolution being discussed by the Derby Philosophical Society, including the ideas of Charles Darwin's grandfather, Erasmus Darwin, and Jean-Baptiste Lamarck. Spencer was largely self-educated and worked for a while as a railway engineer while also trying his hand at writing for radical political journals. Though Spencer was to become more conservative in his political opinions in later life, he maintained a liberal distrust of the state becoming overinvolved in matters of personal freedom.

Spencer believed that all of reality could be understood in entirely naturalistic terms and that the developments produced by the operations of natural forces tended towards improvement and progress. One of the political consequences of Spencer's evolutionary views as applied to society was his belief that society would eventually become so highly evolved that there would no longer be any need for a state to oversee people's lives.

It was Spencer who coined the phrase 'survival of the fittest'. He believed that unfit sections of society would eventually disappear through evolution and argued against any state interference that would prevent this, though he was not opposed to private acts of charity.

Spencer became one of the most widely read thinkers of the late nineteenth century, with his works selling over a million copies (Figure 9.1).

He died in 1903.

Box 9.1 (cont.)

Fig. 9.1 Herbert Spencer

the universe becomes more and more complex and differentiated over time. There is no need for a divine agency to arrange this: it is a purely natural phenomenon, according to Spencer.

Spencer's conception of psychology

Spencer's view of consciousness seemed to have something in common with the double-aspect view of Spinoza, which was discussed in Chapter 8. We saw, in that chapter, that early psychophysicists, such as Fechner, subscribed to a view called *panpsychism*, according to which consciousness or mentality is present in some form throughout nature. (This, as we shall see, is also a view that Darwin toyed with.) The whole thrust of Spencer's evolutionary view was that of continuous development from the simple and homogeneous to the complex and heterogeneous. The sudden appearance of mind at a discrete point on this continuum seemed to run counter to the whole idea of continuity. The attachment of consciousness only to humans was perfectly compatible with the Cartesian view of nature as an insensate machine, to which, in the case of some individuals, the property of consciousness might be added, but it appeared, to Spencer, to be incompatible with the evolutionist view of nature not as a machine but as a self-developing or unfolding organism. The idea of continuous development seemed to demand that what was seen at the higher, more sophisticated end of the evolutionary spectrum must have been contained, even if only in embryonic form, at earlier stages.

The view of mentality to which Spencer subscribed seemed, then, to require that nature had not merely an outer aspect, but an inner one too. Spencer, indeed, stated this explicitly, claiming that "Feeling and nervous action ... are the inner and outer faces of the same change" (Spencer, *Principles of Psychology*, quoted by Smith 1982, p. 70). Just as a given quantity of heat is equal to a given amount of motion – they are the same things seen from two different perspectives – so, says Spencer, is a given amount of physical activity equivalent to the mental or psychological feelings that are associated with it. They are the same thing seen from two different perspectives: one objective and physical, the other subjective and psychological (Smith 1982).

If we accept that the subjective mental world is the inner, experiential, side of objective nervous-system activity, then it follows that, as nervous systems themselves change, evolve, and become more complex, so the mental states that are equivalent to their activity should also change, evolve, and become more complex. More complex and differentiated creatures will therefore have more complex and differentiated mental states than simpler and more homogeneous ones. The mental worlds of these relatively primitive creatures will consist of undifferentiated and generalised feelings, perhaps of only comfort or discomfort. The mental worlds of more evolved creatures will be more complex. Instead of the undifferentiated feeling of discomfort, more evolved creatures will experience different types of discomfort – hunger, pain, excess cold or heat – with, of course, more differentiated feelings of comfort and satisfaction when these needs are assuaged.

It was on the basis of more primitive states of consciousness that the more complex states of consciousness evolved:

> We have seen that it [the mind] consists largely, and in one sense entirely, of Feelings. Not only do Feelings constitute the inferior tracts of consciousness, but Feelings are in all cases the materials out of which, in the superior tracts of consciousness, Intellect is evolved by structural combination. (Spencer, *Principles of Psychology*, quoted by Smith 1982, p. 68)

Effectively, then, the mental world consists of basic feelings, each of which is the inner aspect of a physiological event in the nervous system. More complex states of mind are the result of the fitting together of these basic feelings into more complex arrangements. In his view of the mind as consisting of basic states that are put together according to association, Spencer follows the empiricism of Locke and Hume, which was discussed in Chapters 5 and 6.

Thus, even within the same individual we have a process of evolution in which the undifferentiated feelings of the baby become more complex and evolve into intellect. How does this evolution of thought happen? Evolution teaches us, said Spencer, that creatures that adapt better to their environments are more likely to survive than those that are less well adapted. The same goes, he argued, for mental states and degrees of consciousness. Those mental states that are adapted to the environment are likely to persist, whereas those that are not so adapted are likely to disappear. Thoughts that are more complex and coherent mirror the complexity of the environment more accurately than simpler, less coherent ones, and so are more likely to survive.

The organism's mental world comes to reflect the external world through the formation of relationships or connections between thoughts, and these mental connections have their objective counterpart in the formation of physical con-nections in the nervous system. These internal relations adapt to, and reflect, the relations between things in the outer environment in ever greater detail, complexity, and differentiation. Spencer puts it thus:

> we see that Life is definable as the continuous adjustment of internal relations to external relations. And when we so define it, we discover that the physical and the psychical life are equally comprehended by the definition. We perceive that this which we call Intelligence, shows itself when the external relations to which the internal ones are adjusted, begin to be numerous, complex, and remote in time or space; that every advance in Intelligence essentially consists in the establishment of more varied, more complete, and more involved adjustments; and that even the highest achievements of science are resolvable into mental relations of co-existence and sequence, so co-ordinated as exactly to tally with certain relations of co-existence and sequence that occur externally. (Spencer, *First Principles of a New System of Philosophy*, p. 84)

A true idea is one that corresponds more closely to external reality and is thus more useful to the organism in guiding its behaviour:

> what we call truth, guiding us to successful action and the consequent maintenance of life, is simply the accurate correspondence of subjective to objective relations; while error, leading to failure and therefore towards death, is the absence of such accurate correspondence. (Spencer, *First Principles of a New System of Philosophy*, p. 85)

In his emphasis on the association of ideas, Spencer is firmly within the empiricist tradition, and in his view that "every act of knowing is the formation of a relation in consciousness parallel to a relation in the environment" (Spencer, *First Principles of a New System of Philosophy*, p. 86) he anticipates the **connectionism** of Thorndike and contemporary neuroscience (Leslie 2006). The prefiguring of Thorndike's **Law of Effect**, which is discussed in more detail in Chapter 16, can be seen clearly in the following quotation:

> Suppose, now, that in putting out its head to seize prey scarcely within reach, a creature has repeatedly failed. Suppose that along with the group of motor actions approximately adapted to seize prey at this distance, the diffused discharge is, on some occasion, so distributed throughout the muscular system as to cause a slight forward movement of the body. Success will occur instead of failure; and after success will immediately come certain pleasurable sensations with an accompanying large draught of nervous energy towards the organs employed in eating etc. . . . . On recurrence of the circumstances, these muscular movements that were followed by success are likely to be repeated: what was at first an accidental combination of motions will now be a combination having considerable probability . . . Every repetition of it will . . . increase the probability of subsequent repetitions; until at length the nervous connexions become organized. (Spencer, *Principles of Psychology*, quoted by Leslie 2006, p. 126)

Thorndike too was to attribute animal learning to the gradual stamping in of a physical connection that associated a particular stimulus with a particular response into the nervous system, and in so doing paved the way for the **stimulus–response behaviourism** of Watson. We can see here that very similar ideas were being put forward by Spencer decades earlier.

The picture painted by Spencer, then, is that of a creature that is shaped by its environment. As a result, the organism is no longer seen as an autonomous creature with its own goals, but as a resultant of environmental forces:

> readers must have perceived that the doctrines developed [here] . . . are at variance with the current tenets respecting the freedom of the Will . . . [T]hat every one is at liberty to desire or not to desire, which is the real proposition involved in the dogma of free will, is negatived [*sic*] by the analysis of consciousness . . . From the universal law that, other things being equal, the cohesion of psychic states is proportionate to the frequency with which they followed each other in experience, it is an inevitable corollary that all actions whatever must be determined by those psychical connexions which experience has generated . . . Considered as an internal perception, the illusion results from supposing that at each moment the ego, present as such in consciousness . . . is something more than the aggregate of feelings and ideas which then exists. (Spencer, *Principles of Psychology*, quoted by Leslie 2006, p. 128)

In other words, if one accepts that animals evolve by adapting to their environments, then there is no room for free will or autonomy. The animal, from a psychological point of view, is nothing more than a collection of associations or relations that have been driven by the relations in the external environment. Even the self or ego, says Spencer (echoing Hume's assertion that the self is nothing more than a bundle of sensations; see Chapter 6), is nothing more than "the aggregate of feelings and ideas". As we shall see later in this chapter, this view of the organism as something determined by the action of the environment upon it was to be criticised by William James.

Spencer and Lamarck

We have seen, then, that Spencer believed that organisms evolved by adjusting themselves to their environmental circumstances. In both the mental realm and the behavioural realm, certain connections within the nervous system of the organism would be strengthened under the influence of the environment upon it. But in what way might this process of adaptation result in evolution? How would it lead species to mutate and for different species to be descended from common ancestors? The adaptations that had altered the inner connections of one generation of organisms would have to be preserved and passed on to succeeding generations. This is called the **inheritance of acquired characteristics**. According to this view, the characteristics acquired by an organism during its lifetime are passed on to its offspring, and these offspring in turn acquire characteristics in the course of adjusting to the environment and pass *these* changes on to *their* offspring. Thus, little by little, and from generation to generation, adjustments accumulate, leading to the emergence of new and different species.

The idea of the inheritance of acquired characteristics is particularly associated with Jean-Baptiste Lamarck (1744–1829), an evolutionary theorist who pre-dated Darwin, but it is now known not to occur: the blacksmith's son does not inherit the muscular strength that his father has acquired in the course of his daily occupation. Though Lamarck, and Spencer, were right in recognising the existence of evolution, they were wrong about the way in which it worked.

But, given the fact that acquired characteristics are not inherited, Spencer's view of evolution as the adjustment of organisms to their environment can no longer hold, as there is no means for transmitting any such adjustments to future generations. The moulding of organisms by the environment cannot tell the story of evolution. There must be something else, and this something else is the accidental variations in organisms which are then *selected but not made* by the environment. This is the view that Darwin put forward and which William James used to criticise the ideas of Spencer.

Spencer and Darwin

As stated at the start of this chapter, evolutionary ideas had been around long before Darwin, and Spencer himself developed his ideas before Darwin published any of his work. What Darwin contributed was not the idea of evolution, but the process by which evolution comes about. For Darwin the main driver of evolution was **natural selection**.

The basic idea behind natural selection is as follows. Not all members of a species are the same: there is variation within a species – some birds have longer beaks than others, some mammals are bigger or faster than others. Now, assuming that there is competition between individual animals for resources – food, mates, etc. – some individuals will be more successful in producing offspring than others. The offspring will inherit the characteristics of their parents. In the next generation, if these offspring continue to be reproductively successful, the characteristics will continue to be passed on and, perhaps, even become more extreme. What we have here is called **descent with modification**. All we need for natural selection to operate is that parental characteristics are inherited by offspring and that individuals should have differential reproductive success. Over many generations, certain characteristics – those that are associated with greater reproductive success – will become more prevalent within the population, whereas other characteristics – those that are associated with a lack of reproductive success – will become less prevalent or perhaps disappear altogether.

The important thing to see here is that there is an element of randomness in natural selection. There is natural variation between individuals and in the inheritance of parental characteristics (offspring are not perfect copies of their parents). It is these accidental, random variations upon which natural selection operates.

Though Darwin famously developed his ideas through observation of the natural world, as, for example, on his famous voyage on the *Beagle*, his observations of selective breeding by farmers were also of great importance. Think of how a farmer may want to breed cattle that produce the most meat: he will select the best meat-producing animals to mate with one another so as to produce offspring that are good for meat, and then the best of the offspring will be chosen to breed with one another so as to produce, in their turn, offspring that are even better for meat. By deliberately selecting those animals for breeding, the farmer, over generations of selective breeding, will produce an animal that gives considerably more meat than previous generations.

Human beings have been selectively breeding animals for centuries – not only livestock for meat, but different breeds of dog or horse, each with characteristics that suit it for a particular job or environment. Whereas in the case of domesticated animals it is humans who make the selection of which animals will breed, in evolution it is nature that, in effect, makes the selection (hence *natural selection*), although, of course, there is no conscious choice in this, it is just the outcome of natural circumstances favouring some animals more than others.

The element of randomness in Darwinism was one of the major things that differentiated it from previous theories of evolution. As we saw in the introduction to this chapter, pre-Darwinian theories of evolution had thought of evolution as the unfolding of a predetermined plan or programme according to which higher and more sophisticated creatures necessarily evolved from lower and simpler ones. For some, this plan of evolution was the unfolding of a divinely

Box 9.2 **Charles Darwin**

Charles Robert Darwin was born in Shrewsbury in 1809. As a child he showed an early interest in the natural world. He went to study medicine at the University of Edinburgh, but was squeamish about surgery and neglected his medical studies in favour of his own informal studies of nature. He also attended meetings where evolutionary ideas were discussed and became aware of the evolutionary theory proposed by his own grandfather, Erasmus Darwin.

Following Darwin's unsuccessful medical studies, he was sent by his father to the University of Cambridge with a view to Darwin's getting a degree so that he could become an Anglican cleric. After graduating Darwin was offered the position of ship's naturalist aboard H.M.S. *Beagle* on its voyage to South America. It was during this voyage, during which Darwin kept detailed notes on all his observations, that Darwin began to consider the possible role of evolution in the geographical distribution of different species.

It was Darwin's subsequent reading of the work of Thomas Malthus (1766–1834) that finally led him to the idea of natural selection. Malthus had published *An Essay on the Principle of Population*, in which he argued that the growth of population would, at a certain point, be checked by the scarcity of natural resources. It was this idea, that competition for limited resources would result in differing levels of reproduction, that was the final element that Darwin needed to develop his theory of natural selection.

While Darwin was working on his theory to ready it for publication, however, he became aware that another scientist, Alfred Russel Wallace, had also, independently, hit upon the idea of natural selection as the means of evolution. Darwin quickly produced a brief report of his ideas, and Darwin's and Wallace's papers announcing natural selection were published together at the same meeting of the Linnean Society in 1858. It was only the following year that Darwin finally published *On the Origin of Species*, which was an instant popular success and sold out shortly after publication.

For the remaining years of his life, Darwin continued work upon and expand his theory of evolution, though he was increasingly plagued by ill health (Figure 9.2). He died of heart failure at his home, Down House, in Kent in 1882.

Box 9.2 (cont.)

Fig. 9.2 Charles Darwin

ordained plan of creation, but for others, such as Spencer, there was no need to invoke any deity to explain evolution. For him, as we have seen, the tendency of evolution to produce ever more complex and differentiated creatures was simply the outcome – though a *necessary* outcome – of natural forces of cause and effect.

Darwinian natural selection differed from this outlook not merely in giving no role to a deity in evolution, but in denying that there is any overall pattern to evolution at all, divinely ordained or not. To put it bluntly, the evolution of human beings was not the result of an inevitable tendency of evolution to produce higher species, but an accident – the fortuitous result of random variations in the inheritance of physical characteristics and reproductive success. It could have been otherwise.

This view of evolution undermined not only ideas of human progress, whether secular or religious, but also another much cherished idea of ancient ancestry. Up until Darwin, going right back to the ancient Greeks, there was an approach to all sorts of phenomena that we might call **essentialism**. It was thought that everything is what it is because it embodies certain characteristics that constitute the essence of the class of things to which it belongs. It was thought that there are essential characteristics that all people embody and in virtue of which they are human beings. Similarly there were thought to be essential characteristics of dogs, cats, and everything else. Of course, real actual human beings will embody the essential characteristics to a greater or lesser degree, but we can think of the essence as a kind of template of the ideal human being that we strive towards. The variations between individual people in virtue of which they depart from this ideal is just so much noise and error. It is a mistake, an imperfection in the realisation of the human ideal. The Darwinian approach to evolution changed things round completely – variation was not an error, it was the engine of change. Indeed, for Darwinism, there were no fixed ideal types towards which nature aspires. Everything is change, movement, flux. It was the element of randomness, of unpredictability, that Darwin introduced into his picture of nature that was, as we shall see in Chapter 14, to prove so attractive to William James.

The organism and its environment

We have seen above that, for Spencer, in true empiricist fashion, our complex thoughts and mental states are ultimately constructed from basic feelings and sensations. One class of sensations that was particularly important in Spencer's theory was the sensation of force that we experience when we engage in any movement or physical interaction with the world. When we act upon the world, we have sensations of muscular effort and of the corresponding resistance of the environment to that effort. This is almost ubiquitous throughout nature:

> Excluding the lowest animals ... there are none but what have, at every moment of their lives, some impression of resistance. (Spencer, *Principles of Psychology*, quoted by Smith 1983, p. 9)

It is from this physical interaction with the world and the concomitant sensations of force and resistance that accompany it that we get all our ideas and knowledge, according to Spencer:

> Thus, Matter, Space, Motion, Force, all our fundamental ideas, arise by generalization and abstraction from our experiences of resistance. Nor shall we see in this anything strange if we contemplate, under its simplest aspect, the relation between the organism and its environment. Here is a subject placed in the midst of objects. It can learn nothing of them without being affected by them. Being affected by them implies their action upon its surface ... And the sensation of resistance through which this fundamental action is known, becomes the mother-tongue of thought; in which all the first cognitions are registered, and into which all symbols afterwards learnt are interpretable. (Spencer, *Principles of Psychology*, vol. 2, p. 236)

All our most fundamental ideas, then, come through physical contact with the environment. It is precisely through the sensation of resistance that, according to Spencer, the organism comes to distinguish itself from its environment. This evolutionary understanding of the organism in relationship with its environment is fundamentally different to the Cartesian view of the mind as a disembodied consciousness. For Descartes, as we saw in Chapter 4, the self can be known in isolation from the external world, indeed it can be known even if there is no external world at all, the world's existence being susceptible to the method of doubt that Descartes employed in his effort to find true and certain knowledge. For Spencer, however, it is only through its experience of the surrounding environment that the organism comes to self-consciousness at all, i.e. comes to differentiate between itself and the external world. The self cannot be experienced or known prior to, or in isolation from, experience or knowledge of the environment. We have here an example of what is sometimes called **animal–environment mutuality**.

William James welcomed Spencer's emphasis on the mind's place in nature, in contrast to the Cartesian disembodied mind:

On the whole, few recent formulas have done more real service of a rough sort in psychology than the Spencerian one that the essence of mental life and of bodily life are one, namely, 'the adjustment of inner to outer relations'. Such a formula is vagueness incarnate; but because it takes into account the fact that minds inhabit environments which act on them and on which they in turn react; because, in short, it takes mind in the midst of all its concrete relations, it is immensely more fertile than the old-fashioned 'rational psychology' which treated the soul as a detached existent, sufficient unto itself, and assumed to consider only its nature and properties. (James, *Principles of Psychology*, vol. 1, p. 6)

But, although Spencer recognised that the organism acted on its environment and experienced the sensations of force and resistance that accompanied such action, his main emphasis seemed to be on the environment acting upon the organism. Spencer tended to talk of the organism adjusting or adapting to the environment, and therefore of its mental world and the connections therein coming to correspond to the connections between things in the outer, physical world. For Darwinians, such as James, this view, although it rightly recognised the importance of the organism in its environment, seemed to do away with any autonomy on the part of the organism itself. And for James, the autonomy of the organism was essential to the Darwinian view of nature because spontaneous variations in thought and behaviour were precisely the raw material that was necessary for natural selection to work upon. If the organism was entirely determined by its environment, it seemed to James, there would be none of these unpredictable differences. So, the organism had to act on its environment, not merely have the environment act upon it.

This view of the organism as active is apparent in James's view of knowledge. Whereas Spencer thought that the knowing organism simply reflected the truth of the relations that the environment imposes upon it, for James the organism plays an active role in making those relations:

The knower is an actor, and co-efficient of the truth on one side, whilst on the other he registers the truth *which he helps to create*. Mental interests, hypotheses, postulates, so far as they are bases for human action – *action which to a great extent transforms the world* – help to *make* the truth which they declare. (James, 'Remarks on Spencer's definition of mind as correspondence', p. 18)

James's view that the organism is not only changed by the environment, but in its turn changes the environment is one that chimes with Darwin's own thinking. It is particularly apparent in his study of earthworms (Darwin, *The Formation of Vegetable Mould*).

Many species of earthworm burrow into the earth by consuming whatever is in their way. The nutritious part of what is consumed is digested and the remainder is excreted and becomes vegetable mould or topsoil. For Darwin, this process was particularly interesting because it showed how even a lowly creature such as the earthworm changes its environment. Topsoil is not something that just exists in the environment of its own accord, so to speak, but is something that is created by the activity of animals (see Costall 2004; Reed 1982). Over a long period of time, the topsoil could build up gradually so as to have a profound impact on the environment. The action of earthworms also plays an important role in breaking down larger pieces of stone and the skeletons of dead animals. In so doing, worms improve the quality of the soil for the subsequent growth of plants:

> Worms prepare the ground in an excellent manner for the growth of fibrous-rooted plants and for seedlings of all kinds ... They mingle the whole intimately together, like a gardener who prepares fine soil for his choicest plants. In this state it is well fitted to retain moisture and to absorb all soluble substances, as well as for the process of nitrification. (Darwin, *The Formation of Vegetable Mould*, pp. 309–10)

Another aspect of Darwin's study of earthworms was their use of leaves in lining and blocking their burrows. One of the reasons for doing this is to keep cold air out of the burrow. The worms, in enriching the soil, make the environment more hospitable for the plants whose leaves they need to line their burrows. There is a relationship of reciprocity between the worms and their environment. The worms do not merely adapt to their environment in a passive way, they also have a role in changing their environment. The animal and the environment are not two things that are separate from one another but are intimately related to one another in a web of mutual influences.

Darwin and consciousness

If the organism has an active role to play in altering its environment, then the question of consciousness arises – are animals merely machines, as Descartes maintained, or not? Darwin's study of earthworms provides insight into the extent to which animals can be said to have consciousness or intelligence. Darwin noted that the earthworms' adaptive behaviour of lining their burrows with leaves was not carried out in a purely mechanical fashion but exhibited a considerable degree of flexibility:

Worms are poorly provided with sense organs, for they cannot be said to see, although they can just distinguish between light and darkness; they are completely deaf, and have only a feeble power of smell; the sense of touch alone is well developed. They can therefore learn little about the outside world, and it is surprising that they should exhibit some skill in lining their burrows with their castings and with leaves, and in the case of some species in piling up their castings into tower-like constructions. But it is far more surprising that they should apparently exhibit some degree of intelligence instead of a mere blind instinctive impulse, in their manner of plugging up the mouths of their burrows. They act in nearly the same manner as would a man, who had to close a cylindrical tube with different kinds of leaves, petioles, triangles of paper, &c, for they commonly seize such objects by their pointed ends. But with thin objects a certain number are drawn in by their broader ends. They do not act in the same unvarying manner in all cases, as do most of the lower animals; for instance, they do not drag in leaves by their foot-stalks, unless the basal part of the blade is as narrow as the apex, or narrower than it. (Darwin, *The Formation of Vegetable Mould*, pp. 312–13)

Darwin supplemented his naturalistic observations with experiments, in which he cut leaf-like shapes of different forms from pieces of paper to see how the worms would cope with different shapes and also examined how they performed when presented with leaves of different shapes. Some leaves have their narrowest point at the tip, whereas others have their narrowest point at the base. Darwin found that the worms always tended to pull the leaf from the narrowest point into the burrow. This, of course, is the best way of getting the leaf into the burrow, as obviously the narrowest point will fit more easily into the mouth of the burrow than will the thicker portion. In other words, the worms did not simply pull the leaves by their tips in all cases or by their bases in all cases, but varied their behaviour so as to pull the leaf by the thinnest part regardless of whether it was the tip or the base. They exhibited behaviour, in other words, that was flexible and adapted to the demands of the task.

On the small number of occasions on which the worms dragged leaves by their thickest parts, this too was the best way of getting them into the burrow. Some species of pine, for example, have needles that come in pairs and are joined at the base. In this case the worms tended to pull the pair of needles by the base at which both were joined to one another rather than by the tip of one of them. This would be the most efficient method since, if one needle was dragged by the tip, the other alongside it could prevent progress by digging into the ground. Darwin also noted that, when using pine needles to line their burrows, the earthworms pressed the sharp tips of the needles into the surrounding cylindrical walls of the burrow, so that they would not be injured or inhibited when re-entering the burrow. Darwin marvelled at the 'skill' of the earthworms in constructing their burrows in this way, especially as the pine whose needles they used was not native to the area.

> If worms are able to judge, either before drawing or after having drawn an object close to the mouths of their burrows, how best to drag it in, they must acquire some notion of its general shape. This they probably acquire by touching it in many places with the anterior extremity of their bodies, which serves as a tactile organ. It may be well to remember how perfect the sense of touch becomes in a man when born blind and deaf, as are worms. If worms have the power of acquiring some notion, however rude, of the shape of an object and of their burrows, as seems to be the case, they deserve to be called intelligent; for they then act in nearly the same manner as would a man under similar circumstances. (Darwin, *The Formation of Vegetable Mould*, p. 97)

For Darwin, then, animal behaviour was not purely mechanical, but exhibited intelligence and flexibility. In this way, Darwin's evolutionary thought conflicted with the Cartesian view of nature. We saw in Chapter 4 that, for Descartes, animals were no more than complex machines. Although Descartes believed that animals could feel pain and other basic sensations, they were not capable of intelligent thought – that was the property of the rational mind, the non-material mind that only humans possessed. For, Darwin, however, the mind was part of the natural world, not something remote from it. It was something that was manifested in an organism's activity within its environment rather than something that existed solely in the interior of the organism, as the Cartesian–Lockean 'way of ideas' seemed to suggest (see Chapters 4 and 5). The mind was in the world, not merely in the organism.

The flexibility of action – its use of different means to reach the same end – was also the mark of the mental for James, who adopted "the principle that *no actions but such as are done for an end, and show a choice of means, can be called indubitable expressions of Mind*" (James, *Principles of Psychology*, vol. 1, p. 11). The same criterion was urged by Darwin's colleague, George Romanes (1848–94), who noted that "the distinctive element of mind is consciousness, the test of consciousness is the presence of choice, and the evidence of choice is the antecedent uncertainty of adjustive action between two or more alternatives" (Romanes, *Mental Evolution in Animals*, p. 18). This flexibility of behaviour is contrasted with mechanical, reflex behaviour: "when certain springs of action are touched by certain stimuli, the whole machine is thrown into appropriate action; there is no room for choice, there is no room for uncertainty; but, as surely as any of these inherited mechanisms is affected by the stimulus with reference to which it has been constructed to act, so surely will it act in precisely the same way as it always has acted" (Romanes, *Mental Evolution in Animals*, p. 18).

But is the animal intelligence manifested in flexible behaviour really an indication that animals are conscious in the way that humans are? Darwin himself struggled with this issue and had no clear answer as to when consciousness might be said to arise in nature. Some writers, such as the philosopher James Ferrier, suggested that, though animals may be capable of feeling basic sensations and thus have basic sensory consciousness, they did not have a sense of self in the way that humans did (Smith 2010). In other words, though animals might be said to be acting in a 'thoughtful' manner in the sense that their behaviour was not simply mechanical, they did not realise that they were acting in a thoughtful manner. Humans, on the other hand, not only act with intelligence, they *know* that they are acting with intelligence. They have a sort of 'reflective' consciousness in which they are aware of the nature of their own actions, rather than simply performing them. They are self-aware.

Darwin did not agree with such arguments. He asks "can we feel sure that an old dog with an excellent memory and some power of imagination, as shown by his dreams, never reflects on his past pleasures in the chase?", and points out that "this would be a form of self-consciousness" (Darwin, *Notebooks*, quoted by Smith 2010, p. 110). Darwin also cites several cases of animals that seemed to show evidence of feeling shame or guilt, again indicating an awareness of self: "Jenny [an orang-utan] will often do a thing she has been told not to do – when she thinks the keeper will not see her – but then she knows she has done wrong and will hide herself" (Darwin, *Notebooks*, quoted by Smith 2010, p. 116).

Romanes also believed that the continuity between species proposed by evolution carries with it the consequence that all aspects of mental life are not restricted to humans:

> I hold that if the doctrine of Organic Evolution is accepted, it carries with it, as a necessary corollary, the doctrine of Mental Evolution ... from wholly unintelligent animals to the most highly intelligent, we can trace one continuous gradation; so that if we already believe that all specific forms of animal life have had a derivative origin, we cannot refuse to believe that all the mental faculties which these various forms present must likewise have had a derivative origin. (Romanes, *Mental Evolution in Animals*, p. 8)

Animals, then, were not simply machines devoid of consciousness or thought. Mentality was a quality that was present throughout a large section of the natural world, though exactly how far was difficult to say. Nevertheless, the evolutionary approach constituted a break with earlier, mechanistic views of nature, and viewed nature as a self-developing organism rather than as a piece of intricate clockwork. The contemporary evolutionary theorist Richard Dawkins used the metaphor of the blind watchmaker to point up the way in which Darwinian evolutionary theory dispensed with the idea of a divine craftsman who created nature according to a predetermined plan. But Darwinian theory, in viewing the natural world in organic rather than mechanistic terms, not only did away with the watchmaker, it did away with the watch as well.

Conclusion

In the course of this chapter we have considered two important aspects of the evolutionary approach to psychology. Firstly, the evolutionary approach asserts that the mental is only understandable in terms of the organism's relationship with its environment. The Cartesian idea that the mind resides in the interior of the person and is somehow cut off from the world, a passive spectator, is completely rejected. Mind is part of nature.

Secondly, mind, as a part of nature, is to be found throughout the animal kingdom. There are, of course, gradations of mentality in different species just as there are gradations of bodily characteristics, but mentality of some kind is a property of much of the natural world. Nature, then, is not a machine. The Cartesian (and, indeed, Galilean) world-view separated the mental world from the physical world. The latter was purely mechanistic whereas the former operated according to the rules of rationality rather than the rules of physics. But the evolutionary view hinted at something different: an overcoming of the separation between mind and body and between organism and environment such that animals were no longer just seen as machines within the grand machine of nature. Thinking things were not machines at all, but nor were they disembodied minds. They were organisms that somehow fused the physical and the mental.

This organic, as opposed to mechanistic, approach to psychology was to feature greatly in the work of future psychologists, notably Dewey (see Chapter 15). But it is also to be found in the work of Skinner (see Chapter 16), and in contemporary proponents of 'embodied cognition' (see Chapter 18). Other psychologists, however, maintained, in different ways, important aspects of the Cartesian world-view: behaviourists, such as Watson (see Chapter 16), who viewed animal (and human) learning as something essentially mechanistic, and cognitive theorists, such as Fodor (see Chapter 17), who viewed the mind as something that could be understood in its own terms in isolation from the environment in which it was situated.

Revision questions

1. Why did Spencer believe that evolution was progressive?

2. How, according to Spencer, does an organism's mental world come to reflect the external world?

3. What is natural selection?

4. How did the Darwinian theory of evolution differ from earlier theories of evolution?

5. Why was William James critical of Spencer's view of evolution?

6. What conclusions did Darwin draw from his study of the behaviour of earthworms?

References

Costall, A. (2004). From Darwin to Watson (and cognitivism) and back again: the principle of animal–environment mutuality. *Behavior and Philosophy*, 32, 179–95.

Darwin, C. (1888). *The Formation of Vegetable Mould through the Action of Worms*. New York: Appleton.

James, W. (1878). Remarks on Spencer's definition of mind as correspondence. *Journal of Speculative Philosophy*, 12, 1–18.

James, W. (1890). *The Principles of Psychology*, vol. 1. New York: Henry Holt.

Leslie, J. C. (2006). Herbert Spencer's contribution to behavior analysis: a retrospective review of *Principles of Psychology*. *Journal of the Experimental Analysis of Behavior*, 86, 123–9.

Reed, E. S. (1982). Darwin's earthworms: a case study in evolutionary psychology. *Behaviorism*, 10, 165–85.

Romanes, G. J. (1883). *Mental Evolution in Animals*. London: Kegan Paul, Trench and Co.

Smith, C. U. M. (1982). Evolution and the problem of mind. Part I: Herbert Spencer. *Journal of the History of Biology*, 15, 55–88.

Smith, C. U. M. (1983). Herbert Spencer's epigenetic epistemology. *Studies in the History and Philosophy of Science*, 14, 1–22.

Smith, C. U. M. (2010). Darwin's unsolved problem: the place of consciousness in an evolutionary world. *Journal of the History of the Neurosciences: Basic and Clinical Perspectives*, 19, 105–20.

Spencer, H. (1872). *Principles of Psychology*, vol. 2, 2nd edn. London: Williams and Norgate.

Spencer, H. (1874). *First Principles of a New System of Philosophy*. New York: Appleton.

10 Freud and psychoanalysis

Timeline

1871	Wilhelm I becomes emperor of a united Germany
1882	Anti-Jewish pogroms in Russia
1897	First Zionist congress is organised by Theordor Hertzl
1905	Einstein's special theory of relativity
1915	Einstein's general theory of relativity
1922	Mussolini becomes Italian Prime Minister
1935	Anti-Jewish Nuremberg Laws come into effect in Germany
1938	Germany annexes Austria

Sigmund Freud

1856	Born in Freiberg, Moravia
1860	Family move to Vienna
1873	Studies medicine at the University of Vienna
1885	Works at the Salpêtrière Hospital in Paris
1899	Publishes *The Interpretation of Dreams*
1909	Lectures in America
1910	Founding of the International Psychoanalytic Association
1920	Publishes *Beyond the Pleasure Principle*
1938	Freud's apartment is searched by the Gestapo and his daughter, Anna, is held for questioning; the Freud family escape to London
1939	Dies in London

Introduction

We saw in Chapter 7 that Schopenhauer and Nietzsche questioned the Enlightenment idea that human beings are motivated by rational thought and argued instead that we are driven largely by unconscious urges. Schopenhauer and Nietzsche envisaged the unconscious as not only hidden from conscious inspection, but as *qualitatively different* from conscious thought: it operated according to its own bizarre logic and did not follow the path of reason. Conscious rationality was, far from being the most important influence on our actions, merely the tool of the unconscious drives and existed solely to serve their ends. These ideas, as we shall see in this chapter, were also at the root of Freud's view of the mind, but he attempted to give them a new, biological, interpretation that owed something to the psychophysical ideas of Helmholtz and Fechner.

The biological background

For Freud, the basic drive behind our behaviour is the drive to minimise stimulation within the nervous system. This, as we shall see, is the fundamental conception that underlies the whole Freudian view of the world. Our nervous system, as a result of stimulation, becomes excited and full of energy. Though the precise nature of this nervous energy was not clear to Freud, as a materialist he had no doubt that it was some form of physical energy. In this, Freud's position was completely in accord with the principles put forward by leading German physiologists of the day, such as Helmholtz (in whose laboratory Freud's own teacher, Brücke, had worked). As we saw in Chapter 8, Helmholtz and his colleagues argued that there was no such thing as a spiritual 'life force' that animated living things, but that everything, including the energy coursing through the nervous systems of people and animals, was purely physical.

Fechner too (see Chapter 8) thought of each living organism as full of psychophysical energy, but there was a more profound point of contact between Freud and Fechner than the general concept of nervous energy. Both had, in addition, similar ideas of what the organism does with this nervous energy. According to Fechner, the organism seeks to maintain a state of equilibrium at which it has neither too much nor too little psychophysical energy, either of which would lead,

Box 10.1 Sigmund Freud

Sigmund Freud was born in 1856 in the town of Freiberg in Moravia (then part of the Austro-Hungarian Empire, now part of the Czech Republic). His family moved to Vienna in 1860, and Freud was to live in the city until 1938, when he was forced to leave to escape the Nazis. Freud was the eldest of eight children and was his mother's favourite. The young Freud was a gifted pupil at school, showing a passion for literature, particularly the works of Goethe and Shakespeare, which he retained throughout his life. In 1873, Freud went to study in the medical faculty of the University of Vienna, and carried out research in the physiological laboratory of Ernest Brücke. Brücke was a friend and colleague of Helmholtz and shared with him a materialistic and anti-vitalist philosophy. This was a view that Freud, too, was to adhere to all his life.

After graduating in 1881, Freud worked in hospitals to gain the experience that would allow him to set up his own medical practice. Of particular importance for Freud's intellectual development were the months (October 1885 to February 1886) that he spent working in the Salpêtrière Hospital in Paris. Here Freud worked under the tutelage of Jean-Martin Charcot (1825–93), a neurologist particularly famous for his work on hysteria, the causing of an apparently physical illness by psychological means. This work made a deep impression on Freud, and on his return from Paris he set up his own medical practice in Vienna and started treating hysterical patients.

Freud's setting up of his own medical practice had more to do with financial necessity than vocation. Indeed, Freud would have been happy to remain a laboratory researcher, but he needed a greater income than a pure research career would provide in order to marry his fiancée, Martha Bernays. They married in 1886 and had six children, one of whom, Anna, went on to become a noted psychoanalyst in her own right.

Although psychoanalysis attracted a growing number of adherents, Freud was intolerant of criticism, and this led to heated disagreements with early followers of psychoanalysis, such as Carl Jung (1875–1961) and Alfred Adler (1870–1937), both of whom split from Freud in order to develop their own forms of depth psychology.

The Nazis had declared that psychoanalysis was a 'Jewish science' and Freud's works had been publicly burned. So, when Hitler annexed Austria in 1938, Freud had little choice but to leave the city where he had spent nearly all his life (Figure 10.1). Even then, it was only possible for Freud to get out because he was, by that time, an internationally well-known figure who had powerful and high-profile followers prepared to intervene on his behalf. Freud left Vienna for

Box 10.1 (cont.)

London, where his son Ernst had set up home. Freud, now in the advanced stages of mouth cancer – he had been an obsessive cigar smoker for most of his adulthood – and in almost continual pain, was warmly received in London and made a Fellow of the Royal Society of Medicine. He died in his son's home in Hampstead on 23 September 1939 at the age of 83.

Fig. 10.1 Sigmund Freud

ultimately, to death. Fechner believed that pleasure results when psychophysical energy is directed so as to bring the organism closer to a state of stability. Pain or displeasure is due to too much or too little energy in the system, or to incorrect distribution of that energy, leading to disequilibrium. All living things, according to Fechner, in seeking to maintain equilibrium, effectively seek to gain pleasure and to avoid pain (Ellenberger 1956).

Freud believed that his own view of our basic biological drives was essentially the same as Fechner's, and remarked that "Fechner has advocated a conception of pleasure and 'pain' which in essentials coincides with that forced upon us by psycho-analytic work" (*Beyond the Pleasure Principle*, p. 3). However, despite Freud's endorsement of Fechner's basic position, there was a crucial difference between their positions. Whereas for Fechner energetic *equilibrium* was the goal of the organism's self-regulation, for Freud the goal was the *minimisation* of energy within the nervous system. Of course, this is a sort of equilibrium – the energy within the system is kept close to zero – but Fechner's original conception is compatible with a high absolute quantity of energy within the system, as long as it is regulated in a way that ensures stability. Freud's concern, however, was not merely with stability, but with the overall amount of stimulation within the system.

Pain, then, according to Freud, is that which accompanies an increase in nervous or psychophysical energy whereas pleasure is what accompanies its diminution. The goal of the organism is to avoid increases in excitation, and the nervous system can be defined as "an apparatus which has the function of getting rid of the stimuli that reach it, or of reducing them to the lowest possible level; or which, were it feasible, would maintain itself in an altogether unstimu- lated condition" (*Instincts and their Vicissitudes*, p. 199).

This view – that the function of the nervous system is to discharge psycho- physical energy – is the cornerstone of Freud's psychology, and it stems from his original training in physiology. Indeed, Freud's original goal was to under- stand psychology in purely physiological terms, and he outlined a plan for doing so in a work that has become known as the *Project for a Scientific Psychology*. It is a work that Freud abandoned and which was not actually published until the 1950s, long after Freud's death. However, though Freud abandoned the attempt to reduce psychology to physiology, he nevertheless retained much of the intellectual and theoretical framework that he had erected in the *Project*, but translated its main ideas from the physiological to the psychological level.

The *Project for a Scientific Psychology*

We have seen above how Freud, following the likes of Helmholtz and Fechner, believed the nervous system to be activated by some sort of physiological energy. Though he did not know what this energy was, in the *Project* Freud called it '**Q**'. He also formulated an early version of the view that an organism tries to get rid of the energy within it. This he called "*the principle of neuronic inertia*, which asserts that neurones tend to divest themselves of quantity *(Q)*" (*Project*, p. 356).

The main source of excitation of the nervous system comes from the surrounding environment and an organism seeking to reduce such excitation can, for example, flee from the source of stimulation. Freud points out, however, that some nervous excitation is internal rather than external in origin. Basic biological needs, such as hunger and sex, are not merely responses to the organism's surroundings, but emerge from within the organism itself. There is no running away from this inner-generated, or 'endogenous', Q. In order to get rid of this stimulation, the organism has to find an object in the environment that will satisfy the particular need.

The fact that basic needs can only be relieved by certain environmental objects necessitates a change in how the organism deals with its psychophysical energy. If it is to be able to move through the environment so as find an object that will lead to satisfaction, an organism cannot simply discharge all its energy. If this were the case, it would no longer be able to move. The organism has to store some energy if it is to be mobile. The amount of energy stored should not be too great – this, as we have seen, will lead to pain and instability – but rather just enough to enable the organism to perform behaviours that will satisfy the **instinctual drives**. It is the storing of Q that, according to Freud, results in the development of a relatively stable psychological 'self' or **ego**. The ego is, at the most basic physiological level, a subset of neurons that are more or less permanently energised.

The development of this ego, this stable core of energy-filled neurons, is beneficial to the organism as it, paradoxically, facilitates the ultimate goal of the organism, the minimising of nervous excitation. Firstly, the ego is not merely a store of Q but it can, according to Freud, effectively control the way in which energy flows through the system. The natural inclination of any system is to discharge Q immediately. But such immediate discharge – into some sort of motor activity, say – will not always bring satisfaction because the required object may not be present. Indeed, in such cases, says Freud, the futile attempt to satisfy a need when the means for its satisfaction are not actually there will lead to an increase in unpleasure rather than its decrease. By storing Q, drawing Q to itself until it can be discharged in a way that will achieve satisfaction, the ego actually prevents the build-up of Q that is experienced as pain.

But there is another, even more pressing need for the development of the ego. If there was no energy stored in the organism, it would be unable to flee from sources of stimulation in the environment. It would be a completely passive entity wholly at the mercy of its surroundings and this would almost certainly lead to overwhelming pain and unpleasure.

Pain, however, is not only evoked by present stimulation, but by the activation of painful memories. In an anticipation of some of the ideas of contemporary neuroscience, as well as the 'connectionism' of Thorndike (see Chapter 16), Freud hypothesised that neurons become altered in such a way that, once Q has passed through one neuron to another, it becomes easier in the future for Q to travel down that same path. This, according to Freud, is how memory and learning occur: neural pathways are changed through experience so that the passage of stimulation down them is facilitated. Due to this neural facilitation caused by previous experience, objects or perceptions that originally gave rise to a painful experience will tend, by producing stimulation in now facilitated pathways, to give rise to painful experiences themselves. We have here a third reason for the development of the ego – it can avoid the reactivation of painful memories by directing attention away from the objects, thoughts, or perceptions that might evoke them. As we have seen, the flow of Q between two neurons can be made easier if Q has flowed between them in the past, but it is also the case, according to Freud, than Q is attracted to an already charged neuron. In other words, neurons that are already charged with Q will attract Q from other neurons towards them. The ego, as we have already seen, is nothing but a core of charged neurons. This means that the ego can effectively inhibit the transmission of Q down its normal pathways (i.e. the path of least resistance, which has been created due to previous transmission of Q) and attract Q towards itself. In this case, Q is no longer free-flowing, but becomes 'bound' to the ego.

In this physiological hypothesis about the movement of Q throughout the nervous system we find the roots of many of the concepts that Freud was later to transform into psychoanalysis. We have, first of all, one of the most important of all Freudian ideas, that of **repression**. The ego actively prevents the re-evocation of painful memories by directing one's mental energies away from them and towards other things. Freud admits in the *Project* that he cannot say how this process of repression has arisen, although he believes that he has identified the mechanism by which it is carried out.

A second major psychoanalytic idea that we find here is the distinction between what Freud was later to call the **pleasure principle** and the **reality principle**. The pleasure principle, which Freud sometimes calls the pleasure–unpleasure principle, is the idea, which we have already encountered, that the organism is essentially motivated to avoid pain, which here is identified with the build-up of Q in the nervous system. But, as has already been mentioned, the discharging of Q, and the resulting return to as low a state of stimulation as possible, is not always immediately feasible. An appropriate object is needed to satisfy the organism's needs, and it is here that the reality principle comes into play. When an organism is sexually aroused, it may conjure up sexual fantasies, or when hungry it may think of food. But these are unreal and will not satisfy the organism's needs. It has, therefore, to distinguish between the real presence of satisfying objects and mere fantasies of them. This conflict between desire and reality was to become the essential dynamic of psychoanalysis.

Thus, psychoanalytic concepts, such as repression, the pleasure principle, and the reality principle, have their grounding in Freud's attempt to understand psychology in terms of neurophysiology. As we have seen, the concept of the ego, too, is originally a physiological one, and refers to a group of neurons that are semi-permanently charged with nervous energy.

Box 10.2 **Freud and Jewishness**

Though he was an avowed atheist, Freud nevertheless felt that his identity was strongly Jewish. In his autobiography, Freud stated: "My parents were Jews, and I have remained a Jew myself." Freud was a lifelong member of the B'nai B'rith, a Jewish social and charitable organisation, and he not only socialised there, but also gave the first public presentation of his theory of dream interpretation at the organisation's Vienna branch. He did not accept royalties on the Hebrew or Yiddish translations of his works. In a country where many Jews had converted to Christianity so as to assimilate more fully with the majority population, such declarations and actions amounted to a strong statement of identity.

In many parts of Europe, Jews had been subject to institutionalised anti-Semitism for centuries – they were not, for example, allowed to enter certain professions, and there were restrictions on their movements and where they could live. But the late nineteenth century was a period of increasing liberalism towards the Jews in Vienna, and, in 1867, Jews were officially granted full political rights.

Box 10.2 (cont.)

There was, nevertheless, an undercurrent of anti-Semitism in many aspects of Viennese life that manifested itself in periodic backlashes against the Jewish population. This included the election of an outspoken anti-Semite, Karl Lueger, as mayor of Vienna in 1897.

Freud himself experienced anti-Semitism as a student at the University of Vienna, where gentile students expected Freud to feel inferior to them. But instead of acquiescing in this role as inferior, Freud all the more resolutely clung to his Jewish identity. It seems that his status as something of an outsider, because of his Jewishness, was something that Freud was willing to accept. Freud believed that his marginal status contributed to his independence of thought.

The problems with the *Project*

We have, in the previous section, outlined the major aspects of Freud's attempt to ground his psychology in the neurophysiology of his day. But why did Freud abandon the *Project* and move to a purely psychological theory? One reason was the inability of his physiological hypothesis to explain conscious experience. Although Freud believed that most of what goes on in the nervous system is unconscious, there were some neurons – Freud called them 'perceptual neurons' – whose energising and discharge gave rise to conscious, qualitative experience. But Freud was at a loss to say *why* this was the case: "No attempt can be made . . . to explain how it is that excitatory processes in the perceptual neurones . . . involve consciousness" (*Project*, p. 372).

A second reason for the abandonment of the physiological project, and one that Freud himself felt much more keenly than the problem of conscious experience, was the difficulty in accounting for repression (and other psychological **defence mechanisms**) in a mechanistic way. The problem (as noted by Sirkin and Flemming 1982) is that Freud's mechanistic account of repression was based on the idea that the ego, a stable core of activated neurons, redirected Q by drawing nervous energy towards itself, so that the Q did not activate painful memories. But this is a *goal-directed* activity, and this is difficult to square with a purely mechanistic theory.

The problem faced by Freud becomes clear if we think of ego's effect on Q as analogous to the effect of a planet's gravitational field on objects. A planet's gravitational field draws objects towards it indiscriminately; it does not differentiate between one object and another. If, then, the operation of the ego was a purely mechanistic affair, it would distort the passage of Q in the same way in all instances; it would simply draw the passing Q to itself in the same way that a planet draws an object to itself. In this case *all* memories would be repressed, not just painful ones. But Freud wants to say that the ego inhibits the passage of Q not in an automatic or unthinking way, but in a purposive and goal-directed way. The ego, in other words, seems to act not just as a mechanism, but as an *agent* with a particular purpose. It is the directed nature of repression (and other defence mechanisms) that Freud was unable accommodate within his mechanistic neural model.

From the *Project* to psychoanalysis

Instinct and libido

How, then, were the physiological ideas of the *Project* transformed into the psychological concepts of psychoanalysis? What was described as endogenous Q in the *Project* became, in psychonanalysis, transformed into the concept of instinct. Like endogenous Q, "an instinctual stimulus does not arise from the external world but from within the organism itself" (*Instincts and their Vicissitudes*, p. 198), specifically from processes occurring within bodily organs. Instincts, like endogenous Q, require external objects to satisfy them. Of particular interest to the psychoanalyst are the sexual instincts. The energy that lies behind sexual instincts is called **libido** and the goal of sexual behaviour is the discharge of libido, just as, in the *Project*, the organism tried to divest itself of Q. The discharge of libido produces "organ pleasure" (*Instincts and their Vicissitudes*, p. 204). As discussed below, Freud believed that libido is not only associated with the sexual organs, but with other bodily structures, such as the mouth and the anus.

The ego and the id

The source of all our instinctual energy is originally unconscious. This aspect of the psyche Freud called the **id** (German for 'it'), and its activity, like that of most of the neurons as conceived in the *Project*, is concerned with immediately discharging energy so that a state of quiescence can be achieved. It operates according to the pleasure principle. The conscious ego develops out of this id in order to mediate between the insatiable demands of the id and what is actually possible. It operates according to the reality principle. The psychoanalytic ego is a transformation onto the psychological plane of the neural ego of the *Project*. This permanently charged group of neurons, as we saw, also operated according to the reality principle by inhibiting the immediate discharge of Q until a suitable object had been found for the satisfaction of the organism's needs. "The ego," said Freud, "represents what may be called reason and common sense, in contrast to the id, which contains the passions" (*The Ego and the Id*, pp. 249–50).

Sexuality and neuroticism

Despite the change from neurophysiology to psychology, the main features of Freud's approach remain relatively constant throughout – the conflict between instinctual demands and the demands of reality and the concomitant repression or control of instinctual energy to prevent its immediate and direct expression. How, then, does this framework give rise to the types of neuroticism with which psychoanalysis is primarily concerned, in particular the so-called **Oedipus complex?**

Box 10.3 **Freud and sex**

Freud sometimes encouraged the view that the Viennese medical establishment was too conservative to acknowledge the importance of sexuality, and that their outraged respectability hindered the acceptance of psychoanalysis. Such a picture, however, is rather misleading. In fact sexuality, far from being a topic ignored or brushed under the carpet by the medical and scientific establishment, was one of the most debated topics of the time in Austria and Germany. In 1886, Richard von Krafft-Ebing (1840–1902), professor of psychiatry at Graz and later at Vienna itself, published his *Psychopathia Sexualis*, in which he sought to classify the different types of sexual activity and coined the terms 'sadism' and 'masochism'.

Albert Moll (1862–1939), a Berlin neurologist, published one of the first scientific investigations of homosexuality (*Contrary Sexual Feeling*) in 1891 and, as well as

Box 10.3 (cont.)

overseeing new editions of Krafft-Ebing's *Psychopathia Sexualis* after the latter's death, published a work (*The Sexual Life of the Child*) on the sexuality of children in 1908, only a few years after Freud's own work (*Three Essays on the Theory of Sexuality*, 1905) dealing with the same subject.

The ideas of Krafft-Ebing and Moll removed the topic of sexuality from the realm of morality to the realm of medicine and treated sexual urges not as sudden deviant eruptions, but as manifestations of relatively permanent drives. They argued that the suppression of these drives could give rise to mental illness while also recognising that unconstrained abandonment to them was not compatible with a civilised society.

In addition to this scientific interest in sexuality, there were, in the German-speaking world, political movements advocating feminism (Helene Stöcker, 1869–1943) and the acceptance of homosexuality (Magnus Hirshfeld, 1868–1935), as well as pessimistic cultural critiques denouncing the increasing feminisation of men in modern society (e.g. *Sex and Character*, 1903, by Otto Weininger). Far from being unique, the interest in sexuality that characterised psychoanalysis was very much in tune with the preoccupations of the society in which it was invented.

In the environment in which Freud worked, just as in today's society, it seemed natural to associate childhood with innocence. Freud, however, argued that children are sexual beings, that they have sexual desires. Our mistake, according to Freud, is to equate 'sexuality' with 'adult sexuality', with its association of genital sexual intercourse. This is not the sort of sexuality that Freud attributes to children. Rather, for Freud, the genitals are only one focus of sexuality, a focus that becomes predominant only as the child gets older. Sexual pleasure is derived from various erotogenic zones of the body. An erotogenic zone is "a part of the skin or mucous-membrane in which stimuli of a certain sort evoke a feeling of pleasure possessing a particular quality" (*Three Essays on the Theory of Sexuality*, p. 323). Of course, the genitals are a focus of sexual pleasure for the child as is evidenced by the high incidence of masturbation among infants. It is nevertheless important to keep in mind that this is not sexual in the sense of a substitute for sexual intercourse with another person or as the accompaniment to some erotic fantasy. It is purely a matter of pleasurable sensations caused by stimulation of particular parts of the body.

One erotogenic zone that captures the attention of the young child is the mouth. The instinct for self-preservation requires that the child feed at the mother's breast, but it so happens that feeding does not merely give the child nourishment, but sexual pleasure too: "The child's lips . . . behave like an erotogenic zone, and no doubt stimulation by the warm flow of milk is the cause of the pleasurable sensation" (*Three Essays on the Theory of Sexuality*, p. 322). This pleasure, originally tied to feeding, becomes independent and something that the child seeks for in its own right. One of the most common ways in which this is done is the child's sucking of its own thumb.

The anus is another erotogenic zone, and it comes to be a major focus for the child as it begins to learn to control its bowels:

> Children who are making use of the susceptibility to erotogenic stimulation of the anal zone betray themselves by holding back their stool till its accumulation brings about violent muscular contractions and, as it passes through the anus, is able to produce powerful stimulation of the mucous membrane. In so doing it must no doubt cause not only painful but also highly pleasurable sensations. (*Three Essays on the Theory of Sexuality*, p. 326)

In the normal course of development, the genitals will become, after puberty, the predominant erotogenic zone of the adult. In some cases, however, the person will remain fixated on one of the other erotogenic zones, and this will be manifested in adult behaviour. A child that has received too much pleasure or been overindulged in the course of feeding may remain fixated on the mouth and lips as a source of pleasure and this may be manifested in excessive smoking, drinking, or eating in adulthood. An overemphasis on the control of one's bowels in order to receive anal pleasure may be manifested in adulthood in a neurotic attempt to retain obsessive control over all aspects of one's life and relationships.

The Oedipus complex

We have seen in the above section how sexual experiences at an early age, if the bodily areas associated with them remain the predominant focus for sexual and sensual pleasure, may be manifested in neurotic adult behaviour. But, for Freud, the neurotic is only at one extreme of a psychological spectrum rather than being qualitatively different from the normal adult. We are all, thought

Freud, influenced by the sexual experiences, i.e. experiences of bodily pleasure, that we encounter in childhood.

At the centre of these experiences are the child's parents: it is they who feed, comfort, and discipline the child, and are the sources of both pleasure and punishment. For Freud, the roots of all neuroticism lie in the child's relationship with its parents. Freud claimed, on the basis of dream analysis, as well his wider clinical experience, that young boys will direct sexual impulses towards their mothers and young girls towards their fathers. To the boy, his father becomes a competitor for the mother's affections just as the mother is seen as a competitor for the father's affections by the girl. The child will fantasise about the disappearance or death of the competitor parent. Over time, children will eventually realise that they cannot compete with the competitor parent and will identify with them. They will become role models rather than competitors. Freud believed that it is through this coming to maturity and identifying with, rather than competing with, the same-sex parent that the young adult will be able to form a sexual relationship with an adult other than the originally desired opposite-sex parent.

Nevertheless, these incestuous and murderous desires, if not fully resolved, can remain lurking in the unconscious. They cannot, of course, be consciously acknowledged by the neurotic adult. It is simply not acceptable to admit to oneself a sexual attraction to one parent and a death wish towards the other parent. These desires are, therefore, repressed and can only manifest themselves in disguised and distorted ways in adult life. They may be present in dreams, in which the unconscious and unresolved sexual desires of childhood are played out in symbolic form, or they may reveal themselves in everyday behaviour. One woman reported by Freud (*The Interpretation of Dreams*, p. 220), for example, experienced great anxiety about leaving her mother alone in the house and would rush home as quickly as possible from any engagement that obliged her to leave the house. This exaggerated and neurotic concern for her mother stemmed, says Freud, from her childhood wish that her mother would die and thus cease to be a competitor for the affections of the father. This wish had never been fully resolved and so remained within the young woman's unconscious. She could not, of course, acknowledge this desire consciously, but the feeling of guilt that it generated was manifested in neurotic overprotectiveness of the mother.

Freud believed that these feelings of sexual desire and rivalry directed at one's parents were a universal part of human nature, and that they had been recognised, albeit in a non-scientific way, prior to the invention of psychoanalysis by the ancient Greek playwright Sophocles (Figure 10.2), in his play *Oedipus Rex* (or *Oedipus the King* in some translations).

Fig. 10.2 Sophocles

The story of Oedipus, as recounted by Sophocles, is as follows. Laius, king of Thebes, and his queen, Jocasta, have a son, Oedipus. An oracle warns Laius that he is destined to be killed by his son and so Oedipus is left by his parents to die on a mountainside. The infant Oedipus is, however, rescued by shepherds and is brought up as a prince in the city of Corinth. As a young man Oedipus hears the same prophecy from the oracle that his father heard: that he, Oedipus, is destined to kill his own father and marry his mother. Believing that his father and mother are the king and queen of Corinth, Oedipus leaves the city for Thebes thinking that in removing himself from his father and mother he will avoid fulfilling the prophecy. On the way to Thebes, however, he gets into a fight with a man at a crossroads over who should have right of way. This results in Oedipus killing the man who, unbeknownst to him, is his real father, Laius. On his arrival at Thebes, Oedipus himself becomes the king and marries the widowed queen, his mother, Jocasta. Again, Oedipus has no idea that Jocasta is his mother just as Jocasta has no idea that Oedipus is her son, believing him to have died on a mountainside when an infant. It is only later, when the gods send a plague to punish Thebes for harbouring within it the murderer of Laius, that Oedipus slowly realises that he himself is the murderer and that, moreover, Laius was his father and Jocasta is his mother. Gripped by remorse, Oedipus blinds himself and leaves Thebes forever.

With the murder of a father by his son, who subsequently married his mother, it is clear why Freud's theory of the sexual attraction of a boy to his mother with accompanying hostility to the father was to be labelled the Oedipus complex. But it is not merely a superficial resemblance between the Oedipus legend and our own parent–child relations that impressed Freud. On the contrary, Freud believed that Sophocles had shown remarkable psychological insight – an insight that would only be recovered by psychoanalysis centuries later – into a universal aspect of human nature. It is because of this insight, and because the playwright touches something deep within all of us, says Freud, that the tragedy of Oedipus has such enduring power:

> His fate moves us only for the reason that it might have been ours, for the oracle has put the same curse upon us before our birth as upon him. Perhaps we are all destined to direct our first sexual impulses towards our mothers, and our first hatred and violent wishes towards our fathers; our dreams convince us of it. King Oedipus, who has struck his father Laius dead and has married his mother Jocasta, is nothing but the realised wish of our childhood. (*The Interpretation of Dreams*, p. 223)

But there is, thinks Freud, something deeper and more general that Sophocles has to teach us than the vicissitudes of relationships between parents and children, and the aggression and sexual tension with which they are fraught. It is that we cannot escape our fate. The oracle has informed Laius that he will be killed by his son and Oedipus that he will kill his father. Both men do what they can to defy their fate, but they cannot escape their destiny: the prophecy is ultimately fulfilled. This is the heart not only of the tragedy of Oedipus, but of all tragedy. Its essence is to be found in the futile struggle of human beings to escape the fate which the gods have decreed for them. But the struggle will never succeed, fate will always triumph, and, Freud concludes, "resignation to the will of God and confession of one's own helplessness is the lesson which the deeply-moved spectator is to learn from the tragedy" (*The Interpretation of Dreams*, p. 222).

Box 10.4 **Freud and the Ancients**

Freud's interest in the ancient Greeks is attested to by his naming the Oedipus complex after the Greek mythological figure, but Freud's fascination with the ancients was much deeper than simply borrowing a bit of terminology from Sophocles. In some of his works, Freud refers to the libido as *Eros*, the Greek god of love. For some Greek thinkers, such as Plato, Eros was not merely concerned with sex, but was interpreted in a more metaphysical sense as a force or power that held things together. Freud was himself to give this deeper metaphysical significance to the libido when he remarked that "the libido of our sexual instincts would coincide with the Eros of the poets and philosophers which holds all living things together" (cited by Tourney 1965, p. 81). The sexual union of two human beings was just one manifestation of this wider natural force. Opposing this life force was Freud's death instinct, which is sometimes referred to, though never by Freud himself, as Thanatos (the Greek god of death). This is the force that creates disunion, that destroys and breaks things up.

That nature is ruled by two such opposing principles or forces – one creative, life-giving, and unifying; the other destructive, death-inducing, and divisive – is an idea that has its roots in the thought of the ancient Greek philosopher Empedocles (c. 495–435 BC). He held that the universe was governed by Love and Strife, and Freud himself recognised that "The two fundamental principles of Empedocles – Love and Strife – are, both in name and in function, the same as our two primal instincts, *Eros* and *Destructiveness*, the former of which strives to combine existing phenomena into ever greater unities, while the latter seeks to dissolve these combinations and destroy the structures to which they have given rise" (cited by Tourney 1965, pp. 84–5).

Box 10.4 (cont.)

Freud, of course, did not believe in the existence of Eros or Thanatos as actually existing gods, but he did believe that ancient myths, although not literally true, contained kernels of truth. In particular, he believed that, because these myths were the inventions of human beings, they constituted projections of the human psyche onto external reality. In ancient Greek myth, for example, Zeus becomes king of the gods by castrating his own father, Kronos, after Kronos has murdered all of his other children, apart from Zeus, who succeeded in hiding from his vengeful father. For Freud this symbolised the rebellion of the son against the father, the son's fear of castration by the father, and the son's ultimate victory by doing to the father what he feared the father was going to do to him.

Freud's fascination with ancient civilisations was not only manifested in the psychological concepts that he developed, but also in his keen interest in archaeology. The late nineteenth and early twentieth centuries saw a wealth of archaeological discoveries, including excavations at Troy and Knossos, and Freud took a keen interest in the most recent finds. He also collected antiquities, mainly statuettes of Greek, Roman, and Egyptian gods, and his consulting room in Vienna became crammed with these ancient artefacts. Freud liked to compare the work of the psychoanalyst with that of the archaeologist: both excavated beneath the visible surface to find remnants of the past that lay buried under more recent layers of material.

It is this fatalistic view of the human condition that resonates deeply with Freud. He, like Sophocles, believes that we cannot escape our destiny. Freud, of course, does not believe in the existence of gods on Mount Olympus who decide our fate, but instead nature itself is the source of our inevitable path through life. We are part of nature, we have instincts and desires within us that are provided by nature, and, try as we may, we cannot escape these impulses that are the motivating forces behind our thoughts and actions. To think that we can escape them is to believe that, somehow, we are above nature, that we can defy the natural order of things. But such hubristic attempts to oppose what must be are bound to fail just as surely as the attempts of Oedipus and Laius to avoid their fates. Freud's view of the human condition, then, is essentially a tragic one.

Schopenhauer and Spinoza

Freud's philosophical outlook, then, is one of intense pessimism: human beings are essentially weak creatures condemned to a fate from which they can never escape. There are, in this bleak world-view, deep affinities between Freud and Schopenhauer (Gupta 1975; Young and Brook 1994). We have already seen in Chapter 7 how Schopenhauer prefigured many of the ideas of psychoanalysis, such as the importance of the unconscious, the pre-eminence of the irrational in driving our thought and action (Schopenhauer's concept of the Will), and the repression of these irrational urges. But all of these similarities stem from the same basic pessimistic understanding of the universe and of the place of human beings within it.

Another thinker with whom Freud has a marked affinity is Spinoza (Bernard 1946; Brecher 1933). We have already seen in Chapter 8 that the panpsychism of Spinoza formed the philosophical underpinning of Fechner's psychophysics, and we have already seen in this chapter how the underlying concept of psycho-physical energy, along with the organism's striving to maintain this energy in some sort of stable equilibrium, was the cornerstone not only of Freud's early physiological *Project* but of his mature psychoanalysis as well. This energy, being entirely natural, is as subject to the causal laws of nature as anything else. Thus, Freud believed that our psychological life is determined rather than free, and this is another aspect of his thought that he shared with Spinoza. I will now explore these two themes – **determinism** and **pessimism** – in a little more detail.

Determinism

Everything that we do, think, or say, argues Freud, is determined rather than freely chosen: "there is nothing arbitrary or undetermined in the psychic life" (*The Psychopathology of Everyday Life*, p. 282). Freud admits that we undoubtedly have the strong impression of deciding the course of our own actions in a completely free way, but perhaps, he says, this impression of free will is not quite as widespread as we might think. Take any really important decision that we have to make in our lives – whether to move house, to take up a job offer, to become involved in a relationship. If we are honest in reflecting upon these types of decision, they are the very opposite of freely chosen in some completely arbitrary and unrestricted way. We may weigh up the reasons for and against alternative courses of action, but we are not then free to choose arbitrarily. Rather, the understanding of the pros and cons forces us to take one particular course of action rather than another. Having weighed up the reasons for and against, one *must* act in a certain way. One's choice is determined rather than free.

If real free will, voluntarily and arbitrarily chosen courses of action, exists at all, says Freud, it will only be in connection with our most "trivial and indifferent decisions". Only with respect to what does not really matter do we ever feel that we could have acted in another way, that there was nothing directing us to a particular course of action. Even in these trivial cases, however, the feeling that one could have acted differently is no guarantee that this is indeed the case. We may be unaware of any conscious motives forcing us to act in a particular way, but, says Freud, this only shows the limits of conscious motivation. It is unconscious motivation that is primarily determines our behaviour.

Spinoza once remarked that a stone thrown through the air would, if it were conscious, believe itself to be moving of its own accord. For Spinoza, and for Freud, human beings are in a comparable situation: we may feel ourselves to be free, but this tells us nothing about the true state of affairs. In reality, all our thoughts and actions are determined.

The causally determined nature of our psychological life was an important principle for Freud because, if our behaviours and thoughts were the result of purely free choice or of chance, then there would be no possibility of understanding them. It is only because they obey causal laws that they have any rhyme or reason. Completely free choice, unconstrained by any desire or impulse, would not constitute liberation from mechanism but condemnation to randomness and meaninglessness.

From a practical point of view, too, it was important for Freud to believe that thoughts and actions are determined rather than chance. Many of Freud's therapeutic tools, such as free association or the interpretation of dream symbolism, depend on the assumption that nothing in our psychological life is accidental. By asking the patient to free-associate – to say whatever comes into his or her head – the analyst, Freud believed, is provided with a rich and meaningful source of data that will, it is hoped, shed some light on the patient's problems, rather than a procession of haphazard thoughts. Similarly with the interpretation of dreams: the dream content is not just random; it is there for a reason. Thus, by interpreting this content, the analyst can try to get at the underlying reasons for its being there in the patient's dream consciousness. The therapeutic techniques, as well as the philosophical underpinnings, of psychoanalysis are predicated on psychological determinism.

Pessimism

One corollary of this deterministic view is an intense pessimism concerning humanity and its place in the universe. We are part of the natural world and we are filled with instinctual libidinous energy, which we are compelled to release in whichever way we can. We are not in control of what we do, regardless of how we feel, but are determined in every part of our psychological life by unconscious instinctual desires and drives. We are not the masters of our own destinies, but are condemned to the fate laid down for us by nature.

But there are other aspects to Freud's pessimism. We have already seen that he, following Fechner, viewed the essential goal of any organism as the reduction of stimulation – and stimulation, of any sort, is synonymous with pain and discomfort. Everything that we do – from our most basic sexual desires to the most exalted artistic and scientific endeavours – is ultimately about ridding ourselves of pain. This is a view of life that is entirely negative; even pleasure is not a positive thing in its own right, but is merely the discharging of irritating energy within the organism. The ultimate goal of all our actions is the achievement of a state of quiescence in which we are at last free of any external stimulation or inner drive, a goal that we can never quite achieve because we are constantly being disturbed and threatened by hostile external forces or internally generated impulses. This is a vision that bears comparison with Schopenhauer's bleakly pessimistic depiction of the incessant struggle of life and its endless suffering. Suffering, and the attempt – necessarily futile – to avoid it, is at the root of Freud's world-view as well.

This grim view of existence reaches its apotheosis in Freud's theory of the death instinct. As we have seen in the preceding sections of this chapter, Freud proposed that our thoughts and actions were driven by sexual instincts or the libido, sometimes referred to as 'Eros', as well as instincts for self-preservation. Freud, however, later came to the view that this earlier categorisation of the instincts could not account for all the facts of human activity. He augmented his theory of the instincts with what he called the **death instinct** (this is sometimes referred to as 'Thanatos', the Greek god of death, to contrast with 'Eros', the Greek god of love). This was a controversial step, and not all of Freud's previous adherents followed him in making it. Indeed, Freud himself admitted that his ideas on the death drive were "speculation" and "often far-fetched". Rather than a firm theory, Freud presents the formulation of the death instinct as "the exploitation of an idea out of curiosity to see whither it will lead" (*Beyond the Pleasure Principle*, p. 26). We can thus understand it as an extension of many of the central themes of psychoanalysis, which Freud had earlier developed.

We have already seen that, according to Freud, the goal of all organic action is the discharge of energy so as to return to a state of quiescence. But Freud now takes this way of thinking to its logical extreme. What is the ultimate state of quiescence, when an organism is no longer subject to the pain and discomfort of the external world, when it finally achieves peace? It is, of course, death. All life originally evolved from a lifeless and inert state, and it is to this state that all life ultimately strives to return. Freud puts it thus:

> This final goal of all organic striving ... must rather be an ancient starting point, which the living being left long ago, and to which it harks back again by all the circuitous paths of development. If we may assume as an experience admitting of no exception that everything living dies from causes within itself, and returns to the inorganic, we can only say "*The goal of all life is death*". (*Beyond the Pleasure Principle*, p. 47)

But this return to the inanimate state is not to be achieved in any old way, but by the internally determined route that is characteristic of the organism in question. "The instincts of self-preservation," says Freud, "are part-instincts designed to secure the path to death peculiar to the organism ... the organism is resolved to die only in its own way ... Hence the paradox comes about that the living organism resists with all its energy influences (dangers) which could help it to reach its life-goal by a short way (a short circuit, so to speak)" (*Beyond the Pleasure Principle*, p. 47).

We see in this quotation not only an expression of Freud's pessimism – the idea that the goal of life is death – but of his determinism and fatalism: death must be arrived at in a particular way, the organism must fulfil its natural destiny just as Oedipus and Laius had to fulfil their destinies.

Psychoanalysis as therapy

As well as a theoretical explanation of human thought and behaviour, psycho-analysis is a form of therapy in which patients are treated for their problems. At first sight, the therapeutic use of psychoanalysis seems difficult to square with Freud's deterministic, pessimistic, and tragic view of human nature. After all, if we are condemned to fulfil our fate, if there is no escaping our biological destiny, and if all our thoughts and actions are determined anyway, there seems little scope for overcoming one's problems. It would seem to follow from Freud's wider philosophical views that there is nothing we can do about our problems, since they are inevitable parts of our destiny. In view of Freud's general philosophy, of what sort of benefit could therapy possibly be?

We have seen that Freud concurred with the message of *Oedipus Rex*: we cannot escape our destiny, and "resignation" and "confession of one's own helplessness" seem to be the only options. But we are not completely at the mercy of our passions: from the irrational id, we have developed the rational ego to allow us to cope with the demands of reality. And it is in this island of reason and common sense that a small amount of comfort might be found. "Psycho-analysis," said Freud, "is an instrument to enable the ego to achieve a progressive conquest of the id" (*The Ego and the Id*, p. 476). Its aim is to bring to consciousness what was previously unconscious so that "[w]here id was, there ego shall be" (*Dissection of the Personality*, p. 504). Thus, though Freud laid great emphasis on the role of the unconscious in our lives and the relatively small part played by consciousness, the only hope of the neurotic is to enlarge the territory of consciousness. It is important, therefore, to realise that Freud did not celebrate the unconscious and its sexual impulses, as some of his readers, erroneously, have thought. Freud was a rationalist who nevertheless accepted that human beings were not, by and large, rational creatures, and who wanted to make them more rational.

The impulses that lurk within the unconscious are severed from what is actually possible and reasonable: they are "exempt from mutual contradiction" (*The Unconscious*, p. 159), so that it is possible to have several impulses all of which are mutually incompatible with one another; they are "*timeless*; they have no reference to time at all" (*The Unconscious*, p. 160); and they "pay just as little regard to *reality*" as they do to time (*The Unconscious*, p. 160). Given their incoherent and confused character, there is no doubt that someone at the mercy of these impulses would find it difficult to cope with life. And it is to allow the psychoanalytic patient to cope with life – to be capable of both "enjoyment and work" (*A General Introduction to Psychoanalysis*, p. 393) – that is the goal of psychoanalysis. Thus, in practical terms, the therapeutic aim of psychoanalysis as Freud saw it is a modest one – it is not to produce a miracle cure, to promise personal fulfilment or happiness, or to completely remove conflict and unhappiness. It is merely to remove the obstacles that prevent someone from living a normal, humdrum, everyday existence. It is to replace abnormal unhappiness with normal unhappiness. This is, as Freud notes (*A General Introduction to Psychoanalysis*, p. 396), merely a quantitative change in the patient's level of psychological health rather than a qualitative one.

This transition to a state of comparative health is what is achieved by the ego taking over control of energies that were once completely under the control of the id:

> The decisive change for the better ... is accomplished by the change in the ego under the influence of the physician's suggestion. In the course of the work of interpretation, which translates unconscious into conscious, the ego grows at the expense of the unconscious; it learns forgiveness toward the libido, and becomes inclined to permit some sort of satisfaction for it. (*A General Introduction to Psychoanalysis*, p. 394)

This modest therapeutic goal, which recognises that we cannot transcend our irrational nature completely, but that we might lessen its hold on us through understanding it, is one that Freud shares with Spinoza. Bernard (1946, p. 107) points to the "astonishing agreement of both thinkers on what might be called the question of *therapy*". Spinoza states, in the *Ethics*, that "The more an emotion is known to us the more it is within our power and the less the mind is passive to it." Spinoza later reiterates the same point, saying that the "remedy for emotions ... consists in a true knowledge of them ..." (cited by Bernard 1946, p. 107). For Spinoza "an emotion or passion of the mind *is a confused idea*" (cited by Brecher 1933, p. 390) and "The impotence of man to govern or restrain the emotions I call 'bondage', for a man who is under their control is not his own master" (Spinoza, *Ethics*, Bk IV, Preface). It is the goal of Spinoza's philosophy to release the mind from 'bondage' to the emotions and their confusion so that the person may live his or her life according to the dictates of reason. For Spinoza, according to Brann (1972a), "[r]eason and its underlying insight may help man to overcome the onslaught of his own emotions" (p. 194), and "[r]eason is a knowledge of the rules of the game of nature" (p. 194).

Reason, then, for Spinoza, first and foremost allows us to understand the true wellsprings of our emotions and impulses. We realise that our motivations do not spring from a free choice or a whim on our part but are as thoroughly determined as anything else in the natural world. This is what is meant by understanding the 'rules of the game of nature'. Such understanding leads to a kind of acceptance. According to Spinoza, "In so far as the mind understands all things as necessary, so far has it greater power over the emotions, or suffers less from them" (*Ethics*, Bk V, Prop. VI). When we understand our emotions as necessary parts of our natural being we are less troubled by them, we do not reproach ourselves as much, but, as Freud said in an earlier quote, we are inclined to 'forgive' the libido.

Schopenhauer, too, sees the unhappiness of the human predicament as stemming from emotions and desires that cannot be satisfied. As we saw in Chapter 7,

---

Box 10.5 **Freud and the arts**

Freud believed that the wellsprings of creative art lie deep within the subconscious and that works of art were sublimations of instinctual urges that had been channelled towards creative and aesthetic ends. He famously tried to interpret artworks by Leonardo da Vinci and Michelangelo from a psychoanalytic point of view. But not only was Freud interested in the arts, artists were deeply interested in Freud and psychoanalysis. The techniques used in psychoanalysis, such as free association and the interpretation of dreams, were supposed to provide an insight into the unconscious psychological forces behind the neurotic's thought and action. Many creative artists thought that, by appropriating these techniques themselves, they could get closer to the unconscious forces that were manifested in their own artistic production.

No artistic movement showed more interest in psychoanalysis than Surrealism. André Breton, one of the founders of the Surrealist movement, worked as an aide in a psychiatric ward during World War I, and was introduced by one of the doctors to the works of Freud. Breton became fascinated with the idea of using free association to produce a steady stream of verbal material without the intrusion of the conscious mind, and believed that it provided a way in which literature could get at the deep unconscious urges that had been repressed by respectable society. Indeed, Breton advocated that this automatic, uninhibited approach to composition should be followed in all the arts.

Breton travelled to Vienna to meet Freud in 1921, but the two men seemed to misunderstand one another and the meeting was a disappointment. Breton found Freud unresponsive and eager to get back to seeing his patients; Freud, for his part, found little connection between the French poet's artistic schemes and psychoanalysis. This mutual incomprehension is perhaps not difficult to understand. The surrealists saw themselves as a revolutionary movement in which art, through giving vent to the unconscious urges that were repressed by conventional, bourgeois society, could lead the way to a new and freer society. The last thing that Freud wanted, however, was to give free rein to unconscious impulses: the whole point of psychoanalysis was to understand and gain a measure of control over them.

Schopenhauer locates the source of these emotions in the unconscious Will, a concept that has many similarities to the Freudian id. Schopenhauer (vol. 3, p. 127) speaks of the "unrest" that is felt in the organism when "the will . . . again fills the consciousness through wishes, emotions, passions, and cares". Emotions and desires, therefore, disturb our ability to see things clearly and objectively: "The intellect is really like the reflecting surface of water, but the water itself is like the will, whose disturbance therefore at once destroys the clearness of that mirror and the distinctness of its images" (vol. 2, p. 430). The Will is "the antagonist of knowledge" (vol. 3, p. 128) and from it springs all our suffering.

The remedy for our suffering is to see things clearly, as they really are, without the distorting and disturbing effects of our own selfish desires. This is only possible when we turn away from the demands of the Will and thereby still the disturbances caused by emotion. When the mirror-like surface of the intellect becomes flat and calm again, it reflects reality as it really is, and ourselves with it. We now see things in a different light, we accept ourselves for the weak and inconstant creatures that we are. The person who realises this, and who no longer labours under the self-serving and self-centred illusion that we exist in order to be happy, "will now find the world in harmony with his insight, although not with his wishes. Misfortunes of every kind and magnitude, although they pain him, will no longer surprise him . . . This will give him indeed a wonderful composedness in all that may happen . . ." (Schopenhauer, vol. 3, p. 162).

We cannot remove the incessant demands of the Will, just as the psychoanalytic patient cannot eliminate the urgings of the id, because they are essential parts of us as natural beings. All we can do in such a situation is to understand and accept the nature of our predicament. When we do this we will cease to be as disturbed by our own drives as we were formerly and will be able to meet the emotional conflicts of life with a degree of equanimity. Though we can never divorce ourselves completely from our desires, perhaps by distancing ourselves a little from them, we can attain a small measure of self-acceptance and contentment.

Schopenhauer's view of the therapeutic effects of self-understanding are, therefore, similar to those of Spinoza and of Freud. As thoroughgoing determinists, they all accept that we cannot change our characters and cannot somehow step outside the law-governed universe of nature of which we are a part. We are *not* free, but we can understand and accept the world of nature of which we are a part and cease to struggle futilely against it. It is only then, when we no longer see ourselves in an unrealistic way and demand impossible goals, such as happiness or the satisfaction of our desires, that we can concentrate on the apparently more mundane, but nevertheless more real, aspects of life and to find ourselves capable of "enjoyment and work".

Conclusion

We have now seen how Freud's original neurophysiological approach to the mind metamorphosed into a psychological theory that was itself part of a more wide-ranging philosophical view of the place of human beings in nature. Throughout the development of his thought, Freud retained a materialistic and naturalistic world-view according to which human beings, and their thoughts and actions, are subject to the same deterministic laws as anything else in the natural world. From this deterministic view sprang Freud's pessimism and his tragic view of the human condition. His determinism was something that Freud shared with Spinoza and Schopenhauer, with whom he also shared a belief in the therapeutic effect of self-understanding as a means of reducing the painful hold of one's irrational desires.

Revision questions

1. How was Freud's work informed by the ideas of Fechner?
2. What did Freud mean by Q and what was its role in his early attempts to ground psychology in physiology?
3. Why did Freud abandon the *Project for a Scientific Psychology*?
4. What is the pleasure principle?
5. What is the reality principle?
6. How do the psychoanalytic ideas of *id* and *ego* emerge from Freud's earlier physiological approach to psychology?
7. What is the Oedipus complex?
8. In what ways does Freud's thought have affinities with the ideas of Spinoza and Schopenhauer?

References

Bernard, W. (1946). Freud and Spinoza. *Psychiatry*, 9, 99–108.

Brecher, E. M. (1933). Discussion: conatus in Spinoza's *Ethics*. *Psychological Review*, 40, 388–390.

Brann, H. W. (1972a). Schopenhauer and Spinoza. *Journal of the History of Philosophy*, 10, 181–96.

Ellenberger, H. F. (1956). Fechner and Freud. *Bulletin of the Menninger Clinic*, 20, 201–14.

Freud, S. ([1885]/1954). *Project for a Scientific Psychology*, trans. E. Mosbacher and J. Strachey. In M. Bonaparte, A. Freud, and E. Kris (eds.) *The Origins of Psycho-Analysis: Letters to Wilhelm Fliess, Drafts and Notes, 1887–1902*. London: Imago, pp. 347–445.

Freud, S. ([1905]/1991). *Three Essays on the Theory of Sexuality*, trans. J. Strachey. In S. Freud, *The Essentials of Psycho-Analysis*. London: Penguin, pp. 277–375.

Freud, S. (1913). *The Interpretation of Dreams*, trans. A. A. Brill. New York: Macmillan.

Freud, S. (1914). *The Psychopathology of Everyday Life*, trans. A. A. Brill. London: T. Fisher Unwin Ltd.

Freud, S. ([1915]/1991). *Instincts and Their Vicissitudes*, trans. J. Strachey. In S. Freud, *The Essentials of Psycho-Analysis*. London: Penguin, pp. 197–217.

Freud, S. ([1915]/1991). *The Unconscious*, trans. J. Strachey. In S. Freud, *The Essentials of Psycho-Analysis*. London: Penguin, pp. 142–83.

Freud, S. ([1920]/1991). *Beyond the Pleasure Principle*, trans. J. Strachey. In S. Freud, *The Essentials of Psycho-Analysis*. London: Penguin, pp. 218–68.

Freud, S. (1920). *A General Introduction to Psychoanalysis*, trans. G. S. Hall. New York: Boni & Liveright.

Freud, S. ([1923]/1991). *The Ego and the Id*, trans. J. Strachey. In S. Freud, *The Essentials of Psycho-Analysis*. London: Penguin, pp. 439–83.

Freud, S. ([1933]/1991). *Dissection of the Personality*, trans. J. Strachey. In S. Freud, *The Essentials of Psycho-Analysis*. London: Penguin, pp. 484–504.

Gupta, R. K. (1975). Freud and Schopenhauer. *Journal of the History of Ideas*, 36, 721–728.

Schopenhauer, A. ([1818]/1909). *The World as Will and Idea*, vols. 2 and 3, trans. R. B. Haldane and J. Kemp. London: Kegan Paul, Trench, Trubner & Co.

Sirkin, M. and Flemming, M. (1982). Freud's 'Project' and its relationship to psycho-analytic theory. *Journal of the History of the Behavioral Sciences*, 18, 230–41.

Spinoza, B. ([1677]/1949). *Ethics* (J. Gutman, ed.). New York: Hafner.

Tourney, G. (1965). Freud and the Greeks: a study of the influence of classical Greek mythology and philosophy upon the development of Freudian thought. *Journal of the History of the Behavioral Sciences*, 1, 67–85.

Young, C. and Brook, A. (1994). Schopenhauer and Freud. *International Journal of Psychoanalysis*, 75, 101–18.

Other works consulted

Brann, H. W. (1972b). Freud as philosopher. *American Imago*, **27**, 122–39.

Ellenberger, H. F. (1970). *The Discovery of the Unconscious.* New York: Basic Books.

Esman, A. H. (2011). Psychoanalysis and Surrealism: André Breton and Sigmund Freud. *Journal of the American Psychoanalytic Association*, **59**, 173–81.

Gay, P. (1988). *Freud: A Life for Our Time.* London: Macmillan.

Kaplan, D. M. (1989). Surrealism and psychoanalysis: notes on a cultural affair. *American Imago*, **46**, 319–27.

Oosterhuis, H. (2012). Sexual modernity in the works of Richard von Krafft-Ebing and Albert Moll. *Medical History*, **56**, 133–55.

Sengoopta, C. (1992). Science, sexuality, and gender in the *fin de siècle*: Otto Weininger as Baedeker. *History of Science*, **89**, 249–79.

Storr, A. (2001). *Freud: A Very Short Introduction.* Oxford: Oxford University Press.

11 Wundt and the birth of experimental psychology

Timeline

1837	Telegraph invented by Samuel Morse
1856	First fossil remains of Neanderthal Man discovered
1865	Mendel presents his findings on genetic inheritance
1871	Bismarck becomes German chancellor
1895	Discovery of X-rays by Wilhelm Roentgen in Germany
1911	Roald Amundsen becomes the first person to reach the South Pole

Wilhelm Wundt

1832	Born in Neckarau, Germany
1852	Studies medicine at the University of Heidelberg
1855	Carries out physiological research with Helmholtz
1874	Publication of *Principles of Physiological Psychology*
1879	Opens experimental psychology laboratory at Leipzig
1900–20	Publishes *Völkerpsychologie* (10 volumes)
1920	Dies in Grossbothen, near Leipzig

Introduction

Wilhelm Wundt (1832–1920) is generally regarded as the father of experimental psychology. A glance at the opening chapter of virtually any introductory psychology textbook, which usually contains a brief history of psychology, will almost certainly refer to the importance of his book *Principles of Physiological Psychology* (1874; English translation by E. B. Titchener, 1910) and, in particular, of the laboratory that he set up in Leipzig in 1879. The Leipzig laboratory is usually held to be the first experimental psychology laboratory and was important not only for the research that was carried out there, but for the large number of psychologists, both European and American, that trained there. For many psychologists in America, a trip to Leipzig to learn the new experimental methods was an important part of their education.

But the questions that Wundt sought to answer through these laboratory techniques cannot be fully understood in isolation from his philosophical presuppositions, and these, as Wundt himself says in the Preface to *Principles of Physiological Psychology*, owed much to Kant. In Chapter 6 we saw how Kant and Hume differed in how they sought to account for our experience. For Hume, experience essentially consisted of elementary sensations that were linked together through a mechanical process of association. Kant, on the other hand, believed that one could never account for the ordered nature of experience in this way. The fundamental flaw of empiricism, for Kant, was its willingness to accept sensory experience as fundamental rather than recognising that there must be even more fundamental structuring principles lying behind sensory experience for it to exist in the first place.

Box 11.1 Wilhelm Wundt

Wilhelm Maximilian Wundt was born in Neckarau, near Mannheim, in southwestern Germany, in 1832, the son of a Lutheran minister. He studied medicine at Heidelberg and, after gaining his medical degree, worked as an assistant to Helmholtz when the latter moved his physiological laboratory to Heidelberg. It was here that Wundt learned about the experimental techniques and instrumentation that he was to later adapt to psychological research.

Box 11.1 (cont.)

Fig. 11.1 Wilhelm Wundt

Box 11.1 (cont.)

After a brief appointment at Zurich, Wundt moved to Leipzig, where he set up his psychological laboratory. Initially this was nothing more than a room that Wundt used to store the pieces of equipment that he had acquired. It was more convenient for Wundt to perform experimental demonstrations in the room where the equipment was already housed rather than moving it around to different locations in the university and so the room, almost by accident, became a psychological laboratory and was officially recognised as such by the university.

Wundt was a man of regular habits: he would write in the morning, visit the laboratory after lunch, then he would go for a walk before delivering a lecture in the late afternoon. During the walk he would compose his lecture and then deliver it without notes but with plenty of sarcastic humour. He never travelled far, though many scientists and thinkers came to visit him, and he disliked the superficial trappings of academic life, such as attending conferences, which he did his best to avoid. His preference was for a quiet, scholarly life (Figure 11.1).

Wundt worked at Leipzig for 43 years and became rector of the university in 1889. He died in 1920.

Wundt, too, recognised that experience was not simply the registration and association of sensations. Like Kant, he believed that some active structuring processes or principles had to lie behind our experience. We can identify the following, broadly Kantian, themes in Wundt's psychology.

1. The mind *actively* constructs experience

Hume thought of the human mind as essentially the passive recipient of incoming sensations. The very term 'impressions', which Hume used to describe our sensations, carries with it the sense that the mind is something like a wax tablet onto which the external world imprints its mark. Some of these impressions may then become associated with others if, for example, they frequently occur together. But this association is, again, a purely passive process: things that regularly occur together or that resemble one another just automatically become associated. The perceiving subject plays no effective role in all this; he or she is simply receptive to the regularities that occur in nature.

For Wundt, however, this was, at best, only half the story. Though he accepted that association of the type described by the empiricists was indeed an important part of human psychology, he argued that in many cases the structuring of the basic elements of experience is not merely the result of outside influences impinging on the passive subject, but is done *actively* by the subject. This active structuring he called **apperception** and it is accompanied by "a feeling of activity" that "does not merely follow the combinations as an after-effect produced by them, but ... precedes them so that the combinations themselves are *immediately recognized as formed with the aid of the attention*" (*Outlines*, pp. 249–50, italics in original). And this attentional process of apperception is what Wundt says brings any mental content to "clear apprehension" (*Outlines*, p. 209). It is because of this emphasis on the activity of the subject in bringing about the apperceptive **synthesis** that Wundt's position is sometimes referred to as **voluntarism**: for Wundt "volitional activities are the type in terms of which all other psychological phenomena are to be construed" (*Logik*, vol. 3, p. 162, quoted by Mischel 1970, p. 7). Kant, too, speaks of "an active faculty for the synthesis" of the sensations (*Critique of Pure Reason*, p. 144). The broad Kantian theme of the active structuring of experience, then, is a basic presupposition of Wundt's psychology. And, as with Kant's structuring principles, Wundt's apperceptive processes are not themselves part of experience, but lie behind it. They "are everywhere the conditions of our experience, but for this very reason it is inadmissible to call them 'experience' itself" (*Outlines*, p. 126).

2. The mind *creatively* constructs experience

Not only is the structuring, or synthesis, of psychological elements active, for Wundt it is also creative. That is, the resulting complex mental state is something over and above the elements that make it up: "compounds contain more than the sum of their parts – e.g. the arrangement of those parts, which, by definition, cannot be a property of the parts themselves" (*Outlines*, p. 101). The basic empiricist mechanism of passive association can produce, at best, a mere combination of individual elements, not a new whole. In contrast to the simple combination of elements, Wundt called the putting together of elements into a new whole 'fusion', which "is *psychological* and is not to be confused with the simple addition of simple elements to one another" (*Outlines*, p. 111).

The idea that the synthesis of elements produces something more than the sum of their parts is essential to the Kantian outlook. For Kant, raw sensory data are not spatial or temporal. It is the structuring principles of the mind that organise sensory data *in* space and time. The way in which the elements are structured results in complex experience that has qualities not possessed by the elements themselves.

Wundt's idea of psychology and its relation to natural science

The scientific revolution, which gave birth to modern science, was underpinned by the distinction between primary and secondary qualities. This distinction, which we have already encountered in connection with Galileo, Descartes, and Locke, differentiated the objective, physical aspects of the world, such as the wavelength of light, from the subjective effects, such as the experience of colour, that were caused by them. The physical aspects of the world were the primary qualities, and, as they could be measured, were the subject matter of **natural science**. The subjective effects, the secondary qualities, were, however, deliberately left out of the natural-scientific world picture. This is not to say that they were thought to be non-existent, just that it was not the business of natural science to investigate them. The business of science was to give an objective, mathematical account of the universe and so, by definition, the subjective was left to one side.

For Wundt, it was the business of psychology to complement natural science by investigating how experience depended on the subject. Psychology and natural science both investigate the same thing, the world of experience. But natural science is concerned with "objects in their objective relations to one another" (*Outlines*, p. 361), and, in seeking an objective account of experience, removes all the subjective factors that contribute to its construction. In so doing, natural science does not investigate immediate experience as it is actually had by the subject, but an abstraction that is derived from this experience. Psychology, on the other hand, has as its subject matter the "immediate contents of experience" (*Outlines*, p. 29). It investigates these contents "in their relations to all the other contents of the experience of the knowing subject" (*Outlines*, p. 361) and "in regard to the attributes which this content derives directly from the subject" (*Outlines*, p. 3). This view of psychology as investigating the contribution of the subject to immediate experience is a direct manifestation of the Kantian idea that experience is actively constructed by the subject, and is not simply a record of external events impacting on the mind.

Wundt's view of psychology as being distinct from natural science is of particular importance when we consider the relationship between psychology and one particular natural science, physiology. Wundt recognised that the way in which experience was structured must have a physiological basis and, having worked with Helmholtz, he was himself trained in physiology. He also recognised that some physiological findings might be of use to the psychologist. Nevertheless, he did not seek a physiological explanation of immediate experience. The physiological and psychological domains were to be kept separate and Wundt sought an account of psychological phenomena that remained entirely within the psychological domain: "There is only one kind of causal explanation in psychology, and that is the derivation of more complex psychical processes from simpler ones" (*Outlines*, p. 28). For example, some aspects of our experience present themselves to us with greater strength and vividness than others, and this is a psychological phenomenon. It is with reference to other psychological phenomena, such as attention, and not to the structure of the nervous system, that we have to account for the greater vividness of some mental contents than others. Physiology, like other natural sciences, completely dispenses with the contribution of the subject in its explanations and devotes its attention to purely objective, physical processes. This is perfectly proper, but it is not psychology.

Wundt's view of psychology is, therefore, anti-reductionist. He claims that a "psychology that starts with such a purely physiological definition depends . . . not on experience but, just like the older materialistic psychology, on a metaphysical presupposition" (*Outlines*, p. 17). Given that psychology is the science of experience as it depends upon and is structured by the subject, to take as one's starting point a position that explicitly excludes the subject is seriously misguided. For Wundt, only those blinkered by certain dogmatically held philosophical beliefs can fail to appreciate the specific features of psychology that prevent it starting from, or being reduced to, physiology or any other natural science. Psychology has to study mental phenomena in their own terms.

Wundt's view of psychology is also anti-positivist (Danziger 1980). A major feature of **positivism** is the idea, attributed to Francis Bacon, that, through the observation of events, we can begin to discern regularities that relate one set of observations to others (see Chapter 1). Given one set of observations, then, we will be able predict what other observations will follow. But, for Wundt, such an approach to science was unsatisfactory because, in merely connecting observations to one another, it did not seek to get behind the observations and discover the deep underlying causes that give rise to them. Some schools of psychology, such as behaviourism, did subscribe to a positivist approach to science. Given a certain regime of reinforcements, rats will, for example, reliably behave in a certain way. We can thus predict and control their behaviour. But an explanation of this conditioning in terms of an underlying cause is not something in which behaviourism is interested. Indeed, to infer the existence and nature of some hidden cause that was not actually observed would, for hardline behaviourism, be metaphysical speculation. The antipathy towards such speculation leads the positivist to stick closely to the data themselves and not to go behind them. But Wundt emphatically *does* want to get behind the data. It is not enough to note that on some occasions perception is clearer than others: the question is why this should be so. For Wundt, like Kant, phenomena are not simply given to obser-vation (as Hume and his positivist followers would have us believe), but are themselves the outcome of more fundamental processes that it is the job of science and philosophy to elucidate. To fail to do this would be merely to remain at the most superficial level of surface experience.

Wundt, therefore, sought not merely to describe, but to give causal explan-ations of psychological phenomena. As we have seen, however, Wundt believes that it would be illegitimate to explain psychological phenomena as being caused by physiological events. Psychological explanations must be in purely psycho-logical terms. Thus, Wundt is committed to the idea of **psychic causality**, the idea that some psychological phenomena are the causal outcomes of other psycho-logical phenomena. Our complex experience, for example, is the causal outcome of active and creative structuring processes. The ultimate goal of psychology for Wundt was, then, to explain experience in terms of fundamental laws of psychic causality.

Psychological experiments

For Wundt, as we have seen, psychology was essentially the science of immediate experience. But this experience was not a simple matter; it was complex and constructed from numerous elements: "The immediate contents of experience which constitute the subject-matter of psychology, are under all circumstances processes of a composite character" (*Outlines*, p. 29).

One example that Wundt himself gives is that of hearing a simple tone. On the face of it, this might seem to be one of the most basic and irreducible experiences that one can imagine. But, as Wundt points out, we don't simply hear a tone, but hear a tone coming from some location (*Outlines*, p. 32). Even the most basic

Box 11.2 **Wundt's laboratory**

Though some of the topics investigated and methods used in Wundt's laboratory would be familiar to the contemporary experimental psychologist, there are also marked differences between the Wundt's experimental psychology and that of the present day. There was, for example, little demarcation between experimenter and participant in Wundt's laboratory, and the same person would frequently fill both roles within the same experiment. To the extent that the roles were differentiated, it was that of participant that was thought to be of greater importance. It was, after all, the participant who was actually the source of data, and reliable and accurate data depended on the skill, training, and attention of the participant. The role of the experimenter, on the other hand, was merely to administer the task and present stimuli. The greater prestige of the participant role was reflected in the fact that Wundt himself more often took part in experiments as a participant than as an experimenter (Figure 11.2).

Fig. 11.2 Research in Wundt's laboratory

Box 11.2 (cont.)

Wundt's experimental psychology also was interested in individuals rather than populations of individuals. The research institutes around which German universities were based were relatively small and Wundt's laboratory was no exception. These circumstances favoured the thorough study of small numbers of participants and, though general patterns of performance were of interest, the details of each individual performance were of at least equal importance. It was only with the expansion of student numbers, initially in American universities, that the testing of large numbers of anonymous participants really took off: there was now a ready supply of experimental participants.

---

sensory experiences, situated in space and time, turn out to be more complex than we think. And this structuring of even basic sensory experiences in space and time brings to mind the broadly Kantian character of Wundt's philosophy.

How, then, is the psychologist to go about investigating such composite experience? One part of psychological investigation is to break down experience into its constituent parts, the "*psychical elements*, or the absolutely simple and irreducible components of psychical phenomena" (*Outlines*, p. 32). These elements, however, are not things that we actually experience; our actual experience is complex and structured. The only way, then, to get at the fundamental elements is to infer their existence by abstracting from the experience that we do actually have. The other aspect of psychology, which for Wundt was actually the more important, was, having identified the experiential elements, to find out how they are in fact put together and organised to give rise to the sort of experience that we have.

As one might expect, given Wundt's status as the father of experimental psychology, careful and controlled laboratory experiments constituted an important method for identifying both the elements of experience and the way in which they were structured by the subject. It is often suggested, however, that Wundt's experiments were very different from those carried out by contemporary psychologists. In particular, it is frequently thought that, whereas modern psychologists use objective measures of psychological phenomena, Wundt relied primarily on subjective introspective reports for his data. According to Sternberg (1998), for example: "For Wundt, the optimal method by which a person could be trained to analyze ... sensory experiences was a form of self-observation called **introspection**, which involves looking inward at pieces of information passing through consciousness ..." (p. 45).

This emphasis on Wundt's use of **introspection** often goes together with mention of psychology's eventual rejection of introspection because it was not objective and, as a result, there could be little agreement about what the method actually discovered. Investigators in one laboratory might introspect upon their experience and come up with one description while investigators in another laboratory might come up with a completely different description of the same experience. There seemed to be no way of deciding between the different observers as to the true nature of the phenomenon. According to this story, the subjectivity of Wundt's original experimental psychology led to its demise and its eventual replacement by the more rigorous and objective psychology that exists today.

It is, however, simply not true that Wundt thought that introspection, or indeed laboratory experimentation of whatever sort, was the principal way to investigate psychological phenomena (Danziger 1980). Indeed, as we shall see in the following chapters, Wundt criticised some of his former students, such as Titchener and Külpe, for their excessive use of introspection. Most of the work that was actually carried out in Wundt's laboratory made use of what today psychologists would think of as 'objective' measures, such as reaction times, though, as has been pointed out (Costall 2006), reaction times themselves are really just a form of subjective report in which the participant reports his or her awareness of the stimulus by pressing a button rather than by giving a verbal response.

When Wundt did actually use some form of introspection, it was rather different from what one might expect. The image that many modern psychologists typically have of introspection is of an investigator, seated in an armchair, who, after being presented with stimuli, reports in great detail his or her resulting subjective experience. The image is not far removed from that of the caricature of a wine taster, who waxes lyrical about the flavours and textures he or she is experiencing. But this does not characterise the type of study carried out by Wundt and his students. Danziger (1980) notes that, of 180 studies published in the Wundt laboratory journal, only four made any great use of introspection in the sense of extensive description of subjective experience. More often, when some sort of subjective report formed part of the investigation, it was relatively brief and served as a check as to whether participants in the study were paying attention or, if there were marked individual differences in performance, as a possible source of insight as to why these differences might have arisen. In other cases, subjective reports were simply judgements of stimulus magnitude, such as whether one light was brighter than another. The use of introspection, then, was far less extensive than the textbook account of Wundt's psychology suggests and the 'introspection' itself seldom bore much of a relation to the exaggerated picture of it that psychologists often hold today.

The methods that Wundt actually did use in his research were developed from those that he learned in his training at the physiological laboratory of Helmholtz. Physiological manipulations, for example, could be used to produce variations in the participants' experiences, such as producing sensory stimuli of greater or lesser magnitude. It is important to bear in mind, however, that, though Wundt made use of physiological methods and titled his most famous work *Foundations of Physiological Psychology*, he was primary interested in the psychological for its own sake, not as something to be reduced to, or equated with, physiological functioning. Wundt's psychology is physiological in that it turns physiological methods to psychological ends.

One illustration of this is Wundt's use of reaction times. (An 'objective' method frequently used by Wundt and, of course, still frequently used by contemporary experimental psychologists.) Reaction times had been used by Helmholtz and other physiologists as a way of measuring how quickly impulses were transmitted along a particular nerve. Wundt, however, applied it to psychological phenomena, such as decision-making. He took a choice reaction-time task, in which one has to decide which of several buttons to press in response to a stimulus, and a simple reaction-time task, in which one simply presses the same button regardless of the stimulus that appears and which, therefore, does not involve the decision-making of the choice task. By subtracting the reaction time in the simple task from the reaction time in the choice task we arrive at a measure of the time taken to make the decision itself. The extent to which speed of decision-making can be related to physiological variables such as speed of nerve conductance is not Wundt's concern; he is interested in the nature of the psychological phenomena themselves.

Other experiments carried out in Wundt's laboratory, far from being exercises in meandering introspection, are strikingly similar to those performed by modern cognitive psychologists. For example, Wundt, as we have seen, believed that attention was a fundamental aspect of the active structuring processes that produced organised experiences. He therefore wanted to know how much information could be attended to by subjects at the one time. He sought to answer this question by very briefly displaying an array of letters and numbers to participants and seeing how many of the items they could report immediately afterwards. In doing this, Wundt prefigured the now classic experiments on **iconic memory** carried out by Sperling in 1960.

Another aspect of attention that has interested modern experimental psychologists is the extent to which attention can be divided between different tasks at the same time. This, too, was investigated by Wundt. Participants watched a swinging pendulum and, at some time during its course, a bell would ring. The participants had to say at which point of the pendulum's swing they had heard the bell. Wundt found that the bell was always estimated to have rung at a later point of the pendulum's swing than had actually been the case. It appeared, therefore, that the participants could not simultaneously monitor the position of the pendulum and pay attention to the bell, but had to switch attention from one to the other. By the time they had switched attention to the pendulum after hearing the bell, the pendulum had moved on and the bell was consequently estimated to have rung at this later point in the trajectory.

Though Wundt did not use introspection extensively, preferring instead methods similar to those of later cognitive psychologists, he nevertheless did not think that introspection was completely without value. He did, however, think that it could only be used under very restricted circumstances.

One of Wundt's criticisms of introspection echoes that of Comte and others: "the very *intention to observe*, which is a necessary condition of all observation, modifies essentially the rise and progress of psychical processes" (*Outlines*, p. 25). When you deliberately try to observe yourself, then, you unavoidably contaminate and change those very psychological processes that you are trying to observe. Of course, we may sometimes be aware of what's going on in our minds without consciously setting out to observe them. We are aware of our mental states as they occur, in passing. So, for example, if I feel happy, I am aware that I am happy, even though I am not reflecting on my happiness at the time. The problem is that when I do reflect on it, it changes, yet it would seem that I do need to reflect on it if I am to be able to describe it to others as part of a psychological investigation.

How, then, can we give mental states the attention that is necessary to provide a verbal report of them without corrupting them at the same time? One attempt to get round this difficulty has been to make use of **retrospection** rather than introspection that is contemporaneous with the mental phenomenon of interest. Rather than observe the mental event as it is taking place, we reflect upon it in memory and thus avoid altering the event itself. This is the solution proposed by, among others, J. S. Mill, who fully acknowledged the strength of the argument against introspection that was concurrent with the mental state that was its object. William James, too, thought that retrospection, imperfect though it might be, was the pre-eminent source of insight for the psychologist.

Retrospection, however, was also criticised by Wundt. Memory, after all, can be unreliable and introduce distortions of its own in the subsequent recall of an event. The natural sciences avoid this problem by observing and recording events as they happen, not in memory. If psychology is to be of similar standing to the natural sciences, it, too, should avoid over-reliance on fallible memory in making its observations. A further problem with retrospection is that it is unsystematic: we just have to wait until circumstances happen to produce a certain mental state in us before we can investigate it. To try, deliberately, to bring that mental state about would, of course, give rise to the same contamination that occurs with deliberate observation of a mental state. This reliance on the spontaneous occurrence of the phenomena of interest is, again, unlike the natural sciences that psychology seeks to complement. Natural sciences can often, through experimental manipulation, produce the relevant phenomena to order, and even those natural sciences that make use of naturalistic observations can safely permit investigators to choose deliberately the times and places where their observations are likely to be fruitful.

For Wundt, then, if introspection was to be a legitimate source of insight for a properly scientific psychology, it could not rely on the memory of past psychological states; it had to be immediate, or as close to immediate as possible. In order to reduce the contamination of the mental states under investigation through introspection, Wundt argued that it should only be carried out by trained observers. Many of the researchers working in Wundt's laboratory were themselves trained introspective observers and they often served as participants in each others' experiments. Wundt, and other early psychologists, are often criticised for this use of trained observers, but the almost exclusive reliance on naïve participants characteristic of much modern psychology is itself a relatively recent development in the history of psychology and is not without its own problems. Given the problems with introspection that have been described above, the use of trained observers proves to be not only justified but perhaps necessary for introspective studies.

Criticism of the use of trained observers often assumes that they were trained to look for specific things in their experience and, therefore, that they were bound to find exactly what the experimenter had trained them to find. But this is not how Wundt's observers were trained. They were, rather, practised in giving immediate, spontaneous reports of their experience. Such observers, Wundt reasoned, would not feel self-conscious or spend time groping for words, but would be able to describe their experiences with a minimum of thought and effort and so would not contaminate those experiences by deliberately reflecting on them to too great an extent.

The occurrence of these experiences, however, cannot just be left to luck. If the observations made in introspective studies are to be systematic and, thus, on a par with the observations made by natural scientists, the experiences to be studied have to be produced in a controlled way. There would, after all, be little point in having trained observers only to have them taken by surprise by the spontaneous occurrence of the experience they were supposed to be studying. The experiences had to be produced when the observer was ready for them, in a relaxed but attentive state. The use of physiological techniques of the sort that he had learned under Helmholtz allowed Wundt to produce, and, importantly, reproduce again and again, experiences that could be investigated by trained observers under such optimum circumstances. Not only could the same observer undergo the same experience on several occasions (and thereby produce a more detailed report than would have been possible with only one presentation), but different observers could undergo the same experience and their reports compared and cross-checked with one another.

There was, however, one drawback associated with these methods: they dramatically restricted the phenomena that could be explored using them. Complex experiences and psychological phenomena just could not be reliably produced in the laboratory using physiological techniques. Only the simplest psychological phenomena, such as basic sensory states, were amenable to the sort of rigorous methods that Wundt thought essential for proper scientific investigation. Higher mental processes, such as language and reasoning, could not be investigated through introspection. The required states could not be produced on demand and, even if they could, they were so complex that they would be virtually impossible to observe and report in the non-reflective, spontaneous way that was necessary to avoid contamination of the state under observation. In addition, with increasing complexity there came increasing scope for personal and idiosyncratic interpretations of the material that was presented, scope that was not there when observers were presented with simple sensory stimuli. Cross-checking reports from different observers of complex phenomena could not, therefore, serve as a guarantor of the integrity and trustworthiness of observations.

In his emphasis on controlled stimuli, on the replicability of experiments, and even in terms of some of the specific experiments that he carried out, Wundt is indeed a precursor of modern experimental psychology. But there are also important differences between Wundt and much of contemporary psychology.

Many of the strictures that he placed on the use of introspection, for example, also applied to any laboratory study. It was not just trained introspective observers who were not naïve as to the purpose of the experiment in which they were taking part; no experimental participants were naïve in Wundt's experiments. The preference of today's experimental psychology for naïve participants and Wundt's for skilled, knowledgeable ones is not due merely to differences in taste or in the relative ease with which different sorts of participants can be recruited. Nor does this difference in the characteristics of participants unequivocally mark an 'advance' in the methods of modern psychology over the less sophisticated approach of an early psychologist. The difference stems, rather, from a deep-seated divergence in the ways in which they view the human subject.

For Wundt, as we have seen, the human subject is understood as a purposeful being that actively structures its experience. In order for the participant to structure his experience in the appropriate way, it is clearly necessary for the participant to know something of the aim of the experiment. Simply bombarding the participant with apparently arbitrary stimuli is, unless one is very lucky, unlikely to permit the active structuring of meaningful experience that is the centre of human psychology. Knowledgeable, skilled participants are therefore *necessary* for any worthwhile psychological experiment. The use of naïve participants, on such a view, would not just be ill-advised but would be a *mistake*. It would be an irredeemable flaw in one's experiment.

Contemporary experimental psychology's preference for naïve participants, on the other hand, arises from an essentially empiricist view of the human subject as the passive recipient of sensory stimulation, a view to which the Kant-influenced Wundt was completely opposed. The participant does not actively do anything; things are done to the participant. And because associating stimuli and being responsive to them are, according to this view of the human subject, essentially mechanical and automatic processes, introducing knowledge about the aim of the experiment is bound to lead to complications. It would distort the pure associative processes, which are at the core of human psychology, with too much thinking on the part of the subject. The ideal participant is a sort of blank slate, devoid of knowledge or experience, upon which the stimuli delivered by the experimenter can be impressed with a minimum of complicating factors. Of course, not all experimental psychologists would explicitly endorse such a view, and many would repudiate it. Nevertheless, the use of naïve participants does imply a certain view of the human subject, a basic philosophical presupposition, that differs from the views of many of the founders of psychology, Wundt included.

Cultural psychology

As has already been mentioned, Wundt's strict requirements for laboratory experiments meant that only simple psychological phenomena could be experimentally investigated. Higher mental processes

> are unapproachable by means of experiment in the common acceptance of the term. These facts are the *mental products* that have been developed in the course of history, such as language, mythological ideas, and customs. (*Outlines*, p. 27)

This did not mean that such phenomena could not, however, be investigated by the psychologist. On the contrary, it was essential that they were targets of psychological enquiry. The psychologist's task was, after all, to discover the principles according to which human experience was structured, and, though some of these structuring principles may be inherent in the individual mind, others are collective features of cultures and societies as a whole. The study of cultural phenomena Wundt called **Völkerpsychologie**, and he devoted at least as much time to this aspect of psychology as he did to experimental psychology. (His *Völkerpsychologie* stretches to 10 volumes.) It was through the examination of the cultural products, such as language and myths, of different societies at different times that the *collective* structuring principles of human thought could be discerned. Take, for example, language. When we express our thoughts, we express them through a medium, such as a language. But different languages have different conceptual resources that mould and partially determine the thoughts that can be expressed in them. As an analogy, think of how the same emotion, anger for example, can be expressed in language, in painting, or in music. The medium itself, whether it be sound or paint, in some ways shapes the content of the expressed emotion and, indeed, becomes part of that content. The same is true, albeit on a subtler level, with different natural languages. Language structures our thoughts. But it is also true that our thoughts structure language: it changes over time as a result of new concepts and ideas that come to be expressed using it. So we have a reciprocal relationship between our thoughts and the medium through which these thoughts are expressed. One constantly influences the other. For example, Wundt believed that primitive languages were more directly tied to perceptual experience than were languages with more sophisticated grammatical structures. Thus, more primitive languages both reflected and gave rise to what he called 'concrete thought'.

But it is not simply the case that a given society or linguistic community partially structures the way in which its individual members think; in addition to this, there are thoughts that can only be said to be 'owned' collectively: "we may speak of the interconnection of the ideas and feelings of a social community as a *collective consciousness*" (*Outline*, p. 349). Of course, Wundt did not mean by this that there existed a mysterious entity that existed apart from individuals, but only that certain thoughts can only exist and be had by more than one person. If, for example, you and your friend intend to meet at the cinema tonight, we might ask "Who has the intention?" The answer is: you and your friend. You do not have one intention and your friend another intention; you both share one and the same joint intention. A joint intention of this sort is a very simple example of a thought, idea, or mental state that *cannot* be had by an individual. It might be objected that there are two separate courses of physiological events, one happening in your brain and one happening in your friend's brain, and therefore that there are two separate thoughts, one had by you and one had by your friend. But, as we have seen, this would merely be an example of the sort of physiological reductionism that Wundt disparaged as dependent on a materialist "metaphysical presupposition" and which betrayed a faulty understanding of the nature of psychology. As collective psychological phenomena depend on the relations between individuals, Wundt believed that different sorts of societies, a tribal society or an industrialised society for example, would produce different collective thoughts and ideas.

For Wundt, the above aspects of mental life could not be investigated in a laboratory. After all, the required analysis is at the level of whole societies and their development in historical time, not at that of individual participants tested over a few hours or even weeks. But to disregard such phenomena because they cannot be studied experimentally would be to ignore a vast area of crucial psychological importance just because of a rigid attachment to one particular method. What the psychologist has to do is apply a method that is suitable to phenomena under investigation, not restrict the phenomena that can be investigated in order to fit in with a preordained method.

Conclusion

Wundt's vision of psychology, then, is wide-ranging, both in terms of subject matter and in the plurality of methods that it requires. To describe Wundt as 'the father of experimental psychology', therefore, although not wrong, implies that his conception of psychology was far narrower than it actually was. He neither thought that experimentation was the major method of psychological science nor that the phenomena of psychology should be restricted to what one can study in the laboratory. Even in his laboratory work he used both objective methods and subjective reports when he thought they were appropriate. Some of Wundt's students, however, did have a more restricted view of psychology and its methods, and we shall examine them in the next chapter. This narrower view, which has come to influence contemporary experimental psychology to a greater extent than that of Wundt, rested upon an empiricist view of knowledge and the human subject that was wholly at odds with Wundt's Kantian philosophy. Again, the philosophical presuppositions of psychologists determined the way in which they thought the new science should develop.

Revision questions

1. How was Wundt's approach to psychology influenced by the philosophy of Kant?

2. Why did Wundt think it illegitimate to try to reduce psychology to physiology?

3. What strictures did Wundt place on the use of introspection in experiments?

4. What other methods, besides introspection, did Wundt use in his experiments? Give an example of an experimental task to illustrate your answer.

5. Why did Wundt think it necessary to use trained and knowledgeable experimental participants rather than naïve ones?

6. What sort of phenomena did Wundt think were amenable to experimental investigation and what sort of phenomena did he think could not be investigated in the laboratory? What were his reasons behind this distinction?

7. How did Wundt think that psychological phenomena that could not be studied in the laboratory should be investigated?

References

Blumenthal, A. L. (1975). A reappraisal of Wilhelm Wundt. *American Psychologist*, **30**, 1081–8.

Costall, A. (2006). 'Introspectionism' and the mythical origins of scientific psychology. *Consciousness and Cognition*, **15**, 634–54.

Danziger, K. (1979). The positivist repudiation of Wundt. *Journal of the History of the Behavioral Sciences*, **15**, 205–30.

Danziger, K. (1980). The history of introspection reconsidered. *Journal of the History of the Behavioral Sciences*, **16**, 241–62.

Kant, I. ([1781]/1989). *Critique of Pure Reason*, trans. N. Kemp Smith. London: Macmillan.

Mischel, T. (1970). Wundt and the conceptual foundations of psychology. *Philosophy and Phenomenological Research*, **31**, 1–26.

Sternberg, R. J. (1998). *In Search of the Human Mind*. Orlando, FL: Harcourt Brace.

Wundt, W. (1902). *Outlines of Psychology*, 2nd edn, trans. C. H. Judd. Leipzig: Wilhelm Engelmann.

Wundt, W. (1910). *Principles of Physiological Psychology*, 2nd edn, trans. E. B. Titchener. New York: Macmillan.

12 Titchener, introspection, and positivism

Timeline

1841	New Zealand is made a British colony
1857	Indian Mutiny against British rule
1869	Mendeleyev publishes his periodic table of the elements
1901	First Nobel Prize ceremony is held in Stockholm
1911	Rutherford discovers the atomic nucleus
1928	All women over 21 given the vote in the UK

Edward Bradford Titchener

1867	Born in Chichester, West Sussex
1885	Studies philosophy and physiology at Oxford
1890	Studies under Wundt at Leipzig
1892	Goes to Cornell as head of the new psychological laboratory
1904	Founds the Society of Experimentalists as an alternative to the American Psychological Association
1901–5	Publishes *Experimental Psychology: A Manual of Laboratory Practice* (4 vols.)
1921	Publishes *A Textbook of Psychology*
1927	Dies in Ithaca, New York

Ernst Mach

1838	Born in Chirlitz–Turas, Moravia
1867	Professor of Physics at the University of Prague
1886	Publishes *The Analysis of Sensations*
1895	Professor of the History and Philosophy of Science at the University of Vienna
1901	Retires from academia; becomes member of the Austrian parliament
1916	Dies in Haar, Germany

Introduction

The importance of Wundt in the development of psychology was not confined to his own research and writing, but in the large numbers of future psychologists who were trained in his laboratory. But these students did not always merely reproduce Wundt's ideas; they took certain aspects of his thought and changed them to fit in with their own philosophical presuppositions, which sometimes differed from those of Wundt. In this chapter I will discuss the work of one of Wundt's former students, Edward Bradford Titchener (1867–1927), who provides a prime example of how differing philosophical presuppositions, both about the nature of the mind and the nature of science, lie behind and are manifested in individual psychologists' approaches to their work.

The example of Titchener is particularly significant because, until recently, in textbooks there was often confusion between Wundt and Titchener. It was suggested that their approaches to psychology were basically the same and ideas and pronouncements expressed by Titchener were often thought to be expressions of Wundt's psychology by one of his students. This, however, is far from the truth (Leahy 1981). In fact there were many important differences in their approaches.

As we saw in the previous chapter, Wundt's view of psychology can be characterised as follows. It sought to explain experience with reference to active psychological principles that caused experience to be structured in certain ways. These structuring principles were not themselves experienced, but their nature could be inferred through psychological investigation. Such investigations used a variety of methods. Relatively simple psychological phenomena could be investigated experimentally, through introspection and performance measures, such as reaction time; more complex psychological phenomena could not be investigated in this way, but could be studied by examining cultural products such as language and myth.

As we shall see in the course of this chapter, Titchener's psychology differed from Wundt's in almost every one of these features. Titchener did not seek to explain experience as the causal effect of active structuring principles, but tried to identify and describe the fundamental elements of which experience was composed; he did not believe that inferring the existence of hidden psychological forces behind experience was scientific at all, but was metaphysical speculation; and he did not believe that complex psychological phenomena were outside the scope of laboratory investigation, but believed that there was one method that should be applied to all psychological phenomena: experimental introspection. For Titchener, then, psychology *was* experimental psychology using controlled and systematic introspection.

Box 12.1 **Edward Bradford Titchener**

Edward Bradford Titchener was born at Chichester in West Sussex, UK, in 1867. He went to Oxford in 1885, where he studied philosophy and, later, physiology. It was this combination of subjects that had formed the basis of Wundt's physiological psychology and the research being carried out in his laboratory in Leipzig and Titchener duly went to Leipzig to work in Wundt's laboratory.

Wundt was 35 years older than Titchener and was already a highly respected scientist. The laboratory was hierarchically organised, with Wundt very much at the helm, and Titchener was subsequently to run his own laboratory in the same top–down manner. It was at Leipzig that Titchener, along with several other young members of the laboratory, fell under the influence of positivism, particularly as espoused by Mach, even though this did not sit well with Wundt's own philosophical outlook.

After two years in Leipzig, Titchener returned to Oxford as a lecturer in biology, but his real interest lay in psychology. Psychology was, at that time, not recognised as an academic subject by Oxford (indeed, there was a great deal of opposition to the emerging discipline), and so Titchener left for the United States, where he took over the running of the psychological laboratory at Cornell University. He remained there for the rest of his career (Figure 12.1).

Titchener had strained relations with the newly founded American Psychological Association because he believed that its increasing emphasis on mental testing and child and abnormal psychology meant that it was departing from what he saw as the core of scientific psychology: the experimental introspective study of general psychological phenomena. He set up his own informal group, often referred to as 'The Experimentalists', to provide a forum for those who shared his view of psychology.

Titchener had a rigid sense of decorum and could be somewhat aloof from his colleagues. He always felt something of an outsider in America and taught wearing his Oxford gown, from which an assistant had to remove cigar ash prior to each lecture. In contrast to his rather distant relations with his fellow academics – some of whom claimed never actually to have seen him – Titchener had a great deal of time for his students and, despite his haughty manner, was a dedicated and helpful teacher. He died in 1927.

Box 12.1 (cont.)

Fig. 12.1 Edward Bradford Titchener

Why, then, did Titchener disagree with Wundt about the methods and goals of psychology? It might appear as though their differences of opinion about the applicability of introspection, say, were just a reflection of relatively superficial personal preferences concerning method. This, however, is not the case; their differing views of psychology, its goals, and its methods are motivated by conflicting philosophical presuppositions about the mind and science.

We saw in the previous chapter that important parts of Wundt's basic philosophical orientation were Kantian. This is why discovering the nature of the mind's structuring processes was, for him, the essential goal of psychology. It was also one reason why introspection could not be the only method of investigation in psychology. Although introspection might yield useful descriptions of experience, the most important processes in psychology were not themselves part of experience. One had to infer what was going on behind the scenes, so to speak, to account for the nature of experience, and much of this was not, *in principle*, possible to introspect upon. Other methods, in addition to introspection, that could allow the psychologist to infer the nature of the structuring processes were therefore not only legitimate but necessary.

Although Titchener studied under Wundt, his basic philosophical orientation was that of empiricists like Locke and Hume. Thus, even though he adopted some of the methods of Wundt, the ways in which these methods were used and the questions that they were used to answer differed from the approach of his teacher. But, in addition to the traditional empiricism of the seventeeth and eighteenth centuries, Titchener was strongly influenced by a modern variant of empiricism that won many adherents in the early twentieth century. This was the positivism of Mach and Avenarius.

The influence of positivism

In the early twentieth century, when Titchener was writing, a new and radical form of positivism was increasing in popularity. As well as Titchener, it was to have a major influence on numerous other psychologists, such as William James and many behaviourists. This version of positivism was associated, in particular, with Richard Avenarius (1843–96) in Zurich and a group of philosopher-scientists in the Austro-Hungarian empire, of whom Ernst Mach (1838–1916) was the most prominent. Mach was a physicist, a philosopher, and a psychologist. His position was resolutely anti-metaphysical in that he viewed experience as the foundation deeper than which science could not go. In the traditional empiricism of Locke, for example, perceptual experience is thought of as an internal mental event that is caused by external objects. Though we never see the objects themselves, we can infer their existence through the subjective effects that they produce in us. For Mach, however, the inferred existence of unseen and unexperienced objects is unwarranted metaphysical speculation. This is to go beyond and behind experience. Instead, Mach turned round the order of priority and argued that what we call things or objects are just names for relatively permanent groups of experiential elements: "Bodies do not produce sensations, but complexes of elements (complexes of sensations) make up bodies" (*The Analysis of Sensations*, p. 29). The same approach is taken with respect to the self or ego: "[t]he primary fact is not the ego, but the elements (sensations) ... The elements constitute the I" (*Analysis*, p. 23). Although the concept of the self or ego, like the ideas of permanently existing objects that cause our sensations, might have some use in everyday life, in science and philosophy "The ego must be given up" (*Analysis*, p. 24). Mach's stance clearly echoes that of Hume, who argued that the self was nothing more than the name for a "bundle or collection of different perceptions" (*Treatise*, p. 252).

According to Mach, then, what fundamentally exists are basic sensory 'elements':

> For us, therefore, the world does not consist of mysterious entities, which by their interaction with another, equally mysterious entity, the ego, produce sensations, which alone are accessible. For us, colors, sounds, spaces, times, ... are provisionally the ultimate elements, whose given connexion it is our business to investigate. (*Analysis*, p. 29)

Some of these combinations of elements we *call* things and others we *call* mental states, but to assume that there is a thing in itself lying behind the elements, or a mind that has 'mental states' is just metaphysics: "the reference to unknown

---

Box 12.2 **Ernst Mach**

Ernst Mach was born in Moravia (then part of the Austro-Hungarian empire, today part of the Czech Republic) in 1838. He studied physics at the University of Vienna and then held posts at Graz and Prague before returning to a professorship in Vienna (Figure 12.2). As a student Mach had also taken extra classes in physiology and worked in a laboratory where the new ideas of Müller, Helmholtz, and Fechner on the relationship between the physiological and the psychological were a topic of intense discussion.

Box 12.2 (cont.)

Fig. 12.2 Ernst Mach

Box 12.2 (cont.)

Mach made important contributions to physics, particularly on the speed of sound, and the ratio of an object's speed to the speed of sound is today known as its Mach number. Mach's positivistic philosophy of science was also influential. Mach questioned the idea that Newton's physics provided us with absolute truths about the fundamental nature of the universe. Instead, he argued, we should think of the laws of physics as merely convenient ways of describing complex patterns of observations. The truth of any scientific statement, then, is not fixed and absolute but is a matter of its providing a shorthand description of sensory experience that is useful for a particular purpose. Mach stated: "No point of view has absolute, permanent validity. Each has importance only for some given end" (*Analysis*, p. 37). It was Mach's suggestion that Newtonian physics might be valid only relative to a particular viewpoint that, said Einstein, provided the starting point for his theory of relativity.

Mach's positivism also had political influence among many left-wing thinkers in Russia. Indeed, its popularity was such that Lenin felt compelled to combat its growth by writing a book, *Materialism and Empirico-Criticism*, in which he attacked Mach's ideas as being incompatible with Marxism's dialectical materialism.

Mach retired from the university in 1901 after suffering a stroke, but he remained active, and became a member of the Austrian parliament, where he championed liberal views. He died in 1916.

---

fundamental variables which are not given (things-in-themselves) is purely fictitious and superfluous" (*Analysis*, p. 35). In Kantian terms, there are no noumena, only phenomena.

Mach's radical views of the nature of what fundamentally exists had important implications as to what the goal of science was. If all that actually exists are the phenomena and there is nothing behind the phenomena that causes and, hence, explains their existence, then a certain sort of science – explanatory science – becomes impossible. Instead of *explaining* experience in terms of hidden forces and entities, the scientist has to *describe* experience, and how different parts of experience are related to one another: experience is composed of basic elements and "it as the sole task of science to inquire into the connexion and combination of these elements" (*Analysis*, p. 312).

So, rather than a comprehensive explanatory framework, the goal of positivistic science is economical description. One consequence of this ambition is the idea that the same elements should be used to describe all levels of phenomena. Basic physical events, higher-order mental events, perhaps even social events all had to be ultimately describable in terms of the same basic constituent elements. And for Mach these elements were sensations. If we are being truly rigorous, we must admit that all the phenomena that we experience are complex or simple arrangements of basic sensations. (Again we can hear the echo of Hume and his assertion that all the contents of consciousness can be traced back to sensory experience.) All the sciences, therefore, deal with essentially the same basic things, sensations in more or less complex arrangements, and this means that there is essentially one scientific method. What differentiates one science from another are not qualitative differences in method or subject matter, but merely quantitative differences in the level of abstraction and generality at which they try to describe their common subject matter, and the different points of view from which they try to describe it.

Titchener's view of psychology

Given that all experience is composed of basic elements, for Titchener the ultimate goal of psychology was the breaking down of complex psychological experiences to discover the basic elements of which they are composed. "The first object of the psychologist," says Titchener, "is to ascertain the nature and number of mental elements. He takes up mental experience, bit by bit, dividing, until the division can go no further. When that point is reached, he has found a conscious mental element" (*An Outline of Psychology*, pp. 15–16). We saw in the previous chapter that Wundt, too, considered the discovery of mental elements to be an important part of psychological investigation. But for Wundt this was merely a preliminary to the study of the creative synthesis that put the elements together to produce complex experience. For Titchener, on the other hand, it was the central task of experimental psychology.

Titchener's approach to psychology is called **structuralism**. He likens the task of the psychologist to that of the anatomist who attempts to discover the structure of the body by vivisection. Similarly, the psychologist seeks to discover the structural components of the mind, the basic elements of which experience is composed:

> The primary aim of the experimental psychologist has been to analyze the structure of mind; to ravel out the elemental processes from the tangle of consciousness … to isolate the constituents in the given conscious formation. His task is a vivisection, but a vivisection which shall yield structural, not functional results. He tries to discover, first of all, what is there and in what quantity, not what it is there for. ('Postulates', p. 450)

The way in which this is done is through systematic and controlled introspection. Indeed, Titchener goes so far as to say that "[e]xperimental introspection is … our one reliable method of knowing ourselves; it is the sole gateway to psychology" (*Outline*, p. 32). We see here a marked contrast with Wundt, for whom introspection was merely one method among many. It is true that Titchener mentions in passing that cultural psychology, and the examination of myths and customs, does play a role in psychology, but this is something very different from Wundt's *Völkerpsychologie*. For Titchener, myths, laws, and customs are merely the records of "introspections made in common by the members of a social group" (*Textbook*, p. 33). These cultural phenomena, then, were not qualitatively different from the phenomena studied experimentally.

Why, then, did Titchener put so much more stress on introspection than did Wundt? One of the reasons stems from his positivist-influenced view of science. For Titchener, the methods, and indeed the subject matter, of psychology are of a piece with those of the other sciences. And the scientific method essentially consists of observation. Given that each person has access to only his own mind, the observation of mental processes necessarily takes the form of introspection. For Titchener, unlike critics of introspection, there is nothing mysterious or problematic about this: all scientists observe phenomena, and the experimental psychologist is no different: "introspection may be as impersonal, as objective, as matter-of-fact, as is the observation of the natural sciences" ('Prolegomena', p. 434). Whereas some critics of introspection, such as Comte, believed that it must involve a sort of splitting of the self in two (the psychologist must somehow observe himself in the course of his experience), for Titchener this is simply a misunderstanding. The psychologist does *not* have to observe himself experiencing, he simply has to observe his experience. This is no different from, for example, the naturalist observing animals in the wild. The naturalist does not have to psychologically split himself in two and observe himself in the course of observing; he simply observes the animals, which are in this case the objects of his experience. Introspection does not involve observing oneself in the act of observing any more than any other sort of scientific observation.

It is also not the case, according to Titchener, that introspection is any more prone to differences of opinion or subjective bias than any other sort of scientific observation. Scientists in any discipline disagree about the phenomena that they have observed and they attempt to resolve these disagreements by carrying out further investigations with the express purpose of clarifying the nature of the problematic phenomena. Psychology, too, does this, and it is to make this possible that scientific introspection has to be carried out under properly controlled conditions.

Like the participants in Wundt's experiments, Titchener's introspectors were not naïve subjects. Just like any other scientific observers, introspective observers had to be trained. Astronomers, for example, have to be trained to make useful and reliable observations; observation is not simply a matter of a naïve viewer gazing up at the night sky. The same goes for a biologist examining a specimen through a microscope. For Titchener psychology was no different.

Contrary to present-day psychology, in which it is assumed that the naïve observer is less likely to produce biased responses in accordance with what he or she thinks is expected of them, for Titchener the opposite was true. The naïve observer was likely to have certain presuppositions about the nature of the phenomena that he was observing, and these would be likely to contaminate any report that was given. It is the trained observer who is more able to strip away these preconceptions and to give a report of the phenomena as they actually appear:

> We observe because we are interested in the result of our observation: some chance occurrence has suggested to us an explanation of particular events, and we are interested to discover, by systematic enquiry, whether the explanation is correct. The trained observer, psychologist or physicist or what not, can take the suggestion for what it is worth; he does not allow it to affect his observation. But the beginner is exceedingly liable to be led by interest into partiality; and so to see, not what really happens, but what he desires or expects to see happen. (*Outline*, p. 45)

It is important to note here how Titchener's attitude to introspection, and indeed the attitude of many psychologists in the early twentieth century, differs from that of many psychologists today. The experimental psychologist of today stresses the use of 'objective' measures such as reaction time (although, as we have seen, many of these 'objective' measures involve an element of subjective report, albeit delivered by non-verbal means). Introspection is therefore seen as something subjective and lacking in rigour and hence as not properly scientific. Rather than relying on relatively direct introspective reports of mental phenomena, the nature of mental processing is inferred from participants' objective and measurable performances on experimental tasks. For Titchener, however, exactly the opposite was the case. To be truly scientific in the sense of positivism, one has to stick as closely to the data as possible. Any attempt to infer the existence or nature of unseen processes that are not themselves the data of experience is to flirt with metaphysics. After all, what could be more factual, more rigorous, more scientific than the actual facts of experience as they are presented directly to the subject? Far from being unrigorous or fanciful, it is introspection, according to this reasoning, that is the most truly scientific mode of psychological investigation; it is the postulation of mysterious hidden processes that are never actually observed or experienced that is vague and fanciful. By the standards of Titchener and positivism much current experimental psychology would be considered unscientific and metaphysical.

Attention

The difference in approach between Wundt and Titchener can, perhaps, be best seen by examining a specific example of a psychological phenomenon. The case of attention makes the differences very clear. In the previous chapter we saw how Wundt thought of attention as part of the active structuring of experience. It therefore had causal efficacy: attention actually did something. It was a prime example of the psychic causality that was so important to Wundt. Titchener's view of attention, however, was markedly different.

For Titchener, attention is really a property of sensations; it "is identical with sensory clearness" (*Textbook*, p. 267). Whereas for Wundt attention was an active process that explained certain aspects of experience, for Titchener it was simply a word that we use to communicate the fact that some sensations are clearer than others; it is not a psychological power that explains why some sensations are clearer than others. Rather than something that explains, attention is itself just another name for something that was itself in need of explanation: explanation in terms of the relative strength and clearness of certain sensations and images and the physiological conditions that are necessary for such clearness.

Indeed, Titchener specifically argues against those psychologists who (like Wundt) viewed attention as a type of mental activity that has causal efficacy. Such a psychologist

> has gone beyond introspection, and has drawn inferences from the phenomena of consciousness to the existence of something behind consciousness which introspection

does not reveal, he has been forced, in spite of his resolve, to leave the ground of psychology proper and to appeal for help to some science which is not psychology. The science to which he appeals is metaphysics. (*Outline*, pp. 126–7)

As a statement of positivist psychology, this could not be clearer: to infer the existence of psychological processes that are not themselves the direct object of experience is to indulge in metaphysics.

But it is not the case that Wundt merely infers the existence of active structuring processes from the structure of experience; he also claims that active apperceptive processes are accompanied by "a feeling of activity" (Wundt, *Outlines*, p. 249). Thus, at least certain aspects of the active mind are experienced. Though we cannot observe the workings of the apperceptive processes as part of experience (they are, after all, what makes experience in the first place), we can, nevertheless, catch sight in experience of the fact that they are working. This is because they are active and, therefore, accompanied by sensations of effort. We are now back on the firm ground of experiential data. But the fact that we might feel sensations of effort or activity does not, for Titchener, show that there is an active mental process lying behind these sensations. These 'sensations of effort' are by and large simply bodily sensations, "sensations of tendinous strain" (*Outline*, p. 132). When we introspect closely, says Titchener, we find only these sensations and the affective or emotional colouring (e.g. whether they are pleasant or unpleasant) with which they are tinged. There is no sensation of effort or activity at all. As he puts it elsewhere:

When I am trying to attend I … find myself frowning, wrinkling my forehead etc. All such … bodily sets and movements give rise to characteristic sensations. Why should not these sensations be what we call 'attention'. (*Textbook*, p. 266)

Attention, effort, activity – all of these are not the names of psychological processes that cause experience to be structured in a certain way. They are just the names that we give to certain sorts of bodily sensations.

The demise of the psychological subject

Just as Titchener could find no evidence for active and causally efficacious psychological processes, he could find no evidence for the psychological subject that was the locus of these processes. When we think of the self or the ego, says Titchener, we should have to confess that we think, not of the peculiar way in which our mental experience hangs together, but of a thing, a permanent and active something which lives within our body and directs its movements. Yet introspection reveals no trace of this 'thing'. (*Outline*, p. 306)

The self, just as Hume and Mach had said, was merely a group of sensations, not the seat of activity or causal powers:

Your 'self,' the self that you perceive at this moment, is probably composed of pressures, temperatures, strains, breaths, etc.; that is, a certain total effort or comfortableness or headachiness: together with the visual perception of hands and clothes. That is you, as you perceive yourself ... this mass of felt sensations is yourself. (*Primer*, p. 225)

And it is because there is no such thing as the self, as a causal agent, that no psychological phenomena can be explained by reference to it. Whereas Wundt wanted to explain psychological phenomena as the being the outcome of active structuring processes on the part of the psychological subject, for Titchener there was no such subject and, hence, no such form of explanation. The only explanation that could be offered was with reference to the physiological body.

The demise of positivistic structuralism

Titchener's structuralism, then, was extremely austere. There were no psychological self or psychological processes that had any effect at all on the world. There was no causality either, nor any volition. There were just the basic elements of experience conjoined in various ways in various connections and contexts. These elements of experience do not stand in need of explanation; they are, rather, those fundamental things in terms of which we can account for everything else. Strictly speaking, the elements themselves are meaningless; they are not good or bad or ugly or beautiful, they just *are*. Qualities such as these do not exist in the world of positivistic science. For the positivistic psychologists, therefore, questions of meaning and of value had no place in a properly scientific psychology. The *real* world of experience, which it is the job of science to describe, is the world of bare sensation, devoid of value and meanings.

This assumption of a world of events and things that are, in themselves, meaningless constitutes another difference between the psychology of Wundt and that of Titchener. For Wundt believed that experience is full of values and meanings: we experience things as good or bad or beautiful; we do not just experience bare, meaningless sensations. The reason that our experience is meaningful is that the process of creative synthesis that structures it *produces* meaning and value. It is important to realise that, for Wundt, we do not have meaningless experience and then project meaning onto it; rather, the very act of structuring experience itself by the psychological subject means that our experience is inherently meaningful. This structuring is genuinely creative in the sense that it does not merely join together basic meaningless elements but produces a sense that is over and above the elements themselves.

If Wundt is right, and experience is inherently meaningful, this creates a serious problem for positivism. Positivism was to stick to the bare facts of experience and to be totally rigorous in doing so. But what are the pure facts of experience? It is undeniable that we do not, for the most part at least, experience meaningless sensations. On the contrary, we experience things as having meanings and values. The very content of our actual experience contradicts the positivist description of that experience. The way out of this impasse, for the positivist, is to claim that our normal everyday meaningful experience is deceptive, adulterated as it is with purely subjective factors such as significance and value, and that behind this actual experience is the more basic experience of pure, meaningless sensations.

According to Titchener, the psychologist seeks "a world scoured clean of belief and inference and all such evaluative accretion" (*Systematic Psychology*, p. 32). These things – belief, inference, value – are distorting additions to real experience. But the positivist here is involved in something close to a contradiction: he is forced to deny the basic facts of experience in favour of something that we do not actually experience. On the other hand, Wundt, far from claiming that experience of meaningless elements was prior to, and more basic than, our actual meaningful experience, would have argued the opposite: our meaningful and value-laden experience is primary and meaningless elements are abstractions from this experience. They are what remain once all meaning has been removed.

It is this recognition that the world of meaningless physical elements is an abstraction from a larger experiential whole that meant that Wundt could not accept that a natural scientific approach to psychology was possible. The whole point of natural science is that the subject features nowhere in it. Wundt therefore thought of psychology not as a part of natural science, but as a complement to it. Natural science studies experience with no reference to the subject, and psychology studies experience as it depends upon the subject. It is because positivist psychologists such as Titchener believed that psychology *was* part of natural science that they were forced, by the logic of their own position, to deny the reality of meaningful experience and to postulate the existence of a meaningless experience that was somehow more real and more basic than the experience that we actually have.

This denial of meaning and the associated search for pure elements was one of the reasons that the introspection associated with Titchener eventually fell out of favour. According Titchener's student, E. G. Boring:

> Introspection with inference and meaning left out as much as possible becomes a dull taxonomic account of sensory events which, since they suggest almost no functional value for the organism, are peculiarly uninteresting to the American scientific temper. (Boring 1953, p. 174)

In other words, it was unclear what the point of a 'periodic table' of mental elements, even assuming that such a thing was feasible, actually was. It was doubtful whether enumerating the basic constituents of experience would really help us to understand the human mind. Titchener's type of introspective psychology was also out of kilter with an increasing emphasis on applied psychology. Breaking down complex experiences into individual elements did not seem to have significance for clinical and educational applications, for example. And it was precisely questions about clinical and educational applications that psychologists, in the 1920s and 1930s, were increasingly being expected to answer. The role of the psychologist was changing and introspectionism seemed irrelevant to these new problems.

The internal logic of the positivist introspectionist approach was also part of its downfall. We have already seen that Titchener, unlike Wundt, denied the existence of mental causality. Mental states did not cause one another or, indeed, anything else. But if this were the case, some began to ask, why bother investigating mental states at all? – they seem to be mere **epiphenomena**. The apparent impotence of mental states combined with the new emphasis on applied questions led to an increasing emphasis on the study of behaviour instead of mental states and thus paved the way for the rise of behaviourism.

Revision questions

1. How and why did Titchener's attitude to introspection differ from that of Wundt?
2. For Mach, what are the ultimate constituents of the empirical world?
3. What, for positivists, was the goal of science?

4. What, for Titchener, was the goal of psychology?

5. How did Titchener respond to criticisms of introspection?

6. Why did Titchener prefer to use trained rather than naïve observers?

7. How, according to Titchener, should we understand the phenomenon of attention?

8. Why did Titchener's introspective structuralism fall out of favour?

References

Boring, E. G. (1953). A history of introspection. *Psychological Bulletin*, 50, 169–89.

Danziger, K. (1979). The positivist repudiation of Wundt. *Journal of the History of the Behavioral Sciences*, 15, 205–30.

Hume, D. ([1739–40]/1978). *A Treatise of Human Nature*, 2nd edn (L. A. Selby-Bigge, ed., revised by P. H. Nidditch). Oxford: Oxford University Press.

Leahy, T. H. (1981). The mistaken mirror: on Wundt's and Titchener's psychologies. *Journal of the History of the Behavioral Sciences*, 17, 273–82.

Mach, E. (1914). *The Analysis of Sensations*, trans. C. M. Williams. Chicago, IL: Open Court.

Titchener, E. B. (1898). The postulates of a structural psychology. *Philosophical Review*, 7, 449–65.

Titchener, E. B. (1906). *Experimental Psychology: A Manual of Laboratory Practice*, vol. I. New York: Macmillan.

Titchener, E. B. (1907). *An Outline of Psychology*. New York: Macmillan.

Titchener, E. B. (1912). Prolegomena to a study of introspection. *American Journal of Psychology*, 23, 427–48.

Titchener, E. B. (1919). *A Primer of Psychology*. New York: Macmillan.

Titchener, E. B. (1921). *A Textbook of Psychology*. New York: Macmillan.

Titchener, E. B. (1929). *Systematic Psychology: Prolegomena*. New York: Macmillan.

Wundt, W. (1902). *Outlines of Psychology*, 2nd edn, trans. C. H. Judd. Leipzig: Wilhelm Engelmann.

13 Gestalt psychology

Timeline

Franz Brentano

Max Wertheimer

Kurt Koffka

Wolfgang Köhler

Franz Brentano

Brentano advocated a scientific and empirical, as opposed to a speculative and metaphysical, approach to the questions of psychology and philosophy: for Brentano, "the true method of philosophy is none other than that of the natural sciences" (cited by Smith 1994, p. 31). Nevertheless, Brentano cautioned against simply importing methods and techniques from other fields of science into psychology – one had to adapt one's method to fit the subject matter that was under investigation. The laboratory methods that had been developed in the physiological research of Helmholtz, for example, could not just be applied indiscriminately to psychology. Indeed, such methods were, for Brentano, extremely limited. Laboratory experimentation, he argued, could only deal adequately with basic mental states, such as sensation, that were directly produced by an external stimulus. More important classes of mental phenomena, such as willing and imagination, which are a consequence of internal rather than external processes, could not be investigated experimentally. But for Brentano, this did not mean that one could not investigate them scientifically. He pointed out that experimentation is only one aspect of science and that there are perfectly valid non-experimental sciences whose methods would be more suited to a psychological subject matter.

Box 13.1 **Franz Brentano**

Franz Clemens Brentano (1838–1917) was born in Marienburg, Germany, to a Catholic family of Italian descent. The family was an educated one and previous generations had contained notable intellectuals and writers. Brentano studied philosophy at Berlin, Würzburg, and Munich, before completing his thesis at Tübingen.

Brentano trained for the Catholic priesthood, and was ordained a priest in 1864. There was, however, considerable conflict within the Church at this time. It had been proposed that the principle of papal infallibility – according to which the Pope's judgement on matters of Catholic belief was infallible – be made an official Church doctrine. Not all Catholics, however, agreed with this position. Some of the most cogent opposition came from the bishops and priests of Germany, among them

Box 13.1 (cont.)

Fig. 13.1 Franz Brentano

Box 13.1 (cont.)

Brentano, who wrote a philosophical and historical treatise arguing against the proposed doctrine. The pro-infallibility faction, however, won the day and the doctrine of papal infallibility became the official dogma of the Catholic Church. Brentano had been struggling with religious doubts for some time and the proclamation of papal infallibility was the impetus that led him to question other Church dogmas. Brentano resigned from the priesthood in 1873 and finally left the Church altogether in 1879. During his time as a priest, Brentano had continued to teach philosophy at Würzburg and, in 1874, accepted a professorship at Vienna. In was in this year that his most famous work, *Psychology from an Empirical Standpoint*, was published.

Austrian law prevented anyone who had ever taken priestly vows from marrying and so, in order to marry his fiancée, Brentano, though no longer a priest, had to renounce his Austrian citizenship and marry abroad. Renouncing his Austrian citizenship meant that he had, in addition, to resign his professorship (Figure 13.1). He was allowed to continue teaching under the auspices of the University of Vienna, but without receiving a salary. He tried without success to get his professorship back and finally left Austria in 1895. Brentano first lived in Italy but left at the start of World War I. The war pitted Italy against Austria and Germany. Brentano had pacifist leanings and, moreover, felt that he belonged, in some way, to all three of these countries. He moved, therefore, to neutral Switzerland, where he died in 1917.

Brentano's published output was relatively small and his main influence seems to have been through his teaching. He was, by all accounts, an inspiring and charismatic teacher and many of his students went on to become notable thinkers in their own rights. His former students included Edmund Husserl, founder of phenomenology (see Box 13.2 below), Sigmund Freud, founder of psychoanalysis, and Thomas Masaryk, first president of Czechoslovakia.

Brentano's idea of a non-experimental science owed much to his training in the philosophy of Aristotle (Polkinghorne 2003), which formed an important part of the Catholic theology that Brentano studied for the priesthood. Aristotle's vision of science included descriptive sciences, such as botany, in which one classifies plants into various types according to their different characteristics. This descriptive approach, in which the goal is to develop a taxonomy or classification of phenomena rather than to arrive at an explanation, was, for both Brentano and Aristotle, every bit as scientific as carrying out experiments. It was the approach that Brentano believed was most suitable for psychology. Psychology, said Brentano, "seeks to specify exhaustively the elements of human consciousness and, as far as possible, their interconnections" (cited by Macnamara and Boudewijnse 1995, p. 408).

This type of **descriptive psychology** must precede any attempt to give causal explanations for psychological phenomena. After all, we must know what the different types of mental states and processes actually are before we try to explain them:

> without having distinguished the different fundamental classes of mental phenomena, psychologists would endeavour in vain to establish their laws of succession. (*Psychology from an Empirical Standpoint*, pp. 44–5)

Brentano's psychology, then, would involve the painstaking description of different mental phenomena, just as the botanist would painstakingly collect and describe different types of plants. According to Brentano, the psychologist will, through such descriptions, begin to discern patterns and connections among the different examples under consideration and, at this point, can then start to divide the phenomena into different classes. For Brentano, this perception of patterns is not done through a process of formal induction, but is grasped through insight – we just begin to see, become aware of, the different patterns and commonalities among the things that we are investigating. Brentano's idea of a descriptive psychology laid the foundations for the later development of **phenomenology** (see Box 13.2).

Brentano and method: inner perception

There is, however, an important difference between the psychologist and the botanist. The object of the botanist's inquiry is something external and relatively stable; the act of observation does not alter its characteristics. But Brentano believed that the deliberate introspection of mental states changes those very states that one is trying to introspect upon. According to Brentano, "[i]f someone is in a state in which he wants to observe his own anger raging within him, the anger must already be somewhat diminished, and so his original object of observation would have disappeared ..." (*Psychology from an Empirical Standpoint*, p. 30). But though the deliberate introspection of mental states is, therefore, not a reliable method for the psychologist, we can, said Brentano, gain

Box 13.2 **Phenomenology**

One of the most influential schools of thought to emerge from Brentano's teaching is phenomenology, which was founded by one of Brentano's students, Edmund Husserl (1859–1938). Husserl defined phenomenology as the science of how things appear to us in conscious experience. Phenomenology is not concerned, at least initially, with giving an explanation of our experience. Instead, it seeks to describe that experience and to identify the essential characteristics of each different type of conscious phenomenon. It thus has something in common with Brentano's descriptive psychology and its taxonomic approach.

A phenomenological description demands that we must, if only temporarily, suspend all our preconceptions as to what we think the phenomenon in question should be like in order to describe it as it actually is. If not, our description is likely to be coloured or distorted by these preconceptions. Husserl calls the suspension of preconceptions 'bracketing' them and the process of doing so he calls 'the phenomenological reduction'.

Phenomenology has been particularly influential in Germany, through the work of Martin Heidegger (1889–1976), and France, through the work of Jean-Paul Sartre (1905–80). It is also one of the major schools of thought in qualitative approaches to psychology and, through the work of Maurice Merleau-Ponty (1908–61), forms the philosophical background to much recent research in embodied cognition.

knowledge of our own mental states through what he called **inner perception**. For Brentano, this is the core of psychology:

> Psychology, like the natural sciences, has its basis in perception and experience. Above all, however, its source is to be found in the *inner perception* of our own mental phenomena. We would never know what a thought is, or a judgement, pleasure or pain, desires or aversions, decisions and voluntary intentions if we did not learn what they are through inner perception of our own phenomena. Note, however, that we said that inner *perception* and not introspection, i.e. inner *observation*, constitutes this primary and essential source of psychology. These two concepts must be distinguished from one another. (*Psychology from an Empirical Standpoint*, p. 29)

Inner perception differs from introspection in that, though we do not focus on the mental state that we are experiencing, we nevertheless grasp its nature while we are undergoing it. According to Brentano (again drawing on Aristotle), when you have a certain experience, you are not only aware of the object of that experience, but of the fact that you are having that experience. For example, as I look out of the window at the tree on the pavement opposite, I am aware of the tree: it is the object of my experience. But I am also aware of the fact that I am seeing the tree (and that I am not hearing or touching it). I am also aware of the fact that it is *I* (and not someone else) who is having this visual experience. Nevertheless, my experience, my act of seeing, is not the focus of my attention – the focus of my attention is the tree – and it is only in passing, as it were, that I am also aware of my mental act. Brentano puts it thus:

> It is a universally valid psychological law that we can never focus our *attention* upon the object of inner perception [i.e. the mental process] . . . It is only while our attention is turned toward a different object that we are able to perceive, incidentally, the mental processes that are directed towards that object. (*Psychology from an Empirical Standpoint*, p. 30)

For Brentano, it is true of every mental act – perceiving, willing, thinking, reasoning, judging – that as well as being primarily directed towards an object other than itself, there is a part of consciousness that is aware of the particular act itself that is taking place. This incidental awareness of our own mental acts is, for Brentano, something immediately given and immune to error. The data of psychology, then, are surer than the potentially misleading observations of other sciences.

Intentionality

For Brentano, then, when we are engaged in a mental act there are two contents of consciousness. One is the object of consciousness, such as colours, people, animals, and things; the other is the act of consciousness itself, for example the act of seeing, remembering, or judging. This distinction between a mental act and the object of that mental act is a crucial one for Brentano and is the basis for his most famous contribution to psychology and the philosophy of mind: his theory of **intentionality**. It is intentionality, according to Brentano, that is the essential characteristic of mental acts and processes. Mental states and processes have intentionality; non-mental states and processes do not have intentionality. By the term 'intentionality' Brentano does not mean that mental processes are carried out deliberately or on purpose, but that they are directed towards an object. Or, to put it another way, they are *about* things. My act of seeing the tree, for example, is directed towards the tree, it is about the tree; my thoughts, as I write these words, are *about* Brentano; my hearing of someone working in their garden outside is directed to that person; my image or memory of a holiday in Venice is directed towards that holiday, it is about that holiday. Physical things, however, do not have intentionality in this sense. A table, for example, is just a table; it makes no sense to ask what the table is about or what its object is. It's not about anything or directed at anything, it just is what it is. Mental acts, by contrast, are always about something other than themselves: my act of seeing is not directed at my act of seeing, but at the tree outside the window; my act of remembering is not concerned with remembering itself, but with events and experiences that I have undergone in the past.

Intentionality is thus, for Brentano, the defining characteristic of the mental. "Every mental phenomenon," says Brentano, "is characterized by ... reference to a content, direction toward an object ..." He goes on to state: "No physical phenomenon exhibits anything like it. We can, therefore, define mental phenomena by saying that they contain an object intentionally within themselves" (*Psychology from an Empirical Standpoint*, pp. 88–9).

This idea that mental states and processes have intentionality but physical states and processes do not is one that is still at the centre of many debates today concerning the relationship between the mind and the brain. It poses a problem for those who would wish to identify mental processes with physical processes occurring in a brain (or, indeed, a computer) because they have to explain how it is possible, despite what Brentano says, for some physical states or processes to have this elusive characteristic of *aboutness*. Exactly how this might come about – if, indeed, one believes that it does – is a matter on which there is no consensus.

Ehrenfels and 'gestalt-quality'

We have seen, then, that Brentano believed that psychology should be a descriptive science that catalogues the different types of mental phenomena. In the course of his investigations, one of Brentano's students, Christian von Ehrenfels (1859–1932), believed that he had discovered an aspect of conscious experience that no one had noticed before. He called it the *gestalt-quality*, and he defined it as a perceptual quality associated with the presentation of a complex of perceptual elements. Though each element could be perceived in the absence of the others, there seemed to Ehrenfels to be an added quality when the complex was perceived as a whole, a quality that was characteristic of the ensemble rather than any of the individual elements themselves.

One example of gestalt-quality suggested by Ehrenfels was a melody. This is a new perceptual quality that is something over and above the perception of the individual notes themselves. We can, for example, transpose a melody from one key to another so that the individual notes are now completely different from those in the original key. Nevertheless, we can still perceive the melody when it is played in the new key. This, in fact, was one of the tests that Ehrenfels himself proposed to determine whether a particular perceptual quality was or was not a gestalt-quality: if one changes the elements while keeping the relations between them unaltered and the quality remains unchanged, then it is a gestalt-quality. The gestalt-quality, then, is a new perceptual quality that arises when one perceives the appropriate perceptual elements and which is determined not by the intrinsic characteristics of these elements (e.g. the absolute pitch of musical notes), but by the relationships between them.

We have seen that it was in trying to fulfil Brentano's goal of an exhaustive, descriptive psychology that Ehrenfels discovered the gestalt-quality. There are, however, more profound links between the ideas of Brentano and the idea of gestalt-quality. The roots of this influence go back to the Aristotelian philosophy in which Brentano was so thoroughly schooled and which formed the subject matter of his earliest published works. One of the central questions of both ancient and mediaeval philosophy was the nature of so-called **universals**. This was concerned with the question of what makes a thing the sort of thing that it is. What, for example, makes a dog a dog? What is the quality that a particular dog shares with other dogs but which is not to be found in cats and people? It was Aristotle's answer to this question that formed the ultimate philosophical foundation of the gestalt approach.

One possible answer to the question of what makes a thing a particular type of thing is that it is made out of a particular type of stuff. This works for gold, for example: what makes gold gold is that it is made out of a particular type of material. It is this that differentiates it from, say, silver or iron. But when we consider dogs, this answer won't work: dogs are made out of the same sort of stuff as cats and, for that matter, people. What distinguishes dogs from cats or people is not the **matter** out of which they are made, but *the way in which that matter is organised.* This is what Aristotle called the **form** and it is the form that matter takes rather than the matter itself that defines particular types, classes, or species of things. Indeed, Aristotle's idea of a taxonomic science, which as we have seen influenced Brentano, is a systematic attempt to classify natural phenomena according to their forms so that those with the same or similar forms are grouped together and those with different forms are kept separate.

This distinction between basic matter and the form into which that matter is organised is mirrored in Ehrenfels's distinction between foundational perceptual elements (e.g. musical notes), which are analogous to Aristotelian matter, and the gestalt organisation (e.g. the melody), which is analogous to the form that is given to that basic matter.

Gestalt psychology

In the 1920s, a group of psychologists took Ehrenfels's idea of the gestalt-quality, made it more radical, and turned it into a more general psychological theory, which came to be known as Gestalt psychology. The three psychologists most closely associated with Gestalt psychology are Max Wertheimer (1880–1943), Kurt Koffka (1886–1941), and Wolfgang Köhler (1887–1967) (see Box 13.3 for biographical information), and they radicalised Ehrenfels's insight in the

Box 13.3 Major Gestalt psychologists

Max Wertheimer was born in Prague in 1880. He originally started to study law, but changed to psychology and philosophy, which he pursued in Prague, Berlin, and Würzburg. It seems that, in studying law, Wertheimer became interested in the psychology of courtroom testimony and he completed his thesis on the ability to detect lying. Wertheimer's other main interest was music and he was not only an accomplished violinist, but also composed sophisticated pieces from an early age. His musical interests are apparent in his first psychology publications, which examine the music of the native peoples of Sri Lanka. Though such music might have been dismissed as crude by Western Europeans of the time, Wertheimer argued that it had a complex structure and that earlier phrases in the melody set up 'expectations' that were then fulfilled or completed by later parts. Although Wertheimer had, at this time, not explicitly formulated the idea of a perceptual Gestalt, it is clearly foreshadowed in the idea that different parts of a melody fit with one another to form a complete whole.

Wertheimer later claimed to have had a sudden insight concerning the nature of perceived motion when, during a train journey, he noticed that two flashing lights at a station produced the illusion of one single light moving back and forth. This illusion became known as the phi phenomenon, and Wertheimer carried out extensive research on it, often with the assistance of Koffka and Köhler (see below). Wertheimer worked at the universities of Frankfurt and Berlin but, in 1933, became alarmed at the rise of Nazism. He left Germany and subsequently settled in the United States, where he continued to teach and research. He died of a heart attack at his home in New York in 1943.

Box 13.3 (cont.)

Kurt Koffka was born in Berlin in 1886. He worked at a number of German universities, including Berlin and Frankfurt, and also worked extensively in the United States, where he finally settled in 1927. Koffka is credited with writing the first article in English on Gestalt psychology, which was published in the *Psychological Bulletin* in 1922. He also extended the principles of Gestalt psychology to child development, arguing that the child does not learn through association, but through responses to whole situations. He died of a heart attack in 1941.

Wolfgang Köhler was born in Estonia in 1887. He studied both psychology and physics and, in 1913, was appointed director of Prussian Academy of Sciences Anthropoid Station on the island of Tenerife. It was here that he carried out his celebrated research into problem-solving in chimpanzees. He returned to Germany in 1920 and worked at the universities of Göttingen and Berlin. In 1933, the Nazis began to dismiss academics of Jewish origin or those who held anti-Nazi views and to replace them with Nazi sympathisers. Köhler, by this time a professor and director of the Psychological Institute in Berlin, protested against these measures and tried to have some of the dismissed staff reinstated. He was, however, unsuccessful and, despairing of being able to change the situation, emigrated to the United States. He continued to work there until his death in 1967.

following way. Ehrenfels had thought of the gestalt-quality as an additional perceptual quality that stood alongside the perceptual qualities associated with the individual elements that made up the whole. The elements and the Gestalt were of equal importance. For the new Gestaltists, however, the Gestalt had primary importance. They argued that perceptual elements did not exist independently or have their own inherent qualities, as Ehrenfels believed, but only had the qualities that they did have in virtue of the place that they had in the context of the gestalt configuration. Wertheimer defined the new, radical view in the following way:

The fundamental 'formula' of Gestalt theory might be expressed in this way: There are wholes, the behaviour of which is not determined by that of their individual elements, but *where the part-processes are themselves determined by the intrinsic nature of the whole.* It is the hope of gestalt theory to determine the nature of such wholes. (Wertheimer 1925, p. 2, my italics)

Against the constancy hypothesis

The Gestaltists' insistence that there were no independently existing perceptual elements apart from the whole of which they were part went against a long-held philosophical assumption. As far back as empiricists such as Locke, for example, we find the idea that our complex perceptions are made up from the combination of simple sensory ideas or sensations. These simple ideas or sensations are defined by their own, intrinsic characteristics. The sensation of white, for example, resists any further analysis or definition – it just *is* the sensation of white. Whenever we see a white thing, it produces this sensation in us; whenever we hear a C-sharp, it produces that same sensation in us. The various sensations can, of course, be combined in different ways, but the sensations themselves are unaltered by these combinations: white combined with red is the same as white combined with black; it is still the same sensation of white in all cases. Similarly, a C-sharp combined with a G is the same as a C-sharp combined with an A. The overall combination into, say, a chord may be different in its final effect, but the basic sensation of the C-sharp is the same in all cases. This idea – that a particular stimulus stimulating a particular sense organ will always produce the same basic sensation – is sometimes called the **constancy hypothesis.** It is something with which the Gestalt psychologists completely disagreed and its rejection lies at the heart of the Gestaltist approach to psychology.

What, then, are the arguments and evidence that the Gestaltists mobilise in combating the constancy hypothesis? The first source of evidence is simply reflection on our own sensory experience. The Gestaltists placed great emphasis on looking directly at our actual experience. Indeed, according to the phenomenologist Aaron Gurwitsch, this demand was one of the defining factors of Gestalt psychology:

> Gestalt theory gives an absolute primacy to immediate observation, as opposed to every theoretical consideration. The question no longer concerns what *ought* to be given ... but rather concerns what *is* actually given, what is accessible to direct observation. (Gurwitsch 1966, p. 23)

When we examine our normal perceptual experience we find that it does not consist of atomistic elements that are unvaryingly produced by the same stimuli time after time. Things are perceived differently depending on the context in which they are found: a colour appears brighter when placed beside a dark colour than when placed beside one that is even brighter than itself. Wertheimer himself points out that the same musical note is perceived differently depending on the melodic context in which it occurs:

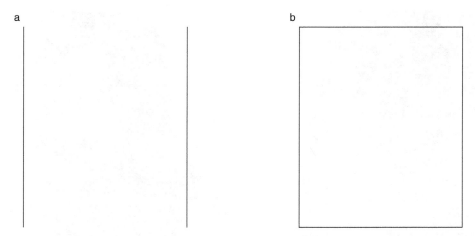

Fig. 13.2 Alteration in the perception of lines as a function of perceptual context

> Is it really true that when I hear a melody I have a *sum* of individual tones ... which
> constitute the primary foundation of my experience? Is not perhaps the reverse of this
> true? ... [W]hat I hear of each individual note ... is a *part* which is itself determined by
> the character of the whole ... The flesh and blood of a tone depends from the start upon
> its role in the melody: a *b* as leading tone to *c* is something radically different from the *b*
> as tonic. (Wertheimer 1925, p. 5)

Our experience of a melody, then, does not accord with the constancy hypothesis:
how we perceive the notes is not simply a matter of their own intrinsic characteristics; it is a question of the role that they play within the whole. And it is not
simply the case that the whole is more than the sum of its parts, it is that the whole
determines what those parts are because outside the context of the whole they
would not have the characteristics that they do have.

Even a moment's reflection on very simple perceptual experiences will reveal,
according to the Gestaltists, the problems with the constancy hypothesis. Take, for
example, two lines, such as those shown in Figure 13.2a. They are perceived as two
individual lines, parallel and separate from one another. If we add two more lines,
as in Figure 13.2b, the two original lines are now perceived differently: they are
perceived as sides of a square rather than just two independent lines. Nothing about
the lines themselves has changed – their objective physical characteristics are the
same – but they are now perceived in a different context. It is this context, and the
role that they play within it, that determines how the lines are perceived, either as
sides of a single figure or as independent elements.

Ambiguous figures, such as the Rubin vase (see Figure 13.3), also provide
evidence against the constancy hypothesis. This figure can be seen either as a

Fig. 13.3 The Rubin vase

white candlestick against a black background or as the black silhouettes of faces in profile against a white background. But, though the same figure can be perceived in two completely distinct ways, no change in the stimulus accompanies the change in perceptual experience. Given that the constancy hypothesis claims that the same stimulus will always give rise to the same sensations, the existence of ambiguous figures constitutes, according to the Gestaltists, a powerful argument against it.

A defender of the constancy hypothesis might reply that, though the final *perceptions* of a figure may differ according to context, nevertheless *the basic sensations* are the same. It is the different ways in which these same basic sensations are put together or interpreted that gives rise to different perceptual experiences. According to this view, the unchanging atomistic sensations are present unconsciously even though they are not consciously perceived. We have already encountered a similar view in Helmholtz's idea of unconscious inferences.

This is, however, a view that the Gestaltists thoroughly repudiated as unscientific. There can, by definition, be no evidence in our experience for the existence of these unconscious sensations. Belief in them is, therefore, unscientific; it departs from the facts of perception. The only motivation that one could have for believing in the existence of unconscious sensations, then, is a pre-existing assumption that they must exist simply because one's theory – the constancy hypothesis – demands that they exist.

In addition, because assertions concerning these hypothetical unconscious sensations cannot be checked against the facts of experience, there is no limit to what unconscious sensations can be called in to do. According to Gurwitsch, they "escape all control; they can be neither validated not invalidated by direct observation ... the object of psychology, the immediate data, is renounced in favour of data constructed according to the requirements of a theory" (Gurwitsch 1966, p. 22). Gestalt psychology, on the other hand, does not invent unconscious entities for which there is no evidence, but is rooted firmly in perceptual experience.

For the Gestaltists, then, sensations, far from being the most basic and funda-mental features of perceptual experience, are actually theoretical fictions thought up by psychologists, philosophers, and physiologists because they fit in with what they think *should* be there. They are a product of sophisticated – albeit erroneous – thinking. After all, if atomistic sensations really were primary, we would expect them to be present in the perceptual experience of more primitive species or infants, but this is not the case:

> We have learned to recognize the 'sensations' of our textbooks as products of a late culture utterly different from the experiences of more primitive stages. Who experi-ences the sensation of a specific red in that sense? What the man of the streets, children, or primitive men normally react to is something coloured but at the same time exciting, gay, strong, or affecting – not 'sensations'. (Wertheimer 1925, p. 6)

In other words, the untutored, direct experience is of an object as a whole, not of a collection of atomistic elements.

Gestalt organisation

If we accept that we perceive not a concatenation of sensations, but an organised whole, the question then arises as to the nature of this perceptual organisation. The Gestaltists claimed to have identified certain laws or principles according to which our perceptual experience is organised. Wertheimer (1925) notes that features that have similar characteristics tend to be grouped together. Figure 13.4a, for example, tends not to be seen as an array of individual black and white dots, but as columns of black dots alternating with columns of

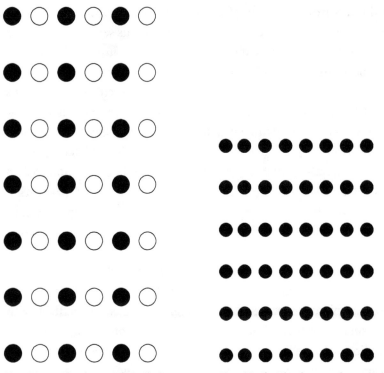

Fig. 13.4a The factor of similarity   **Fig. 13.4b** The factor of proximity

white dots. This feature of our experience was called the **factor of similarity** by Wertheimer. But this is only one of the factors that are at work in perceptual organisation. Sometimes it is those features that are closest to one another that tend to be perceived together. Figure 13.4b depicts an array of black dots, but they do not tend to be seen just as an array of individual elements, but as a series of horizontal lines. Note that the dots are all black and so cannot be grouped together according to the law of similarity. The distances between them, however, are shorter in the horizontal dimension than in the vertical dimension and so those that are closest together tend to be perceived as part of the same perceptual unit. Wertheimer called this the **factor of proximity**.

Another example of Gestalt organisation is depicted in Figure 13.5. This tends to be perceived as two lines crossing over one another rather than two pointed shapes, such as > and <, touching one another at a single point. It would appear that, because the contour of segment B continues smoothly that of segment A, they tend to be perceived as parts of the same line. This is sometimes called the **principle of good continuity**, and it is the principle that underlies the effectiveness of camouflage, whether it occurs naturally or through human design. If the

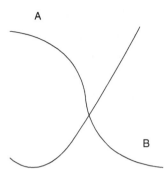

Fig. 13.5 The factor of good continuity

perceptual features of your covering continue those of your background in a smooth and relatively unbroken fashion, then an observer will tend to perceive you as part of the background against which you stand; you and the background will form a single perceptual entity.

All of these individual examples (similarity, proximity, good continuation) are just manifestations of the one overall principle of gestalt organisation, which is sometimes referred to as the principle of **Prägnantz**. According to this principle, our perceptions will tend to form as good a gestalt pattern as possible. It makes no sense to ask which of the Gestalt laws (e.g. similarity or proximity) is the stronger in any absolute sense. The factors that predominate in any situation will be those that produce the most stable and organised perception, and this will be different on different occasions. This point is emphasised by Koffka:

> Psychological organization will always be as 'good' as the prevailing conditions allow. In this definition the term 'good' is undefined. It embraces such properties as regularity, symmetry, simplicity, and others. (Koffka 1935, p. 110)

Organisation in nature

Having now described the principles according to which our perception is organised, we are still left with the question of where this organisation comes from. For empiricists, who believe in atomistic sensations, the answer is clear – organisation comes from the association of perceptual elements. This association arises in the course of our experience: discrete perceptual elements that tend to occur together, for example, become associated with one another over the course of time and, eventually, are perceived as parts of the same object or event.

For the Gestaltists, however, associationism cannot account for the structured and meaningful nature of our perceptual experience because the associations that it envisages are completely arbitrary. It is a matter of definition of the atomistic approach that *nothing is intrinsically connected with anything else* in our perceptual experience. After all, if there were such intrinsic perceptual connections, then association would not be needed to put together what is essentially separate. But if association is arbitrary there is no reason why any sensation occurring simultaneously or in succession with any other should or should not be associated together.

The atomistic approach, then, cannot account for our structured and meaningful experience. If sensory atoms are associated in an essentially arbitrary way then it is difficult to understand how anything stable and meaningful would arise from such associations. There is nothing to guide these associations – no indication of what goes with what – and so the resulting perceptual experience would just be as jumbled and meaningless as the atoms from which it was constructed. If there is anything to guide these associations – any indication as to what goes with what – then we have, in effect, abandoned the atomistic approach because some perceptual elements are perceived as being more closely related than others and are, therefore, not discrete, independent atoms of experience.

But as well as such theoretical arguments against atomistic associationism, the Gestaltists produced experimental evidence to support their criticisms. Participants were presented with complex shapes in which were embedded commonly seen figures. Figure 13.6, for example, contains within it the numeral '4'. If empricisim were correct and we group together the elements of our perceptual experience that we have encountered together most commonly in the past, then the figure 4 should

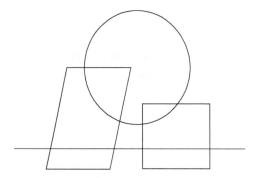

Fig. 13.6 The hidden figure '4'

have been immediately obvious to the participants. But it was not. Indeed, not only did they not spontaneously spot the figure 4, but when they were told specifically that the figure 4 was hidden in the shape, they still had great difficulty in finding it (Köhler 1947).

Both logical argument and empirical data, then, are difficult to square with the idea that perception is organised according to associations based on past experience. The Gestaltists argued instead that our perceptual experience is *intrinsically structured and meaningful.* It does not require organisation to be imposed upon it because it is already organised in itself. This is, perhaps, one of the most difficult, and radical, notions of gestalt psychology: the idea that the perceptual field is **self-organising.** Throughout the history of thought about perception, the predominant idea has been that perception has to be organised *by* something. In the case of the empiricists, as we have seen, this organisation is done through the laws of association. According to Kant, on the other hand, our experience is organised by inbuilt mental structures that embody space, time, and causality. Despite the major, and obvious, differences between empiricists and Kantians, however, both schools of thought regarded the raw sensory input to the mind as something essentially disorganised, chaotic, and meaningless. Though they differed on the means whereby such input was to be organised, they nevertheless agreed that it had to *be organised* by some process or other.

This similarity of outlook was recognised by Wertheimer:

> For centuries the assumption has prevailed that our world is essentially a summation of elements. For Hume and largely also for Kant the world is like a bundle of fragments, and the dogma of meaningless summations continues to play its part. (Wertheimer 1925, p. 9)

It is precisely this outlook – that the empirical world is disorganised and has to be structured by us – that is rejected by the Gestalt psychologists. And that is why it is so difficult to grasp: it goes so radically against the grain of the majority of thinking about the mind. In place of an essentially chaotic perceptual world, the Gestaltists give us a perceptual world that is *intrinsically structured.* According to Gurwitsch, Gestalt theory "does not admit any primary raw materials in need of being organized by means of subjective acts, *the multiplicities are considered grouped at the very outset*" (Gurwitsch 1966, p. 30, my italics). The same point is made by Wertheimer:

> *The given is itself in varying degrees "structured" ... it consists of more or less definitely structured wholes and whole processes with their whole-properties and laws, characteristic whole tendencies and whole-determinations of parts.* (Wertheimer 1925, p. 14)

When various perceptual features are grouped together as belonging to one object and others as belonging to another object, this is not because we *impose* this grouping on the perceptual input, it is because this grouping is *already there* in the perceptual input itself.

The idea that natural phenomena somehow organise themselves into coherent structures may seem mysterious at first, but self-organisation is, in fact, found throughout nature. Köhler (1947) pointed out that, in nature, the free dynamic interplay of forces tends to produce order rather than disorder – when we mix oil and water together, they will separate into distinct layers, but there is no organising entity that has to do the separating. Similarly, no one or thing has to organise the snowflake into a six-sided figure; that is simply the result of physical forces that operate throughout nature acting on particular material. Or, to use another example that was a favourite of the Gestaltists, no one organises a soap bubble into its spherical shape: it is a self-organising phenomenon. The spherical shape is simply the most stable form into which the molecules can combine given the physical forces acting upon them. The organisation and structure emerge *naturally* from the forces at work in the physical world, and the action of these forces tends to produce order rather than disorder.

This is the way in which the Gestaltists viewed perceptual organisation. Like any other natural phenomenon, the phenomena of perception tend to naturally organise themselves into the most stable and coherent structures, and it is the goal of the psychologist to describe the laws or principles according to which such structuring takes place. According to Köhler:

> As the physicist is accustomed to say that surface tension tends to reduce the area of liquid surfaces, so we say that in the sensory field grouping tends to establish units of certain kinds rather than others. Simple and regular wholes, also closed areas, are formed more readily and more generally than irregular and open wholes. The order of sensory fields, in this sense, shows a strong predilection for particular kinds of organization, just as the formation of molecules and the pull of surface forces in physics operate in specific directions. (Köhler 1947, p. 145)

The idea that some perceptual organisations are more *natural*, are more stable, simple, clear – are, in short, better Gestalts – than others is shown by our own perceptual experience. Consider the arrangement of black and white dots in Figure 13.4a, which illustrate the effect of similarity. In theory there is no reason why one should not see this arrangement as a series of horizontal lines composed of alternating black and white dots rather than alternating columns composed either of uniform black dots or uniform white dots. Indeed, when one thinks about it, there are many other possible ways in which this array could be seen: as a collection of completely individual dots not organised into lines or columns, as a series of diagonal lines composed of alternating black and white dots, for example. Nevertheless, we do not see the figure in this way: it seems as though the perceptual field naturally organises itself in a certain way regardless of our intentions or wishes. We can *try* to see the figure in one of the many possible non-preferred ways – such as horizontal lines of alternating black and white dots – but it is difficult to hold on to this perception and there is always a tendency to switch back into the preferred perception.

It is in this context that the various Gestalt 'laws of organisation' have to be understood. Our perceptual fields naturally and spontaneously organise them-selves according to such factors as similarity, proximity, and good continuity. *We do not impose such organisation on our perceptions; they come to us ready formed.* The Gestalt laws of organisation, then, are not *explanations* of perceptual organisation that is imposed on chaotic material, but *descriptions* of the ways in which the perceptual world spontaneously self-organises.

Extension of the basic Gestalt principles

Although the basic ideas of the Gestalt approach were developed in connection with perception, it soon became apparent to many Gestalt psychologists that the principles that had been uncovered could be generalised to other areas of psy-chology as well. The psychology of problem-solving was one area that saw a particularly famous, and fruitful, application of gestalt principles: Köhler's (1925) chimpanzee studies.

In applying Gestalt principles to problem-solving, Köhler was combating the same brand of associationist thinking that had been prevalent in percep-tual theory. Associationist theories of problem-solving, which had been pro-posed by Thorndike (see Chapter 16), claimed that an animal, when placed in a problem situation, will produce a series of random behaviours. Some of these behaviours, purely through luck rather than any reasoning on the part of the animal, will lead toward the solution of the problem. The association of this response with a successful outcome will make it more likely to occur in the future so that, when the animal is again faced with the same problem, it will be able to solve it ever more quickly. It is important to note that, for Thorndike, this sort of learning required no intelligence – it relied on the purely mechanical association of a fortuitous response with a successful out-come. There is, according to this view, no intrinsic connection between the problem situation, the response, and the outcome; they all become associated with one another through purely arbitrary connections in a way that is analogous to the arbitrary association of atomistic sensory elements in empiricist perceptual theories.

The Gestaltists' response to associationist theories of problem-solving was analogous to their response to associationist theories of perception. Just as perception, for the Gestaltists, involves seeing an integrated and coherent whole figure, so learning and problem-solving involve seeing and understanding the configuration of the whole problem situation. We can see this approach at work in Köhler's chimpanzee studies.

Köhler observed how chimpanzees in a cage learned to use objects to reach for food outside the cage. In one particular instance, a chimpanzee called Sultan, who had learned to reach for food with a single bamboo stick, was presented with food that was beyond the reach of a single stick. Sultan had managed to use one stick to push a second stick along the ground outside the cage to touch the desired food but, as the two sticks were not connected, he could not use this method to actually succeed in retrieving the food. After an hour of doing this, Sultan seemed to have given up on getting the food and was left on his own to play with the sticks. In so doing he brought the two sticks into alignment with one another and then pushed the thinner stick inside the thicker one to produce a single long stick. At this point he ran excitedly to the bars of the cage and used this new implement to retrieve the banana that was outside the cage but was outside the reach of either of the sticks on its own.

It appeared to Köhler that Sultan had suddenly realised that pushing one stick inside the other was the solution to retrieving the food. Rather than a progressive and gradual association of different random behaviours, it appeared that the chimpanzee had suddenly 'seen' the connections between the different parts of the problem and, therefore, how the problem could be solved. Köhler referred to this seeing of connections as **insight**. This term has sometimes been misinter-preted as suggesting that the chimpanzees had some mysterious intellectual ability, but all that Köhler meant by the term was that they had been able to perceive the whole problem situation and what was demanded to solve it. It is less a question of higher-level thinking than a question of simply seeing what things go together, what things feel 'right' in the sense that a symmetrical figure is more 'right' than an asymmetrical one.

The insight displayed in problem-solving is analogous to the perception of Gestalts in that it often involves the reconfiguration of a problem situation. We have already encountered perceptual configurations, such as the Rubin vase (Figure 13.3), which have more than one stable perception. We see the figure one way, as a vase against a black background, and then, suddenly, without necessarily any effort on our part, our perceptual field reconfigures itself so that we now see the silhouettes of two faces. The reconfiguration of a perceptual figure is analogous to the reconfiguration of a problem situation, to suddenly seeing it in a different way: Sultan suddenly saw that the two sticks could be pushed together to create one long stick. No longer were the sticks seen as two individual items; they were now seen as complementary parts of a larger whole. They now played a different functional role within the problem situation just as the black areas of the Rubin vase play a different functional role (i.e. part of a single black background or two silhouettes) depending on the way in which the figure is seen. In this way, the ideas that had originally been developed in the study of perception were applied by Gestaltists to a wide range of psychological topics.

Conclusion

We have now seen how Brentano's descriptive psychology and Ehernfels's subsequent discovery of the gestalt-quality ultimately led to the development of Gestalt psychology, with its questioning of the idea that states of mind are built up from atomistic sensations. The Gestalt psychologists argued that there was simply no evidence anywhere in our experience for such a position. Indeed, not only was there no evidence *for* the sensationalist position, there was actually a mass of evidence *against* it and the constancy hypothesis which underpinned it. For the Gestalt psychologists, perceptual experience, and, by extension, the rest of our mental states, was far more readily understandable in terms of intrinsically structured wholes. Such structures were not imposed on a chaos of individual elements, but were intrinsic to the wholes themselves. In the next chapter we shall see how another psychologist, William James, exemplified, in his own way, this anti-atomistic trend in his approach to what he called the 'stream of consciousness'.

Revision questions

1. How, according to Brentano, does inner perception differ from introspection?

2. What did Brentano mean by 'intentionality'?

3. What did Ehrenfels mean by 'gestalt-quality'?

4. What is the constancy hypothesis and why did the Gestalt psychologists disagree with it?

5. Describe some of the principles of Gestalt organisation. Why did the Gestaltists think that such principles applied to our perceptual experience?

6. How were Gestalt ideas applied to problem-solving?

References

Brentano, F. ([1874]/1973). *Psychology from an Empirical Standpoint*, trans. A. C. Rancurello, D. B. Terrell, and L. L. McAlister. London: Routledge.

Gurwitsch, A. (1966). Some aspects and developments of Gestalt psychology. In Gurwitsch, A., *Studies in Phenomenology and Psychology*. Evanston, IL: Northwestern University Press, pp. 3–55.

Koffka, K. (1935). *Principles of Gestalt Psychology*. London: Routledge.

Köhler, W. (1925). *The Mentality of Apes*. London: Routledge.

Köhler, W. (1947). *Gestalt Psychology*. New York: Liveright.

Macnamara, J. and Boudewijnse, G.-J. (1995). Brentano's influence on Ehrenfels's theory of perceptual gestalts. *Journal for the Theory of Social Behaviour*, 25, 401–18.

Polkinghorne, D. E. (2003). Franz Brentano's psychology from an empirical standpoint. In R. J. Sternberg (ed.) *The Anatomy of Impact: What Makes the Great Works of Psychology Great*. Washington, DC: American Psychological Association, pp. 43–70.

Smith, B. (1994). *Austrian Philosophy: The Legacy of Franz Brentano*. La Salle, IL: Open Court.

Wertheimer, M. (1925). Gestalt theory. In W. D. Ellis (ed.) (1938) *A Source Book of Gestalt Psychology*. London: Routledge and Kegan Paul, pp. 1–11.

14 William James and the stream of consciousness

Timeline

1846–8	US–Mexican War
1859	Darwin publishes *On the Origin of Species*
1860	Abraham Lincoln elected president
1861–5	American Civil War
1876	Defeat of Custer and 7th Cavalry at the battle of Little Bighorn
1884	Mark Twain publishes *The Adventures of Huckleberry Finn*
1901	Assassination of US President McKinley

William James

1842	Born in New York
1860	Studies painting
1864	Goes to study medicine at Harvard
1865	Goes to Brazil as part of scientific expedition
1870	Suffers serious breakdown
1872	Starts teaching physiology at Harvard
1889	Made Professor of Psychology
1890	Publishes *The Principles of Psychology*
1902	Publishes *The Varieties of Religious Experience*
1907	Publishes *Pragmatism*
1910	Dies in Chocorua, New Hampshire

Introduction

The Gestaltists, as we saw in the previous chapter, argued against the psychological atomism that was inherent in both classical empiricism, of which Titchener was the modern incarnation, and Kantianism, of which Wundt was the representative. They were not, however, the only ones to find fault with these views: William James also disagreed with atomism. His approach, however, derived not from the Aristotle-influenced descriptive psychology of Brentano but from empiricism itself. For James, as we shall see, classical empiricism of the type exemplified by the likes of Locke and Hume was simply not empiricist enough. It had claimed to be true to the facts of experience, but had failed to live up to its own principles. It had, for example, claimed that experience was made up of atomistic sensations when no such things were ever actually found in our experience. If only, thought James, empiricists had had the courage of their convictions, they would have seen that our mental life does not consist of discrete elements but is an interconnected flux. It was a more radical empiricism, one that really did try to do justice to the facts of experience, that lay at the foundation of James's approach to psychology. The essence of this anti-atomistic approach to consciousness is exemplified in James's central idea of the **stream of consciousness.**

Like the Gestaltists, James believed that structure did not have to be imposed on experience by bringing together disconnected elements, but rather that experience was itself inherently structured. We can, indeed we must, break up the stream of consciousness into parts and regions by focusing on one aspect of experience rather than another because we cannot take in all aspects of the rich flux of experience at once. But this breaking up of the stream into parts is something *we* do after the fact: experience does not come to us in parts.

James's willingness to take experience at face value coupled with his belief that our awareness of the richness of experiential reality is necessarily limited meant that he was unwilling to dismiss any idea or thought out of hand. No matter how unorthodox or outré an idea might be, if, for James, it seemed to have a genuine basis in the concrete experience of someone, it was worthy of consideration. This attitude led James to investigate areas of experience, such as altered states of consciousness or religious mysticism, that seldom figured in the research interests of more conventional academics.

In describing consciousness as a stream, James was attempting to get at the *what* of consciousness, its fundamental characteristics. But he was also interested in the *why* of consciousness, the reason for its existing in the first place. The answer to this question was, for James, rooted in biology and evolution, and it is to this aspect of his thought that we now turn.

Box 14.1 **William James**

William James was born on 11 January 1842 in New York City. His father, Henry James Sr, was a restless individual and, as a result, the family was frequently on the move. William and his siblings – the novelist Henry James was one of his brothers – never stayed in one school, or even one country, for very long. The children received not only home schooling, but also, at various points, attended schools in Switzerland, France, and Germany, as the family moved back and forth between the USA and Europe. By the time William was 16, the family had lived at 18 different addresses.

James himself was a restless spirit and throughout his life he was predisposed towards freedom, change, and impulsivity. His sister, Alice, compared him to "a blob of mercury" because "you cannot put a mental finger upon him" (cited by Menand 2001, p. 74). This characteristic is evident in the number of times that James changed his mind about which career to pursue. His early inclination, at the age of 18, was to be an artist and he had private painting lessons. Surviving drawings by James show him to have been a talented draughtsman. James's interests, however, switched from art to science and he studied chemistry, before moving to anatomy and physiology, and then to medicine. Before completing his medical degree, however, James decided that he wanted to be a naturalist and set off for the Amazon as part of a scientific expedition investigating the geographical distribution of animal species. James returned from the expedition having realised that he did not want to be a naturalist after all and completed his medical training, although he never subsequently practised medicine (Figure 14.1).

James's inability to find a direction for his life, as well as recurring physical illnesses, plunged him into depression. He went to Europe in search of a cure and, in his spare time, attended courses in physiology in Berlin, which stimulated his interest in the newly emerging field of physiological psychology. A few years later he finally found a measure of stability when he was appointed as an

Box 14.1 (cont.)

instructor in physiology at Harvard. He was to continue working at Harvard for the rest of his academic life. James was, nevertheless, uncomfortable at times with the formality of university life and preferred walking in the woods and climbing in the Adirondack Mountains to university functions and parties. It was on one of these climbs, at the age of 58, that James seriously strained his already damaged heart. His steadily worsening heart condition resulted in his death ten years later, in 1910.

Fig. 14.1 William James

The mind and evolution

James studied biology before turning to psychology and philosophy, and Darwinian ideas of evolution permanently coloured his thought. The crucial lesson of Darwinism, as James saw it, was that the natural world was not something fixed or predictable, but was, on the contrary, constantly transforming itself. Pre-Darwinian thinkers had believed that the different animal species were each created according to their own unchanging patterns, as if there was a specific template for a lion or a chimpanzee which was embodied by the individual members of these species. But Darwin showed the opposite to be the case – the natural world, far from containing species characterised by fixed attributes, was a scene of continuous change. Species evolved into new species with different features rather than just repeating the same unchanging patterns from generation to generation. Fluidity and not stability was nature's most notable feature.

The engine of this change was variation in individual organisms. Some of these variations prove to be successful for survival and reproduction, and therefore continue, whereas others are not successful, and consequently disappear. Other evolutionary thinkers prior to Darwin had also believed this, but Darwin's fundamental insight, according to James, was his realisation that these variations arose *spontaneously from within the organism* rather than being produced by the environment. James accused other thinkers – who believed themselves to be Darwinian – of failing to see this crucial point. Herbert Spencer, for example, argued that the mind was essentially shaped by the environment, and that our thoughts and ideas were ultimately the products of environmental influences. This way of thinking was, for James, of a piece with pre-Darwinian theories of evolution, according to which the environment not only selected those giraffes with long necks as the fittest, but somehow produced the long necks by having the giraffes strive to reach food high in the trees (James 1880). What Spencer had failed to do, according to James, was to differentiate between the *production* and the *selection* of characteristics in evolution. Darwin's great achievement was to have distinguished these two roles. According to Darwin, the environment selects those variations that are most successful – the fittest – but it does not produce them. The variations are produced spontaneously by the organism itself. Exactly how and why these variations arise is, from the point of view of evolution, irrelevant; it is what happens to variations *after* they appear that is important.

For James, the same points that were true of bodily variations were also true of the mind. He believed that a truly Darwinian view of the mind requires that the mind freely produce thoughts, ideas, and actions from within itself to provide raw material for the selection carried out by the environment. Spencer's view, that the mind was a passive entity onto which the environment stamped its mark, was incompatible with Darwinian evolution. Of course, James recognised that both our previous experience and our genetic inheritance *influence* our thoughts, but he argued that they do not *determine* them. Our thoughts, he said, spring from an "active originality and spontaneous productivity which Spencer's law so entirely ignores" (cited by Perry 1936, p. 478). For James, there is not only a space for novelty and unpredictability in Darwinian evolution, novelty and unpredictability are essential to it.

The knowing mind, then, is not, for James "simply a mirror floating with no foot-hold anywhere … passively reflecting an order that he comes upon and finds simply existing". It is "an actor", it is "in the game, and not a mere looker-on" (James 1878, p.17). It generates thoughts and performs actions that may, or may not, meet with success in the selecting environment. But though they spring spontaneously from the organism, these thoughts and actions are not simply arbitrary. They are in the service of the organism's own interests, whether these are basic biological interests or, in higher forms of consciousness, more complex cultural and moral interests. James points out, however, that the very existence of 'interests' at all requires the existence of consciousness. In a purely mechanical universe devoid of consciousness, nothing has interests or goals; events merely happen, determined by previous events in a causal chain. We cannot say that its erosion by wind and rain is detrimental to a rock's interests, since a rock is not the sort of thing that has any interests at all, but is an inert piece of matter. We also find the same absence at the biological level: the brain and other organs, for example, have no concerns about the survival of their owner; they have no concerns at all, since they do not think. For an organism to have any interests at all it has, at some level, to *care* about its own survival. Such an organism need not possess a fully reflective human consciousness, but consciousness of some sort is essential.

With the arrival of such a consciousness, the question of survival is no longer just one of merely theoretical interest, as if the consciousness were a "mere looker-on", but "has now become an imperative decree" (James 1890, vol. 1, p. 141). Survival has now become a goal that the organism is impelled to realise. A conscious organism does not simply choose a course of action while remaining indifferent to the consequences – it predicts what those consequences will be and chooses the actions whose consequences further its own interests. The conscious mind, says James, is "a fighter for ends" (James 1890, vol. 1, p. 141). Consciousness, then, allows us to make novel choices as to those actions that, we believe, are most in accord with our own interests.

A Darwinian view of knowledge: pragmatism

This Darwinian view of the mind – as a producer of novel thoughts and actions, which are then selected by the environment – was expanded by James into a more general theory of knowledge, which he called **pragmatism**. He was at pains to point out that pragmatism was not exclusively his own idea and explicitly credited C. S. Pierce with formulating its essential idea in a series of lectures called 'How to make our ideas clear' (1878). Pierce and James (and, as we will see in the next chapter, 'Dewey and functionalism') believed that ideas were not merely descriptions or representations of the external world, but that they had an essential role to play in the organism's struggle for survival. Ideas were not pictures in the head, but tools for practical living, they were "rules for action" (James, *Pragmatism*, p. 25).

In emphasising the concrete and practical nature of our ideas James, along with other pragmatists, was reacting against the prevailing metaphysical philosophy of the time, which he criticised as being too abstract and woolly. It invoked grandiose sounding terms – such as God, or Reason – as if they were the final solutions to age-old philosophical problems. But, for James, such high-flown language was less an answer to real questions than an escape from the difficulty and messiness of everyday life. When faced with a problem about which course of action to follow, the injunctions to "follow God's will" or to "act rationally" are both equally empty, because they do not actually tell us what to do. What you have to do when faced with abstractions like God and Reason is to "bring out of each word its practical cash-value, set it at work within the stream of your experience" (*Pragmatism*, p. 28). What does following the will of God or the dictates of reason actually amount to in terms of concrete action? – this is the important question for the pragmatist. Any abstraction that cannot be translated into concrete effects in the empirical world is just empty verbiage. From the pragmatist perspective, then, "[t]heories ... become instruments, not answers to enigmas ..." (*Pragmatism*, p. 28). They tell us how the world would be different if one theory were acted upon rather than another, and thus guide our action.

The evolutionary aspect of pragmatism is clear – ideas are there to help us to survive and flourish in our environments. But there is also another important affinity between pragmatism and Darwinism: the emphasis on the future rather than the past. For James, pragmatism does not mean any particular dogma or creed, but a general "attitude of orientation . . . [t]he attitude of looking away from first things, principles, 'categories', supposed necessities; and of looking towards last things, fruits, consequences, facts" (*Pragmatism*, p. 29, italics in original). This is in accord with what James identified as the crucial aspect of Darwinism – the supreme importance of the selection of variations and the irrelevance of how those variations were created. For Darwinian evolution, as we have seen above, the source of variations in organisms is of minor importance. It is what happens to these variations once they arrive on the scene that is important. A similar mindset characterised pragmatism: where ideas come from does not matter, it is their consequences and, in particular, whether they help us to survive and prosper, that determines their worth. The future and not the past, whether in terms of organisms or ideas, is the crucial thing for the Darwinian and the pragmatist. (It was in this pragmatic spirit – as a tool that might help him to recover from severe depression – that James treated the idea of free will; see Box 14.2 for more information.)

Box 14.2 Depression and recovery

James suffered from bouts of depression throughout his life. In his mid-twenties, he later admitted to a friend, he had contemplated suicide on several occasions. There was, however, one particular occasion, in 1870, when James suffered an almost complete mental and physical breakdown. James's biographer, Richardson, describes it as "a defining moment in his life" (Richardson 2006, p. 117). James himself recorded the experience much later in *The Varieties of Religious Experience*, in which he gives an account of a breakdown suffered by an 'anonymous correspondent'. Suddenly, when thinking about a patient seen in an asylum, ". . . I became a mass of quivering fear," said the correspondent. He continued: "After this the universe was changed for me altogether. I awoke morning after morning with a horrible dread at the pit of my stomach, and with a sense of the insecurity of life that I never knew before . . ." (*Varieties*, p. 160). James later told the French translator of the *Varieties* that the 'anonymous correspondent' was none other than James himself.

Box 14.2 (cont.)

There are many factors that may have contributed to James's breakdown – his lack of direction in life, his poor physical health, the recent death of a much-loved cousin – but, as well as these personal factors, there was also a philosophical component. All James's scientific reading seemed to suggest that future was, in its entirety, causally determined by the past and that nothing could be done to change anything. It also suggested that James was completely at the mercy of his physical ailments. This vision of a deterministic universe was one that James found demoralising, but, during his convalescence, his reading of the French philosopher Charles Renouvier provided a spur towards recovery. Renouvier defended the idea of free will and his arguments convinced James to at least think and act as if free will were true. "My first act of free will," James wrote in his diary, "shall be to believe in free will" (Richardson 2006, p. 120). Though James's recovery was by no means sudden, and though he was always prone to depression, it is from this moment that James himself dated a new mental strength and health in his life.

This emphasis on the destination of ideas – the kind of future to which they lead, rather than their origin – was a major change in orientation from the prevailing tradition in Western thought. In previous chapters we have seen how empiricists and nativists argued about the ultimate source from which our ideas spring, whether that is experience or innate characteristics, as if this source was somehow indicative of an idea's truth. For the pragmatist, however, this question is completely irrelevant to the worth, or lack of worth, of any idea. Where an idea or thought comes from tells us precisely nothing about its value. Only its future practical consequences can tell us that.

For James, the job of the conscious mind – the reason that it evolved – is that it enables the organism to foresee to a greater extent what these consequences might be. When faced with a novel situation, one in which habitual responses are not evoked, an organism will be uncertain as to how to respond. The conscious mind will help to incline the organism towards those actions believed to have positive consequences. The mind, as we saw in the previous section, is "a fighter for ends", and the ideas that it generates are tools that serve those ends.

The stream of consciousness

Consciousness, then, has a biological purpose in promoting an organism's ability to survive and flourish in its environment. This is the *why* of consciousness, the reason for its existence. But James was just as interested in the *what* of consciousness – what is consciousness actually like? What are its defining characteristics? Tackling the *what* of consciousness was one of the major tasks of James's classic work, *The Principles of Psychology* (1890). When trying to grasp the nature of consciousness – indeed of any psychological phenomenon – James's primary method of investigation was introspection:

> *Introspective Observation is what we have to rely on first and foremost and always.* The word introspection need hardly be defined – it means, of course, the looking into our own minds and reporting what we there discover. *Every one agrees that we there discover states of consciousness.* (*Principles*, vol. 1, p. 185, italics in original)

The introspection that James had in mind, however, was rather different from that practised by the likes of Titchener, with its highly controlled laboratory settings. Though credited with setting up the first psychological laboratory in the United States (at Harvard in 1875), James himself was temperamentally unsuited to painstaking experiments. He admitted that the precisely controlled work of Fechner, Wundt, and Titchener could shed light on psychological phenomena but remarked that there was "little of the grand style" about them and their approach (*Principles*, vol. 1, p. 193), and he confessed in a letter to another psychologist, Hugo Münsterberg, that "I naturally hate experimental work" (*Letters*, p. 301). The detailed, methodical approach of the laboratory scientist simply did not accord with James's more free-wheeling personality. "He had," according to Perry (1936, vol. 2, p. 52), "the old-fashioned attitude of the 'naturalist' who collects facts out of doors instead of in a laboratory."

James's introspection was more informal than that carried out in the laboratories and consisted, at least in his own practice, of thoughtful reflection on one's own mental states. Rather than attempt to analyse conscious experience into more basic elements – an approach which, as we shall see, he thought fundamentally misguided – James sought to provide descriptions or metaphors that captured some of the essential characteristics of mental life. It is one of those metaphors, the stream of thought or **stream of consciousness**, which forms the core of James's psychology.

When we reflect on our own conscious experience, says James, we find that it does not consist of atomistic sensations or discrete mental states. What we find, rather, is a continuous flow of thoughts and feelings that run into and merge with one another. Both empiricists and Kantians had assumed that mental states consisted of disconnected elements that have to be joined together in some way. But James found that such a view was simply out of kilter with our actual experience:

> Consciousness, then, does not appear to itself chopped up in bits. Such words as 'chain' or 'train' do not describe it fitly as it presents itself in the first instance. It is nothing jointed; it flows. A 'river' or a 'stream' are the metaphors by which it is most naturally described. *In talking of it hereafter, let us call it the stream of thought, of consciousness, or of subjective life.* (*Principles*, vol. 1, p. 239, italics in original)

Even seemingly abrupt transitions from one thought to another are not simply the replacement of one discrete state by a new one: the relationship that ties them together, the fact of transition itself, is part of our consciousness. When, on a quiet afternoon, we suddenly hear a crash of thunder, we do not simply have a discrete experience of quiet followed by a discrete experience of the thunder as if there were no connection between these experiential states. According to James, "[i]nto the awareness of the thunder itself the awareness of the previous silence creeps and continues; for what we hear when the thunder crashes is not thunder *pure*, but thunder-breaking-upon-silence-and-contrasting-with-it" (*Principles*, vol. 1, p. 234). Even very different mental states, then, are experienced as related to one another, although such relationships may be ones of change and contrast.

It is because the transitions from one relatively stable thought to another may be rather fleeting that we do not notice them and erroneously conclude that there are only discrete states of consciousness. James tries to capture this contrast between fleeting and stable states of consciousness in another of his characteristic images. Our stream of thought, says James, seems to consist of **substantive parts,** thoughts or experiences that are relatively fixed, steady, and salient, and **transitive parts,** which lead up to the substantive ideas. James likens these different parts of the stream to the flights and perchings of a bird as it flies from branch to branch:

> Like a bird's life, it seems to be made of an alternation of flights ... *Let us call the resting-places the 'substantive parts,' and the places of flight the 'transitive parts,' of the stream of thought.* (*Principles*, vol. 1, p. 243)

The transitive parts of consciousness are often overlooked when we reflect on our own mental lives. When writing these words, I am aware of a whole host of thoughts and associations, words and turns of phrase, that pass rapidly through my mind and coalesce into the words that I type on the screen. But the arrival at the final sentence that I type onto the screen seems to erase my awareness of the fleeting passage of thoughts and associations that led up to the composition of that sentence. If, however, we are more careful and attentive in reflecting on our own conscious experience, says James, we will find the transitive parts of consciousness are there just as surely as are the more substantive ideas that they join together.

The fringe of consciousness

The transient parts of consciousness noticed by James constitute one aspect of what he calls the **fringe of consciousness**. This refers to all those aspects of consciousness that we are only dimly aware of at any given moment. James notes that whenever we are aware of a particular thought or thing, we are simultaneously aware of a multitude of other things besides. I am currently aware of the words that I am writing on the computer screen in front of me – they are the *focus* of my consciousness – but I am also dimly aware of the sunshine outside the window, of the pressure on my back from the seat that I am sitting on, of being slightly hungry, of the wall behind the computer screen. But more important than these incidental impressions are a whole host of other thoughts and feelings that are related directly to the focus of my consciousness: an awareness of what I have previously written in this chapter, an awareness of the direction in which the chapter is going, an awareness of James himself, and the general tenor of his ideas, and of how these ideas relate to the ideas of other psychologists and philosophers.

According to James:

> Every definite image in the mind is steeped and dyed in the free water that flows round it. With it goes the sense of its relations, near and remote, the dying echo of whence it came to us, the dawning sense of wither it is to lead. The significance, the value, of the image is all in the halo or penumbra that surrounds and escorts it ... (*Principles*, vol. 1, p. 255)

It is this awareness "of relations and objects but dimly perceived" (*Principles*, vol. 1, p. 258) that gives meaning to our thoughts. Indeed, for James, the meaning of a thought simply *is* how it relates to other thoughts, ideas, and experiences within the stream of consciousness. So, though the thought itself is the focus of our consciousness, it would be devoid of significance were we not also aware, in the fringe of our consciousness, of a vast web of vaguely perceived relations that this thought has with the rest of the stream of consciousness. It was the overlooking of these crucially important fringe relations by other psychologists that motivated James to argue for "the re-instatement of the vague to its proper place in our mental life" (*Principles*, vol. 1, p. 254).

As has already been noted, it is difficult to notice the fringe relations because they are, by definition, vague and fleeting. There are, however, instances in which the fringe relations themselves are thrown into relief and become more obvious to us than they would be normally. One such instance is the so-called tip-of-the-tongue phenomenon, in which you search for a word but can't quite find it. You may have a hazy awareness of the word – perhaps the initial letter, or how many syllables it contains – and you know instantly whether any candidate word is or is not the one that you have been looking for. You are also aware of the word's meaning and of other words that are a bit like it (but are not the precise word that you want). You are, in other words, aware of the fringe of relations that surround the sought-for word without the word itself coming into clear, focal consciousness. Indeed, it is precisely the absence of the sought-for word that causes you to become more acutely aware of the ideas and associations around it. If the desired word is finally found, its discovery is characterised by a feeling of rightness, a sense that the word 'fits' with the thoughts and ideas that constitute its fringe. Incorrect words, on the other hand, do not fit with these fringe relations; there is a sense of disharmony that means that the word can immediately be rejected.

The self

The stream of consciousness, and the fringe in particular, is crucial in James's account of the self. It was, in James's view, the same ignorance of the connections in consciousness that we have already seen with respect to the transitive parts of consciousness that led some earlier thinkers to reject the existence of the self. Hume had famously enquired into his own experience and had failed to come across any impression corresponding to his idea of the self:

> For my part, when I enter most intimately into what I call *myself*, I always stumble on some particular perception or other, of heat or cold, light of shade, love or hatred, pain or pleasure. I never can catch *myself* at any time without a perception, and never can

observe anything but perception . . . I may venture to affirm of the rest of mankind, that they are nothing but a bundle or collection of different perceptions, which succeed each other with an inconceivable rapidity, and are in a perpetual flux and movement. (*Treatise of Human Nature*, p. 252)

Though Hume came across perceptions of things, he did not find anything in his experience that corresponded to the self. The most that could be said was that the self was nothing more than a flux of perceptions.

James was opposed to idea that the self is just a name for an incoherent jumble of different perceptions and sensations. But he was also opposed to the Kantian idea that the self is something transcendental that lies outside the stream of experience. For James, the self was an empirical fact: we *have* a sense of self, and therefore this sense of self must somehow be part of our stream of experience, but it must be something more coherent that Hume's bundle of sensations. What, then, is it?

There are several aspects of selfhood that James identified within the stream of consciousness. At the most general level, the **empirical self** – what we feel ourselves to be – can be identified with all that we are "tempted to call by the name of *me*" (*Principles*, vol. 1, p. 291). "*In its widest possible sense*," says James, "*a man's Self is the sum total of all that he* CAN *call his*, not only his body and his psychic powers, but his clothes and his house, his wife and children, his ancestors and friends, his reputation and works, his lands and horses, and yacht and bank-account" (*Principles*, vol. 1, p. 291, italics in original).

James's account of the self is resolutely empirical – it seeks to describe just what the sense of self is to us as it appears in our consciousness. And, when we do reflect on our consciousness of self, we find, according to James, that "between what a man calls *me* and what he simply calls *mine* the line is difficult to draw" (*Principles*, vol. 1, p. 291). Sometimes material possessions seem to be an important part of our sense of self, and when they are damaged we feel a sense of personal loss. The same goes to an even greater extent for our family and friends – our sense of self is often so closely bound up with them that their loss hurts us as keenly as any injury to our own bodies. When a bereaved person says that it feels as though a part of them has died along with the deceased person they are not, for James, speaking metaphorically.

Other people are not merely part of our sense of self in that we identify, at least partially, our own well-being with theirs; they also define our sense of self in the sense that how we experience ourselves is, to some extent, mediated by their views of us. How other people see us – whether we are respected or despised, loved or hated – is an important factor in how we experience ourselves. This is what James calls the **social self**:

> Properly speaking, *a man has as many social selves as there are individuals who recognize him* and carry an image of him in their mind. To wound any one of these his images is to wound him. (*Principles*, vol. 1, p. 294, italics in original)

Here we can see how James expands the normal concept of self to include people and things that are, strictly speaking, outside ourselves – or at least outside our bodies. But, we naturally think, surely the self – the *real* self – cannot be tied up with other objects and other people. Surely the real self is something 'inner' rather than something 'outer'; something that is completely personal to each individual.

For James there is indeed a core of selfhood that is not attached to external things. James calls it the **spiritual self**. But this spiritual self is not something mysterious or other-worldly. What we feel as being our innermost self is, for James, just a specific, circumscribed portion of the stream of consciousness. In particular, James suggests that the sense of self is nothing more than the fringe awareness of certain bodily sensations: *"our entire feeling of spiritual activity, or what commonly passes by that name, is really a feeling of bodily activities whose exact nature is by most men overlooked"* (*Principles*, vol. 1, pp. 301–2).

The sense of self, then, *is* a matter of sensations. To this extent, Hume was right. But he was wrong in thinking that these sensations were nothing more than an incoherent jumble. Because our sensations are not isolated atoms, but are part of a ceaselessly flowing and interconnected stream of consciousness, the self has some stability and continuity over time. The bodily sensations that James identifies with the innermost sense of self are simply the most continuous aspect of the stream since they are there throughout our conscious life. Whether this experiential continuity is underpinned by continuity of the same thinking substance or soul is, pragmatically speaking, irrelevant. What matters in concrete terms is the continuity of experience itself. In this respect, James's account of the self bears some similarities with that given by Locke in his *Essay concerning Human Understanding*. Locke, like James, locates the continuity of the self in the continuity of experience rather than in the continuity of an unknowable substance. Of course, this continuity of certain aspects of the stream of consciousness is not something that we are focally aware of all the time. The continuity of bodily sensation on which the sense of self relies is part of the fringe or margin of consciousness and it is because of this that, for James, it has gone unnoticed by previous thinkers.

The selectivity of consciousness

Consciousness, then, for James, is a rich and constantly changing web of inter-connected ideas, thoughts, and feelings, and there is much more to it than what we are focally aware of at any given moment. This is just as well: we could, if we were fully and clearly aware of all of this richness, become overwhelmed by the sheer abundance of our own streams of experience. Indeed, James suggests that this *is* what the experience of an infant is like: it is "a blooming, buzzing confusion" (*Principles*, vol. 1, p. 488), which the infant, through its development, learns to make sense of.

But how is this sense-making arrived at? How does a chaotic flux generate coherent thoughts and experiences? The answer, for James, lies in the mind's selectivity. Though there is a mass of thoughts, feelings, and relations within the stream of experience, the mind selects certain aspects of that stream to attend to:

> Millions of items of the outward order are presented to my senses which never properly enter into my experience. Why? Because they have no *interest* for me. *My experience is what I agree to attend to.* Only those items which I *notice* shape my mind – without selective interest, experience is an utter chaos. Interest alone gives accent and empha-sis, light and shade, background and foreground – intelligible perspective, in a word. It varies in every creature, but without it the consciousness of every creature would be a gray chaotic indiscriminateness, impossible for us even to conceive. (*Principles*, vol. 1, pp. 402–3)

James's view of the mind's selectivity is underpinned by a very different idea of experience from that put forward by empiricists and Kantians. For both of these groups, complex and coherent conscious experience is built up from discon-nected atoms of experience. The connections between ideas and feelings are thought to be *added* by the mind itself; they are not actually there in the basic sensory or experiential input itself. Both Kantians and empiricists, then, view the mind as analogous to a mosaic artist, taking small, isolated elements and putting them together to create an organised whole picture. The corresponding analogy for James is that of the mind as a sculptor: the mind does not put things together, but it selects, emphasises, and discards the material that is in front of it:

> The mind . . . works on the data it receives very much as a sculptor works on his block of stone. In a sense the statue stood there from eternity. But there were a thousand different ones beside it, and the sculptor alone is to thank for having extricated this one from the rest. Just so the world of each of us, howsoever different our several

views of it may be, all lay embedded in the primordial chaos of sensations ...
(*Principles*, vol. 1, p. 288)

The mind, then, for James, does not *add* structure and connectedness to the stream of experience – the structure and connectedness are *already there* in the stream of experience itself. What the mind does is focus on some of this content rather than other parts of it. The mind *finds* rather than makes connections.

The case of space

Nowhere is the idea that structure is inherent in experience more clearly demonstrated than in James's treatment of space perception. The chapter on space perception is the single largest chapter in the whole of the *Principles* and one commentator (Barzun 1983) has called it James's single greatest achievement in psychology. James's target is the Kantian approach to space perception. For Kant, as we have seen, sensory information is not inherently spatial, but is organised into a spatial form by us. The spatial framework is in the mind rather than in the perceptual matter itself. Psychologists of James's own time reiterated this Kantian position. Wundt, for example, following Kant, claimed that space is "one of the a priori functions with which consciousness is endowed" (cited by James, *Principles*, vol. 2, p. 278). Empiricists also believed that spatiality had to be added to experience by the experiencer. For thinkers such as Helmholtz, for example, we have to *infer* the external spatial characteristics of objects on the basis of the internal stimulation of our sense organs and nervous system. The spatiality of the external world is not something given directly in experience, but is something added by the mind itself.

But for James the opposite is the case. James's approach, we must remember, is to reflect on experience as it immediately appears to us, and when we do that, says James, we find that a spatial quality is intrinsic to our experience from the outset. This spatial quality may be rather vague and disordered, but it is *there* in our immediate experience. Consider looking at the blue sky on a sunny day, says James, "[t]he *extent* of the blue which I at this moment see, seems to be an attribute given quite as immediately" as the brightness of the blue (James, 1879, p. 68). To be sure, the sense of spatial extent given when we look at the blue sky may be nothing more than an indefinite feeling of "vastness", as James calls it, but it is intrinsically spatial nonetheless.

Even non-visual sensations have a spatial quality intrinsically associated with them: "[t]he squeaking of a slate-pencil is less spatial than the voluminous reverberations of a thunderstorm; the prick of a pin less so than the feeling of a warm bath; a little neuralgic pain, fine as a cobweb, in the face, far less so than the heavy soreness of a boil or the vast discomfort of a colic or lumbago" (James, 1879, p. 70).

For James, thinkers of the Kantian persuasion have confused the spatial character of sensation – of all sensation – with well-defined spatial relations. The Kantians think that, unless sensations are fitted into a well-defined spatial framework in which all the relationships are clear and fully articulated, there is no spatiality at all to our experience. But this is a mistake, according to James – it fails to distinguish that essential sense of vastness, which is the fundamentally spatial aspect of our experience, from the more precise awareness of spatial relationships that may be built upon it. Our basic sense of spatiality has nothing to do with precise ordering. When, says James, a man looks at the world upside down through his legs "the spatial *relations* of what he sees – distances, directions, and so forth – will be very uncertain, positions and measurements vague; but who will pretend that the picture, in losing its *order*, has become any less spatial?" (James, 1879, p. 72).

Reflection on our own experience, then, reveals a primitive impression of spatiality in all our sensations. But it also reveals an absence of any awareness of our own minds adding spatiality to non-spatial sensory input. James points out that there is nothing in our experience to support the Kantian idea that space is somehow constructed rather than found directly in experience: "I am conscious of no such Kantian machine-shop in my mind ... I have no introspective experience of mentally producing or creating space" (*Principles*, vol. 2, p. 275). The Kantian view does not accord with our direct experience, and James, therefore, describes it as "mythological".

James recognises that our sense of spatial relations is often more precise than just a vague feeling of voluminousness, but this more refined awareness is not a matter of importing into the stream of experience something that is external to it, but rather of developing greater attentional and discriminative abilities. We become able to make discriminations within our previously undifferentiated spatial awareness; we can divide that space into several sub-spaces that are related to one another in precise ways; we can quantify and measure these spaces. All of these aspects of our more refined spatial perception, however, are parts of the original stream of experience: the distinctions and relationships *are really there* in our sensory world and what we learn to do is to attend to them and perceive them. We do not create them.

Pluralism and altered states of consciousness

The stream of consciousness, then, is for James, a rich, ever-changing complex of interrelated thoughts and feelings. Only some of these thoughts and feelings can be the focus of conscious awareness at any one time, whereas others are merely vague apprehensions on the fringe of consciousness. Still others are completely ignored. The richness of the stream, and the accompanying necessity of selective consciousness, meant that, for James, we can never grasp the empirical world in its entirety. The idea of absolute knowledge, which had been the goal of science and philosophy for centuries, was dismissed by James as rationalistic fantasy: we can never grasp the whole of reality all at once because as soon as we focus on one aspect of experience, others fade into the background and become part of the fringe. When those things that were on the fringe now receive our full attention, what was previously our focus now becomes part of the fringe. And this is with respect only to our own experience. Different people, even those living in the same time and place, will have different goals and purposes, and it is in accord with these goals and purposes that they will select out certain aspects of reality for attention. When one also includes people living in widely different cultures and historical epochs, to say nothing of non-human organisms, one is faced with an almost infinite multiplicity of viewpoints on reality, all of which have been extracted from the same raw material. Continuing his sculptor metaphor, James exclaims:

> Other sculptors, other statues from the same stone! Other minds, other worlds from the same monotonous and inexpressive chaos! My world is but one in a million alike embedded, alike real to those who may abstract them. How different must be the worlds in the consciousness of ant, cuttle-fish, or crab! (*Principles*, vol. 1, p. 289)

Complete and absolute knowledge would somehow have to encompass all of these different – sometimes competing, sometimes incommensurable – goals, purposes, and perspectives. On James's view, this is beyond the grasp of finite human minds.

This awareness that there is a multiplicity of different perspectives on reality and that none has a monopoly on truth is the core of James's **pluralism**. It is because he recognised the irreducibility of different points of view that James was more interested in, and tolerant of, unorthodox ideas than many in his position would be. He was, for example, greatly interested in psychic research (see Box 14.3). One of the unorthodox points of view that particularly interested James

---

Box 14.3 James and psychical research

In the Victorian era there was a great interest in séances, mediumship, and psychic phenomena of all kinds. Nowhere was this more prevalent than in New England and by the 1870s James had started to investigate claims of spirit rappings, in which the spirits of the dead were alleged to communicate with the living through knocking on solid objects. James was no dupe: he did not accept uncritically the claims of mediums. He noted, for example, that the medium at one séance was nothing more than a 'deciever' who produced the rapping noises alleged to be produced by a spirit by the surreptitious cracking of her knee joint. Nevertheless, despite such fraudulent claims, James maintained his interest in the possibility that there might be some phenomena that lay outside the accepted commonsense or scientific picture of the world. He speculated that mediumship and automatic writing, in which the protagonists felt themselves to be under the control of another personality or acting outside of their own conscious will, might be related to psychopathological phenomena, such as multiple personality. Such interests did not always meet with the approval of his colleagues, some of whom believed that James had abandoned scientific rigour for superstitious nonsense.

On a trip to England in 1882–3, James met the founders of a new organisation, the Society for Psychical Research, which had as its aim the scientific investigation of supposed psychic phenomena. The founders of this organisation neither accepted claims of psychic phenomena at face value nor did they simply dismiss them out of hand. Their goal was to collect evidence in an objective yet open-minded way. This was James's own attitude to psychic phenomena, and, on his return to the United States, he set up an American branch of the organisation. He was elected president of the original Society for Psychical Research ten years later.

---

came in the form of a self-published pamphlet called 'The anaesthetic revelation and the gist of philosophy'. In this pamphlet, the author – a farmer and circus strongman called Benjamin Paul Blood – claimed to have had a mystical experience while under the influence of nitrous oxide (laughing gas) used as an anaesthetic by his dentist. According to Blood:

> It was in the year 1860 that there came to me, through the necessary [medical] use of anaesthetics, a Revelation or insight of the immemorial Mystery which among enlightened peoples still persists as the philosophical secret or problem of the world. (Blood 1920, p. vii)

James's pluralism meant that he was reluctant to simply reject Blood's claims without further consideration. Instead, he wanted to find out for himself what the nature of the nitrous oxide experience was. James accordingly underwent several sessions with nitrous oxide as well as collecting reports from others who had experienced its intoxicating effects. James, like his correspondents and like Blood himself, felt an altered, expanded, state of consciousness when under the influence of nitrous oxide:

> With me, as with every other person of whom I have heard, the keynote of the experience is the tremendously exciting sense of an intense metaphysical illumination. Truth lies open to the view in depth beneath depth of almost blinding evidence. The mind sees all the logical relations of being with an apparent subtlety and instantaneity to which its normal consciousness offers no parallel; only as sobriety returns, the feeling of insight fades, and one is left staring vacantly at a few disjointed words and phrases, as one stares at the cadaverous-looking snow peak from which the sunset glow has just fled, or at the black cinder left by an extinguished brand. (James 1882, p. 206)

For James, this sense of mystical enlightenment could be understood in terms of the stream of consciousness. We have already noted that James saw the mind as selecting certain aspects of the stream of consciousness to attend to in greater detail. Those aspects on which we are focused constitute our most clear and explicit awareness, whereas those of which we are only vaguely aware constitute the fringe of our consciousness. Among these fringe aspects of consciousness are, as we have seen, a vast network of relations – connections, associations, transitions – which constitute the surrounding context in which any substantive idea exists. It is this context – these relations – that give sense and meaning to any idea or thought that we might have. What happens, according to James, in the altered state of consciousness produced by nitrous oxide is that more of these relations are available to consciousness than is normally the case:

> states of mystical intuition may be only very sudden and great extensions of the ordinary 'field of consciousness'. .... the field widens and the relations of its center to matters usually subliminal come into view, the larger panorama perceived fills the mind with exhilaration and sense of mental power. (James 1910, p. 85)

As a result of this widening, "the sense of *relation* will be greatly enhanced" (James 1910, p. 87). It is this enhanced sense of relation within the stream of consciousness that gives rise to the feeling of illumination and enlightenment: relations of which one was not normally aware, or only vaguely aware, now come into full, explicit awareness. And since the sense of meaning consists in these relations, everything suddenly seems more meaningful and significant than is normally the case. "Normal human consciousness," James concluded, "is only a narrow extract from a great sea of possible human consciousness, of whose limits we know nothing ..." (James 1898, p. 194).

Related to James's interest in anomalous states of consciousness was his interest in the psychology of religion, which he investigated in *The Varieties of Religious Experience* (1902). In fact, James thought that his experiences under nitrous oxide were similar to those experienced by religious mystics; the means were different – ingestion of a psychoactive substance, on the one hand, and meditation and prayer on the other – but the final state of illuminated consciousness was, in many respects, similar in both cases. Religious mysticism and nitrous oxide intoxication both induced an expanded state of consciousness and an enhanced sense of the meaningfulness of existence.

In one important respect, however, the experiences of religious mystics and those under nitrous oxide were rather different. Whereas James found that the thoughts he had written down while intoxicated seemed, on returning to normal consciousness, to be incomprehensible gibberish, the experiences undergone by religious mystics tended to have a lasting effect on the way that they led their lives. Religiously inspired mystical experiences became more integrated with the rest of the person's ongoing stream of consciousness than was the case with nitrous oxide experiences. The content of mystical experiences seemed to those who had undergone them to 'fit' in some way with their everyday consciousness and, because of this dovetailing, the mystical states were experienced as being, in some way, real. Other altered states of consciousness, such as dreams, do not tend to fit with the rest of our experience and are therefore classed as illusory. In this respect at least, nitrous oxide intoxication had more in common with dreams than with religious experience.

Conclusion

We have now seen how the central metaphor of the stream of consciousness is used by James to illuminate a range of psychological phenomena: our sense of meaning derives from the connections, often dimly perceived, that ideas and experiences have with other parts of the stream; our sense of self depends on the temporal continuity of certain parts of the stream; even apparently anomalous

phenomena such as mystical experiences are understandable in terms of awareness of connections within the stream.

The idea that the connections between different parts of experience are fundamental to our thought processes was shared by John Dewey. Dewey, along with
James (and C. S. Pierce), was also one of the great exponents of pragmatism, and
it is Dewey's distinctive contribution to psychology and philosophy that is the
subject of the next chapter.

Revision questions

1. How did pragmatism's view of knowledge differ from most preceding theories of knowledge?

2. How did James's approach to introspection differ from the introspectionism of Titchener?

3. James argued that consciousness was like a 'stream'. To what extent was he correct?

4. What did James mean by the 'fringe' of consciousness? Give an example to illustrate your answer.

5. How did James think of the self and how do his views on the self compare with those of Locke and Hume?

6. What, according to James, is the role of attention in our experience of a coherent world?

7. Why did James believe in a pluralistic approach to reality?

8. How, in terms of the stream of consciousness metaphor, did James try to understand mystical experiences?

References

Barzun, J. (1983). *A Stroll with William James*. Chicago, IL: University of Chicago Press.

Blood, B. P. (1920). *Pluriverse*. Boston, MA: Marshall Jones.

Hume, D. ([1739–40]/1978). *A Treatise of Human Nature*, 2nd edn (L. A. Selby-Bigge, ed., revised by P. H. Nidditch). Oxford: Oxford University Press.

James, W. (1878). Remarks on Spencer's definition of mind as correspondence. *Journal of Speculative Philosophy*, 12, 1–18.

James, W. (1879). The spatial quale. *Journal of Speculative Philosophy*, 13, 64–87.

James, W. (1880). Great men and their environment. In W. James (1897) *The Will to Believe and Other Essays in Popular Philosophy*. New York: Longmans Green, pp. 216–54.

James, W. (1882). On some Hegelisms. *Mind*, 7, 186–208.

James, W. (1890). *The Principles of Psychology*, 2 vols. New York: Henry Holt.

James, W. (1898). Consciousness under nitrous oxide. *Psychological Review*, 5, 194–6.

James, W. ([1902]/1982). *The Varieties of Religious Experience*. London: Penguin.

James, W. ([1907]/2000). *Pragmatism*. In W. James *Pragmatism and Other Writings*. London: Penguin.

James, W. (1910). A suggestion about mysticism. *Journal of Philosophy, Psychology, and Scientific Methods*, 7, 85–92.

James, W. (1920). *The Letters of William James*, vol. 1 (H. James, ed.). Boston, MA: Atlantic Monthly Press.

Menand, L. (2001). *The Metaphysical Club*. London: HarperCollins.

Perry, R. B. (1936). *The Thought and Character of William James*, vol. 1. London: Oxford University Press.

Richardson, R. D. (2006). *William James: In the Maelstrom of American Modernism*. Boston, MA: Houghton Mifflin.

15 Dewey and functionalism

Timeline

1865	Abolition of slavery in the US
1867	Karl Marx publishes the first volume of *Das Kapital*
1881	US President Garfield is assassinated
1911	Revolution in China overthrows the emperor and establishes a republic
1933	Franklin D. Roosevelt becomes US President
1941	Japanese bombing of Pearl Harbour; US declares war on Japan
1949	Communists take power in China
1959	Cuban Revolution

John Dewey

1859	Born in Burlington, Vermont
1884	PhD in philosophy from Johns Hopkins
1894	Appointed Professor of Philosophy at the University of Chicago
1896	Publishes *The reflex arc concept in psychology*; establishes the Laboratory School at the University of Chicago
1904	Leaves Chicago to take up professorship at Columbia University
1919–20	Lectures in Japan and China
1925	Publishes *Experience and Nature*
1928	Visits schools in the Soviet Union
1930	Retires from Columbia University
1937	Chairs the Trotsky enquiry committee
1952	Dies in New York

Introduction

In this chapter I will introduce the work of John Dewey (1859–1952) (see Box 15.1) and an approach to psychology called **functionalism**. (Dewey himself preferred the term 'instrumentalism', but 'functionalism' tends to be the term most commonly used to refer to this approach.) Functionalism can be contrasted with the structuralist approach, exemplified by Titchener. Whereas structural psychology was an attempt to codify the structural elements, such as basic sensations, that went together to make complex states, the functionalists argued that there were no such elements. They argued that psychological phenomena should be understood in terms of processes and functions rather than fixed structural features.

This basic functionalist idea is present in Dewey's thought in the following ways. Firstly, because psychology is to be understood in terms of processes rather than structures, the things that it deals with are not defined by their intrinsic characteristics, but by the functions that they perform. We should not, then, speak of memory, for example, as if it were a thing, but rather of the process of remembering. In addition, there are no parts of this process that are intrinsically memorial; anything – sensations, emotions, cognitions – that plays a role in the process is, for as long as the process lasts, part of what we call memory. Secondly, functionalists believe that psychological phenomena can only be understood as part of a broader network of connected processes. If we want to understand more about something in psychology, we should not attempt to narrow our focus and isolate it from everything else as if we were looking though a microscope. On the contrary, we should expand our field of view to see how that process functions within the wider context of other processes within the organism and the environment. When we do this, says Dewey, we find that many of the dualisms that have bedevilled philosophy – such as those between body and mind or between thought and action – do not reflect deep-seated metaphysical differences, but only differences of function. According to Dewey, when we see processes in context we find that they are not opposed to one another, but are necessary parts of an overall process. I hope to show in the course of this chapter how Dewey's functionalist approach allows him to reconcile what were previously thought to be opposing sides of philosophical dichotomies. First of all, however, let us consider the roots of Dewey's approach. There are two important currents of thought feeding into Dewey's functionalism: Darwinian inspired pragmatism, and the ideas of the philosopher G. W. F. Hegel.

Darwin and pragmatism

Dewey, along with William James and C. S. Peirce, was an exponent of pragmatism. Pragmatism, as we saw in the previous chapter, was influenced by Darwin's evolutionary theory. For Dewey, the lesson of evolutionary theory was as follows:

> The entire significance of the evolutionary method in biology and social history is that every distinct organ, structure, or formation, every grouping of cells or elements, has to be treated as an instrument of adjustment or adaptation to a particular environing situation. Its meaning, its character, its value, is known when, and only when, it is considered as an arrangement for meeting the conditions involved in some specific situation. (*Studies in Logical Theory*, p. 15)

The pragmatists tried to apply this lesson to our ideas. Our ideas, like our bodies, can only be understood in terms of how they allow us to adapt to, and come to grips with, our environment and to make sense of our experience. Already we can see the affinities between pragmatism and functionalism – both understand mental states in terms of the functions that they perform rather than as static entities. But whereas the organs of the body can be looked at either in terms of their structure – their size, weight, material composition – or in terms of the functions that they perform, this is not so with psychological phenomena. For the functionalists, there were not analogous mental 'organs' that existed apart from the functions that they performed.

In arguing this view, the functionalists departed from centuries of thought in psychology and philosophy, which had traditionally viewed the mind as being composed of different **faculties** – cognition, feeling, and will, for example – which were pre-existing structures or parts. For functionalism, however, these 'faculties' are just names for different types of mental *activity*. They do not exist apart from the actions that they perform in the way that a heart can still exist apart from its function of pumping blood. This is because the 'faculties' are not the names of things that perform certain actions but are in fact just names for the actions themselves. We have no faculties of thinking, feeling, or willing in just the same way that we have no faculties of running, dancing, or walking. These are just the names for certain types of action. Of course, it is the case with running, dancing, and walking that there are certain anatomical prerequisites that enable the performance of these activities, but we do not refer to the legs as the 'faculty of running'. In the same way, we would not refer to the brain as the faculty of thinking or willing. Indeed, just as the legs can perform a variety of

Box 15.1 John Dewey

John Dewey was born in the small town of Burlington, Vermont, in 1859. After graduating from the University of Vermont, he worked briefly as a schoolteacher before studying for a PhD in philosophy at Johns Hopkins University. As part of his undergraduate degree, Dewey had studied physiology and had been greatly impressed by the course text, written by Thomas Huxley, a well-known and vociferous supporter of Darwinism. It was Huxley's conception of the organism as a whole composed of interrelated and interdependent parts that, Dewey said, stimulated his interest in philosophy. The philosophy of Hegel, which he subsequently encountered at Johns Hopkins, provided an intellectual framework within which Dewey could work out his vision of the mutual interconnectedness of things.

Dewey developed an interest in education while working at the universities of Michigan and Chicago, and it was at Chicago, in 1896, that he established the Laboratory School to try out some of his pedagogical ideas. Dewey's wife, Alice, was the school principal. It was through this school that Dewey established his reputation as a pioneer of progressive education. Dewey was opposed to traditional approaches to education which imposed a preconceived curriculum on the child regardless of its inclinations and interests, but he was, however, equally opposed to child-centred learning, which took its cue from the spontaneous impulses of the child. For Dewey, what was needed was a way of integrating the curriculum with the interests of the child rather than just emphasising one or the other.

Dewey resigned from the University of Chicago in 1904 after disagreements with the university president over the running and funding of the school and moved to Columbia University, New York, where he continued to write and teach on a wide variety of subjects (Figure 15.1). Although by nature a rather shy person, Dewey did not shrink from voicing his opinion on contemporary political questions, and he wrote many articles in the popular press in which he examined topical issues. He became something of a public intellectual and was frequently invited to lecture abroad, notably in Japan and China, where he stayed for two years. Dewey retired from teaching in 1930, but continued his academic and political interests. He died on 2 June 1952, at the age of 92.

Box 15.1 (cont.)

Fig. 15.1 John Dewey

functions, so can the brain. And it is the functions, rather than the physiological substrate, in which functional psychology is interested.

Again, the pragmatic element in functionalism is clear. For pragmatism, as we have seen, ideas have to be understood in terms of the tangible effects that their truth would have on the empirical world. Even abstract metaphysical terms have to be translated into their concrete 'cash value' if they are to have any meaning. Psychological phenomena, then, are not to be understood as shadowy faculties lying behind overt actions, but as the actions themselves.

Hegel

A second major influence on Dewey was the philosophy of G.W.F. Hegel (1770–1831) (see Box 15.2). Dewey was attracted to Hegel's ideas because they seemed to offer a way in which many of the divisions, such as that between body and mind, which characterise Western philosophy might be overcome. Hegel claimed to show how seemingly opposed entities could be reconciled in an overarching synthesis. The Hegelian **synthesis** viewed each side of a dichotomy not in opposition to one another, but in a **symbiotic relationship** with one another. Here is what Dewey himself says about what attracted him to Hegel's philosophy:

> Hegel's thought ... supplied a demand for unification that was doubtless an intense emotional craving, and yet was a hunger that only an intellectualized subject matter could satisfy ... divisions by way of isolation of self from the world, of soul from body, of nature from God ... were an inward laceration ... Hegel's synthesis of subject and object, matter and spirit, the divine and the human, was ... no mere intellectual formula; it operated as an immense release, a liberation. ('From absolutism to experimentalism', p. 19)

Though Dewey's later thought was less explicitly influenced by Hegel that his earlier work, Dewey nevertheless admitted that Hegel and the Hegelian approach had left a "permanent deposit" ('From absolutism to experimentalism', p. 21) in his way of thinking.

Hegel believed that the contradictions that afflicted philosophy were the result of not taking a wide enough perspective. Focusing too narrowly on any given phenomenon prevents us from seeing how things are related to one another. Philosophers have tended to take one side of a dichotomy – for example, either

---

Box 15.2 **Georg Wilhelm Friedrich Hegel**

Georg Wilhelm Friedrich Hegel was born in Stuttgart in 1770. He studied theology at the University of Tübingen and then worked as a private tutor in Switzerland and Frankfurt. He then moved to the University of Jena in 1799 and it was there that he completed his first major philosophical work, *The Phenomenology of Spirit*. At this time, Napoleon's army was conquering large parts of Europe, and Hegel worked on the book as the battle of Jena was fought in the surrounding countryside and streets. He finished the book on 13 October 1806, the day that the French forces finally occupied the city.

As a result of the war, the University of Jena was closed, and Hegel left the town to work briefly as a newspaper editor before becoming a school headmaster in Nuremberg for nine years. During this time he continued to publish and his reputation increased as a result. He returned to academia in 1816, taking up the chair of philosophy in Heidelberg. In 1818, he was invited, by the Prussian minister of education, to take the chair of philosophy at the University of Berlin, a position that he held until his death in 1831, at the age of 61. He was, at the time of his death, the most revered philosopher in the German-speaking world.

Hegel was deeply influenced by two somewhat opposed trends in European thought: the Enlightenment and Romanticism. The Enlightenment had emphasised individual liberty, rationality, and progress whereas the Romantics had emphasised the importance of community, nature, and the emotions. Much of Hegel's philosophy tried to find a way of reconciling what he considered to be the valuable aspects of each approach in an overall synthesis. This is seen in Hegel's view of politics and history – without doubt the most influential aspect of his philosophy – in which he argues that individuals can only fully reach their potential in a society which is an expression of their needs and desires. Such a society is not something that is opposed to the autonomy of the individual, but is in fact necessary for that autonomy to be realised. It was this vision of the state as embodying the aspirations of the people that was a decisive influence on Karl Marx (1818–83) and the development of socialism.

---

mind or body – and to emphasise that one thing as the most important and to denigrate, or deny the existence of, the other side of the dichotomy. Descartes, for example, emphasised the importance of the rational mind whereas materialists have emphasised the importance of the physical body. But if we take one side of a dichotomy and really think about what it entails then, according to Hegel, we will see how its existence necessarily implies the existence other side of the dichotomy. The two sides of the dichotomy are recognised as forming a system or a structure in which both are indispensable. It was Hegel's conviction that, as we learn more about the world and our place in it, we will come to see how dichotomies and divisions can be resolved by a more all-encompassing viewpoint from which the essential relatedness of apparently conflicting things becomes apparent. This way of reconciling philosophical divisions is called **dialectic**.

The dialectic in action

To illustrate how Hegel's dialectic resolves philosophical divisions let us take the related dichotomies of body/mind and thought/action as examples. The mind is traditionally thought of as the seat of thought and rationality whereas the body is the physical thing that behaves and acts. As we have already seen in the chapter on Descartes, there is for many thinkers a problem of how the thoughts in the mind become translated into, or cause, the actions of the body.

But let us think a bit more deeply about the apparently contrasting sides of these divisions. For example, what does having a thought really entail? The dominant view in Western philosophy, which we see exemplified by Descartes and Locke, is that thinking is having ideas, which are representations of the external world, in the mind. But for Hegel this is erroneous – when we examine the matter from a broader perspective we realise that thoughts are not just representations inside one's head, but that thoughts require outward expression. Take, for example, artistic or musical creation. Artistic or musical thinking does not consist simply of having representations in one's head; it consists, rather, in the ability to express certain ideas or feelings in paint or sound. Frequently the artist or composer will not have a clear idea of what the finished piece will be like before actually engaging in its creation. It is in the process of trying to express it that the thought itself becomes clarified and developed. This is also true of more abstract thought – it too demands expression, not merely to express what is already determinate and fully thought out, but for the idea itself to *become* determinate and fully thought out. Think, for example, of writing an essay or similar piece of work. You may have a rather vague idea of what you want to say at the outset, but it is only in the saying of it that the idea becomes fully developed and clarified. This, then, is how Hegel views thought – it is a matter of expression rather than simply having inert 'ideas' or representations within the mind, because those ideas only reach their full actuality in the act of their expression.

We can see here how the division between thought and action breaks down in the philosophy of Hegel. Thought and action are not two separate things opposed to one another, one of which exists in the physical world and the other of which exists in some shadowy mental world. Rather, thought and action are two sides of the same coin: thought *is* what we express in action and action just *is* the expression of thought.

But this view of thought has a wider implication for the mind–body problem as a whole. Because thought requires expression, it requires a material medium within which that expression can take place – there is no art without the medium of paint or stone in which the artistic idea can be expressed and no music without the medium of sound in which the musical idea can be expressed. This also goes for more abstract thought: it cannot exist without its expression in some sort of physical medium, and this means that thought is necessarily embodied. The whole Cartesian idea of a disembodied mind which thinks its rational thoughts in isolation from the physical world is, from the Hegelian point of view, completely wrong-headed. The mind, as the thinker of thoughts, *must* be embodied because those thoughts require expression in a material medium. And the most important medium for the expression of thoughts is the body itself: it is through its language, gestures, and actions that our thoughts are most readily expressed. The mind, then, is not something essentially separate from the body, but requires the body for its own expression.

But just as there would be no mind without a body in which it is expressed, so there would be no body without the mind that it expresses. This is not to say, of course, that without minds there would be no physical matter in the universe. What is meant, rather, is that the human body is more than just physical matter – it is physical matter that is coherently organised in such a way to express and instantiate a human mind. Unless it served the function of embodying the mind, the human body would not be the human body.

Returning to our example of artistic expression might make this clearer. We have already seen that artistic ideas cannot exist fully without their expression in some material medium, such as paint. But it is equally true that there would be no paintings without the artistic ideas that they express and embody. There would, of course, still be pigments, and bits of matter of different colours, but they would not be *paintings* – they would just be unorganised materials. Similarly, there would of course still be sound if there were no musical ideas, but there would be no music without musical ideas because music just is the organisation of sound in such a way that it embodies and expresses a certain musical idea. The same goes for the human body, then, which just is an organisation of material substance in such a way that it expresses and embodies the human mind.

Hegel, thus, sought to overcome dichotomies by showing how one side of a dichotomy was, in fact, not simply opposed to the other side, but was necessary for its existence. From this dialectical perspective, mind and body, thought and action, are revealed as being mutually dependent on one another rather than as opposed sides of a metaphysical divide.

The dialectic in Dewey's thought: critique of the reflex arc concept

We can see the results of Dewey's Hegel-influenced functionalism in one of his most famous papers, 'The reflex arc concept in psychology' (1896). The idea of the **reflex** arc is that an organism, when presented with a sensory stimulus, will produce a reflex motor response to it. The reflex arc concept goes back at least to Descartes and many thinkers proposed that all behaviour could be thought of as a complex of stimulus–response reflex arc units, simple behaviour involving just a few reflex arcs and complex behaviour requiring a more sophisticated ensemble of reflex arcs working together.

Dewey argued, however, not merely that intelligent behaviour was too complex to be explained by such mechanical stimulus–response connections, but that the very concept of the reflex arc was itself fundamentally flawed. It was flawed because it was a reflection of precisely the sort of philosophical dichotomies that, Dewey believed, could be overcome by Hegel's dialectical approach. According to Dewey, the dualism of stimulus and response was a "distinct echo" of "the older dualism of body and soul" ('The reflex arc concept in psychology', pp. 357–8). The stimulus tended to be thought of as a discrete sensory event and the response as a discrete bodily movement, and this mirrored the older Cartesian distinction between the perceiving mind and the acting body. According to Dewey, we must overcome this residual dualism by conceiving of sensations, thoughts, and acts in functional terms, as mutually dependent parts of a larger whole rather than distinct processes defined by their own intrinsic characteristics.

To illustrate his view, Dewey takes the example of a young child reaching out towards a candle, an example that had been extensively discussed by James in the *Principles of Psychology*. According to the stimulus–response view, the stimulus, say the seeing of a light, simply serves to unleash a motor response, a movement, towards the source of the light. The stimulus and response are considered purely in isolation from one another: on the one side, there is a visual sensation and, on the other, a movement of the arm. But, says Dewey, when we think about this strict division, we find that it cannot hold. Vision is, in fact, essential for the ongoing control of the arm, whereas the movement of the arm determines the target that vision must monitor:

> the ability of the hand to do its work will depend, either directly or indirectly, upon its control, as well as its stimulation, by the act of vision … The reaching, in turn, must both stimulate and control the seeing. The eye must be kept upon the candle if the arm is to do its work; let it wander and the arm takes up another task. In other words, we now have an enlarged and transformed coördination; the act is seeing no less than before, but it is now seeing-for-reaching purposes. ('The reflex arc concept in psychology', p. 359)

The sensation and the response are, then, inextricably intertwined with one another – seeing is not just something separate from action, it is something that stimulates and controls action, and it is action that determines the target of our seeing, it stimulates and controls the seeing. "[T]he reflex arc idea," according to Dewey, "is defective in that it assumes sensory stimulus and motor response as distinct psychical existences, while in reality they are always inside a coördination and have their significance purely from the part played in maintaining or reconstituting the coördination" ('The reflex arc concept in psychology', p. 360). Any attempt to understand stimulus and response that ignores their functional interaction within the larger pattern of activity is doomed to failure.

But Dewey goes further than this. He argues that not only are the sensory stimulus and the motor response intimately connected with one another, but that they can only be defined in terms of their reciprocal connections. In other words, the nature of the stimulus is determined not by its intrinsic characteristics but by its relationship with the response, and the nature of the response is determined by its relationship with the stimulus. Dewey gives the following example to illustrate his point. You are walking in a lonely place on a dark night and hear a noise in the undergrowth. You are frightened and start running away from the source of the sound. From the reflex arc viewpoint, one might say that you hear a sound, are frightened by it, and try to escape as if these were three separate states or processes. But Dewey points out that it is the response that determines the nature of the stimulus. It is the act of running away, for example, that defines the sound as something fearful or dangerous: one doesn't hear a sound, decide that it is dangerous, *and then* run away; one decides that it is dangerous *by* running away. An aversive stimulus is precisely that stimulus that produces a flight response. The nature of the response actually *changes* the nature of the stimulus from something indeterminate to something with a determinate value, as aversive or attractive, for example. Until one starts to run from the noise, it is not a fearful or aversive stimulus; these characteristics are conferred upon it by the act of running away.

But the response, too, can only be defined in terms of the stimulus. What makes the running a flight response is that it is away from the stimulus, that it has as its goal the disappearance of the stimulus or the reduction of its intensity. Nothing is a flight response in and of itself – it can only be flight *from* something. Similarly, nothing is an aversive stimulus in and of itself – it is only an aversive stimulus because it provokes a flight response. Thus stimulus and response are not only inseparable from one another, it does not make logical sense to try to characterise one without the other. The dualism of stimulus and response has, Dewey believes, been overcome by a functionalist dialectical approach.

Dewey's application of functionalism in other domains

The method of understanding things in terms of their relationships with one another, which we have just seen in connection with the ideas of stimulus and response, was also applied by Dewey to the wider question of the distinction between mental and non-mental processes. There are, after all, many processes that go on in living things that are not mental or psychological. Digestion and the production of blood cells, for example, are essential to maintaining a human organism, but they are not mental or psychological activities. There must be something other than just contributing to the integrity and growth of an organism that makes certain processes genuinely mental.

In keeping with his functionalist approach, Dewey argues that what makes some organic processes mental is not their intrinsic characteristics, but the role that they play within a wider functional context. In particular, an organic process gains the additional property of mentality through the acquisition of meaning. What this means, for Dewey, is that the process in question is related to other processes and things in certain ways. Meaning requires that a process is not merely undergone, but that it is categorised – it is selected, connected with other things, and differentiated from yet other things. The most obvious way in which this is done is through language. It is not the case that simply attaching a linguistic label to an organic state or process magically turns it into a mental state or process. It is, rather, a question of what is involved in being able to name something. Naming requires not merely that we associate a certain sound with a particular thing, but that we situate that thing within a whole network of references and connections. When a botanist recognises a plant in the course of a country walk, it is not just a matter of applying an appropriate verbal label, but of seeing the plant as an example of a particular type, of understanding that it shares common characteristics with other examples of this type, and of understanding that it differs from other plant species in certain ways. It is through this process of categorisation, of connecting and differentiating, that the plant becomes for the botanist not just any old plant, but a plant with a certain meaning or significance. For Dewey, certain organic processes come to have meaning for us – and thereby become mental processes – in an analogous way.

At first sight this may seem a frankly incredible statement. Surely feeling hunger, for example, is just as much a mental state whether or not one can recognise it as hunger or give it a linguistic label? Surely the intrinsic characteristics of the hunger experience are the same regardless of what one can or cannot say about it? Such responses are, of course, natural when we think of mental states as being defined by their own intrinsic characteristics, but it is the whole point of Dewey's approach to argue against this point of view – mental states are *not* mental in virtue of their own intrinsic characteristics, but in virtue of how they are functionally linked to other processes and things, both within the body and within the environment. According to Dewey, "[t]o term a quality 'hunger', to name it, is to refer to an object, to food, to that which will satisfy it, towards which the active situation moves" (*Experience and Nature*, pp. 259–60). The naming of the physiological state requires the establishment of references to other states and processes, but particularly to the actions that the organism must engage in to deal with this physiological state. In recognising it for what it is, the organic state of a lack of nourishment in the body of the organism becomes a mental state.

Of course the actual bodily state or process is not changed by categorising it, but the organism's understanding and experience of the bodily state or process *is* changed. This is no more than an application of the same of thinking as in the reflex arc paper. Just as running away from a sound in the bushes confers the status of frightening or dangerous upon it, so the categorisation of a certain organic state confers the status of hunger upon it. Of course, the actual objective state of the body is not changed by attaching a label to it, just as the actual objective nature of what is in the bushes is not changed by my running away – there may, after all, be nothing there at all, and the rustling in the bushes caused by a gust of wind. But what we are concerned with here is how things and processes feature in our experience, what their psychological force or meaning is, and that *is* a function of how they are understood to connect to other things and processes. Hunger becomes a mental state, rather than just a lack of nourishment within the organism, when it is so named or recognised and is understood as requiring certain actions to resolve it. For Dewey, then, those organic states that are mental differ from those that are not mental in virtue of their extrinsic connections and relations, not in virtue of intrinsic characteristics.

Consciousness and thinking

Though mental states and processes are concerned with meaning, they are not always fully conscious or explicit. Much of the time meanings are taken for granted, they are already established and understood. For Dewey, we are only tacitly aware of these meanings. Conscious mental states arise from the creation of *new* meaning, of forging new connections between current and past experiences. "Consciousness," says Dewey, "is that phase of a system of meanings which at a given time is undergoing re-direction, transitive transformation ... Consciousness *is* the meaning of events in course of remaking" (*Experience and Nature*, p. 308).

This process of 'remaking' is, for Dewey, a purely natural one. It does not require a transcendental self to carry it out any more than a snowflake needs a self to organise it into a six-sided shape. Dewey believed that the remaking of meaning arises spontaneously through an organism's interaction with its environment. In the course of its activities, an organism will understand new things and situations in the light of its pre-existing knowledge while this pre-existing knowledge may in turn be altered to accommodate the new facts that the organism has discovered. Some pieces of knowledge will fit with earlier knowledge or they will have beneficial consequences in helping the organism to negotiate its environment. They will therefore become part of that organism's stable knowledge. Other pieces of knowledge will not fit with earlier knowledge or help the organism to negotiate its environment. They will consequently become rejected in the battle of ideas and will not form part of the organism's stable knowledge base.

Dewey adopts a pragmatic and functional approach to the question of consciousness. Consciousness is not a thing that effects a process, rather consciousness is the name that we give to that process itself, the process of knitting new knowledge onto old. This is the 'cash value' of the term 'consciousness' – not a mysterious abstraction that lies outside experience, but a concrete, empirical function.

But, in addition to the pragmatic element in Dewey's thought, we can also see the Hegelian strand in his treatment of consciousness. For Hegel, it is conflict or contradiction that is the motor of the dialectical process. It is because there is a contradiction within the very ideas of a disembodied mind and a purely mechanical body that our understanding is forced to reconceptualise body and mind as being necessary for one another's existence. The apparent conflict between the two sides of the dichotomy has to be resolved in higher-level synthesis. It is internal conflicts and contradictions that drive our understanding to ever higher levels as it attempts to resolve them. For Dewey, too, it is because of conflict within our experience that we become conscious of certain facts or portions of that experience. When the stream of our experience is moving smoothly, we do not notice its passing. It is just something there, in the background, that we are not explicitly aware of. When, however, a conflict arises, and one part of our experience does not smoothly cohere with another part, certain contents associated with this conflict become objects of our conscious awareness. We become explicitly aware of them precisely because of their problematic nature. The conflicting parts of our experience are then examined, reinterpreted, accepted, and rejected in a way that preserves the most coherent experience. For Dewey, self-aware thinking just is "the conscious maintenance of the unity of experience, with a critical consideration of the claims of the various conflicting contents to a place within itself" (*Studies in Logical Theory*, p. 50). But again, it is important to note that consciousness is not something that pre-dates these conflicts in experience and their resolution. It is simply is the process of their resolution. Higher-level, more explicit, thought processes are created precisely to resolve conflicts that existed at a lower, less explicit level.

It is this bringing together of different parts of experience that, for Dewey, constitutes conscious thinking. But the way in which Dewey envisages the formation of these connections is very different from some other views that we have already encountered. We have seen, for example, that empiricists such as Locke and Hume, as well as later psychologists such Titchener, believed conscious experience to consist essentially of atomistic sensations. The job of the mind, in particular the process of association, was to arrange these elements together to create a meaningful and coherent experience. Kant and Wundt also assumed that the raw material for experiences was disjointed and incoherent, although they thought that a synthesising ego rather than just mechanical association was necessary to create meaningful experience.

From Dewey's perspective, both of these views are wrong because they start from the mistaken assumption that experience starts with meaningless sensations and that meaning is created by their being put together in a coherent way. But, Dewey points out, if the events are themselves meaningless, then it does not matter which way they are put together – any particular ordering of them is just as senseless as any other. Dewey gives the example of hearing noises outside the window. If they are just random sounds, then the question of whether or not they are coherent does not even arise. If, however, the sounds might be overheard speech, then their order does become important; the question of whether or not they are coherent becomes a live and important one. Sensory information can only be associated and ordered in a meaningful way if it is *already* meaningful, because ordering in a meaningful way just is ordering it in a way that reflects and preserves the meanings that it carries. This is why, for Dewey, thinking cannot be the assignation of meaning to elementary sensory data by their correct ordering and association, but can only be the coordination of already meaningful complexes within a new and larger organisation. "It is not bare coincidence, or bare connection, or bare addition of one [thing] to the other, that excites thought," says Dewey, "[i]t is a situation which is organized or constituted as a whole, and which yet is falling to pieces in its parts – a situation which is in conflict within itself – that arouses the search to find what really goes together and a correspondent effort to shut out what only seemingly belongs together" (*Studies in Logical Theory*, p. 37).

Logic

For Dewey, then, thinking is something that arises in response to specific needs and specific situations in which particular aspects of experience do not cohere. Its success is a matter of solving the problem at hand. This view contrasts with the rationalist view that thinking can be understood in pure, logical terms quite apart from the various concrete situations in which it is actually exercised. According to such a view, the rightness of a piece of thinking is a matter of its conforming to certain abstract logical rules.

Dewey, and other pragmatists such as James, believed that the rationalists had got things the wrong way round. According to the pragmatists, what comes first is the performing of thinking in specific concrete situations, and it is only through the abstraction and generalisation of these procedures that we come up with the idea of general 'formal' laws of logic. The rationalists, they argue, make the mistake of thinking that these laws are somehow primary and that real thought, 'pure' thought, is something unsullied by actual everyday reality. Logic, then, is not about finding some eternal laws of thought that are true in themselves; it is about finding the ways – the successful ways – in which thinking is actually performed.

Dewey and education

Given pragmatism's insistence on the real-world efficacy of ideas, it is not surprising that Dewey was always ready to try to apply his thinking to the political and social problems of his day (see Box 15.3). He was particularly known for his views on education, which embodied the emphasis on the concrete character of thought discussed in the previous section. Dewey's philosophy of education is sometimes referred to as **experiential education** because of its emphasis on concrete experience. It is one of Dewey's criticisms of traditional forms of education that they are prey to dualisms between body and mind, between thought and action, that have bedevilled more abstract realms of philosophy. In the late nineteenth and early twentieth centuries, a good deal of education involved the rote learning of information and the monotonous repetition of drills. The child was completely under the direction of the teacher and was expected simply to absorb the material that was presented by the teacher and then repeat it. For Dewey, this approach was not merely uninteresting and stultifying for the child, it was based on philosophical error: it was guilty of separating body and mind and treated the mind as simply the passive recipient of incoming information.

> In schools, those under instruction are too customarily looked upon as acquiring knowledge as theoretical spectators, minds which appropriate knowledge by direct energy of intellect . . . Something which is called mind or consciousness is severed from the physical organs of activity. The former is then thought to be purely intellectual and cognitive; the latter to be an irrelevant and intruding physical factor. The intimate union of activity and undergoing its consequences which leads to recognition of

---

Box 15.3 **Dewey and politics**

In an address on the occasion of his 80th birthday, Dewey said his faith in democracy was at the heart of his philosophical position. He was not, however, merely an armchair political theorist, but was involved – both through journalism and more direct political activism – in the issues of his day. Dewey himself claimed that it was his wife, Alice, a prominent campaigner for women's rights, who turned his thinking from relatively theoretical problems to the problems of real social life. Another influence in Dewey's political awakening was his move to Chicago, which, at the end of the nineteenth century, was the scene of rapid industrialisation and population growth. There were large immigrant communities, extremes of wealth and poverty, and industrial unrest. All of these factors stimulated Dewey's political interests.

One notable aspect of Dewey's political involvement was his chairing of a commission, in 1937, to investigate charges made against Leon Trotsky by the Stalinist regime in the Soviet Union. Trotsky, who was at the time living in exile in Mexico, had been accused of conspiring against Stalin and the Soviet state. The committee heard testimony from Trotsky and concluded that he was not guilty and that the Soviet regime had tried to frame him. Although the committee's verdict was favourable to Trotsky, Dewey himself angered the former Bolshevik revolutionary by speaking out against violent revolution as a means to a better, more democratic society. Unlike Trotsky, Dewey argued that democratic goals could never be reached by undemocratic means and advocated a steady process of social reform rather than sudden and violent revolution.

---

meaning is broken; instead we have two fragments: mere bodily action on one side, and meaning directly grasped by 'spiritual' activity on the other.

It would be impossible to state adequately the evil results which have flowed from this dualism of mind and body, much less to exaggerate them. (*Democracy and Education*, pp. 164–5)

The 'theoretical' aspect of education, the more intellectual aspects, cannot be separated from the physical and practical aspects. As we have already seen, this is of a piece with Dewey's general philosophy, according to which thought and action are actually necessary for one another's existence – thought is expressed in action, and action is the expression of thought. Separating thought and action reduces the intellectual component of thinking to an abstract exercise that has little connection with concrete reality, and reduces the physical and sensorimotor aspects of education to mechanical movements:

> Even, however, with respect to the lessons which have to be learned by the application of 'mind,' some bodily activities have to be used. The senses – especially the eye and ear – have to be employed to take in what the book, the map, the blackboard, and the teacher say. The lips and vocal organs, and the hands, have to be used to reproduce in speech and writing what has been stowed away. The senses are then regarded as a kind of mysterious conduit through which information is conducted from the external world into the mind; they are spoken of as gateways, and avenues of knowledge. To keep the eyes on the book and the ears open to the teacher's words is a mysterious source of intellectual grace. Moreover, reading, writing, and figuring – important school arts – demand muscular or motor training. The muscles of eye, hand, and vocal organs accordingly have to be trained to act as pipes for carrying knowledge back out of the mind into external action. For it happens that using the muscles repeatedly in the same way fixes in them an automatic tendency to repeat.
>
> The obvious result is a mechanical use of the bodily activities which (in spite of the generally obtrusive and interfering character of the body in mental action) have to be employed more or less. For the senses and muscles are used not as organic participants in having an instructive experience, but as external inlets and outlets of mind. (*Democracy and Education*, p. 166)

This is exactly the sort of thinking that Dewey attacked in his paper on the critique of the reflex arc concept. There he talks about the 'act of seeing' – seeing is *not* simply the passive registration of external or nervous events, it is an activity that is directed towards a particular purpose. But to sever an act from the purpose to which it is directed, to situate it not in a meaningful goal-directed context but in a meaningless and artificial setting is to transform an action into a mechanical performance.

> But when pupils are expected to use their eyes to note the form of words, irrespective of their meaning, in order to reproduce them in spelling or reading, the resulting training is simply of isolated sense organs and muscles. It is such isolation of an act from a purpose which makes it mechanical . . . Drawing, singing, and writing may be taught in the same mechanical way; for, we repeat, any way *is* mechanical which narrows down the bodily activity so that a separation of body from mind – that is, from recognition of meaning – is set up. (*Democracy and Education*, p. 167)

In order to counteract these deficiencies in traditional education, in which the child was treated as a passive recipient of knowledge, Dewey and his colleagues set up a school at the University of Chicago, which put his educational philosophy into practice. This was not just an effort to try to improve upon existing educational practice, but involved the putting into practice a completely different philosophy of education, one that tried to overcome the dualisms inherent in existing educational practice just as Dewey had tried to overcome the dualisms inherent in existing philosophical and psychological theory.

The putting into practice of this educational theory did not, according to Dewey, require the rigid adherence to fixed principles. Rather – and this is very much in the spirit of pragmatism – the specific methods used were worked out by the teachers in the course of their practice. Instead of fixed principles and methods, the school was set up with the more general aims of finding ways in which education could be made to be more continuous with the child's everyday life and the practicalities of life at home and in the rest of society. How this was best done was a matter for exploration by the teachers themselves. We can see, then, that the University Elementary School instantiated the ideas of pragmatism both in its overall mission – to connect education with concrete, everyday existence – and in its approach to implementing that mission – dispensing with fixed principles and leaving it to teachers to find those methods that worked best rather than having a fixed set of methods that were worked out in advance in a purely theoretical setting.

In effect, much of the lessons in the school involved practical tasks, such as sewing and weaving and cooking. These tasks formed the core of the lessons not because it was expected that the children would go on to become weavers or cooks, but because they provided a practical and concrete focus for tuition in science, history, and mathematics. In sewing and weaving, for example, the children would be presented with the raw materials – flax, cotton, wool – in unprocessed form and have to work out how to transform them into usable fibres and cloth. In so doing, they learn about the natural properties of these materials and about the technology that is involved in processing them. They learn about the history of that technology – from spinning wheels for wool to sophisticated looms – and the impact that it had on society. They also learn about the geographical distributions of the different raw materials and the climatic conditions necessary for their production. "You can," concludes Dewey, "concentrate the history of all mankind into the evolution of the flax, cotton, and wool fibers into clothing" (*The School and Society*, p. 36). What could be somewhat abstract instruction in science and history is made concrete by connecting it with the hands-on tasks of sewing and weaving. In organising education in this way, the school put into practice the pragmatist principle according to which all our ideas, even the most abstract, ultimately derive their sense and meaning from their connection with concrete practical reality. Learning, therefore, is no longer a mechanical activity that has little sense for the child, but something that is endowed with meaning through its connection with the concrete reality outside the classroom.

Conclusion

We have now seen how Dewey's pragmatic philosophy was manifested in his functional approach to psychology. According to this view, mental states are defined not by intrinsic characteristics, but by the functions that they perform within a larger coordinated pattern of activity. Even seemingly opposed things, such as stimulus and response, can, on deeper reflection, only be understood in terms of their relationships with one another. This emphasis on the interrelations between states and processes in Dewey's thought was, in part, an expression of the profound effect that the ideas of Hegel had upon him. It also meant that, in order to be understood, any thought or action had to be considered with respect to the concrete situation within which it arose. After all, thinking and behaviour evolve – in a dialectical relationship with the environment – purely to allow the organism to cope with its surroundings. This relationship between an organism's activity and its concrete environment was also the concern of behaviourism, although, as we shall see in the next chapter, their pragmatic approach to psychology was rather more uncompromising than that of either James or Dewey.

Revision questions

1. How does functionalism differ from structuralism?
2. What is the dialectic and how can it resolve dichotomies between thought and action and between mind and body?
3. How did Dewey criticise the concept of the reflex arc?
4. What, according to Dewey, makes some biological processes also mental processes?
5. What, according to Dewey, is consciousness?
6. How were Dewey's philosophical ideas reflected in his views on education?

References

Dewey, J. (1896). The reflex arc concept in psychology. *Psychological Review*, 3, 357–70.

Dewey, J. (1899). *The School and Society*. Chicago, IL: University of Chicago Press.

Dewey, J. (1903). *Studies in Logical Theory*. Chicago, IL: University of Chicago Press.

Dewey, J. (1916). *Democracy and Education*. New York: Macmillan.

Dewey, J. (1929). *Experience and Nature*. London: George Allen & Unwin.

Dewey, J. (1930). From absolutism to experimentalism. In G.P. Adams and W.P. Montague (eds.) *Contemporary American Philosophy: Personal Statements*. New York: Russell & Russell, pp. 13–27.

Dewey, J. (1939). Creative democracy. In J. Dewey (1988) *The Later Works, 1925–1953*. Carbondale, IL: Southern Illinois University Press.

16 Behaviourism

Timeline

1889	Opening of the Eiffel Tower in Paris
1903	Marie Curie is the awarded the Nobel Prize in Physics
1922	Stalin becomes General Secretary of the Soviet Communist Party
1936–9	Spanish Civil War
1945	Atomic bombs dropped on Hiroshima and Nagasaki
1954	Racial segregation is made illegal in the U.S.
1962	Cuban missile crisis
1975	Pol Pot and the Khmer Rouge take power in Cambodia
1989	Tiananmen Square massacre

Edward Lee Thorndike

1874	Born in Williamsburg, Massachusetts
1885	Studies psychology at Harvard under William James
1889	Becomes an instructor at Teachers College, Columbia University
1911	Publishes *Animal Intelligence*
1912	Elected president of the American Psychological Association
1931	Publishes *Human Learning*
1939	Retires from Columbia University
1949	Dies in Montrose, New York

John Broadus Watson

1878	Born near Greenville, South Carolina
1908	Becomes Professor of Psychology at Johns Hopkins University
1913	Publishes *Psychology as the Behaviorist Views It*
1915	Elected president of the American Psychological Association
1920	Is forced to resign his position at Johns Hopkins because of an extra-marital affair; goes to work in advertising
1924	Publishes *Behaviorism*
1958	Dies in New York

Burrhus Frederic Skinner

1904	Born in Susquehanna, Pennsylvania
1928	Studies psychology at Harvard
1943	Develops the air crib
1948	Appointed Professor at Harvard; Publishes *Walden Two*
1953	Publishes *Science and Human Behavior*
1957	Publishes *Verbal Behavior*
1971	Publishes *Beyond Freedom and Dignity*
1976	Publishes *About Behaviorism*
1990	Dies in Cambridge, Massachusetts

Introduction

In the previous chapter we saw how pragmatism emphasised the connection of ideas with their practical consequences and how functionalism, exemplified in the work of Dewey, applied this approach to psychology. For the functionalists, mental states had to be understood in terms of the functions that they performed, and these functions were a matter of allowing an organism to survive in its environment. The idea of a pure realm of consciousness, completely divorced from the practical demands of action, was rejected; mental states could only be studied validly in connection with the behaviour to which they were intrinsically connected. This strain of thought was taken to a more radical conclusion by behaviourism. To the most radical of the behaviourists – and both J. B. Watson and B. F. Skinner, two of the thinkers to be discussed in this chapter, described themselves as radical behaviourists – functionalism had not gone far enough. It was not simply the case, as the functionalists had argued, that one cannot talk about mental states without also talking about behaviour, but that so-called 'mental states' were nothing more than types of behaviour. Before examining the ideas of Watson and Skinner, however, we turn to one of the important precursors of behaviourism, E. L. Thorndike.

E. L. Thorndike: against introspection

Edward Lee Thorndike (1874–1949) was an important forerunner of behaviourism, and many of the ideas that are associated with the later behaviourism of

Box 16.1 Edward Lee Thorndike

Edward Lee Thorndike was born in Williamsburg, Massachusetts, in 1874, the son of a Methodist preacher. He started to study literature at Harvard but, upon reading William James's *Principles of Psychology*, he decided, after also attending some of James's lectures, to switch exclusively to psychology. Thorndike started research on learning in chicks, but animals were not allowed in the psychology laboratory and so he carried out the research in his own room until stopped by his landlady. Alternative accommodation for the chicks was found in the basement of William

Box 16.1 (cont.)

James's house, apparently to the annoyance of Mrs James but to the delight of the James children. Thorndike continued his work on animal learning at Columbia University (Figure 16.1), and the resulting thesis was published as *Animal Behavior*. This work inaugurated the laboratory study of animal behaviour.

Fig. 16.1 Edward Lee Thorndike

Box 16.1 (cont.)

Thorndike believed that his work on learning had implications for educational psychology. Contrary to prevailing ideas of rote learning, Thorndike argued that, because of the Law of Effect, children needed some reward for learning to take place and that mere repetition with no positive outcome was ineffective. He also claimed that his research showed that there was little skill transfer from the study of one subject to another and concluded that human intelligence consisted of an array of specific abilities, rather than one, general intelligence. He advocated, and designed, several educational tests so that children's progress could be measured numerically and developed a series of dictionaries to be used in school. He died in 1949 in Montrose, New York, where he had set up a community for like-minded colleagues and their families.

Watson can be found in Thorndike's work. In particular, Thorndike argued against the use of introspection of mental states as an important method in psychology, and maintained that overt, objectively observable behaviour should be the focus of psychology's investigation.

Thorndike paved the way for behaviourism as an outspoken proponent of the view that psychology should investigate – perhaps not exclusively, but to a large extent – observable behaviour. Thorndike's emphasis on observable behaviour rather than subjective, introspective reports was largely pragmatic or methodological: he did not deny the existence of mental states, as Watson was later to do (indeed, he defined psychology as "the science of mental facts or of mind" (Thorndike, *Elements of Psychology*, p. 1)), but he argued that the study of such states, especially through introspection, was a largely unproductive way of doing psychology.

Thorndike had several reasons for proposing that psychology should concentrate on behaviour rather than introspection. Firstly, from a practical point of view, introspection restricts the scope of psychology to adult humans – it can tell us nothing about the psychology of animals or of children who have not yet mastered language to a high degree. A reorienting of psychology from subjective introspection to the study of overt, objective behaviour would, for Thorndike, have the practical benefit of enlarging the scope of the discipline to include creatures that are incapable of introspection or communication.

Secondly, according to Thorndike, the apparent superiority of introspection in studying mental states is actually based on a misconception. Proponents of introspection assume that it is the only way in which psychological states can be studied, but, argued Thorndike, this is not the case: there is no reason why mental facts cannot be studied as objectively as anything else. Although a person suffering toothache, for example, may have more data (e.g. sensations from the teeth) at his or her disposal than that available to an outsider, it is possible in principle that "[w]ell-trained outside observers might identify the intensity of John's toothache more accurately than he could" (*Animal Intelligence*, p. 9). We should not confuse experiencing a mental state with knowledge of that mental state.

Thirdly, consciousness is intimately connected with action and behaviour. It is therefore unnatural to cut off the 'mental' sphere from that of behaviour. Even mental states can only be studied in terms of their functional connections with action. Here we see the legacy of functionalism as it fed into behaviourism. Thus, even if one is interested in mental states, one *cannot* study them adequately through introspection as if the mental was a private, subjective realm somehow connected only tenuously linked with the objective world of behaviour. Mental states are fundamentally connected with behaviour. According to Thorndike, "Knowledge of the action-system of an animal and its connections is a prerequisite to knowledge of its stream of consciousness" (*Animal Intelligence*, p. 15).

Without its intimate connection with actual behaviour, consciousness might as well be anything, or nothing. It is in their connection with behaviour that we know states of consciousness and it is therefore only through behaviour that they can be studied. To deny this, and to advocate that consciousness just be studied 'in itself', would be to reduce consciousness to something completely epiphenomenal, that had no effect on the world at all.

Given, then, that mental states have to be studied in connection with overt action or behaviour, what does Thorndike actually believe action to be? It is, according to him, strictly speaking, only some form of muscular movement. This is what any action *really* is:

> All acts are reducible to movements of the body brought about by the contraction and relaxation of muscles . . . The mere act of saying 'Yes' is the same whether it be a slice of bread or a husband that is accepted. The million things a man does from birth to death are at bottom only some thousands of muscular contractions. (*Elements of Psychology*, p. 10)

This definition of behaviour as nothing more that a physical movement will, as we shall see, pose problems in behaviourism's ability to deal with more complex aspects of psychology, such as thinking.

Thorndike and animal learning

Having dispensed with introspection as the primary means of psychological investigation, the way, then, was open to investigate animal psychology in behavioural terms. Thorndike was not the first to interest himself in animal psychology. Scientists such as George Romanes (1848–94), a colleague of Darwin's, published extensive studies of animal thought from an evolutionary point of view. Much of Romanes's data was culled from anecdotal reports from farmers, pet owners, zoo keepers, and others who had close and extensive experience of animals. Many of these reports seemed to suggest that animals may be possessed of quite sophisticated mental abilities. It should be noted, however, that Romanes did not simply believe all these anecdotes uncritically; there were some stories that he rejected as being implausible. Other thinkers, such as Lloyd Morgan (1852–1936), also believed that animals possessed consciousness, and that it played an important role in evolution. He argued that without consciousness and intelligence, animals would not be able to survive to an age at which they could reproduce. As natural selection operates through differential reproductive success, the very existence of natural selection required that animals have intelligence in order to reach the stage of reproduction.

Thorndike, however, believed that the animal behaviour that was reported in these anecdotal accounts was being interpreted in an **anthropomorphic** way that possibly exaggerated the level of thought that was needed to explain the animal's behaviour. In addition, Thorndike also believed that the use of data from anecdotal reports was itself suspect and possibly inaccurate or distorted. For Thorndike, animal behaviour had to be studied under rigorous scientific conditions in the controlled environment of the laboratory (though, as Lloyd Morgan was later to comment, whether the artificial conditions of the laboratory are likely to give a true picture of an animal's range of abilities is arguable to say the least).

When, according to Thorndike, we examine anecdotal reports of animal behaviour "we find it the opinion of the better observers and analysts that these reactions can all be explained by the ordinary associative processes without aid from abstract, conceptual, inferential thinking" (*Animal Intelligence*, p. 20). It is these "associative processes" that were the object of Thorndike's study. The process of association in animals is, of course, an object of legitimate scientific investigation in its own right, but, says Thorndike, the study of these processes in animals will shed light on human psychology too, because, according to Thorndike, "[s]omehow out of these associative processes have arisen human consciousnesses with their sciences and arts and religions" (*Animal Intelligence*, p. 22).

Thorndike developed 'puzzle boxes', pieces of laboratory equipment that would enable him to study animal associative learning in a controlled setting. He would put a hungry animal (cats, chicks, dogs, and monkeys were all used by Thorndike) inside a box from which it had to escape in order to get food. Different boxes could be opened in different ways: the animal might have to push a lever or pull a loop of string, for example. Thorndike found that, at first, animals would produce various behaviours – such as clawing at the bars or sides of the box – in an attempt to escape, and would hit on the correct response by sheer accident. However, over repeated trials, the animals performed the correct response more and more quickly until they performed the correct response almost immediately after being confined in the box.

Such learning would, said Thorndike, normally be couched in terms of the association of ideas, such as mental images of the box, motor representations, and memories of pleasurable feelings. Thorndike, however, envisaged a much more direct connection between an environmental stimulus and a motor impulse that is not mediated by mental states or ideas. The animal, according to Thorndike, merely perceives the current situation and this calls forth the appropriate behaviour.

Thorndike likened this direct connection between situation and response formed by animals to that created by training in a tennis player. The association between seeing the tennis ball come towards you and the production of a shot to hit the ball back over the net is not a matter of conscious thought or 'association of ideas'. Indeed, it is precisely the point of training to minimise the thought and deliberation required so that the expert player returns the shot as instinctively and intuitively as possible. The association, then, lies in the creation of a connection – a physical connection in the nervous system – between the sense impression and the motor impulse without the mediation of thinking and deliberation. The connections between neurons are strengthened or weakened according to whether or not the behaviour has a rewarding outcome and the frequency with which it is produced. These two principles Thorndike calls, respectively, the **Law of Effect** and the **Law of Exercise**. He defines them as follows:

The Law of Effect is that: Of several responses made to the same situation, those which are accompanied or closely followed by satisfaction to the animal will, other things being equal, be more firmly connected with the situation, so that, when it recurs, they will be more likely to recur; those which are accompanied or closely followed by discomfort to the animal will, other things being equal, have their connections with that situation weakened, so that, when it recurs, they will be less likely to occur. The greater the satisfaction or discomfort, the greater the strengthening or weakening of the bond. The Law of Exercise is that: Any response to a situation will, other things being equal, be more strongly connected with the situation in proportion to the number of times it has been connected with that situation and to the average vigor and duration of the connections. (*Animal Intelligence*, p. 244)

Thorndike believed that the pattern of learning shown by his experimental animals was indicative of the gradual establishment of a neural connection rather than insightful thinking. If an animal learned how to escape from the box through rational problem-solving, one would predict a sudden drop in the time taken to escape, which would correspond to the animal's finally cottoning on to the problem's solution. But this is not what is seen. Rather, the animals get progressively quicker over repeated trials. It is this pattern of performance that led Thorndike to attribute the animal's learning to "the wearing smooth of a path in the brain, not the decisions of a rational consciousness" (*Animal Intelligence*, p. 74). Human learning, too, although mediated by ideas to a greater extent than animal learning, was, for Thorndike, essentially a matter of connections being formed in the nervous system. "Learning," said Thorndike, "is connecting. The mind is man's connection system" (*Human Learning*, p. 122). In this sense, then, Thorndike was a precursor of contemporary **connectionist** approaches to psychology and neuroscience, which are also based on the facilitation and inhibition of transmission along neural pathways, and which views these as being moulded by practice and reward.

Thorndike, then, was important in the development of behaviourism because of his emphasis on behaviour, as opposed to introspective mental states, as the most important area of interest for the psychologist. He nevertheless did not reject the existence of mental states, and indeed believed that animals probably did have some minimal form of conscious experience. Thorndike's minimal concessions to mentalism were, however, rejected by Watson. He formulated a radical behaviourism in which consciousness and mental states were not merely reduced in importance, but declared to be non-existent.

Watson's 'behaviourist manifesto'

John Broadus Watson (1878–1958) announced his behaviourist programme in his famous 1913 paper, 'Psychology as the behaviorist views it'. This paper is almost a manifesto for behaviourism in which Watson argues that psychology, in order to fulfil its potential, has to change tack and to focus exclusively on behaviour. Watson characterises the old psychology, against which he defines his new, radical behaviourism, as the science of consciousness and its goal as the analysis of complex mental states into their constituent elements. The method by which the analysis of mental states is to be achieved is introspection and among the older generation of introspectionists Watson mentions Titchener, Wundt, and James (although neither Wundt nor James could fairly be described as analytical introspectionists). Psychology, for Watson, must reject this method if it is to make any progress.

There were several reasons behind Watson's rejection of introspection. He believed, first of all, that its subjective nature meant that it could never give us any reliable facts. An example, to which Watson alludes in his 1913 paper, illustrates what he saw as the problem. In the early years of the twentieth century, there was a dispute between different groups, one with Titchener in the

Box 16.2 John Broadus Watson

John Broadus Watson was born in a small village near Greenville, South Carolina, in 1878. His alcoholic father left the family home when Watson was 13 and he was raised by his mother, a devoutly religious Southern Baptist. Watson studied psychology and philosophy at Furman University, a local Baptist institution, and, upon graduation, considered studying to become a church minister. Before Watson could enrol on the required theology course, however, his mother died and Watson abruptly changed his plans and went to do postgraduate work in psychology at the University of Chicago. In the bustling city of Chicago, Watson moved ever further away from his Southern Baptist background, and his dismissal of 'consciousness' in psychology as nothing more than a residue of the 'soul' may have been as much a revolt against his own upbringing as it was against the introspectionism of Titchener.

Box 16.2 **(cont.)**

Fig. 16.2 John Broadus Watson

Box 16.2 (cont.)

In 1908, Watson moved to Johns Hopkins University in Baltimore as professor of psychology. In 1915 he became, at the age of 36, the youngest President of the American Psychological Association. However, his successful career at Johns Hopkins was cut short after it became known that Watson was having an affair with one of his research assistants, Rosalie Rayner, whom he subsequently married. Rayner's grandfather was a prominent local businessman and her uncle was a US Senator and the affair featured extensively in the local newspapers. The scandal surrounding the affair forced Watson to resign his position.

After leaving academia, Watson found work in a Madison Avenue advertising agency and rapidly worked his way up to senior positions (Figure 16.2). Though no longer working in academic psychology, Watson continued to publish articles on psychology in popular magazines. In 1957, the year before his death, Watson received a special award from the American Psychological Association to mark his contribution to psychology. Watson, who had never completely forgiven the academic world after being forced out of his professorship, sent his son to pick up the award instead of going himself.

United States and another in Würzburg in Germany, which centred on the question of imageless thought, i.e. whether one could have a thought that did not give rise to some sort of sensory image. Introspective observers with Titchener's laboratory claimed that thought was always accompanied by a sensory image whereas the Würzburg group claimed to have experienced imageless thoughts. But how could one decide between the different subjective reports? Could it not be the case that one of the groups was using introspection in a faulty way? And if so, which one? In *Behaviorism* (1924a) Watson reiterated his dissatisfaction with the subjectivity of introspection:

> As a result of this major assumption that there is such a thing as consciousness and that we can analyze it by introspection, we find as many analyses as there are individual psychologists. There is no way of experimentally attacking and solving psychological problems and standardizing methods. (*Behaviorism*, p. 6)

Given the subjective nature of introspection and the unreliable data that are obtained using it, there is only one thing that the psychologist can do to put the discipline on a firm, truly scientific footing: "What we need to do is to start work upon psychology, making *behavior*, not *consciousness*, the objective point of our attack" ('Psychology as the behaviorist views it', pp. 175–6).

What Watson saw as the subjective, and, hence, unreliable nature of introspection was not his only reason for rejecting it. It was also the case that the questions that introspection was supposed to answer – the nature and number of the basic elements that made up complex mental states – seemed to him trivial and to have no relevance whatsoever to everyday life. Watson contrasted the stagnancy of introspective experimental psychology and its sterile debates with the thriving use of psychology in real life problems and settings:

> those branches of psychology which have already partially withdrawn from the parent, experimental psychology, and which are consequently less dependent upon introspection are today in a most flourishing condition. Experimental pedagogy, the psychology of drugs, the psychology of advertising, legal psychology, the psychology of tests, and psychopathology are all vigorous growths. ('Psychology as the behaviorist views it', p. 169)

The flourishing parts of psychology are concerned with *practical results* rather than enumerating states of consciousness. Introspection, even if it were reliable, would have nothing to tell us about whether, say, one teaching method is more effective than another. The only way to find this out is to experimentally investigate which one has the better *outcome*. What goes on introspectively in the heads of schoolchildren taught according to the different methods is neither here nor there; one method is simply better than another and it allows us to improve the learning of children in school. The purpose of psychology is no longer the description and analysis of consciousness, but "the prediction and control of behavior" ('Psychology as the behaviorist views it', p. 158). Watson's psychology not only uses different methods from the introspectionists, it asks different questions.

There was also a third, more philosophical, reason for Watson's rejection of introspection: the thing that introspection claimed to investigate, consciousness, did not, according to Watson, even exist. The whole idea of 'consciousness' as a special realm that could be investigated by introspection was, for Watson, little more than a modernised version of religious mystification. According to Watson, consciousness was "merely another word for the 'soul' of more ancient times" (*Behaviorism*, p. 3).

Watson believed that behaviouristic psychology, like the other natural sciences, had to be strictly materialistic in its basic view of the universe, and that introspective psychology, with its whiff of dualism, did not, therefore, qualify as a real science. Watson later claimed that "All psychology except behaviorism is dualistic" (*Behaviorism*, p. 4).

In his rejection of introspection, then, Watson went further than Thorndike and claimed not only that introspection was unreliable and useless, but that its very field of investigation was illusory.

Predicting behaviour

When a human being acts – does something with arms, legs or vocal cords – there must be an invariable group of antecedents serving as a "cause" of the act. For this group of antecedents the term situation or stimulus is a convenient term. When an individual is placed face to face with some situation – a fire, a menacing animal or human, a change in fortune – he will do something, even if he only stands still or faints. Psychology is thus confronted immediately with two problems – the one of predicting the probable causal situation or stimulus giving rise to the response; the other, given the situation, of predicting the probable response. (*Psychology from the Standpoint of a Behaviorist*, p. 5)

This passage sums up Watson's general orientation: all behaviour, given the right analysis, can be understood in terms of **stimulus–response** relationships, the stimulus being an object or event in the environment or internal organs of the animal that causes a response, this being any bodily movement on the part of the organism. Psychology's job, as a purely scientific enterprise, is to discover these stimulus–response relationships.

It is important to note that the organism is not here seen as the initiator of behaviour. It is the causal effect of the environment that elicits a response from the organism. And this causal relationship is direct: "The behaviorist claims that there is a response to every effective stimulus and that the response is immediate ..." (*Behaviorism*, pp. 14–15). Watson will have no truck with the idea, which he associates with psychoanalysis, that a stimulus encountered in the distant past can have an effect in the present day. On the contrary, the effect (response) produced by a cause (stimulus) must be as immediate as that of any other physical cause-and-effect relationship, such as the collision of one billiard ball with another or the ripples caused by the throwing of a stone into a pond.

But knowing the relationship between cause and effect, though it may allow us to predict behaviour, is only one part of Watson's vision of psychology, which is not only to predict behaviour but also to control it. Such control would, however, only be possible on the assumption that much of our behaviour is highly malleable. If it were the result of innate, fixed drives and instincts, then there would be little that any applied psychology could do to alter and control it. But Watson believed that a few basic drives – for food and sex, for example – were all that animals and people were born with, and he rejected the idea that more complex or sophisticated aspects of psychology had innate components, stating that, "there is no such thing as inheritance of *capacity, talent, temperament, mental constitution,* and *characteristics*" (*Behaviorism*, pp. 74–5).

In this respect, Watson harks back to the empiricist views of Locke and believes that child's mind is a blank slate at birth. This means that through education and training, we can mould people into whatever sort of person we want them to be. The controlling or moulding of behaviour that Watson envisaged was to be achieved through stimulus–response learning, i.e. the scientist would find out what sort of stimuli produced what sort of response and how responses could be shaped by the presentation of different sorts of stimuli. The behaviorist, says Watson, would then be able to say to society, "If you decide that the human organism should behave in this way, you just arrange situations of such and such kinds" (*Behaviorism*, p. 7).

The stimulus–response learning that Watson envisaged as moulding behaviour followed the principles of conditioned reflexes as investigated by Ivan Pavlov (1849–1936). Pavlov differentiated between **unconditioned reflexes**, which are simple, direct, and natural responses to specific stimuli, and **conditioned reflexes**. These latter were not part of an organism's inbuilt repertoire of behaviours, but were learned. Dogs will automatically start salivating when food is placed in their mouths. This is an unconditioned reflex. Pavlov, however, found that if the dogs heard a bell immediately prior to receiving food, they would come to start salivating to the sound of the bell alone. This was a conditioned reflex, and Pavlov claimed that any arbitrary stimulus could be turned into a conditioned stimulus. Both types of response were, said Pavlov, entirely a function of physiological connections in the nervous system; there was no need to supplement a physiological explanation with supposedly mental processes.

Watson himself famously tried to use Pavlovian principles to condition fear in a 9-month-old infant, Albert B, or 'Little Albert' as he is sometimes referred to in the literature (Watson and Rayner 1920). Albert was happy to play with a white rat, but after Watson had made a loud, frightening noise by banging a metal bar with a hammer every time Albert touched the rat, the infant started to cry and show fear when the rat came close. Though it is sometimes suggested that Albert's conditioned fear generalised to all white or furry objects, such as a rabbit of which he had previously been unafraid, the results of Watson and Rayner's study were not as clear-cut as is sometimes supposed. Fear reactions to the rabbit were not consistent and even fear reactions to the rat were much reduced when Albert encountered it in a different room from the one in which the conditioning had taken place. Watson also had to 'refresh' Albert's conditioned fear of the rat several times by repeating the pairing of the loud noise with Albert's touching of the rat.

Behaviourism and thinking

Although Watson contended that movements of limbs or of the whole body are the most common responses to stimuli, he nevertheless recognised that not all responses take the form of obvious, overt behaviours. He recognised that along with overt or explicit responses that are easily observable, there are also implicit responses "wholly confined to the muscular and glandular systems inside the body" (*Behaviorism*, p. 15) that cannot be observed without specialised instruments. These are, nevertheless, behavioural and entirely physical responses to stimuli and, as such, are observable at least in principle. In this sense, they differed from the events that non-behaviourists believed took place in the immaterial realm of the mind: these were not observable, even in principle. Their inaccessability was not a matter of practicalities, but a matter of metaphysical necessity. But implicit responses did not differ intrinsically from explicit ones; they were merely "hidden from the eye" (*Behaviorism*, p. 15).

Watson gives the following example to illustrate what he means by implicit responses:

> A child or hungry adult may be standing stock still in front of a window filled with pastry. Your first exclamation may be "he isn't doing anything" or "he is just looking at the pastry." An instrument would show that his salivary glands are pouring out secretions, that his stomach is rhythmically contracting and expanding, and that marked changes in blood pressure are taking place – that the endocrine glands are pouring substances into the blood. (*Behaviorism*, p. 15)

All of this may indeed by true, but isn't there something missing? Isn't the hungry person doing more than just being subject to physiological changes in salivation and blood pressure? Isn't the hungry person thinking, "Those pastries look good"? It would seem that Watson's analysis leaves out the very process of thinking itself, but Watson proposed an analysis in which thinking can find a place within the behaviourist scheme of things. For Watson "what the psychologists have hitherto called thought is in short nothing but talking to ourselves" (*Behaviorism*, p. 191); it is "subvocal talking" (*Behaviorism*, p. 194).

But what is this 'talking to ourselves'? According to Watson, the learning of language – or the learning of 'language habits' – occurs in the same way as learning a motor response, such as withdrawing one's hand when a certain stimulus is presented. The infant naturally produces vocal reflexes, some of which will, fortuitously, sound similar to words, and the adult will try to get the child to associate the vocalisation with the object named by the word and will try to shape the child's response so as to get ever closer to the word that it approximates. The responses that are learned are, perhaps, more complex than those involved in simply moving the hand – they involve the larynx, cheek, tongue, throat, and chest musculature all interacting in a coordinated way – but they are different in terms of complexity, or quantity, rather than quality. It is these "muscular habits learned in overt speech" that are, according to Watson, "responsible for implicit or internal speech (thought)" (*Behaviorism*, p. 192). But other muscular responses, such as shrugging the shoulders, can also become part of this complex of motor habits. Indeed, so complex is the organisation and coordination, the substitution of actions for words, such as shaking or nodding the head for 'yes' and 'no', that Watson concludes that "man both talks and thinks with his whole body just as be does everything else with his whole body" (*Behaviorism*, p. 180). It is when we activate some of these complex motor responses implicitly, when we make "subvocal use of our language organization" (*Behaviorism*, p. 194), that we are thinking.

Even thinking, then, for Watson, is assimilated to a complex of physical movements or muscular activations. Such muscular activity may be invisible to the casual observer, but it is just as objective, just as physical, as larger movements that are more easily observed. There is no need to envisage it taking place in some subjective, inner world just because it is difficult to detect. It takes place in the same world as any other sort of behaviour, and that is the only world that there is: the physical world described by natural science.

The radical behaviourism of B. F. Skinner

Skinner, like Watson, did not believe in the existence of mental states as traditionally conceived. His viewpoint was one of radical behaviourism "in which the

Box 16.3 **Burrhus Frederic Skinner**

Burrhus Frederic Skinner was born in Susquehanna, Pennsylvania, in 1904, the son of a lawyer. At college his studies concentrated on literature rather than science and his original ambition was to become a writer, but as Skinner himself admitted, his youthful attempts at novel writing were 'disastrous'. Musing on his failure as a writer, Skinner came to the conclusion that, though literature could describe people's behaviour, only science could really understand it. He decided to study psychology at Harvard and arrived there in 1928, at the age of 24. At Harvard, Skinner adopted a rigid schedule of work in order to make up for his lack of background knowledge in psychology, and in 1938 he completed his doctoral thesis on the concept of the reflex. He taught at the universities of Minnesota and Indiana before returning to Harvard in 1948. He was to remain there for the rest of his career.

Skinner never lost his interest in literature, particularly classic French writers, such as Diderot, Stendhal, and Proust, whose works he read in the original. He was also a keen amateur musician. Along with these cultural interests, Skinner was also very keen on making gadgets and devices to solve practical problems. One of these was the so-called 'Skinner box', or operant-conditioning chamber, in which an animal's behaviour could be reinforced by the automated delivery of food pellets into the box in which the animal was housed. Another device, which was the subject of much misunderstanding, was the 'air crib'. In order to make household tasks easier for his wife upon the birth of their second baby, Deborah, Skinner decided to replace the traditional baby's crib with one of his own making. Rather than have the baby wrapped up in constricting clothes and blankets and placed in stationary crib from where she would be unable to see her mother most of the time, Skinner constructed a mobile compartment, which had a large window, controlled temperature, and plenty of room for the baby to move around. Deborah was able to see her mother while remaining in a safe, warm environment. Skinner's invention was the subject of an article in a women's magazine, in which it was referred to as a 'baby box'. Some people confused this with the Skinner box and believed, completely erroneously, that Deborah had been raised in an operant-conditioning chamber. It was even alleged that she had later committed suicide or become psychotic as a result. In fact, she grew up completely normally and became a successful artist in London.

existence of subjective entities is denied" (*The Shaping of a Behaviorist*, p. 117). Skinner also agreed with Watson that the goal of behaviourism was the prediction and control of behaviour. This goal, as with Watson, was to be achieved through finding the causal antecedents of behaviour. Underneath these surface similarities, however, Skinner's version of behaviourism differed from that of Watson in a number of significant ways. Firstly, Skinner viewed the organism as essentially active, as purposively producing behaviour, rather than the passive recipient of stimuli coming from the environment. Secondly, Skinner's view of causality – and hence his behaviourist reinterpretation of 'mental' processes such as thinking – was considerably more subtle than that of Watson.

The organism as an active entity

We have seen above that Watson thought of behaviour as something that is elicited *from* the organism *by* the environment acting upon it. The organism itself does not actively initiate action (apart from the most minimal and basic movements); behaviour has to be mechanically wrested from it by causal influence of the environment. Skinner, in contrast, sees the organism as actively exploring and operating on its environment. This is why he used the term **'operant'** rather than 'reflex' to designate the crucial component of his view of behaviourism. Rather than a piece of behaviour being triggered by the causal effect of an environmental stimulus, Skinner thinks of behaviour as being 'emitted' by the organism in a purposeful and active manner (*Shaping of a Behaviorist*, p. 58). Skinner is at pains to distinguish his own approach from earlier, reflex-based, forms of behaviourism:

> Possibly no charge is more often levelled against behaviorism or a science of behavior than that it cannot deal with purpose or intention. A stimulus–response formula has no answer, but operant behavior is the very field of purpose and intention. By its nature it is directed toward the future: a person acts *in order that* something will happen, and the order is temporal. (*Shaping of a Behaviorist*, p. 61)

But the question then arises as to where this purpose comes from. The traditional, 'mentalistic' answer, according to Skinner, would be that purpose originates in an act of free will or volition on the part of the organism. Needless to say Skinner completely rejects the idea that behaviour is somehow the outcome of a mysterious mental event. But he also rejects the idea that behaviour is mechanically caused by stimuli in the current environment in the traditional stimulus–response fashion. Even though operant behaviour is purposeful, and not mechanically elicited by the environment, it is nevertheless caused rather than free or spontaneous. Skinner's view of behaviour and its causes is rather more sophisticated than either of these other views.

Purposeful behaviour, causality, and reinforcement

Stimulus–response theorists, such as Watson, thought that the causes of behaviour must be in the immediate environment because their view of causality was one that was rooted in seventeenth-century notions of clockwork and mechanism – of bits of matter pushing and pulling each other. They thought that behaviour was caused through environmental stimuli impinging on the sense organs of the organism in a way analogous to the movement in a previously stationary billiard ball being caused by its being hit by another, moving, billiard ball. Skinner's view of the causes of behaviour, however, owed more to the ideas of Darwin than to seventeenth-century physics.

"Darwin," said Skinner, "discovered the role of selection, a kind of causality very different from the push-pull mechanisms of science up to that time" (*Shaping of a Behaviorist*, pp. 40–1). One of the things that Darwin realised, and which Skinner applied to the learning of behaviour, is that the causal forces that shape evolution were not in the current environment, but were in the past. In Darwinian evolution, organisms produce mutations or variations, some of which are more successful than others. These more successful variations are selected by the environment, and continue to exist; those that are not successful disappear. Skinner applied similar reasoning to the explanation of behaviour. Just like biological variations, behavioural variations are also selected by the environment – some are more successful in allowing the organism to survive and meet its needs than others. These are said to be 'reinforced' and the positive consequences that strengthen the successful behaviour are called 'reinforcers'. And although the timescale over which behavioural selection occurs is much shorter than the evolution of species according to natural selection, the principle is the same: the environment selects successful variations, which continue to be seen, and rejects unsuccessful variations, which become extinct.

Thus, it is the *past consequences* of a behavioural variation – whether it is selected or not – that determine the probability that it will be seen in the future.

What makes this different from the 'push–pull' mechanistic causality that was characteristic of pre-Darwinian science is that the causes of a behaviour lie in the past, in the reinforcement history of the organism, rather than in the present. The explanation of a piece of behaviour is still causal – the behaviour is not the result of a spontaneous act of free will on the part of the organism – but it is not mechanical. The causal explanation of behaviour does not lie in the present environment, but the environment of the past, which has reinforced certain behaviours at the expense of others.

The type of causality that Skinner envisages is *historical* rather than *mechanical*. It is more akin to the causal explanation of a historical event than a physical event. It would be nonsense to say that the cause of the French Revolution, for example, was a single discrete event occurring in a specific time and place. The French Revolution was the result of complex social, economic, and political factors that existed in Europe not only immediately prior to the revolution, but which had developed through the history of Europe and had therefore changed Europe itself. To seek an explanation of the French Revolution requires an understanding of the history of Europe. Skinner's explanation of the behaviour of an organism is analogous – it requires an understanding of the history of the organism.

Skinner's reconceptualisation of mentalistic concepts

Skinner's approach runs counter to the main tradition in Western psychology and philosophy, which traces its origins to Descartes and Locke. According to this main tradition, the mind is a sort of inner space in which mental entities called ideas have their existence. Our knowledge, our thought, perception, and memory – indeed our whole psychology – is to be explained in terms of what goes on inside us. Even the stimulus–response theorists who preceded Skinner thought in terms of inner explanations, although these were reflexes and neural connections rather than 'mentalistic' ideas. For Skinner, however, if we want to know more about human psychology – perception, learning, memory – we must look *outside* the person, to her history and how she interacts with her environment, rather than inside the person.

For Skinner, knowledge, perception, and memory just are different aspects of behaviour, which has been shaped by our reinforcement history. To remember something is not to have an image or thought before one's mind, but to act in a

---

Box 16.4 **The social views of Skinner**

Skinner was keen to apply his ideas to topics of wider social concern, such as education and mental health. He had no doubt that a behaviourist approach to social problems could lead to a better society. Skinner set forth his social views in a novel called *Walden Two*, in which he described a fictional utopian community, which operated according to behaviourist principles.

Though Skinner was caricatured (e.g. by US Vice-President Spiro Agnew) as a fascist or totalitarian for his view that society could be improved by scientifically grounded techniques of behaviour control, a look at the utopian community described in *Walden Two* suggests that Skinner's vision is more akin to an anarchist commune than to a modern totalitarian state: the community is self-governing, rather than subject to the authority of an elite political class; all property, including the means of production, is held in common, and so it is impossible to build up wealth purely for oneself; there is equality between the sexes; and everyone, even the managers and planners, has to do at least some manual work to contribute to the production of the community.

For Skinner, there was nothing inherently totalitarian about behaviour control because he believed that *all* behaviour is under the control of some reinforcement or other. It was only certain *types* of control, such as control through punishment, rather than control per se that he believed to be oppressive. He also believed punishment to be ineffective as a means of behaviour control when compared to positive reinforcement. The dystopian vision of people being shocked to 'condition' their behaviour is absent from Skinner's social ideas. Instead, Skinner believed that, as behaviour is controlled by reinforcement anyway, it makes sense to organise that reinforcement in ways that are beneficial to society, for example through using reinforcement to encourage cooperation.

---

way that has been informed by previous experience. Similarly, having knowledge is being able to *do* something. Having knowledge of French means that we can ask for the time of the next train to Paris when on holiday in France and can then behave in a way that takes into account the reply that the information desk in the station has given to us; it is being able to order a meal in a restaurant, to reserve a room, to hold a conversation on the latest political or sporting events with people that we meet when visiting France, etc. It is, in other words, a matter of being able to *behave* in certain ways, not a matter of 'ideas' inside us. From a Skinnerian point of view, it is important to realise that this behaviour is not merely an outward sign of the knowledge that lurks within the person, it *is* that knowledge; there is no knowledge of French apart from the behaviour of communicating in French. The having of the knowledge is inseparable from its instantiation in actual behaviour.

Perceiving, too, is a type of behaviour: it is behaviour that is under the control of a current stimulus in a certain way. In linking perception specifically to behaviour, Skinner echoes the ideas of Dewey. For Dewey, as we saw in the previous chapter, perception is inseparable from action: to perceive a danger just is to behave in a certain way (e.g. to run away or to hide) in the presence of the stimulus, it is to have behaviour that is under the control of the stimulus in a particular way. The same holds true of Skinner's view of perception: we cannot divorce some supposedly 'inner' process of perception from separate behaviour to which it supposedly gives rise because perception is not an inner process at all, but a matter of acting in certain ways under certain circumstances: we do not run away from a dangerous stimulus *because* we perceive it and interpret it as dangerous; our running away from it *is* (part of) our perception of it. We do not have two things, perception *plus* behaviour. We have one thing, perceptual behaviour.

Verbal behaviour and thinking

There nevertheless seem to be some examples of 'mental' activity in which we appear to be engaged in no overt behaviour – no matter how subtle – whatsoever. We are just 'thinking'. We have seen above that Watson tried to assimilate thinking to some form of behaviour by equating it with subvocal speech, although he also noted that speech involved more than the vocal apparatus. Skinner too believes that covert verbal behaviour is often associated with thought, but does not identify the two in the way that Watson does.

For Watson, as we saw above, verbal behaviour was defined as a particular bodily, muscular habit that was learned in the course of being conditioned by experience. This most obviously involved the structures of the vocal apparatus – mouth, throat, vocal cords – but also involved a far larger group of anatomical structures, including the chest, and potentially extended to the face (in the case of emotional expressions), shoulders (a shrug of the shoulders being a substitute for a vocal utterance), and whole body. But even though he widened the scope of speech to include other bodily actions that could substitute for speech strictly considered, Watson was still tied to thinking in terms of particular physiological activities: thinking was intrinsically attached to speech, which was intrinsically attached to the whole vocal apparatus, even though substitutions could be made.

Skinner's view of verbal behaviour was different from Watson's in that it had nothing to do with any particular anatomical structures. Whereas Watson defined verbal behaviour in terms of its relationship to the anatomical vocal apparatus, in its widest possible sense, Skinner defined verbal behaviour in terms of the type of reinforcement history by which it was shaped. Skinner differentiated between verbal behaviour and the physiological structures that may be used in effecting that behaviour.

Watson's mistake was in thinking that verbal behaviour counts as such simply because it is associated with movements, no matter how subtle, within the vocal tract. A moment's reflection, however, tells us that this view of verbal behaviour is completely unsound: there are many examples of verbal behaviour that have nothing to do with what is going on the vocal tract. Writing is an obvious example that has nothing to do with the vocal apparatus, as is sign language. Conversely there are many sounds and noises that we make using the vocal tract but which scarcely deserve to be designated 'verbal behaviour'. The conclusion that we must come to – and the conclusion that is implied in Skinner's discussion of the matter – is that the involvement or otherwise of the vocal tract is irrelevant as to whether a piece of behaviour is or is not verbal.

What makes verbal behaviour *verbal* behaviour is, for Skinner, nothing to do with the actual behaviour itself taken just as it is – making marks on a piece of paper may be verbal, but it might not be; making noises using one's vocal apparatus is usually verbal, but it need not be. What makes a piece of behaviour verbal, as opposed to non-verbal, is to be sought outside the behaviour itself in its reinforcement history. Specifically, verbal behaviour is that class of behaviour that is "reinforced through the mediation of other persons" (*Verbal Behavior*, p. 2). Skinner goes on to make clear that this means that any behaviour, considered purely as a physical event, could be verbal:

> In defining verbal behavior as behavior reinforced through the mediation of other persons we do not, and cannot, specify any one form, mode, or medium. Any movement capable of affecting another organism may be verbal. We are likely to single out vocal behavior, not only because it is commonest, but because it has little effect upon the physical environment and hence is almost necessarily verbal. But there are extensive written languages, sign languages, and languages in which the "speaker" stimulates the skin of the "listener." Audible behavior which is not vocal (for example, clapping the

> hands for a servant, or blowing a bugle) and gestures are verbal, although they may not compose an organized language. The skilled telegraphist behaves verbally by moving his wrist ... Pointing to words is verbal – as, indeed, is all pointing, since it is effective only when it alters the behavior of someone. (*Verbal Behavior*, p. 14)

Watson, as we have seen, argued that thinking was implicit or covert verbal behaviour. Skinner, too, believes that thinking often takes the form of covert verbal behaviour, but that other sorts of covert non-verbal behaviour, such as the planning of chess moves, also constitute thinking. It just so happens that verbal behaviour lends itself to covert performance more than other sorts of behaviour, but it is not because it is verbal but because it "occurs on a scale so small that it cannot be detected by others" (*Shaping of a Behaviorist*, p. 114) that it is labelled 'thinking'.

For Skinner, however, there is nothing special about covert behaviour, as opposed to overt behaviour, that magically turns it into a special type of activity called thinking. There is a continuum of the degree to which behaviours may be carried out covertly. Let us take verbal behaviour as an example:

> The range of verbal behavior is roughly suggested, in descending order of energy, by shouting, loud talking, quiet talking, whispering, muttering "under one's breath," subaudible speech with detectable muscular action, subaudible speech of unclear dimensions, and perhaps even the "unconscious thinking" sometimes inferred in instances of problem solving. There is no point at which it is profitable to draw a line distinguishing thinking from acting on this continuum. So far as we know, the events at the covert end have no special properties, observe no special laws, and can be credited with no special achievements. (*Verbal Behavior*, p. 438)

There is, then, nothing special about covert verbal behaviour, or indeed covert non-verbal behaviour, that makes it different from its overt counterpart and confers upon it some magical quality of thought. It is simply the same behaviour as the overt variety only performed in a covert fashion. 'Thinking', then, is interpreted behaviouristically as the covert performance of behaviour that can also be overt. But there are other types of 'mental process' that are commonly considered to be part of thinking but which, says Skinner, are not so easily assimilated to covert behaviour. These include abstraction (responding "under the control of a single property or a special set of properties of a stimulus") and generalisation (responding "in a given way to a new stimulus bearing some resemblance to the old"). "These," says Skinner, "are not *behaviors*, covert or overt. They are controlling relations or the changes in probability which result from changes in such relations" (*Verbal Behavior*, p. 438).

We can see here how, for Skinner, activities that are thought to be part of thinking are not really independent activities in their own right, but refer to the *way* in which behaviour is related to reinforcement and stimuli encountered by the organism. 'Generalisation' or 'abstraction' can be an aspect of verbal behaviour or non-verbal behaviour, covert or overt. These terms name not a process or behaviour but qualify behaviour as being controlled or carried out in a certain way; they are adverbs rather than verbs.

And this is the crux of Skinner's analysis of thinking: there is no such thing as an independent behaviour or process called 'thinking'; 'thinking' is a term that we use to qualify behaviours. It may indicate their covert nature or indicate the way in which they are controlled by stimuli, but is not a behaviour in its own right. Any behaviour is an example of 'thinking' as long as it is carried out in a 'thoughtful' manner, i.e. under the control of the relevant variables. The study of thought, then, is nothing more than the study of behaviour:

> When we study human thought, we study behavior. In the broadest possible sense, the thought of Julius Caesar was simply the sum total of his responses to the complex world in which he lived. We can study only those of which we have records. For obvious reasons, it is primarily his verbal behavior which has survived in recorded form, but from this and other records we know something about his nonverbal behavior. When we say that he "thought Brutus could be trusted," we do not necessarily mean that he ever said as much. He behaved, verbally and otherwise, as if Brutus could be trusted. The rest of his behavior, his plans and achievements, are also part of his thought in this sense ... So far as a science of behavior is concerned, Man Thinking is simply Man Behaving. (*Verbal Behavior*, pp. 451–2)

Conclusion

We have seen above how three important psychologists – Thorndike, Watson, and Skinner – sought to redefine their discipline as the study of behaviour rather than the study of mental states or processes. In the case of Thorndike, this reorientation had a practical motivation in that he believed that introspection, as a method of investigating the mental, was restrictive and unreliable. But Watson and Skinner augmented these practical reasons with philosophically based objections to the very idea of the mental. Though both Watson and Skinner tried to redefine mental processes in terms of behaviour – Skinner rather more subtly than Watson – it was the perceived difficulty that behaviourism had in dealing with the more cognitive aspects of human psychology, such as thought and language, that prompted some psychologists to reject behaviourism and to argue that psychology should indeed be the study of mental life. It is this so-called 'cognitive revolution' that is the topic of the next chapter.

Revision questions

1. Why did Thorndike believe that psychology should concentrate on observable behaviour rather than mental states and processes?

2. Describe the Law of Effect and the Law of Exercise.

3. What did Watson believe to be the goal of psychology and how was it to be achieved?

4. What, according to Watson, is thinking?

5. Why did Skinner take the operant rather than the reflex as the foundation of his version of behaviourism?

6. How did Skinner's view of the causes of behaviour differ from that of Watson?

7. How did Skinner's view of verbal behaviour differ from that of Watson?

References

Skinner, B. F. (1957). *Verbal Behavior.* New York: Appleton–Century–Crofts.

Skinner, B. F. (1979). *The Shaping of a Behaviorist.* New York: Knopf.

Skinner, B. F. (1993). *About Behaviorism.* London: Penguin.

Thorndike, E. L. (1911). *Animal Intelligence.* New York: Macmillan.

Thorndike, E. L. (1912). *The Elements of Psychology,* 2nd edn. New York: A. G. Seiler.

Thorndike, E. L. (1931). *Human Learning.* New York: Century.

Watson, J. B. (1913). Psychology as the behaviorist views it. *Psychological Review,* 20, 158–77.

Watson, J. B. (1924a). *Behaviorism.* London: Kegan Paul, Trench, Trubner & Co.

Watson, J. B. (1924b). *Psychology from the Standpoint of a Behaviorist,* 2nd edn. Philadelphia, PA: J. P. Lippincott.

Watson, J. B. and Rayner, R. (1920). Conditioned emotional reactions. *Journal of Experimental Psychology,* 3, 1–14.

Other works consulted

Bakan, D. (1966). Behaviorism and American urbanization. *Journal of the History of the Behavioral Sciences*, **2**, 5–28.

Costall, A. (1993). How Lloyd Morgan's canon backfired. *Journal of the History of the Behavioral Sciences*, **29**, 113–22.

Costall, A. (2004). From Darwin to Watson (and cognitivism) and back again: the principle of animal–environment mutuality. *Behavior and Philosophy*, **32**, 179–95.

Creelan, P. (1985). Watson as mythmaker: the millenarian sources of Watsonian behaviorism. *Journal for the Scientific Study of Religion*, **24**, 194–216.

Harris, B. (1979). Whatever happened to Little Albert? *American Psychologist*, **34**, 151–60.

Lecas, J.-C. (2006). Behaviourism and the mechanization of the mind. *C.R. Biologies*, **329**, 386–97.

Pavlov, I. P. (1928). *Lectures on Conditioned Reflexes: Twenty-Five Years of Objective Study of the Higher Nervous Activity (Behaviour) of Animals*, trans. G. W. Horsley. New York: Liverwright.

Richelle, M. N. (1993). *B. F. Skinner: A Reappraisal*. Hove, UK: Lawrence Erlbaum Associates.

Skinner, B. F. (1959). *Cumulative Record*. New York: Appleton–Century–Crofts.

Skinner, B. F. (1959). John Broadus Watson, behaviorist. *Science*, **129**, 197–8.

Woodworth, R. S. (1952). *Edward Lee Thorndike (1874–1949): A Biographical Memoir*. Washington, DC: National Academy of Sciences.

17   Cognitive psychology

Timeline

1939–45	Second World War
1947	Independence of India and Pakistan from British rule
1955–75	Vietnam War
1963	Assassination of John F. Kennedy
1991	Dissolution of the Soviet Union
2003	Start of Iraq War

Noam Chomsky

1928	Born in Philadelphia
1955	Joins MIT
1959	Publishes critique of Skinner's *Verbal Behavior*
1965	Publishes *Cartesian Linguistics*
1967	Opposes the Vietnam War
1988	Publishes (with E.S. Herman) *Manufacturing Consent: The Political Economy of the Mass Media*

Alan Turing

1912	Born in London
1931–4	Studies mathematics at Cambridge
1939	Joins the code breaking unit at Bletchley Park
1949	Director of the computing laboratory at the University of Manchester
1950	Publishes *Computing Machinery and Intelligence*
1954	Dies in Wilmslow, Cheshire

Introduction

We saw in the previous chapter that the behaviourists, in their different ways, sought to change the focus of psychology from the study of putatively internal mental states to the study of overt behaviour. In particular, mental states were said to be subjective and private and therefore not amenable to objective scientific study whereas behaviour was amenable to objective scientific study. Thorndike argued that mental states were, in any case, only of interest because they are intimately connected with behaviour; if they had nothing to do with how we act then they would be mere epiphenomena. Watson was to take this further: he argued that there were no mental states as traditionally conceived, only behaviour. Cartesian philosophy viewed people as mechanical bodies that were connected with thinking and feeling souls. Watson rejected the existence of the soul or mind and reconceived the human being in a purely materialistic way as only consisting of the mechanical body. As the philosopher Charles Taylor put it, materialism of this sort was "dualism with one term suppressed" (Taylor 1975, p. 81).

This mechanistic view put Watson in the difficult position of having to redefine what were normally thought of as mental states and processes in terms of purely mechanistic behaviour. Thinking, for example, had to be redefined as subvocal speech, and speech itself had to be redefined in terms of physical activity going on within the vocal apparatus, or other parts of the body that were allied to it. But what, then, differentiated between merely making a noise and producing meaningful speech? The traditional answer would have been that speech is the expression of thoughts, desires, intentions, in other words, of mental states. It was the apparent inability of behaviourism to deal with these more complex aspects of human psychology – such as the meaningful use of language – that caused some thinkers to question the adequacy of the behaviourist approach. One of these was Chomsky.

Box 17.1 Noam Chomsky

Avram Noam Chomsky was born in 1928 in Philadelphia. His parents were Jewish immigrants from Ukraine and Belarus. Politics were always a topic of debate in the family and, though Chomsky's parents were fairly moderate in their views, other members of his extended family held radical left-wing views.

Box 17.1 (cont.)

Chomsky's father had taught in Hebrew schools and had published several works on the development of the Hebrew language. Chomsky continued this tradition when he studied philosophy and linguistics at the University of Pennsylvania and did his masters' thesis on grammatical transformations in Hebrew.

Chomsky joined the Massachusetts Institute of Technology in 1955, and has remained there to this day. His work on linguistics draws on the rationalist philosophy of thinkers such as Descartes. Chomsky argues that humans are possessed of an innate language acquisition device because, he believes, environmental stimulation is not enough to account for the speed and proficiency with which children acquire language.

As well as his work in linguistics, Chomsky is noted for his political activism. His political thought is broadly anarchist and he has been an outspoken critic of American foreign policy.

Mental states and representations

At the end of the previous chapter, we considered Skinner's views on language, which were put forward in his book *Verbal Behavior*. It was the highly critical review of this work by Noam Chomsky (see Box 17.1) that was one of the major events in the so-called 'cognitive revolution', which saw cognitivism replace behaviourism as the dominant approach in psychology. Chomsky argued that behaviourism's restriction of investigation to observable events in an attempt to keep psychology scientific was not only artificially restrictive, but completely unnecessary. Many scientists, argued Chomsky, are perfectly happy to deal with unobservable events and processes providing, of course, that they can be related to objective data in a meaningful way:

> take a physicist who wants to figure out what is happening inside the sun. He's concerned with data too, but he does not limit himself to arrangement of data concerning the sun's exterior. He may accept an explanatory theory that he dreamed up about the invisible interior of the sun, which happens to work very well, explains a lot of things, and is continuous with the rest of the physics in some fashion. (Chomsky, quoted in Baars 1986, p. 346)

There is, then, nothing inherently unscientific in trying to explain observable phenomena in terms of things that are themselves not observable. Therefore, argued Chomsky, there is nothing inherently wrong in trying to explain observable behaviour in terms of unobservable mental states. Indeed, Chomsky argued, it is simply not credible to try to explain or predict behaviour solely in terms of environmental stimulation without also considering what is going on inside the organism:

> One would naturally expect that prediction of the behavior of a complex organism (or machine) would require, in addition to information about external stimulation, knowledge of the internal structure of the organism, the ways in which it processes input information and organizes its own behavior. (Chomsky 1959, p. 26)

Behaviourism, then, for Chomsky, looked at language purely in terms of the external stimuli impinging on the organism at the expense of more important factors that exist within the organism.

But, in truth, the behaviourist movement had never been a unified approach, even though Watson's manifesto tried to make it sound this way. There was little in common between Watson and Skinner, for example, in the way that they viewed the organism: for Watson it was the passive instrument of environmental forces whereas for Skinner it was the active emitter of purposeful behaviours. (Indeed, it has been noted (Richelle 1993) that the version of behaviourism attacked by Chomsky had more in common with the stimulus–response behaviourism of Watson than with the operant approach of Skinner, even though it was Skinner that was the ostensible target of Chomsky's critique.) It was also not the case that all behaviourists, or those associated with the approach, had completely ruled out the utility of hypothetical internal states as explanatory constructs in psychology.

One psychologist who did make use of these constructs even before the 'cognitive revolution' was E. C. Tolman (1886–1959), who postulated the existence of **intervening variables**, such as 'demand', 'appetite', and 'motor skill', mediating between environmental stimuli and behaviour. Indeed, Tolman pointed out, the neural connections that Thorndike believed to underlie stimulus–response associations were themselves intervening variables of a sort (Tolman 1938). Tolman's approach is sometimes referred to as *neo-behaviourism* because of its acceptance of internal variables into its explanatory schema.

One of the things that Tolman studied was the ability of rats to learn their way through a maze. Although some psychologists believed that such learning could be accounted for by the building up of stimulus–response chains, which might be likened to a series of directions (e.g. turn left at the first junction, turn right at the second, etc.), Tolman did not believe that this kind of response learning could adequately explain the flexibility of the rats' performances. In particular, thought Tolman, the use of stimulus–response chains would seem to require the rat to go by the same route each time it found its way through the maze in order to get food. But, he said, this was not always the case.

Tolman (1948), in a series of experiments, trained rats to run through one arm of a maze to a food goal. But when, in subsequent trials, the learned route was blocked off, and the rats were provided with several alternative routes, he found that the rats tended to choose the route that led most directly to the goal, even though they had never been down that route before. Tolman proposed that the rats had learned the location of a *place* not merely a set of *responses*. He argued that the rats, in their initial learning, had learned where the food goal was in relation to the surroundings of the laboratory in which the maze was placed. They could then use this information to navigate to the goal via a new route which, by definition, required novel responses. Tolman believed that this spatial knowledge must, somehow, be stored within the organism of the rat itself, in the form of something like a mental map of the whereabouts of the food goal in relation to the rest of the laboratory. In other words, the rats had acquired a **mental representation** of the environment, and they used this representation to guide their behaviour. This mental representation was called a *cognitive map* by Tolman.

Tolman, then, prefigured later developments in cognitive psychology in that he did not merely seek to explain the rats' behaviour in terms of the information and stimuli that were in the environment – i.e. in terms of what was outside the rat – but in terms of what was inside the rat, specifically in terms of stored information that took the form of some sort of mental representation of the outside world.

The supposed existence of mental representations seemed to cognitive psychologists to be able to account for more flexible and sophisticated behaviour than stimulus–response connections alone. It meant that people were not completely determined in their behaviour by what was in the immediate environment – they were not just slaves to the here and now – but that their conduct could be a function of things that were not in the current environment, either because they were no longer, or not yet, present, or because they were abstract ideas or notions that could not be said to exist in the environment at all in any simple, concrete way. People could, for example, pursue future goals and think about possible states of affairs that did not actually exist.

But the cognitive psychologists who embraced the idea of internal representations as explanatory constructs took with them important aspects of behaviourist thinking. As has been noted (Costall 2004) both Watsonian behaviourism and cognitivism believed that behaviour should be understood in terms of mechanistic stimulus–response associations. Cognitivism believed that one had also to understand what went on between the stimulus and the response in the mind of the organism, but the idea of stimulus–response pairing was nonetheless taken for granted. This was understood by some, though by no means all, cognitive psychologists. Bernard Baars, for example, in his book entitled *The Cognitive Revolution*, noted:

> All modern psychologists restrict their *evidence* to observable behavior, attempt to specify stimuli and responses with the greatest possible precision, are skeptical of theories that resist empirical testing, and refuse to consider unsupported subjective reports as scientific evidence. *In these ways, we are all behaviorists.* (Baars 1986, pp. viii–ix, quoted by Costall 2004, p. 182, emphasis added by Costall)

The cognitive 'revolution' was, therefore, not a revolution in the Kuhnian sense (see Chapter 2) because, far from overthrowing all the presuppositions of behaviourism, it continued to operate with them under somewhat altered circumstances. Despite the apparent differences between cognitivism and behaviourism, there was actually a good deal of continuity.

Defining mental representations in terms of observable behaviour meant that one could infer from the observable behaviour itself back to the internal, mental processing that underpinned that behaviour. This, of course, had been an aspect of experimental psychology since the time of Wundt, who used behavioural responses, such as reaction times, as indications of mental processes.

One striking example of this use of behavioural responses to infer the nature of mental processing was in the resurgence of research on **mental imagery**. The study of mental imagery was one of the first things to be attacked by Watson as an example of all that was wrong with what he saw as the old, subjective psychology that he was trying to overthrow. But with the idea that internal mental processes could be inferred from external behaviour, cognitive psychologists believed that they had found a way to rehabilitate the study of imagery in an objective and scientifically respectable way. One of the most cited studies in early cognitive psychology, Shepard and Metzler's (1971) study of mental rotation, gives an example of how this was done.

Shepard and Metzler (1971) presented their participants with pairs of pictures of three-dimensional shapes, such as those shown in Figure 17.1. Sometimes both figures depicted the same shape, albeit in different orientations; sometimes one shape was the mirror image of the other. The participants' task was simply to indicate as quickly as possible whether or not the two shapes were the same or different.

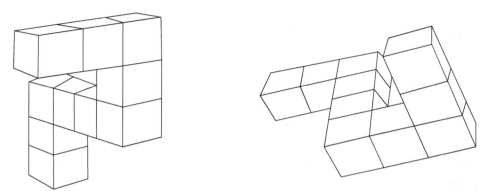

Fig. 17.1 Shapes of the type used by Shepard and Metzler (1971) in their study of mental rotation

Shepard and Metzler found that the time that it took participants to correctly identify two identical shapes as being the same increased linearly as a function of the angular difference in orientation between the two shapes. If the two shapes differed only slightly in orientation the participants tended to respond quickly; if the difference in orientation was larger the participants took longer to respond.

Shepard and Metzler came to the conclusion that the participants arrived at their decisions by mentally rotating a mental image of one shape into the same orientation as the other shape. When the images of the two shapes were in the same orientation, then the participant would be able to see directly whether or not the shapes were the same. It was as if the participants, instead of rotating real shapes in the external world, mimicked this process in their internal, mental world by rotating mental representations of the shapes. This was why it took them longer to respond when there was a greater angular difference between the depicted shapes: it simply takes longer to rotate something, or to imagine some-thing rotating, through a larger angle than it does through a smaller angle. Thus, Shepard and Metzler had used the participants' overt behavioural responses, their response times, to infer the nature of a process that was going on within the minds of the participants.

It should be noted here that the existence of mental rotation was not something that was inferred from the subjective reports of the participants – whether the participants actually had the subjective experience of imagining one shape rotating into alignment with the other was immaterial, because the process could have gone on unconsciously. It was the *behavioural response* of the participant that was the crucial factor in deciding whether a mental process of a particular type was going on and what its characteristics might be.

The Turing test and functionalism

This characterisation of mental states and processes in behavioural terms is nowhere more explicit than in the **Turing test**. Alan Turing (see Box 17.2) was a mathematician and computer scientist who, famously, played a crucial role in cracking the German Enigma code during World War II. "The idea behind digital computers," said Turing, "may be explained by saying that these machines are intended to carry out any operations which could be done by a human computer" (Turing 1950, p. 436). Like a human being carrying out a computation, the digital computer follows a series of rules in a step-by-step manner and manipulates symbols according to these rules. This – the manipulation of symbols according to explicit, formal rules – is the essence of computation. But can all thinking be characterised in this way? And can computers be said to think?

Box 17.2 **Alan Turing**

Alan Mathison Turing was born in London in 1912. When at school, he showed precocious mathematical ability and went on to study mathematics at King's College, Cambridge. During World War II Turing worked at the secret code-breaking unit at Bletchley Park. He was particularly noted for his work on breaking the Enigma code used by German forces. Turing's simple but crucial idea was to rule out any interpretation of the coded message that produced an internal contradiction. In this way the number of possible interpretations that were worth investigating in detail was drastically reduced.

After the war, Turing worked on the development of the first computers to use stored programmes, first at the National Physical Laboratory in London and then at the University of Manchester.

Turing was homosexual and, at that time, homosexual acts between men were illegal. Turing was charged with indecency in 1952 and agreed to undergo hormone treatment to reduce his sexual urges instead of going to prison. This treatment produced side effects, such as impotence.

In 1954 Turing was found dead in his home. The cause of death was found to be cyanide poisoning. Turing's biographers have, in the main, believed that Turing committed suicide by deliberately administering the cyanide to himself, although others have suggested that the poisoning was accidental and stemmed from Turing's storing of laboratory chemicals in his home.

Turing proposed to replace these rather vague questions with something more well defined. Imagine that we have a human who poses questions by typing them into a computer and who receives answers to those questions on her computer screen. Now, the written questions can either be sent to a human, who then types the answers to appear on the questioner's screen, or the answers can be provided by a computer. The question is: can the questioner tell the difference between a human responder and a machine responder? This scenario was called by Turing the *imitation game* and it has become known as the *Turing test*. It was his contention that, if a machine's responses could not be distinguished from those of a human over a reasonable length of time, then we would have to say that the machine was thinking in the same way as the human. It was Turing's prediction that, in the future, this would indeed come to pass:

> I believe that in about fifty years' time it will be possible to programme computers ... to make them play the imitation game so well that an average interrogator will not have more than 70 percent chance of making the right identification after five minutes of questioning ... I believe that at the end of the century the use of words and general educated opinion will have altered so much that one will be able to speak of machines thinking without expecting to be contradicted. (Turing 1950, p. 442)

Turing's prediction may not have come to pass, but the important thing from the point of view of this chapter is not the accuracy of Turing's prediction but the premise on which it stands: thinking is to be defined in terms of the computer's output, its *verbal behaviour*, so to speak. If it behaves in the right way then that means the behaviour must be underpinned by cognitive processing of adequate complexity, and so we can say that the machine is thinking. Though mentalistic concepts have been reintroduced into psychology's vocabulary, there is, far from being a radical break with behaviourism, more of a modification of its tenets. Behaviour – overt, publicly observable, objectively measurable – is still the psychologist's touchstone, so much so that mental processes, such as thinking, are effectively characterised in terms of the behaviour that they permit.

We saw, in Chapter 4 on Descartes and the mind–body problem, that one approach to understanding mental states was to think of them in terms of the jobs that they do – the functions that they serve – rather than the substance in which they inhere. This is called **functionalism,** and it is a philosophical presupposition that lies behind much of cognitive psychology. Rather than describing mental states in terms of certain *intrinsic* characteristics, characteristics that can really only be accessed by the person who is undergoing the states in question, mental states are defined in *relational* terms. In particular, they are defined in terms of the relations that they have as mediating between perceptual inputs and behavioural outputs.

When we define mental states in this way, there are two aspects of the mental that no longer have the significance that they once had. Firstly, the subjective, experiential aspect of a mental state is no longer thought of as a defining characteristic of that state and, accordingly, reports of these subjective aspects are of little interest to the functionalist psychologist. We might think that visual perception could be defined in terms of having certain sensations of colour and light, for example, but for functionalism these are incidental accompaniments to the real business of visual perception, which is taking in information from the eyes and processing it in such a way that I can, for example, reach out and pick up the coffee cup that I see in front of me. The sensations or experiences that accompany this processing are irrelevant. Indeed, it is irrelevant whether there are any sensations or experiences *at all*. Any processing that takes in, transforms, and outputs information in the appropriate way is an instance of visual perception, regardless of whether it is accompanied by subjective, qualitative experiences or not.

A second question that loses its force for the functionalist is that of the substance within which the process is taking place. Any substance that is capable of performing the function in question can be said to have, or be in, mental states. It therefore does not matter that a computer, for example, is made out of entirely different stuff from a human brain. What matters is what the computer *does* and what the human brain *does*. If the computer takes in information and transforms it and produces output in the same way that a human being does, then we have to say, according to functionalism, that the computer has mental states just as much as the human does. Both are performing the same function, therefore both are in the same mental states.

Newell and Simon put it as follows:

> It can be seen that this approach makes no assumption that the 'hardware' of computers and brains are similar, beyond the assumptions that both are general purpose symbol-manipulating devices, and that the computer can be programmed to execute *elementary information processes* functionally quite like those executed by the brain. (Newell and Simon, quoted by Dreyfus 1972, p. 67, emphasis added by Dreyfus)

This functionalist assumption lies behind the Turing test. As we cannot, in the imitation game, tell the difference between a human interlocutor and a machine, we have to say that they are doing the same sort of thing: both receive written questions and produce answers, and in between the input and the output, some processing of the question must take place so as to produce an appropriate answer. Given that, according to functionalism, *this is all that thinking is*, then it must be the case that the machine is thinking in the same sense as the human. The crucial intermediate stage between input and output, during which information is processed and transformed, may be instantiated in very different material structures – the biological brain or the silicon computer – and may be accompanied by subjective experience in one case but not in the other, but, as we saw above, these factors are not important to the functionalist. It is what is *done* not what is doing it that is important in defining a mental state.

This alleged similarity between the human mind and the computer – both take in information, transform it, and produce output – led some to argue that we could find out about the nature of human mental states by trying to instantiate them in computer models. If, for example, human participants behave in a certain way on being presented with information, we can try to create a computer program that will behave in the same way as the human participants when presented with the same sort of information. In this way, because we have to design what goes on between input and output in the computer, we have a way of getting an idea about what goes on between input and output in the human participants. We have created a computer model of human cognitive functioning. This attempt to create computer models of human cognitive functioning was called **artificial intelligence (AI)**. The aim was to take a task that undeniably involved human thinking and intelligence and then create an artefact that could do the same sort of thing.

Two of the strongest early proponents of AI were Herbert Simon (1916–2001) and Allen Newell (1927–92). Unlike Turing, who believed that at sometime in the future we might talk of machines thinking, Simon and Newell, in the late 1950s, believed that there already existed thinking machines:

> It is not my aim to surprise or shock you . . . But the simplest way I can summarize is to say that there are now in the world machines that can think, that learn and create. Moreover, their ability to do these things is going to increase rapidly until – in the visible future – the range of problems they can handle will be co-extensive with the range to which the human mind has been applied. (Simon and Newell 1958, p. 8)

The reason, according to the pioneers of cognitive psychology and AI, that human minds could be compared with computers was that both were *mechanisms* that manipulated symbols, or representations. We use symbols all the time, whether they are pictorial or linguistic, and according to Newell and Simon (1976), this is because the human mind is, at bottom, a symbol-manipulating device:

> The symbol-system hypothesis implies that the symbolic behaviour of man arises because he has the characteristics of a physical-symbol system. Hence, the results of

efforts to model human behaviour with symbol systems become an important part of the evidence for the hypothesis, and research in artificial intelligence goes in close collaboration with research in information processing psychology, as it is usually called. (Newell and Simon 1976, p. 119)

Because computers, too, are symbol-manipulating devices, albeit artificial ones constructed by humans, the one can be used to study the other.

One early example of this symbol manipulation approach to cognition was a program called ELIZA, created by Weizenbaum (1966). This program can be thought of as something akin to the imitation game envisaged by Turing. ELIZA was designed to mimic the interaction of a client with a Rogerian therapist. Rogerian therapy, as founded by Carl Rogers (1902–87), is sometimes called 'non-directive' therapy because the therapist does not seek to force the client in any direction or to impose an interpretation on what the client says. The therapeutic process is about getting clients to open up about their problems so that they themselves come to make sense of their own problems and arrive at a solution. To this end, the non-directive therapist's role is often one of prompting the client to say more about this or that aspect of their lives. It is this sort of interaction that ELIZA was designed to imitate. Here are a couple of illustrative examples:

PERSON	Perhaps I could learn to get along with my mother.
ELIZA	Tell me more about your family.
PERSON	Well, my boyfriend made me come here.
ELIZA	Your boyfriend made you come here?

We can see in the above examples how ELIZA manipulates the incoming information so as to respond with appropriate prompts and further questions. There are a number of relatively straightforward rules that allows the program to do this. In the first example, we see that one of the rules that ELIZA has is that, when one of the incoming questions mentions the name of a family member, ELIZA responds with the request: "Tell me more about your family." Another rule that ELIZA has for transforming an input into a plausible response is simply to turn a statement made by the person into a question, so that the statement "My boyfriend made me come here" on the part of the human receives the question "Your boyfriend made you come here?" in response from ELIZA. In the context of the therapeutic session, this would be understood as a request for more information about the boyfriend and why he made the person come to therapy.

We can see, then, how the whole idea of manipulating symbols (in the above case, linguistic symbols) can produce plausible output that could, at least in theory, be very similar, if not indistinguishable, from human responses. If this were the case then, according to functionalism, the program would be thinking.

Methodological solipsism

Thinking about mental states in functional terms was something that cognitive psychology shared with earlier functionalists such as Dewey. But there was a way in which the new functionalism of cognitive psychology differed from Dewey's earlier functionalism. For Dewey, as we saw in Chapter 15, mental states were not only described in functional terms, but, in addition, the functional relationships in question held between the organism and its environment. The new cognitive psychology rejected this aspect of earlier functionalist thought and conceived of the important functional relationships as existing *within* the organism itself, not between the organism and its surroundings.

One of major thinkers in the rise of cognitivism, Jerry Fodor, characterised the view exemplified by Dewey in the following way:

> The recurrent theme here is that psychology is a branch of biology, hence that one must view the organism as embedded in a physical environment. The psychologist's job is to trace those organism/environment interactions which constitute its behavior. (Fodor 1980, p. 64)

It was this view that Fodor wished to refute. Mental states, he argued, should not be thought of in this way, but should be viewed as entirely internal to the organism and without any necessary connections to the external world. This constituted a return to the Cartesian approach to mind because, as Fodor points out, "Descartes argued that there is an important sense in which how the world is makes no difference to one's mental states" (Fodor 1980, p. 64).

The representational theory of mind upon which cognitive psychology is based can, according to Fodor, be defined in the following terms: to be in a certain mental state is to stand in a certain relation to a mental representation. To believe that it is raining, for example, is to have a certain attitude or relation to the proposition 'It is raining'. To hope that it is raining or to worry that it is raining constitute different relations to the proposition 'It is raining', and hence they constitute different mental states. Whether it actually is raining or not makes no difference to the mental states themselves: they are what they are, and whether they accurately reflect the real state of affairs in the world is a secondary question.

We have already seen, in Chapter 4, that Descartes believed that the mind could be investigated and its existence proved even if there were no external world at all. Fodor himself quotes Descartes with approval:

> At this moment it does indeed seem to me that it is with eyes awake that I am looking at this paper; that this head which I move is not asleep, that it is deliberately and of set purpose that I extend my hand and perceive it ... But in thinking over this I remind myself that on many occasions I have been deceived by similar illusions, and in dwelling on this reflection I see so manifestly that there are no certain indications by which we may clearly distinguish wakefulness from sleep that I am lost in astonishment. And my astonishment is such that it is almost capable of persuading me that I now dream. (Descartes, *Meditations*, quoted by Fodor 1980, p. 64)

What Descartes is here saying is that his perception of the paper in front of himself has nothing to do with whether he really is awake and looking at the paper or whether he is asleep and merely dreaming that he is looking at the paper. In both cases the *perception*, the mental state, is the same, although in one case it may be accurate and in the other illusory.

If this characterisation of mental states is correct, then it is not only legitimate, but actually required, to investigate mental states in their own terms without reference to the surrounding environment. Of course, it is legitimate to ask how sensory information feeds into the creation of representations, but this is merely a question about the *source* of information, it is not a question about the nature of the representations themselves. As Descartes said, there is no intrinsic difference between the truthful representation and the illusory representation. As *representations* they are identical (otherwise one could not be mistaken for the other), in the same way that the portrait of a real person is not intrinsically distinguishable from a portrait of a fictional person. Questions of truth or falsity are external to the representations themselves. The approach to psychology exemplified by Dewey could not be more different. His approach, as we have seen, defines mental states only in terms of their function within the wider context of the organism's interaction with its environment.

It is not only the nature of the representations themselves, but also what is done with them, that, according to Fodor, can be understood without reference to the external world. The nature of the formal computational rules according to which symbolic representations are manipulated is independent of the environment in which the mind exists. We can see how such a view follows from taking seriously the computational theory of mind. A computer manipulates symbols according to the rules encoded in its program. The accuracy, inaccuracy, or downright falsity of the information that the computer is given makes no difference to the way that it works: it still follows the same program, and the workings of that program can, and indeed *must*, be understood without reference to the external world simply because the external world is irrelevant.

This is why Fodor characterises the research strategy of cognitivism as one of **methodological solipsism**. Solipsism is a philosophical position according to which the person believes that he or she is actually the only person in existence and everything else is just an illusion in his or her own mind. Fodor, of course, doesn't actually believe in solipsism, just as Descartes did not believe that there was no external world and that he had no body. Fodor's solipsistic strategy is *methodological* just as Descartes' doubting was methodological. In both cases the point is that we can understand the mind *as if* there were nothing outside it, because, even though in reality there are things outside it, these things are irrelevant to its operation. The psychologist is therefore justified in investigating the mind – the manipulation of symbols according to formal syntactic rules – *as if* there were nothing outside the mind.

The contrast with the earlier functionalism of Dewey is marked. As we saw in Chapter 15, for Dewey a mental state could *only* be defined in terms of relationships between the thinking and feeling organism and its environment. The mental state of being afraid is not the having of an attitude towards a proposition, but is constituted by the perception of a stimulus as fearful, and this perception is, as we saw, not simply an event occurring inside the organism, but is an aspect of its behaviour: its running away from the rustling in the trees is part of its perception of the stimulus as fearful. Relationships with the external world, including acting within that world, are, for Dewey, essential to making a mental state what it is. Mental states cannot, therefore, be understood in isolation from the environment because they are, in part, constituted by relations with that environment.

Criticisms of cognitivism and AI

We have now considered two of the major philosophical underpinnings of cognitivism and AI: firstly, the nature of mind consists in the manipulation of symbolic representations according to formal rules, and, secondly, these representations and rules must be understood in their own terms without reference to the world outside the mind. Both of these suppositions have, however, been questioned by critics of cognitivism and AI.

This cognitivist definition of thinking, and of cognitive processing in general, as a matter of symbol manipulation that mediates between informational inputs and behavioural outputs was not accepted by everybody. Take the example of ELIZA, described above. Would we really want to say that ELIZA understands the input and produces an output in the same way that a human would? Isn't it the case that the program just mechanically moves linguistic symbols around without actually understanding anything? ELIZA might be able to respond to "My boyfriend made me come here" with "Tell me more about your boyfriend", but does it even understand what a 'boyfriend' is? Doesn't the approach to cognition championed by the likes of Turing and Simon leave something out?

Someone who did think that it left something out was the philosopher John Searle. His most well-known (and much discussed) argument against AI and cognitivism is called the 'Chinese room argument' (Searle 1980). It goes as follows.

Searle asks us to imagine that he is locked inside a room that has two holes in the wall by which he might receive messages from outside the room and give messages to those outside the room. Imagine that, from the input slot, Searle receives a series of tablets from outside and that on these tables there are Chinese characters. Searle does not understand Chinese, but he has a large rule-book that tells him what to do when he receives Chinese characters. This rule-book says that if a certain string of characters are passed into the room, then a certain string of other characters should be passed out of the room through the other slot. Searle, then, on receiving a string of Chinese characters, looks in his book, sees the string of characters that has to be passed out of the room, chooses tablets with the appropriate characters from a store of them in the room, and passes them outside through the appropriate slot. Imagine also that, unbeknownst to Searle, the string of characters that he has received constitute a question in Chinese and that the string of characters that he has passed out of the room constitute an answer to that question. To someone outside the room it might appear that Searle understands Chinese: when he receives a question in Chinese, he is able to answer it. But, says Searle, he does *not* understand Chinese. All he is doing is mechanically following a set of rules that say: if a certain string of characters are passed into the room then a certain string of other characters should be passed out of the room.

According to AI and functionalism, however, this is precisely what thinking and understanding is all about: manipulating symbols according to a set of rules. But if Searle cannot be said to understand Chinese by doing this, then neither can any computer. Thinking, argues Searle, must be something more than manipulating symbols according to a series of formal rules. Searle, for his part, argues that the basic tenet of functionalism is wrong and that AI's disregard of the biological foundations of human thought is not just the ignoring of something that is irrelevant to the real business of thinking and cognition, but something that is of crucial importance. In other words, for Searle, the physical nature of the system that instantiates mental states and processes is crucial. We cannot ignore the fact that computers are made of different stuff from brains. The biological nature of the latter, Searle believes, is crucial to its being able to play a part in thinking and cognising.

The second presupposition of cognitivism – its methodological solipsism – has also been questioned, notably by the philosopher Hubert Dreyfus. Dreyfus points out that the situation in which any thinking organism finds itself is, far from being incidental to the business of cognition, actually crucial to it. This is because the sort of tasks that are faced in real life are, unlike a highly constrained task such as playing chess, open-ended and so there is a potentially infinite number of facts that might be relevant to the performance of the task. Dreyfus states the problem thus:

> Open-structured problems, unlike games and tests, raise three sorts of difficulties: one must determine which facts are possibly relevant; which are actually relevant; and, among these, which are essential and which inessential ... What counts as essential depends on what counts as inessential and vice versa, and the distinction cannot be decided in advance, independently of some particular problem ... Now, since facts are not relevant or irrelevant in a fixed way, but only in terms of human purposes, all facts are possibly relevant in some situation ... In any particular situation an indefinite number of facts are possibly relevant and an indefinitely large number are irrelevant. Since a computer is not in a situation, however, it must treat all facts as possibly relevant at all times. This leaves AI workers with a dilemma: they are faced either with storing and accessing an infinity of facts, or with having to exclude some possibly relevant facts from the computer's range of calculations. (Dreyfus 1972, pp. 169–70)

In other words, the situation in which an organism finds itself constrains the number of choices that it can make. The situation itself determines what information is relevant and what actions are possible. Now, if the mind is understood from the standpoint of methodological solipsism, i.e. without reference to the external situation in which cognition takes place, the situational and environmental constraints are taken out of the equation. This means that an AI computer would have to consider an infinite number of facts and possible actions before it could tackle any open-ended task. The factors that would normally cut down on the possibilities and facts that have to be considered have been discounted.

Dreyfus also attacks the assumption that the essence of cognition is the manipulation of symbols according to formal rules. Firstly, the fact that behaviour is regular and predictable does not mean that it is the result of following rules. The orbit of planets around the Sun is regular, orderly, and predictable with a high degree of mathematical precision, but this does not mean, of course, that the planets are actually following rules. In addition, argues Dreyfus, much of our behaviour is driven not by knowledge that can be encoded explicitly in formal rules, but practical knowledge of the sort that resists explicit codification. This is the practical knowledge that is involved in skilled action, such as riding a bike or being good at tennis. This sort of practical knowledge is not a matter of following explicit rules, but of "dispositions to respond to the solicitations of situations in the world" (Dreyfus 2002, p. 367). Again, the role of the situation is crucial: it is in the ability to read the situation and to react appropriately that knowledge lies rather than symbol manipulation in a mental realm with no essential connection to the world.

Conclusion

In this chapter we have seen how cognitivism attempted to remedy the perceived problems of behaviourism by proposing the existence of internal variables that mediated between a stimulus and a response. Nevertheless, despite this difference from behaviourism, there was still a good deal of continuity between cognitivism and behaviourism: the conceptualisation of behaviour in terms of stimulus–response connections was still a part of the cognitive approach. Cognitivism also took overt, observable behaviour as its touchstone, just as the behaviourists did, but it tried to infer from this behaviour the nature of the cognitive processing that lay behind it.

The type of cognitive processing that was said to lie behind behaviour was the manipulation of symbolic representations according to formal rules. It was a form of computation. Because the sorts of activities that went on in a human mind were thought to be the same as those that went on inside a computer, it was thought that computer models could be used to shed light on human cognitive processing through the construction of artificial intelligence programs.

Not everyone agreed with this approach, however. Searle argued that there was more to the understanding of language than the manipulation of symbols, and Dreyfus argued that artificial intelligence, by failing to take account of the environmental situations in which thinking takes place, had ignored a crucial aspect of cognition.

Revision questions

1. On what grounds did Chomsky criticise behaviourism?
2. What is an intervening variable?
3. In what way did cognitive psychology constitute a continuation of behaviourism?
4. What, in the context of cognitive psychology, is functionalism and how does the Turing test exemplify this approach?
5. What is methodological solipsism?
6. Outline Searle's 'Chinese room' argument.

References

Baars, B. J. (1986). *The Cognitive Revolution in Psychology*. New York: Guilford Press.

Chomsky, N. (1959). *Verbal Behavior*, by B.F. Skinner. *Language*, **36**, 26–58.

Costall, A. (2004). From Darwin to Watson (and cognitivism) and back again: the principle of animal–environment mutuality. *Behavior and Philosophy*, **32**, 179–95.

Dreyfus, H. L. (1972). *What Computers Can't Do: A Critique of Artificial Reason*. New York: Harper & Row.

Dreyfus, H. L. (2002). Intelligence without representation: Merleau-Ponty's critique of mental representation. *Phenomenology and the Cognitive Sciences*, **1**, 367–83.

Fodor, J. A. (1980). Methodological solipsism considered as a research strategy in cognitive psychology. *Behavioral and Brain Sciences*, **3**, 63–109.

Newell, A. and Simon, H. A. (1976). Computer science as empirical inquiry: symbols and search. *Communications of the Association for Computing Machinery*, **19**, 113–26.

Richelle, M. N. (1993). *B.F. Skinner: A Reappraisal*. Hove, UK: Lawrence Erlbaum Associates.

Searle, J. R. (1980). Minds, brains, and programs. *Behavioral and Brain Sciences*, **3**, 417–57.

Shepard, R. N. and Metzler, J. (1971). Mental rotation of three-dimensional objects. *Science*, **171**, 701–3.

Simon, H. A. and Newell, A. (1958). Heuristic problem solving: the next advance in operations research. *Operations Research*, **6**, 1–10.

Taylor, C. (1975). *Hegel*. Cambridge: Cambridge University Press.

Tolman, E. C. (1938). The determiners of behavior at a choice point. *Psychological Review*, **45**, 1–41.

Tolman, E. C. (1948). Cognitive maps in rats and men. *Psychological Review*, **55**, 189–208.

Turing, A. (1950). Computing machinery and intelligence. *Mind*, **59**, 433–60.

Weizenbaum, J. (1966). ELIZA: a computer program for the study of natural language communication between man and machine. *Communications of the Association for Computing Machinery*, **9**, 36–45.

18 Modularity, neuroscience, and embodied cognition

Timeline

1952	Start of Mau Mau rebellion in Kenya
1957	Launch of Sputnik 1, first artificial satellite
1966	Mao's Cultural Revolution in China
1974	Nixon resigns over Watergate
1984	Ethiopian famine
1994	Channel Tunnel opens
2001	September 11 attacks on the World Trade Centre and Pentagon

Jerry Fodor

1935	Born in New York
1959	Joins MIT
1968	Publishes *Psychological Explanations*
1983	Publishes *Modularity of Mind*
1988	Joins Rutgers University

Paul M. Churchland

1942	Born in Vancouver
1969	Joins University of Manitoba; Marries Patricia S. Churchland
1983	Joins University of California, San Diego
1984	Publishes *Matter and Consciousness*
1995	Publishes *The Engine of Reason, The Seat of the Soul: A Philosophical Journey into the Brain*

Patricia S. Churchland

1943	Born in British Columbia
1969	Joins University of Manitoba; Marries Paul M. Churchland
1984	Joins University of California, San Diego
1986	Publishes *Neurophilosophy: Toward a Unified Science of the Mind-Brain*
1992	Publishes (with T. J. Sejnowski) *The Computational Brain*

Daniel C. Dennett

1942	Born in Boston
1963	Studies under Gilbert Ryle at Oxford
1971	Joins Tufts University
1991	Publishes *Consciousness Explained*
1995	Publishes *Darwin's Dangerous Idea*

Introduction

In the previous chapter we saw that one of the crucial assumptions behind cognitivism was what Fodor called methodological solipsism. This is the idea, ultimately deriving from Descartes, that the mind is to be understood in its own terms rather than in terms of its connection to the environment. The nature, even the existence, of an environment external to the mind is as irrelevant to a description of its operations as it would be to the description of a computer's programe: the program is still the same program regardless of what is going on outside the computer.

We also saw that one of the corollaries of this view was that all the constraints and structuring of behaviour could not be seen as the effects of environmental or situational factors because these were considered irrelevant to the actual nature of the mind. Structure, even the structure of overt behaviour, had to come from inside the mind. Fodor puts it thus:

> Behavior is organized, but the organization of behavior is merely derivative; the structure of behavior stands to mental structure as an effect stands to its cause. (Fodor 1983, p. 2)

Behaviour, then, has no structure of its own other than that which is derived from the mental structure that lies behind it.

Box 18.1 Jerry Fodor

Jerry Fodor was born in New York City in 1935. After studying at Columbia and Princeton Universities, he taught at the Massachusetts Institute of Technology and then at Rutgers University. Fodor, like Chomsky (of whom he is a strong supporter), was highly critical of behaviourism. In his book *Psychological Explanations* (1968), Fodor argued that philosophers such as Gilbert Ryle and Wittgenstein had mistakenly believed that a rejection of Cartesian dualism meant that one had to embrace a form of behaviourism and that, therefore, mentalistic terms were really about behaviour. Fodor argued that, on the contrary, a representational theory of mind, in which mentalistic terms really did refer to mental states and processes, was perfectly compatible with an anti-dualistic position. The influence of Chomsky is

Box 18.1 **(cont.)**

also apparent in Fodor's *The Modularity of Mind* (1983), in which he argues that Chomsky's idea of a domain-specific module for language acquisition could be applied to other types of cognitive processing. Although Fodor believes in the existence of innate modules, he argues against the idea that they are the result of natural selection and has, in recent work (e.g. *What Darwin Got Wrong*, co-authored with M. Piattelli-Palmarini), been critical of Darwinian theory in general.

Modularity and the mind

If the structure of behaviour depends on the structure of mind, then this raises the question as to what, precisely, is the nature of mental organisation or structure. Fodor's idea, which is shared in its broad outlines by the likes of Chomsky and Marr among others, is that the mind is organised in terms of a collection of **modules**. A module is a functional unit that does a particular task or processes a particular type of information. Chomsky (Fodor 1983) compares mental modules to physical organs: just as physical organs such as the liver and the heart are isolatable structures that perform specific functions, so mental modules can be thought of in an analogous way. This does not mean *necessarily* that they correspond to isolatable brain regions in any simple way (though they might), but rather that they are *functional* units.

Chomsky argues, for example, that there is a specific language unit in the mind that deals only with language and with nothing else. Fodor, too, argues that modules are domain specific – they deal only with a particular type of task or information – and gives as possible visual modules "mechanisms for color perception, for the analysis of shape, and for the analysis of three-dimensional spatial relations ... systems concerned with the visual guidance of bodily motions or with the recognition of faces of conspecifics" (Fodor 1983, p. 47).

The idea of specific modules, each of which works in its own specialised domain, is, for Fodor, the antithesis of the associationistc approach to mind, which is found in empiricism and behaviourism. Rather than seeing the mind as made up of *specialised* units, the associationist views the mind as operating with one *general purpose mechanism*, that of association, which is applied to all manner of information: association works with visual, linguistic, mathematical, haptic information, and whatever else you care to think of. The same process and the same principles explain everything in the mental domain. Any apparent differentiation of structure in the mind – the fact that visual impressions, for example, might give rise to the recollection of other visual impressions rather than haptic impressions – is not to be explained by the pre-existence of a visual module, or group of such modules, but as the *outcome* of the process of association, which results in some things being more closely connected with one another than with others. The structure of the mind is a *result* of the general process of association.

For Fodor, however, and for the other advocates of modularity, the structure of the mind, the existence of particular modules, *precedes* the processing of information. Indeed, it is the existence of such modules that permits the processing of particular types of information in the first place. The structure of mind is the *cause* of the processing that takes place, not the *effect* of the processing.

This is not to say, of course, that modules do not change and develop in the course of their maturation. This is indeed what the likes of Fodor and Chomsky would say. The language 'organ' changes and develops just as do physical organs, but, like physical organs, it is an innate structure that develops according to its own maturational plan rather than being the by-product of some more fundamental process such as association.

But not only does a module do a specific job, dealing with a particular type of information, it does this with minimal interference from other modules. Modules are said to carry out their processing in a relatively automatic way such that knowledge from outside the module cannot interfere or change the way in which it performs its functions. This is called **informational encapsulation**, and Fodor illustrates it with the example of the Müller–Lyer illusion (see Figure 18.1). This illusion is familiar to most psychology students, and a lot of non-psychologists too. Though the two lines are in fact the same length, the one depicted on the left appears longer than the one on the right. Fodor's point is that, even though we know that it is an illusion, and may even know how the illusion works, this does not alter the fact that we are susceptible to the illusion. We *know* that the two lines are equal in length, but we *see* one as longer than the other. This is because, Fodor says, visual processing is modular and is therefore encapsulated from the influence of our higher-order beliefs and knowledge about the illusion.

There are also computational arguments as to why modular organisation is the best for any information processing system. According to Marr:

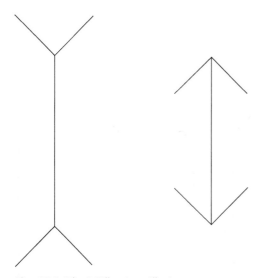

Fig. 18.1 The Müller–Lyer illusion

> Any large computation should be split up and implemented as a collection of small sub-parts that are as nearly independent of one another as the overall task allows. If a process is not designed in this way, a small change in one place will have consequences in many other places. This means that the process as a whole becomes extremely difficult to debug or to improve, whether by a human designer or in the course of natural evolution, because a small change to improve one part has to be accompanied by many simultaneous compensating changes elsewhere. (Marr, quoted by Shallice 1988, p. 18)

So, just as a computer system designed by humans will be more efficient if it is organised as a series of modules, so will an information processing system designed by nature. Because such a system is more efficient, it is more likely to survive. If sub-systems were not relatively independent from one another, for example, it would mean that any item of information might enter into any type of processing, and this would slow down the processing. Taking evasive action when a predator is seen coming towards you will be done more quickly when it operates automatically on the incoming visual information, and extraneous considerations are kept to a minimum.

Of course, though it is the case that we can carry out some cognitive tasks in relative isolation from others (we can, for example, talk at the same time as looking where we are going), sometimes we must coordinate the information from different sensory domains. For this reason, Fodor envisages a set of more general processes that can deal with the output of many different modules. But though this general processing deals with the *output* of modules, it does not *input*

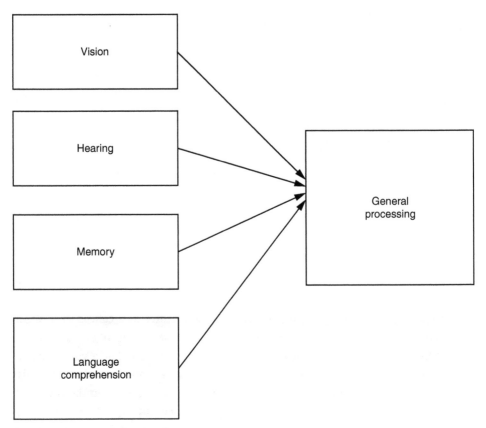

Fig. 18.2 Modular organisation

any of this general information back into the modules, which remain informationally encapsulated. We can, therefore, according to Fodor, think of the structure of the mind as being composed of domain-specific modules that operate relatively independently of one another and which feed their output into more general processing mechanisms. The overall structure might look something like the diagram in Figure 18.2.

Modularity and neuropsychology

In the above discussion of modularity we have assumed that the functional structure of processing is independent of the physical structure in which it is instantiated. But though it is *logically* possible to differentiate functional organisation from physical organisation this does not mean that *in practice* they are completely independent of one another. In particular, because the organisation of the human mind has been shaped by evolution, we would expect that its physical organisation as well as its functional organisation would be relatively efficient. The same also goes, of course, for the design and construction of a computer by human designers and engineers. Though it would be *possible* to implement the functional architecture in any number of ways (and, in theory, in any number of different materials), not all of these implementations would be equally efficient. Some would simply make more sense than others. This fact is recognised by Fodor:

> standing restrictions on information flow imply the option of hardwiring. If, in the extreme case, system B is required to take note of information from system A and is allowed to take note of information from nowhere else, you might as well build your brain with a permanent neuroanatomical connection from A to B. It is, in short, reasonable to expect biases in the distribution of information to mental processes to show up as structural biases in neural architecture. (Fodor 1983, pp. 117–18)

As there are specific roles that are performed by modules, says Fodor, it is reasonable to expect these specific roles to be reflected in neural structures. Modules, then, are not only functionally isolatable, but this functionality may be reflected in physical or anatomical organisation. To put it very crudely, we may expect one functional module to correspond to one particular part of the brain.

If this is the case, then one might expect that damage to circumscribed areas of the brain would impair or destroy the functions of particular modules, while the functions of the other modules would continue relatively unimpaired. Early neuropsychologists, such as Broca and Wernicke, did indeed claim that specific language disorders, or aphasias, were consequent upon damage to particular brain regions (Shallice 1988). They seemed to demonstrate not only that language was separate from other functions, but that even within language, separate functions could be distinguished because they could be differentially impaired as the result of damage to different brain areas. Damage to the left frontal lobe, for example, was thought to result in a form of **aphasia** in which the patient could not produce fluent speech, although some understanding was maintained, whereas damage to more posterior regions in the temporal lobe produced an inability to understand and produce meaningful language, even though the patient could still speak fluently. Different types of visual **agnosia** also seemed to stem from damage to different brain areas: apperceptive agnosia patients could not recognise the visual form of common objects presented to them though, when given the names of objects they could say what the objects were for; associative agnosia patients, on the other hand, could recognise the visual form of objects (they could, for example, produce accurate drawings of them), but did not know what the objects were for.

The preservation of intact cognitive function in some areas with impaired function in other areas is clearly consistent with the modular approach to psychology. If we think of the modular organisation of the mind in terms of a flow diagram of the sort depicted above (see Figure 18.2), then we can see how this is so. Damage to one of the boxes would knock out certain sorts of performance while others would be unaffected. A severe impairment of language, for example, would leave visual and auditory perception unimpaired.

So, by studying the pattern of impairments that resulted from brain damage one could, then, gain an insight into the organisation of the normal human mind. The modular functionalism characteristic of cognitive psychology came to be connected with studies of brain lesions in a field that was called cognitive neuropsychology.

Neuroscientific criticisms of functionalism

The bringing together of the study of the brain with functionalist cognitive psychology did not, for some, pay enough attention to the neural instantiation

Box 18.2 **Paul and Patricia Churchland**

Paul Churchland was born in Vancouver, Canada, in 1942. He studied at the universities of British Columbia and Pittsburgh. It was at the latter institution that he met his future wife, Patricia Churchland. Patricia Churchland was also born in British Columbia and studied at the universities of British Columbia, Pittsburgh, and Oxford. Both then went on to work at the University of Manitoba and the University of California, San Diego. The Churchlands are both proponents of eliminative materialism, according to which increased knowledge of the brain and the nervous system will require us to jettison many of our commonsense beliefs and concepts pertaining to the mind and consciousness. They have argued for this position in many books and articles, notably *Matter and Consciouness* (1988) and *The Engine of Reason, The Seat of the Soul* (1996) by Paul Churchland and *Neurophilosophy* (1986) and *The Computational Brain* (1994) by Patricia Churchland (the latter co-authored with T. J. Sejnowski).

of mental processes. In particular, the differentiation of the functional 'software' of cognitive functions from the neural 'hardware' in which it was instantiated, which was still recognised by many cognitive neuropsychologists, was called into question by thinkers from a neuroscientific perspective, such as Patricia S. Churchland.

Though these levels of description may be perfectly applicable to computers, as indeed one would expect since that is what they are derived from, they are not necessarily applicable to the brain and nervous system, according to P. S. Churchland (1986). In other words, the distinction between structure and function, between hardware and software, which is pretty clear in the case of computers, is not so clear in the case of the brain. Like any other part of the living body, the brain can be looked at on many different levels, and it is dependent on the chosen level of investigation as to what counts as structure and what as function. From one point of view, the activity of the brain is a function of the neurons that make it up. Brain activity is the function and neurons are the structural components in which that function is instantiated. But from another point of view, we can look at the activity of the neuron in terms of the structural components that make it up, such as the axon and dendrites. In other words, what one chooses to regard as functional and what one chooses to regard as structural is relative to the point of view that one adopts.

Moreover, argues P. S. Churchland, the functionalist assumption that the structure of a physical system makes no difference to the functions that it implements is not warranted:

we simply do not know at what level of organization one can assume that the physical implementation can vary but the capacities will remain the same. In brief, it may be that if we had a complete cognitive neurobiology we would find that to build a computer with the same capacities as the human brain, we had to use as structural elements things that behave very like neurons. (*Neurophilosophy*, p. 360)

P. S. Churchland, therefore, argues that the whole metaphor of the mind as a digital computer is misconceived:

The dominant metaphor of our time likens the brain to a computer ... Only in a *very* abstract sense is the brain like a computer: in both the brain and the electronic machine the output is a function of the input and the internal processing of the input. But this is clearly a highly abstract similarity, drawing merely on the presumption of a systematicity between input and output ... Certainly there are profound dissimilarities between brains and standard serial electronic computers ... and it is arguable that for many brain functions the computer metaphor has been positively misleading ...

> Most pernicious perhaps is the suggestion that the nervous system is just the hardware and that what we really need to understand is its 'cognitive software.' The hardware–software distinction as applied to the brain is dualism in yet another disguise. (*Neurophilosophy*, p. 408)

What, then, are the ways in which the brain differs from a computer? The most important one is the way in which processing is carried out. The traditional computer on which the original work in AI and cognitive psychology was based processed information serially, doing one job after another. Computers could do such **serial processing** extremely quickly, much faster than a human being could, which accounted for their superiority over human beings at tasks such as calculation. Other tasks, like searching through data or proving theorems in logic could also be done by a computer with great success. Indeed, one could even say that these tasks, which would take a human being a great deal of time and effort to perform, were done far better by computers. Tasks that people found easy to do, however, were often impossible to implement in computers. The basic processes of visual perception, face recognition, to say nothing of complex sensorimotor control, though done seemingly effortlessly by humans, and indeed by other animals, were, and are, beyond the powers of the most sophisticated computers. This discrepancy between the abilities of computers and the abilities of humans and non-human animals seemed to some to suggest that there was a radical difference between what computers did and what people did (*Matter and Consciousness*, p. 121). In addition, notes P. M. Churchland, the superiority of humans over computers in some tasks, such as face recognition, exists even though neurons are far slower than computers in the speed at which signals are transmitted. The fact that people can do some things faster than computers even though neural transmission times are comparatively slow would seem to indicate that brains work on rather different principles than do digital computers.

Connectionism

The alternative to the digital computer metaphor proposed by many neuroscientists is connectionism. There are two differences between connectionism and traditional AI. Firstly, as we have seen above, the digital computer processes information sequentially. Its power lies in being able to do this very quickly. But the brain, instead of processing information sequentially, seems to process information in *parallel*. In other words, different parts of the brain process different sorts of information simultaneously. Whereas the computer carries out single tasks one after the other very quickly, the brain is, in effect, multi-tasking all the time. **Parallel processing** is the reason why, despite slower transmission velocities, people can still do some tasks much more quickly than can a computer.

The second way in which processing in the brain differs from that in a digital computer is in terms of the role of symbols. Traditional AI and cognitivism, as we have seen, envisaged information processing as the manipulation of symbols according to explicit formal rules. Connectionism, on the other hand, although it subscribes to the basic idea that the brain somehow 'represents' information and states of affairs in the external world, sees this representational function in different terms. Rather than being encoded in symbols, information is said to be represented by a "pattern of activation distributed across a network" of neurons (P. M. Churchland 1986, p. 460).

Rather than individual neurons representing particular items of knowledge it is a network of neurons that do so. Feldman and Ballard state it thus:

> The fundamental premise of connectionism is that individual neurons *do not transmit large amounts of symbolic information*. Instead they compute by being *appropriately connected* to large numbers of similar units. This is in sharp contrast to the conventional computer model of intelligence prevalent in computer science and cognitive psychology. (Feldman and Ballard, quoted in P. M. Churchland 1986, p. 461)

It is because it conceives of information processing as taking place in parallel (rather than sequentially) and as being distributed across a network of neurons (rather than being localisable to a precise location) that the connectionist approach is sometimes called *parallel distributed processing* (or PDP for short).

Here is an example that might help to illustrate the ideas behind connectionism. Think of a picture that is made up of a lot of dots or pixels. We cannot say that it is one of these pixels that represents the face, for example, that is depicted. Indeed, one might not be able to say that any one particular pixel represents *anything* on its own; it is just a dot of a particular colour or shading. It is, rather, the overall arrangement of pixels that represents the face, and the individual pixels only serve a representational function in the context of their overall place in the display and their spatial relationships with the other pixels in the array. It should also be noted that individual pixels could therefore play a role in representing different things depending on the context of the other pixels by which they are surrounded. A single black pixel could play a role in representing the pupil of the eye, a zebra's stripe, or the night sky depending on what the other pixels are doing. This is also so in the case of neurons: a given network might represent different items of information a different times depending on the momentary pattern of activation across the network and the resulting relationships between the individual neurons that make up the network.

Most researchers working within connectionism would nevertheless accept that there is a degree of specialisation in different parts of the brain, particularly with regard to basic sensory processing. The occipital lobe, for example, is concerned with the processing of visual information. However, such localisation of function is still to be thought of in terms of distributed networks, rather than individual neurons.

Although the idea of connectionism has become popular in contemporary neuroscience, it represents a continuation of some of the earlier ideas about learning that we have encountered in previous chapters. We saw in Chapter 16, for example, that Thorndike thought of learning in animals, and, by extension, in humans too, as a matter of the stamping in of connections in the nervous system. The more often that parts of the nervous system were active together, the stronger the physiological connection between them was said to become. Conversely, connections between parts of the nervous system that are not active together will become weaker over time. These ideas were later developed by Donald Hebb (1904–1985), who proposed the following:

> The fundamental physiological assumption of learning is that whenever an impulse crosses a synapse it becomes easier for later impulses to do so. More precisely: when a neuron A fires, or takes part in firing, another neuron B, some change occurs in A or B or both which increases A's capacity to fire B in the future. (Hebb 1958, p. 103)

The enhanced connectivity between neurons results in the creation of cell-assemblies, groups of neurons that mutually influence one another's firing, and cell-assemblies can themselves merge with other such assemblies to form larger networks of interconnected neurons. Such assemblies, argued Hebb, constitute the neural underpinnings of learning.

The location of thought

Connectionism, as described above, constitutes one example of a move away from trying to localise complex psychological processes in narrowly circumscribed brain areas to seeing such processes as the outcome of coordinated activity distributed over extended brain regions. Another manifestation of this trend is seen in Daniel Dennett's critique of attempts to locate consciousness in a specific brain area.

As we saw in Chapter 4, one of the perennial problems that arose from the work of Descartes was the question of how the body and mind interact with one another. Descartes located the point of interaction at the pineal gland in the brain. It was here, he thought, that the physical, mechanistic body made contact with the rational, non-material mind. Although few psychologists and philosophers would subscribe to such a view today (and it's not clear that very many thinkers in Descartes' own time found his solution very convincing), there nevertheless persists, according to Dennett, an idea that consciousness must arise in the brain at a particular location. This is a view that Dennett (1991) calls *Cartesian materialism*. Dennett's point is that, although most neuroscientists and philosophers subscribe to materialism of one sort or another and have therefore rejected Descartes' dualism, there are still vestiges of Cartesian thinking in their ideas. One such vestige is the idea that there is a priveliged location in the brain where 'it all comes together', just as Descartes believed that body and mind came together at the pineal gland.

Box 18.3 Daniel Dennett

Daniel Dennett was born in Boston in 1942. He studied philosophy at Harvard and then, later, at Oxford under the supervision of Gilbert Ryle. He subsequently worked at the University of California, Irvine, and Tufts University, Massachusetts. Much of Dennett's work has focused on removing what he believes to be the confusions that lie in our way of a proper understanding of the mind and in this respect his approach is not dissimilar to that of Ryle. In *Consciousness Explained* (1991), for example, Dennett argued that our ideas on the nature of consciousness still bear the imprint of flawed Cartesian thinking and that it is this residual Cartesianism that makes the problem of consciousness seem especially mysterious. Once Cartesian obstacles have been removed, believes Dennett, the way will be open for a naturalistic understanding of consciousness. Dennett has also emphasised the power of natural selection as an explanatory concept (*Darwin's Dangerous Idea*) and has recently, in *Breaking the Spell* (2006), argued that religious belief may itself be the result of evolutionary forces.

The assumption behind Cartesian materialism is that we can pinpoint a specific time and place in the brain at which consciousness of a particular event occurs. But Dennett's point is that something's coming into conscious awareness is not a discrete event with a precise spatial and temporal location. Consciousness is, rather, the result of processes going on over a period of time in different parts of the brain. We can say that, at a particular time, a person was not conscious of a particular stimulus, and that she was conscious of it 300 ms later, for example, but to try to pinpoint the 'instant' of consciousness with any greater detail, to ask for example, whether consciousness occurred in the brain at 200 ms or 201 ms, is to make a mistake. It is to think that consciousness is an event rather than a process. The only answer to the question of when our subject became conscious of the stimulus is 'over the 300 ms between presentation of the stimulus and the verbal report of its presence'.

And, just as there is no precise temporal location of consciousness, so there is no precise spatial location either. Rather than consciousness rising at a particular place in the brain, it is, says Dennett, "spatially smeared" over the brain. There are, according to Dennett, multiple processing sites and streams, not a single, privileged stream or site of consciouness. Information in any one of these multiple processing streams may enter into conscious awareness depending on the task at hand.

With the connectionists and with Dennett, then, we move towards a view of psychological processes as neural processes extended over space and time. But others, such as Antonio Damasio, seem to go further: for Damasio, it is no longer enough to look just at the brain, even the whole brain; one must consider the brain within the body. He states his position as follows:

> I propose that human reason depends on several brain systems, working in concert across many levels of neuronal organization, rather than on a single brain center. Both 'high-level' and 'low-level' brain regions . . . cooperate in the making of reason . . . The lower levels in the neural edifice of reason are the same ones that regulate the processing of emotions and feelings, along with the body functions necessary for an organism's survival. In turn, these lower levels maintain direct and mutual relationships with virtually every bodily organ, thus placing the body directly within the chain of operations that generate the highest reaches of reasoning, decision making, and, by extension, social behavior and creativity. (*Descartes' Error*, p. xiii)

For Damasio, then, even the most complex psychological phenomena, such as rationality, cannot simply be understood by looking at the brain in isolation; one must look at the brain within the body, for the feelings generated in the organs of the body are all part of the process of thinking. We have now moved even further away from the view of the mind as a collection of discrete modules that process symbols according to syntactic rules without reference to what is going on elsewhere. The body is no longer seen as just a complex piece of machinery that just happens to be attached to the brain or mind, but as something that is a crucial part of our mental lives. It is not simply the case, according to Damasio, that the body is necessary to keep the brain alive, provide it with sensory inputs, and move it around the world, it is, rather, that the body actually plays an essential role in reasoning. Thinking, in other words, does not just occur in the brain, but in the rest of the body too.

Embodied cognition

The general move towards recognising the importance of the body in the psychological is called **embodied cognition**. Cognition, according to this view, involves not only the brain, but the body in which it is housed too and, indeed, the environment within which the organism lives and acts. It is also sometimes called *situated cognition*, because cognition, it is argued, can only be understood with reference to the tangible environmental context within which the embodied organism is situated.

We saw that, for Descartes, cognition takes place in the mind, which is connected in some mysterious way to a mechanical body. The body itself, other than perhaps acting as a conduit for information to get from the external world to the interior of the mind, plays no material role in the business of thought whatsoever. Thinking is essentially a disembodied activity. The symbol manipulation that, for Cartesian-inspired cognitivism constitutes the essence of mental processing, takes place in isolation from the world in the interior of the mind according to its own abstract rules and procedures. The body may be important in getting information to the mind in the first place, but the nature of the body or the way in which it interacts with the environment does not affect the nature of cognition itself. Viewing cognition as an essentially embodied activity, therefore, "would require our culture to abandon some of its deepest philosophical assumptions" (Lakoff and Johnson 1999, p. 3) and, in particular, it "requires us to abandon the idea (common since Descartes) of the mental as a realm distinct from the realm of the body" (Clark 1997, p. xiii).

So, what then does it mean to view cognition as something essentially embodied? Though embodied cognition is a general approach rather than a uniform doctrine, there are two aspects of the approach that I will bring out in the following pages. Firstly, perception and cognition are thought of as being, fundamentally, for the control of action, rather than the gaining of knowledge for its own sake. Secondly, perception and cognition are themselves considered as forms of action, as particular types of behaviour performed upon the organism's environment.

Perception for action

Traditional cognitive science took *knowledge* as its starting point. In so doing it continued the dominant tradition in Western thought. Going right back to Descartes, the goal of much of philosophy and psychology has been to understand how humans, and animals, gain knowledge of the world, how this knowledge might be represented or instantiated in the mind or brain, and whether it was innate or acquired from experience. Empiricists thought that knowledge took the form of internal copies of sensory impressions, cognitivists and AI theorists thought that it took the form of language-like symbols, but despite these major differences, the theoretical orientation of many schools of thought has been towards knowledge. This way of thinking is exemplified in Marr's definition of vision as "knowing what is there by looking" (Marr 1982, p. 3).

But we have also seen examples of another way of thinking about psychology: not in terms of pure knowledge, but in terms of action. We saw this in the work of pragmatists such as James and Dewey, for whom thoughts and ideas are tools that enable us to negotiate our environments. From this point of view, perception is no longer seen as the means of gaining abstract knowledge about the world, knowledge that has only a contingent connection with action; it is, rather, intimately connected with action. Perception, fundamentally, is *for* action. In adopting this view, many embodied cognition theorists have been influenced by psychologists such as Gibson (1979), who argued that we perceive objects not in abstract mathematical or geometrical terms but in terms of the actions that they permit or support. Instead of perceiving a stream as being 1.5 m in breadth, for example, we perceive it as jumpable or not jumpable. These behavioural possibilities were called **affordances** by Gibson. According to Gibson we perceive that the surface of the ground affords walking whereas the surface of the sea does not and that a 5-inch cube affords grasping whereas a 10-inch cube does not. A similar idea was put forward by the Gestalt psychologist Kurt Koffka (1935), who proposed that we perceive what he called the demand characteristics of objects:

> Each thing says what it is . . . a fruit says 'Eat me'; water says 'Drink me'; thunder says 'Fear me'; and woman says 'Love me'. (Koffka 1935, p. 7)

Perception as action

The philosopher Gilbert Ryle (1900–76) distinguished between **knowing how** and **knowing that** (Ryle 1949). Knowing that refers to factual knowledge of the sort that could be expressed in a sentence, knowing, for example, that Paris is the capital of France. Knowing how, in contrast, is the knowledge that is instantiated in performing a skilled action, such as knowing how to ride a bike. This sort of knowledge is not the accumulation of facts but is practical knowledge; it is not instantiated in propositions or statements but in activity. It is the contention of embodied cognition theorists that too much of psychology has focused on knowing that at the expense of knowing how. The goal of perception, according to this view, is knowledge of *how* to act with respect to one's surroundings rather than knowledge *that* a particular state of affairs happens to hold in the world.

But it is not simply the case that embodied cognition theorists view perception and cognition as serving action, they view perception and cognition as themselves forms of skilful action. Skilled activities, such as riding a bike or playing tennis, are essentially *embodied* activities – neither a disembodied brain nor a computer can perform these sorts of activities, because they require a body of a certain sort, which allows interacting with the environment in a particular way. Embodied activities therefore require not only a brain and not only a body but a particular sort of environment too. To attempt to look at such activities only in terms of one or two of these things is to ignore some of the crucial factors that make the skill possible in the first place.

This view of perception as an action performed in the environment, sometimes called animate vision, is contrasted by Clark with the traditional cognitivist approach exemplified in the work of Marr:

> The task [of vision], according to Marr is to construct a rich inner model of the three dimensional visual scene on the basis of the available (two dimensional) input information. Work in Animate Vision, by contrast, depicts the task as, simply, the use of

visual strategies to control behavior, in real-world contexts, at as low a computational
cost as possible. (Clark 1998, p. 8)

As an example of a visual strategy, Clark gives the example of searching the visual
environment for bright yellow when trying to find one's coffee cup because the cup
is bright yellow. We can see in this example that vision is no longer considered in
terms of creating a representation of the coffee cup, let alone of the rest of the visual
scene. It is, rather, a matter of performing a practical task in as simple a way as
possible. When searching for the yellow coffee cup one simply searches for yellow;
other visual characteristics, such as the forms of objects in the environment need
not even be considered, at least during the initial search, because it is only the
colour that matters. The creation of a detailed inner representation is replaced by
quick and efficient behaviour directed to the environment.

A similar view of perception is put forward by O'Regan and Noë (2001):

Instead of assuming that vision consists in the creation of an internal representation of
the outside world ... we propose to treat vision as ... a mode of exploration of the
world that is mediated by knowledge of what we call sensorimotor contingencies.
(O'Regan and Noë 2001, p. 940)

Again, perception is seen as a way of interacting with the world, of probing it for
the information that is necessary for the performance of the task at hand. And
this visual exploration of the world is not a matter of following formal rules of the
sort that characterise the cognitivist approach to mind but is the putting into
practice of sensorimotor knowledge, i.e. of *knowing how* to skilfully explore the
environment.

Viewing perception and cognition as embodied activities situated in an environment dramatically reduces the need to invoke internal mental representations
of the external world in psychological theories. Indeed, some embodied-
cognition theorists, like Gibson (1979) before them, completely reject the idea
of mental representation altogether. According to this radical view, there is no
need to duplicate the world in front of our eyes with a copy of it inside our heads.
Instead of our perception of the world being mediated by representations of it – a
view that goes back to Locke, if not further – why not think of perception as the
gathering of information directly from the world itself?

O'Regan and Noë, two proponents of this view, state it thus:

Under the present theory, visual experience does not arise because an internal representation of the world is activated in some brain area. On the contrary, visual
experience is a mode of activity involving practical knowledge about currently

possible behaviors and associated sensory consequences. Visual experience rests on know-how, the possession of skills.

Indeed, there is no "*re*"-presentation of the world inside the brain: the only pictorial or 3D version required is the real outside version. What *is* required, however, are methods for probing the outside world – and visual perception constitutes one mode via which it can be probed. (O'Regan and Noë 2001, p. 946)

According to this view, there is no need to store large amounts of information inside the organism, because the information needed to control behaviour is outside the organism, in the environment, and only needs to be sampled when needed. The world can, therefore, be thought of as an 'external memory' from which information can be retrieved through the use of skilled perceptual behaviour (O'Regan 1992).

It is only because traditional cognitivism, with its commitment to methodological solipsism, separated the mind from the world that it had to furnish the now isolated mind with representations of the world to make up for the loss of the real thing. But if one thinks of mental processes as going on in the interaction of an organism with its environment, then such extensive representations are no longer needed.

Not all proponents of embodied cognition would agree that their approach completely does away with the need for internal representations of the external world. After all, some (e.g. Clark 1998) argue, not *all* our activities are driven by interaction with our current environment. Some of our thinking, such as planning for the future, is directed to things not present in the here and now. Aspects of cognition such as these, it is argued, therefore require some sort of representation. Nevertheless the representations envisaged in such cases are not the symbolic representations of traditional cognitivism, but are action-based. To think about what one is going to do at the weekend is to simulate mentally the actions that one might perform in the future, not to manipulate abstract symbols according to syntactical rules. Thus, even when recourse is had to representations, they too are not divorced from the nature of embodied action but are simulations of that action without its actual overt performance.

Conclusion

We have seen in this chapter how connectionism viewed cognition as something distributed in the brain. Embodied-cognition theorists went a stage further and viewed cognition as something that was distributed throughout not only the brain but also the rest of the body and the environment in which the embodied organism acted. It is only when not only the brain but also the world and the body are understood as mutually influencing one another that mental states can be fully understood.

The critique of traditional cognitivism by embodied-cognition theorists has elements in common with some of the criticisms voiced by Dreyfus, as discussed in the previous chapter. As we saw, for Dreyfus, one of the problems with AI was that it viewed the mind as independent of any situation. That meant that all the constraints on thought that would normally be provided by the environment and the situation in general had to be built into the computer in the form of explicit rules. But because this situational knowledge is better thought of as practical know-how, of Ryle's knowing how, it is impossible to express it in a finite series of formal rules. The embodied-cognition approach also says a similar thing. Perception and cognition are matters of knowing how to do things, how to obtain visual information from the environment that enables one to find one's coffee cup, for example. This is a matter of tacit knowledge how rather than explicit knowing that.

Revision questions

1. What is a module?
2. Why did Fodor believe that modular organisation at the functional level would also exist at the physiological level?
3. What, according to Patricia and Paul Churchland, is wrong with the computer metaphor for the mind?
4. How does connectionism differ from traditional symbol-based AI?
5. What is 'Cartesian materialism' and what are Dennett's criticisms of it?
6. What are affordances?
7. Why do embodied-cognition theorists believe that mental representations play less of a role in our cognition than traditional cognitive science would suggest?

References

Churchland, P. M. (1988). *Matter and Consciousness*, revised edn. Cambridge, MA: MIT Press.

Churchland, P. S. (1986). *Neurophilosophy: Toward a Unified Science of the Mind/Brain.* Cambridge, MA: MIT Press.

Clark, A. (1997). *Being There: Putting Brain, Body, and World Together Again.* Cambridge, MA: MIT Press.

Clark, A. (1998). Embodiment and the philosophy of mind. In A. O'Hear (ed.) *Current Issues in Philosophy of Mind: Royal Institute of Philosophy Supplement 43.* Cambridge: Cambridge University Press.

Damasio, A. (1994). *Descartes' Error: Emotion, Reason, and the Human Brain.* New York: HarperCollins.

Dennett, D. C. (1991). *Consciousness Explained.* London: Allen Lane.

Fodor, J. A. (1983). *Modularity of Mind: An Essay on Faculty Psychology.* Cambridge, MA: MIT Press.

Gibson, J. J. (1979). *The Ecological Approach to Visual Perception.* Boston, MA: Houghton Mifflin.

Hebb, D. O. (1958). *A Textbook of Psychology.* Philadelphia, PA: W.B. Saunders.

Koffka, K. (1935). *Principles of Gestalt Psychology.* New York: Harcourt Brace.

Lakoff, G. and Johnson, M. (1999). *Philosophy in the Flesh.* New York: Basic Books.

Marr, D. (1982). *Vision.* San Francisco, CA: W. H. Freeman.

O'Regan, J. K. (1992). Solving the "real" mysteries of visual perception: the world as an outside memory. *Canadian Journal of Psychology*, **46**, 461–88.

O'Regan, J. K. and Noë, A. (2001). A sensorimotor account of vision and visual consciousness. *Behavioral and Brain Sciences*, **24**, 939–1031.

Ryle, G. (1949). *The Concept of Mind.* London: Hutchinson.

Shallice, T. (1988). *From Neuropsychology to Mental Structure.* Cambridge: Cambridge University Press.

Glossary

affordances   the action possibilities offered by an object.

a posteriori   an *a posteriori* statement or idea is one that can only be known to be true after empirical observations have been made.

a priori   an *a priori* statement or idea is one that can be known to be true before empirical observations have been made.

agnosia   a neuropsychological disorder in which the patient is unable to recognise previously familiar objects.

analytic statement   a statement that is true by definition or as a matter of logic.

animal–environment mutuality   the view that we can only understand the psychology of an organism in relation to its surroundings.

anomaly   an empirical finding that does not fit with the prevailing paradigm.

anthropomorphism   the attribution of human characteristics to non-human things.

aphasia   a neuropsychological disorder in which the patient has problems in the production or understanding of language.

apperception   the process whereby perception becomes a unified and structured whole.

artificial intelligence   an approach that seeks insight into human intelligence by trying to build computer models that exhibit the same sorts of cognitive abilities as people.

ascetic   someone who denies themselves sensual pleasure, often for religious or ethical reasons.

association of ideas   the combination or linking together of simpler ideas into more complex wholes according to their frequently being encountered in spatial and temporal contiguity.

automata   mechanical replicas of living things.

auxiliary hypotheses   those parts of a research programme that can, according to Lakatos, be altered without affecting the central presuppositions of the research programme.

bad conscience   the feeling of remorse or guilt associated with instinctual drives and which, according to Nietzsche, is the result of Christian morality.

bundle theory of the self   the idea, associated with Hume, that 'the self' is simply the name for a temporary aggregate of associated sensations rather than a permanent and unified entity.

Cartesian   of or relating to the philosophy of Descartes.

Cartesian dualism   the view that the mind and the body are two different sorts of substance. The body is physical but the mind is non-physical.

Cartesian materialism   elements of Cartesian thinking that nevertheless remain in the philosophy of those who reject Cartesian dualism.

categorical imperative   the ethical rule that states that we should only act as we would wish others to act, and which, according to Kant, is binding on all rational actors.

category mistake   erroneously treating an idea of one logical category as if it were a member of another logical category; associated with the philosophy of Gilbert Ryle.

complex ideas   a combination of simple ideas through association to form a composite mental representation, e.g. the complex idea of snow is made up of the simple ideas of white and coldness. Often associated with the philosophy of Locke.

conditioned reflex   a learned response to a stimulus that has been created through associative learning.

connectionism   the idea that learning consists in the formation of connections in the nervous system based on the repeated presentation of stimuli in close spatial or temporal proximity.

constancy hypothesis   the idea that the same stimulation of the same sensory organs at different times will always give rise to the same sensations.

conventionalism   the view that what is correct or true is relative to the wishes and decisions of the community in question rather than being correct or true in absolute terms.

Copernican theory   the model of the universe put forward by the Polish astronomer and mathematician Nicolaus Copernicus (1473–1543), according to which the stationary Sun is the centre of the universe and the planets, including the Earth, orbit around it.

death instinct   a hypothetical drive, postulated by Freud, in which the ultimate goal of an organism's life is the death of the organism.

deduction   reasoning that proceeds from general statements to more specific conclusions.

defence mechanisms   psychological processes, postulated by Freud, to prevent potentially disturbing desires from reaching conscious awareness.

descent with modification   variability in the inheritance of parental characteristics among offspring.

descriptive psychology   an approach to psychology, proposed by Brentano, according to which the psychologist should try to describe the essential characteristics of different mental states and processes before attempting to explain them.

determinism   the view that all events are the necessary effects of antecedent causes.

dialectic   the idea, associated with Hegel, that a concept contains within itself the seeds of its opposite and that it can only be understood in relation to this opposite.

double-aspect theory   the view that the mind and the body are not separate substances but are two attributes of one and the same substance.

ego   the self; in psychoanalysis it is the conscious part of the mind that attempts to fit the organism's unconscious drives with what is actually possible in reality.

embodied cognition   the idea that the body of the organism, and the way that it interacts with the environment, plays an essential role in thinking, perception, and other cognitive processes.

emergent property   a higher-order characteristic that is exhibited by a complex entity but not exhibited by any of its individual parts; the property only comes into being when the parts combine with one another in certain specific ways.

empirical self   what can, according to James, be considered to be a psychological part of a person taken in the widest possible sense. This could include things not normally considered to be part of a person's sense of individuality such as their family or prized possessions.

empiricism   a school of thought that places emphasis on experience, particularly sensory experience, as the means of obtaining and justifying knowledge.

Enlightenment   a period in Western thought, extending from the late seventeenth century to the late eighteenth century, in which science and rationality were championed at the expense of traditional authority.

epiphenomena   side effects of processes or events that do not themselves have any effect on the processes or events that gave rise to them.

epistemological anarchism   Feyerabend's belief that scientific research should not be bound by pre-existing methodological rules and that the scientist should be free to employ different methods and approaches as the situation demands.

epistemology   the branch of philosophy that deals with the gaining and justification of knowledge.

essentialism   the view that different members of a class, such as animal species, are members of that class in virtue of instantiating a fixed essence or quality that is definitive of that class.

experiential education   a philosophy of education, associated with Dewey, that emphasises the concrete, practical experience of the child as against purely abstract exercises or rote learning.

faculties   hypothesised pre-existing mental structures each one of which is associated with a specific process or function, such as reasoning or feeling.

falsificationism   an approach to the philosophy of science, associated with Popper and Lakatos, that locates the rational core of science in the testing of theories to try to prove them false rather than in the attempt to prove them to be true.

feedback loop   the means whereby an activity or process is altered as a result of information concerning its resultant success or failure.

form   the overall plan or ideal that, according to Aristotle, is embodied by an individual thing; the way in which the matter that makes up a thing is structured and organised.

fringe of consciousness   according to James, those aspects of consciousness of which we have only a vague awareness.

functionalism   (1) an approach to psychology, associated with Dewey, according to which the mind should not be understood as a collection of pre-existing faculties but in terms of the functions or activities that it performs or enacts; (2) the philosophical underpinning of cognitive psychology, according to which mental states should be understood in terms of the functions that they perform in mediating between perceptual inputs and behavioural outputs.

gestalt-quality   a perceptual quality that is possessed by a complex of perceptual elements but not by the individual elements themselves. The quality exists in virtue of the relationships between elements and can exist when completely different elements are arranged in a manner that produces the necessary interrelationships between them.

good continuity   one of the factors that governs the way in which perceptual phenomena organise themselves: those perceptual elements that continue seamlessly from one another tend to be perceived as belonging to the same unit.

hard core   those aspects of a research programme that are absolutely fundamental to it and which cannot be altered or rejected without rejecting the whole research programme.

hedonist   someone whose goal in life is the maximisation of pleasure and happiness.

iconic memory   the very short-term retention of sensory stimulation for, at most, a second or two after it has been delivered. Believed to be the retention of the relatively 'raw' stimulation before it has received much cognitive processing.

id   the part of the unconscious mind which, according to Freud, gives rise to sexual and other instinctual desires; it demands immediate satisfaction and is not bound by any laws of rationality or awareness of reality.

idea   (1) an object of thought or perception; (2) (Hume) a faded memory copy of a past perception.

ideas of reflection   knowledge that the mind derives from being aware of its own activities. Associated with the philosophy of Locke.

ideas of sensation   knowledge that the mind derives from being aware of the external world. Associated with the philosophy of Locke.

immaterial   of or pertaining to something that is not made from physical matter.

immaterialism   Berkeley's proposal that there are no material objects that lie behind our perceptions and cause them, but just the perceptions themselves.

impressions   according to Hume, these are the contents of the mind that are caused by objects impinging on the sensory organs of the body.

inattentional blindness   the failure of observers to notice objects or events to which they are not paying attention.

incommensurability   the lack of any common ground between two theories on which they can be compared with one another.

induction   reasoning that proceeds from individual cases to general conclusions.

informational encapsulation   the imperviousness of a psychological module to information that exists outside itself and the sense organs to which it is connected.

inheritance of acquired characteristics   the idea, most notably associated with Lamarck, that offspring will inherit characteristics that were developed by their parents during their parents' lifetimes.

innate ideas   contents of the mind that are said to be present at birth and prior to experience.

inner perception   according to Brentano, this is the ability of the mind to be aware of its own activities while it is engaging in them.

insight   the sudden resolution of a problem by seeing it in a new light rather than by gradual, step-by-step reasoning.

instinctual drives   needs that stem from the biological make-up of the organism.

intellectualist   any approach to psychology or to the philosophy of mind that emphasises the mind's rationality and thinking processes over and above emotions or the biological constitution of the organism.

intentionality   a defining feature of mental states, according to Brentano, in virtue of which they are directed to, or are about, things other than themselves.

intervening variables   mental representations that lie between the reception of a sensory stimulus by an organism and the organism's subsequent behaviour.

introspection   the act of looking into one's own mind and observing one's own mental states and processes as they occur.

just-noticeable difference   the amount that the magnitude of a stimulus has to be increased in order for an observer to be aware that it has increased.

knowing how   practical skill-based knowledge that cannot be expressed in propositions.

knowing that   knowledge of facts or other sorts of information that can be expressed in propositions.

Law of Effect   the idea, put forward by Thorndike, that the successful outcome of a behaviour will make that behaviour more likely to occur in the future in similar circumstances.

Law of Exercise   the idea, put forward by Thorndike, that the more often a behavioural response has been made in a certain situation, the more likely it will be produced in similar situations in the future.

libido   the name given in psychoanalysis to the energy that fuels our sexual instincts and desires.

logarithmic   a non-linear mathematical relationship between two variables such that a constant increase in the magnitude of one variable is associated with progressively smaller increases in the other variable.

logical positivism   an approach to philosophy that came to prominence in the early twentieth century and that disdained metaphysical speculation in favour of founding all knowledge on empirically observed facts and formal logic.

matter   the basic, formless element from which, according to Aristotle, all things are constructed. It is only when matter is imbued with a form that organises and structures it that it can be said to be a thing or an object.

mechanism   the view that the natural universe, and the entities that comprise it, can all be thought of as machines of greater or lesser complexity.

mental imagery   a mental representation that shares important structural properties with perceptual experience such as, in the case of visual imagery, the spatial organisation of information.

mental representation   an internal state of an organism that reflects or mirrors actual or possible states of affairs in the external world.

method of doubt   the method employed by Descartes in his attempt to find certain knowledge. He decided to reject all supposed knowledge that could possibly be doubted in the hope of arriving at knowledge that was immune to any doubt.

methodological solipsism   an approach in cognitive psychology, advocated by Fodor, according to which mental states should be understood without reference to the environment in which the organism is situated.

mind–body problem   the question of how the mind and the body interact with and influence one another.

module   a hypothesised mental structure that is dedicated to a particular task and is only minimally interfered with by other modules or processes.

nativists   psychologists or philosophers who believe that much of our psychology is present at birth rather than acquired through experience.

natural science   the investigation of the empirical world while leaving out the subjective component of experience.

natural selection   the most important evolutionary process, according to Darwin, in which some random mutations among individual organisms prove to be more conducive to reproduction than other random mutations and so are more likely to be passed on to future generations.

nature–nurture debate   the question as to whether psychological features are inborn or whether they are a result of one's upbringing and experience.

Naturphilosophie   a school of thought popular among Romantic thinkers, especially those in late eighteenth- and nineteenth-century Germany, that viewed nature as a whole, interconnected organism rather than a mechanism built up from separable components.

non sequitur   a proposed conclusion that does not actually follow from the argument that is put forward to support it.

noumena   things as they are in themselves as opposed to how they appear to be.

Oedipus complex   the unresolved sexual desire that, according to Freud, a man feels towards his mother.

operant   a piece of behaviour by which an organism operates and has an effect on the environment.

panpsychism   the view that attributes of mind are to be found throughout nature, not just in human beings or animals.

paradigm   the intellectual framework within which normal science takes place, according to Kuhn. A paradigm comprises theoretical concepts, practical methods, and live problems for investigation. The change from one paradigm to another constitutes a scientific revolution or paradigm shift.

parallel processing   the ability of the brain or a computer to operate upon multiple streams of information simultaneously.

personal identity   the continuing existence of the same human being over time.

pessimism   the philosophical position according to which life is inevitably full of suffering and that our desires can never be satisfied.

phenomena   things as they appear to us as opposed to how they are in themselves.

phenomenal self   our sense of self as it appears in experience.

phenomenology   a philosophical approach, founded by Edmund Husserl, which seeks to examine things just as they appear to us in our own conscious experience without being influenced by theoretical presuppositions or expectations.

pleasure principle   the exclusive concern with the immediate gratification of instinctual desires, which Freud argued was the governing motivation of the id, or instinctual unconscious.

pluralism   the idea that no one point of view or approach has a monopoly on truth and therefore that it is good that multiple points of view exist.

positivism   a philosophical school of thought, originally founded by Auguste Comte, that emphasises positive factual knowledge rather than theoretical speculation.

pragmatism   a philosophical approach, associated with James, Dewey, and Peirce, according to which ideas should be considered tools that allow us to cope with the environment and that the worth of an idea lies in the extent to which it enables us to do this.

Prägnantz   the idea, associated with Gestalt psychology, that perceptual phenomena tend to organise themselves into stable configurations.

primary qualities   features of things, such as length and mass, that exist independently of our perception of those features.

property dualism   the view that the mental and the physical are not the properties of two different sorts of substance but are two different kinds of property inhering in one substance.

protective belt   the function served by auxiliary hypotheses in shielding the hard core of a research programme from potentially falsifying observations. It is because the auxiliary hypotheses can be altered to take account of such observations that the hard core can itself remain intact and unaltered.

proximity   one of the factors that governs the way in which perceptual phenomena organise themselves: perceptual elements that are close to one another will tend to be perceived as being parts of the same unified structure.

pseudo-problem   an apparent problem that arises not because of any deep philosophical issues, but due to a misunderstanding of the concepts that are being discussed.

psychic causality   the view, espoused by Wundt among others, that psychological states should be understood as the results of other psychological states rather than physiological processes.

psychoanalysis   the school of psychological thought and clinical method created by Sigmund Freud.

psychophysics   a sub-discipline of psychology concerned with finding out the relationships between the physical intensity of stimuli and the intensity of the sensations to which they give rise.

Ptolemaic cosmology   a model of the universe in which the Earth is the stationary centre around which all other heavenly bodies orbit in circular paths. It is attributed to Ptolemy (c. AD 85–165) of Alexandria in Egypt and was widely accepted in the ancient world and the Middle Ages.

puzzle box   a piece of equipment used by Thorndike to study animal learning. A hungry animal was placed inside a wooden box and had to perform a specific response, such as pressing a lever or pulling on a loop of string, in order to get out of the box and eat the food placed outside.

Q   Freud's designation of psychophysical energy within the nervous system. The organism behaves in such a way as to reduce the amount of this energy.

reality principle   according to Freud, the motivating principle behind the operation of the ego, or conscious mind. It tries to square the instinctual demands of the unconscious id with what is actually possible in reality.

reductionist   someone who seeks to equate psychological processes with physiological processes.

reflex   a behaviour automatically produced in response to a sensory stimulus.

Reformation   the religious movement in Western Europe, instigated by Martin Luther (1483–1546), which rejected the authority of the Roman Catholic Church and replaced it with other forms of Protestant Christianity.

reinforcement   the increased likelihood that an organism will produce a piece of behaviour due to its successful outcome in the past.

Renaissance   an intellectual and artistic movement that characterised much of Western European culture from the fourteenth to the sixteenth century. It was marked by a rediscovery of and renewed enthusiasm for the culture of classical Greece and Rome.

repression   a defence mechanism that prevents forbidden sexual desires from reaching conscious awareness because they would be too disturbing.

research programme   according to Lakatos, the theoretical and practical framework within which science takes place. Research programmes consist of series of theories, each one of which will be an attempt to improve on its predecessor, rather than single monolithic theories.

retrospection   the examination of one's past mental states in memory.

scepticism   the view that human knowledge is fallible and that true and certain knowledge can never be attained.

scholasticism   a term used to describe the philosophy of the Middle Ages, heavily influenced by Aristotle and exemplified by philosophers such as Thomas Aquinas and William of Ockham.

scientific revolution   the replacement of one paradigm by another paradigm.

secondary qualities   perceived qualities of things, such as colour and smell, that exist solely within the mind of the perceiver rather than in the object itself.

self-organising   refers to a system that spontaneously realises a structural arrangement without this having to be imposed on it by an outside agency or process.

self-overcoming   the ability, according to Nietzsche, of higher human beings to control and direct their basic desires and impulses towards other ends.

serial processing   the performance of one task after another by a computer.

similarity   one of the factors that governs the way in which perceptual phenomena organise themselves: perceptual elements that are similar to one another will tend to be perceived as being parts of the same unified structure.

simple ideas   ideas, such as those of basic sensory qualities such as white, that cannot be broken down into more basic constituent parts.

social self   that aspect of our sense of self that depends, according to James, upon how others see us.

specific nerve energies   according to Müller, the qualitatively different sensory component associated with stimulation of different nerves, which is produced regardless of the nature of the external stimulus.

spiritual self   according to James, that part of the sense of self that remains when one gets rid of those aspects of selfhood that are connected with one's possessions, relationships, and social standing. It seems to be the innermost core of the self and James's identifies it with perception of continuing sensations in one's own body.

stimulus–response behaviourism   an approach to psychology most strongly associated with John B. Watson, who argued that our behaviour is causally produced by stimuli in the environment and that learning occurs through the creation and modifications of links between environmental stimuli and behavioural responses.

stream of consciousness   one of James's metaphors to describe conscious experience; it emphasises that our experience is in flux and is not made up of discrete elements.

structuralism   the approach to psychology advocated by Titchener, which sought to break down complex psychological states into the basic mental elements from which they were constructed.

sublimation   the redirection of primitive instinctual desires, such as those for power or sex, towards more elevated cultural or social outlets rather than direct satisfaction.

substantive parts   those parts of the stream of consciousness that, according to James, are relatively stable and persistent over time.

superego   that part of the mind, according to Freud, that is created by the internalisation of moral and ethical codes.

symbiotic relationship   any relationship in which each side depends on the other for its existence.

synthesis   (1) a stage in the dialectic in which, according to Hegel, the opposition between two ideas or principles is overcome at a higher level; (2) the psychological process that, according to Wundt, puts together individual psychological elements, such as basic sensations, to produce a complex and unified psychological whole.

synthetic statement   a statement that tells us something about the way the world is rather than simply being true by definition.

tabula rasa   means 'blank slate' and was used by Locke to describe the mind of the newborn infant, which he believed was devoid of any innate contents.

taxonomy   an organisation of any field of phenomena into categories and sub-categories, such as the organisation of animals into different species.

theory-laden   of observations that are determined, at least in part, by the theoretical beliefs and practices of the observer rather than solely by the observed objects themselves.

theory-neutral   of observations that are not determined by the theoretical beliefs and practices of the observer but by the objects that are observed.

touch teaches vision   the theory, associated with Berkeley, according to which the visual perception of depth and distance is only possible through its being calibrated with respect to physical interaction with objects.

transcendental argument   a type of argument, notably used by Kant, which starts from the way that things actually are and works backwards to discover what must be the case in order for this to be so.

transcendental self   that part of ourselves that is not itself experienced but lies behind our experience and structures it.

transitive parts   those parts of the stream of consciousness that, according to James, are fleeting and serve to join together more stable parts of consciousness.

trichromatic theory of colour vision   the theory that colour vision is the product of three different classes of visual receptors, each of which responds to light of different wavelengths.

Turing test   the name often given to the 'imitation game', a thought experiment devised by Alan Turing, in which a human participant has to decide whether an interlocutor is a human being or a computer.

Übermensch   Nietzsche's name for the highest type of human being, who can master and make use of his own instinctual energies.

unconditioned reflex   according to Pavlov, this is an automatic, unlearned response to a stimulus.

unconscious inference   an influential theory, associated with Helmholtz and J. S. Mill, according to which our conscious perceptions are the outcome of unconscious reasoning.

universals   those qualities or features that are shared by all members of a particular class in virtue of which they are members of that class, e.g. that which makes all red things red, or that which makes all dogs dogs.

verificationism   a theory of meaning, associated with logical positivism, according to which the meaning of an empirical proposition resides in its possible or actual confirmation by the observation of facts.

Völkerpsychologie   the study of psychology through the collective cultural products of different societies and civilisations.

vitalism   the view that living things are animated by some life force or spirit.

voluntarism   a philosophical position, exemplified by Wundt, according to which the mind plays an active and deliberate role in constructing experience.

Will   according to Schopenhauer, the unconscious force that underlies all reality.

will to power   according to Nietzsche, this is the instinctual drive to dominate and control that lies behind human behaviour.

Index

CPSIA information can be obtained
at www.ICGtesting.com
Printed in the USA
LVHW021218180822
726206LV00005B/168